COMMUNICATION
ETHICS NOW

COMMUNICATION ETHICS NOW

EDITED BY
RICHARD KEEBLE

Troubador Publishing Ltd
9 De Montfort Mews
Leicester LE1 7FW, UK
Tel: (+44) 116 255 9311 / 9312
Email: books@troubador.co.uk
Web: www.troubador.co.uk

ISBN: 9781 906221 041

Typeset in 11pt Bembo by Troubador Publishing Ltd, Leicester, UK

Dedicated to the memory of Claude-Jean Bertrand,
Dennis Foy and Peter McGregor

CONTENTS

Looking at communication ethics 'with new eyes'

Cees Hamelink

Imagine yourself as an extra-terrestrial alien visiting planet Earth and using the opportunity to attend the planet's largest gathering on information-communication issues: the United Nations World Summit on the Information Society (2003, Geneva, 2005, Tunis).

In your travel report you refer to extensive debates on political, financial-economic and technological themes. You would also report that in relation to communication and information planet Earth seems to have no moral concerns. Ethics was not on the conference agenda! Obviously, several topics, such as the global digital divide, had moral implications but the political leaders and diplomats never engaged in serious ethical reflection.

This is bizarre, since the material from the second volume of *Ethical Space* that constitutes the contents of this book convincingly demonstrates how lively and relevant today's ethical reflections on communication can be. The chapters of the book cover such an exciting and broad range of topics that I recommend reading them all and not expecting me to summarize and introduce them to you. I rather prefer to use this space for a brief argument about the critical necessity of communication ethics now! The argument has the following five components.

- Contemporary reality is characterised by what Jurgen Habermas has described as "neue Unuebersichtlichkeit", meaning that the full picture of reality escapes us as the world around us becomes more complex and more chaotic. Contrary to popular wisdom the world is not getting any smaller but rapidly expands and gets more difficult to "survey", let alone to understand. This growing complexity implies that for most ordinary information-seekers the dependence upon the professional community of information-providers reaches unprecedented heights. A good reason to monitor the moral justifications those professionals offer for their "selective articulation" of the world's events.

- Information provision is to an ever greater extent the domain of highly trained "spin-doctors" and "perception managers". The growing dependence upon external sources for knowledge about the world runs parallel with the growing skill to manipulate this knowledge. This constitutes a crucial moral concern for journalists and their audiences alike.

- Today's communication environment changes as new mediascapes evolve through innovative technologies and their new uses by younger generations. Users shift from being mere consumers to operating as co-creators of content. This "user-generated content" is increasingly commercially exploited by such mega-corporations as Google and Yahoo. This control poses urgent issues about free speech and intellectual property. Moreover, peer-produced civil journalism and weblog journalism raise challenges to conventional conceptions of professionalism and professional responsibility.

- The reflection on new realities and new dependencies must take place within the historical context of current processes of globalisation, localisation and glocalisation. It all happens at the same time: global impact on local situations, local impact on global developments and the fusion of global and local elements into new glocal formats. For the field of ethics this raises fascinating and perplexing questions about how we should reflect on moral concerns: can the morality of localities (still very strongly present around the globe) be globalised (is universal ethics a realistic proposition?) or should we design new forms of "glocal ethics"? Since moral concerns about the way we communicate inevitably cross borders and we no longer conveniently find the single best answers to moral questions, ethics will have to develop discursive modalities. However, what are the chances of a discursive ethics in a world where a fierce clash of mentalities takes place between the absolutist mind-set and the reflexive mind-set? This is the essential clash we face in today's world: a collision that is more fundamental than rifts between cultures, ethnic backgrounds or religions.

- The absolutist mindset operates with such notions as the absolute truth and absolute certainty. It aspires towards solid moral foundations and sharp dichotomies between good and evil.
- The reflexive mindset proposes that all claims to validity – be they political, moral, or religious – are open to examination and critique. For a global discursive ethics the reflexive mindset is the key requirement. Unfortunately, this mentality is currently worldwide under serious threat from strange bed-fellows such as conservative politicians, fundamentalist religious leaders and a new breed of university manager.

Summing up: the convergence of factors that shape today's provision and use of information-communication contributes to the critical need of ethical reflection. In this exercise the ethicist needs to look "with new eyes" (Proust) at new realities. The prevailing format of "doing ethics" may no longer be adequate. A striking similarity in many ethical studies is the attempt to address moral issues as choices between a limited set of options. Moral questions are often couched in terms of dilemmas for which solutions must be found from deontological, utilitarian or discursive methodologies.

The solutions are usually ambiguous and unsatisfactory. Ethical inquiry needs to be more creative and deconstruct situations that look like dilemmas into configurations of a wide variety of moral options and challenges. We are very fortunate to have such important platforms as *Communication Ethics Now* for this exercise in new forms of reflection!

Cees J. Hamelink
Professor Emeritus Universiteit van Amsterdam

NOTE ON AUTHOR

Cees J. Hamelink studied philosophy and psychology at the University of Amsterdam where he received his PhD degree in 1975. He is currently Professor for Globalisation, Health and Human Rights at the Vrije Universiteit in Amsterdam and Honorary Professor at the University of Queensland, Brisbane, Australia. He is Professor Emeritus of International Communication at the University of Amsterdam, editor-in-chief of the *International Communication Gazette* and president of the Dutch Federation for Human Rights. He has authored seventeen books and published numerous edited books and articles on communication, culture, conflict and human rights.

Creativity, imagination and the ethics of communication

Richard Lance Keeble

The Institute of Communication Ethics (ICE) stresses in its mission statement: "Communication ethics is the founding philosophy for human interaction that defines issues according to their impact on human well-being and relationships."

And it is this caring for people – the desperately poor, the inarticulate, the oppressed – along with a sense that honesty, integrity, clarity, respect for difference and diversity are some of the core principles underlying human interaction and, ultimately, communication ethics that drive the many writings in this volume.

Communication lies at the heart of human experience. After all, we know about our world largely through communication. We engage in discussions with family, friends and colleagues (both on and off-line and via the telephone). We consume books, advertisements, photographs, letters, newspapers, magazines and the broadcast media. Increasingly we use the Internet.

But these are extraordinary times. We face enormous, perhaps unprecedented crises: global warming, mass poverty, environmental degradation, the ever-onward rise of authoritarianism and militarism to name but a few. In order to tackle these issues we need to be able to engage in dialogue, to communicate well, to break down divisions and encourage understanding rather than hatred. And we need to act creatively and imaginatively to inspire new ways of communicating.

This is the context in which the quarterly journal, *Ethical Space: The International Journal of Communication Ethics* (the "voice" of ICE), operates. And this text draws together pieces from the 2005, Volume 2 of the journal. Significantly, *Ethical Space*, since its launch in 2003, has been inter-disciplinary, international, philosophically and theoretically eclectic and rooted in a determination to approach in original ways the pressing political, cultural, environmental issues of today.

COMMUNICATING THE 'NEW IMPERIALISM'

Given that America spends more than all the rest of the world combined on its military – with additional billions of dollars devoted to research and development of armaments and the US/UK-led arms trade fuelling countless conflicts across the globe – it is perhaps not surprising that the opening section "Journalism ethics today" includes chapters on some of the crucial issues involved in reporting of this "new imperialism".

John Tulloch's chapter (using both qualitative and quantitative research strategies) explores the coverage in the UK mainstream media of the so-called "extraordinary renditions". One of those strange euphemistic phrases that clutter the military lexicon of warfare, it denotes the taking of terrorist suspects by the CIA and sundry American intelligence agencies to secret torture prisons around the globe. Usefully Tulloch places his study in an historical, imperial context comparing contemporary reports and commentaries with the coverage of brutality by British forces in earlier conflicts in Kenya and Northern Ireland. He concludes: "In this very British assumption of moral superiority, the dirty work of empire continues." Worryingly, he identifies the extent to which contemplation of the use of torture as a legitimate "weapon" in the fight against "terrorism" has been normalised in the process of the media controversy.

Inauthentic communication is based on lies, secrecy and illusions. Thus one of the many functions of communication ethics is to make visible the invisible. The operations of the CIA and the secret state more widely in both the US and UK have for too long remained veiled behind a cloud of state secrecy and anonymous briefing of journalists by the intelligence services. Investigative journalists bravely exposing the hard facts behind the secret and horrifying "renditions" (in complete contravention of all international, human rights legislation) are clearly outstanding practitioners of ethical journalism and are rightly celebrated by John Tulloch in his chapter.

Following on the theme of human rights, Liz Harrop's chapter examines the journalist's responsibility to promote freedom of expression (particularly at times of conflict) as a fundamental right. Yet, in her study of the US/UK media coverage of the Iraq invasion of 2003, she argues that rather than promote understanding of the "enemy" they indulged in pro-war propaganda. And by filtering communications, distorting facts and compromising access to contrary views, this propaganda violated crucial human rights, including freedom of information, freedom of expression and freedom from discrimination. In effect, Harrop is arguing, controversially, that war propaganda is illegal under international human rights law – though this is rarely acknowledged by the media, governments, or even anti-war campaigners,

Julie-ann Davies's chapter carries on the theme of secrecy examining the growing practice of journalists to use anonymous sources, particularly in the reporting of the "war on terror". She speaks to prominent journalists and whistleblowers on the complex, associated ethical dilemmas and concludes: "But is journalism's first duty to its sources or to its audience? There are no easy answers. Studies have shown that readers find unattributed quotes less credible but it may be difficult for journalists to gain a higher level of public trust unless they address their use of anonymous sources and unattributed quotes."

My own chapter continues the focus on US/UK imperialism arguing that the dominant language of war coverage essentially serves to silence dissident, anti-war views and hide the horrors of "humanitarian" conflicts. It draws on George Orwell's concept of newspeak as outlined in his novel *Nineteen Eighty-Four* and Paul Chilton's notion of nukespeak to trace the origins of what I term "massacrespeak". And as a deliberately "ethical" communicative strategy I begin by exploring the ways in which my personal, subjective experiences and preoccupations have informed my political ideas and activities – and led on to my involvement in debates over communication ethics and peace journalism.

ON EUROMYTHS AND 'DUMBING DOWN'

Simon Cross continues the debate over media standards with a wry, entertaining look at Fleet Street's manufacture of the myth of the "barmy Brussels bureaucrats". But behind the humour, Cross is making a serious point: Euromyths are lies and distortions perpetrated by journalists concerning EU-related issues and dressed up as "facts". Nor are they the exclusive fare of tabloids, concerned only with trivia, gossip and "non-news". The broadsheets also "revel in the pleasure of mobilising Euromythology according to their own particular criteria and partisan interests".

The study of stardom has grown enormously in the academy in recent years while much of the mainstream debate over the "dumbing down" of media standards has focused on the sleaze, trivia and sensationalism usually associated with celebrity coverage. Jane Taylor, in her analysis of the press coverage of the celebrity Carole Caplin, the one-time "personal advisor" to the British Prime Minister's wife, Cherie Blair, explores an intriguing paradox. For at one time, the press, in an archetypal moral panic (dubbed "Cheriegate"), demonised her as a "woman of bad influence". Then soon afterwards they changed tack and celebrated her as an "expert" worth cultivating with one newspaper even giving her a regular column to expound her views. How to explain this? Originally, Taylor draws on the theories of Richard Rorty on language and identity, pragmatism and contingency to show how the coverage can tell us a great deal about the complexities of the hyper-personal: such as the relationship between news and commentary, journalists and their subjects, a newspaper and the expectations of its readers.

Somewhat marginalised from dominant debate over "dumbing down" are critiques of the mainstream media as institutionally racist. Just as John Tulloch, in his earlier chapter, identified the extraordinary weight of 19th century British imperial attitudes on contemporary coverage of US/UK militarism, so Kate Azuka Omenugha shows (through a close content analysis of two Fleet Street newspapers) how the reporting is informed by notions of "otherness" and racial myths, accentuated by the constraints of journalism practice.

Moving away from Fleet Street, Susanne Fengler and Stephan Russ-Mohl, of the Lugano-based European Journalism Observatory, explore the factors behind the "fourth estate's tarnished reputation" in Germany. One of the constant themes of *Ethical Space* is to locate debates over standards within tightly focused political and economic contexts. Significantly here, Russ-Mohl and Fengler suggest that journalists too often see themselves as victims of proprietors' obsessions with "profit maximisation" while a thorough-going, proactive debate within the media and editorial departments over declining standards is well overdue.

Remaining in continental Europe, Angelika W. Wyka examines the history of the media following the 1989 collapse of communism in Poland, Hungary and the Czech Republic and the changes in media standards and journalistic notions of professionalism. At the same time the media were both freed from state control and thrown headlong into a new competitive environment. Wyka suggests that there were positive and negative aspects to this process. She concludes with a call for the reform of editorial and journalistic practices and journalism education. "Only well-educated, professionally sound and responsible journalists will be in a position to increase the respect in which the free means of mass communication are held as democratic institutions."

Tony Harcup highlights democratic practices in his examination of the role of the alternative media and the National Union of Journalists in the promotion of ethical journalism (roles usually ignored in the mainstream debate). And the broadcaster and *Times* columnist Libby Purves ends the section on journalism standards with a lively, heart-felt broadside against the media's daily diet of "unkind intrusions and falsifications" – and she traces the alarming growth of cynicism amongst teenagers.

JOURNALISM ETHICS: HISTORICAL PERSPECTIVES

Martin Conboy, in the introduction to the special edition of *Ethical Space* he edited (Vol. 2, No. 1), commented: "Ethical journalism can only be developed through a dialogic engagement between individual responsibility (of journalist, educator and reader) and the collective burden of institutions and social and political groupings. It also needs to define itself within or against the prevailing pragmatics of the market. Such journalism needs to be popular in the broadest sense of the word for it to provide a suitably critical model for intervention in the contemporary world."

Those issues were explored by a variety of papers at the 9th conference of the International Society for the Study of European Ideas at the University of Navarro, Pamplona in a session entitled "Popular ethics in journalism: Individual burden or collective responsibility?" And a selection of those papers are included here.

Jane Chapman places the consideration of journalism ethics crucially in their historical context, arguing that the French Revolution saw journalism for the first time play a major part in formulating a truly popular ethic of involvement of the citizenry previously excluded from the political life of the nation. She concludes, drawing on the theories of Sandel, that "newspapers provided the crucial narratives by which people made sense of their condition and interpreted their shared experiences at a time of revolutionary upheaval".

Ethical debates in journalism are often framed around notions of professionalisation which emerged in the US and UK towards the end of the nineteenth century and too often leave unproblematised capitalist norms of production. In his own chapter, Conboy returns to the early part of the nineteenth century when the central elements of journalistic discourse were being formulated to argue that both the political economy of the media and its content have ethical implications. He focuses on just one small element of the period's vast outpouring of radical journalism – Wooler's *Black Dwarf* – to highlight its carnivalesque mix of parody, satire and libertarian rhetoric. And Conboy suggests that the journal, while it exposed the limitations of journalism fixed within a capitalist system, also offered a more radical and popular engagement through its textual experimentation.

COMMUNICATION ETHICS AND PEDAGOGY

The next section draws on a selection of papers at the ICE annual conference of 2005 which explored the impact of communication ethical theory on teaching practice. Firstly Raphael Cohen-Almagor analyses the concept of compromise through a discussion of teaching ethics in class. In particular, the chapter addresses the complexities of abortion and Cohen-Almagor discusses critically his own personal experience in teaching this issue in the United States.

Next, John Strain argues that the teaching of professional ethics is important across all disciplines in higher education, not just communication studies. In addition, it highlights the importance of communication in the ethics of all professions and identifies the scope for collaboration across the different professions.

Brian Hoey stresses the value of life coaching principles in resolving some of the problematic ethical issues in the teaching of the creative arts. Finally in this section, Brian Morris draws on the Japanese concept of ba meaning a "place that harbours meaning" while discussing the role his online blog played for his students' final year students doing their multimedia undergraduate projects. Crucially, he found that the blog helped close down the distance between the student and supervisor: "The awareness of the power of a safe and trusting environment, or ba, has become for me an ethical imperative for my project supervision exercised under conditions of high-care."

PR ETHICS AND PEDAGOGY

The ethics of Public Relations theory and practice have been a major concern of ICE since its formation. Here Simon Goldsworthy continues the pedagogy theme arguing that, while "plenty of lush, moralistic vegetation flourishes" in the PR field, education can play only a limited role in inculcating ethical practice. Next, Anne Gregory tackles the question of whether PR can help organisations communicate more ethically with their stakeholders. And she uses a teaching case study to describe how one large Mental Health NHS Trust has implemented its public relations-led involvement policy.

COMMUNICATION ETHICS: PHILOSOPHICAL EXPLORATIONS

The complexities of the philosophical issues underlying communication ethics are explored in the next four chapters. Karen Sanders contrasts the merits of the "freedom paradigm" of the Enlightenment with the authoritarian paradigm of communitarian thought; the possibility of objective, "good" journalism with that of subjective, "bad" journalism. She concludes by arguing that unless "we agree upon what journalism is for we will find it difficult to develop a framework for evaluating the practice of ethical journalism".

Next Kristine Lowe interviews Dr Hallvard Johannes Fossheim of the Oslo Happiness Project which aims to investigate ancient conceptions of the good life and to create greater awareness of ancient insights into ethics. The project was started in 2003 by a group of scholars in philosophy and antique languages. Robert Beckett draws on a vast range of theorists (such as Engels, Habermas, Lyotard, Marcuse, Popper, Sartre) to highlight the relevance of the concept of the dialectic to the formulation of a rigorous ethic of communication. Moira Carroll-Mayer and Bernd Carsten Stahl shift the focus to cyberspace and discuss whether involvement in virtual environments can be used as an excuse from responsibility. Examining in detail the cases of Rusnak and Leeson, two online traders successfully prosecuted in the criminal courts for having lost huge sums of money, Carroll-Mayer and Cartsen Stahl argue there are stimuli unique to cyberspace that induce psychological disturbance and moral ambiguity synonymous with postmodern ennui.

BUSINESS AND COMMUNICATION ETHICS: BEYOND THE CONTRADICTIONS

In another "Face to Face" interview, Kristine Lowe talks to Professor Paul Jackson, of the Manchester Business School, about communication ethics and Corporate Social Responsibility. Intriguingly, Jackson comments that Enron, the company at the heart of one of the biggest financial scandals of all time, had a "beautiful ethical code". Fittingly then the discussion ends the volume highlighting the complexity of the issues involved – and the contradictions at the heart of the human predicament and the ethical search for meaning.

PART 1

JOURNALISM ETHICS TODAY

1

Normalising the unthinkable: The British press, torture, and the human rights of terrorist suspects

John Tulloch

This chapter explores contemporary media coverage of torture by examining in detail the editorial positions taken on the issue of "extraordinary rendition" by UK national daily and weekly newspapers during December 2005. It explores the historic origins of the myths dominating mainstream media coverage of torture drawing on comparisons with UK press coverage of brutality by British forces in previous emergencies, including conflicts in Kenya and Northern Ireland. In addition, it discusses the extent to which the contemplation of the use of torture in anti-terrorism strategies has been normalised in the process of media debate. In conclusion, the 2005 "rendition" controversy suggests that dominant myths surrounding British uses of torture are "alive and well".

"The British have always been coy about torture, and with good reason" David Anderson (2005: 293)

"Opinions which justify cruelty are inspired by cruel impulses" Bertrand Russell (1950)

INTRODUCTION

How much does the recent, and continuing, controversy over "extraordinary rendition" – flying terrorist suspects to countries where allegedly they can be tortured outside Western legal jurisdiction – reflect a change in the moral climate of debate, to allow a contemplation in the public sphere of measures once regarded as outside civilised discussion? Edward Herman suggests that one role of the "mainstream media" is to ease the birth of measures previously regarded as unthinkable:

> Doing terrible things in an organised and systematic way rests on "normalisation". This is the process whereby ugly, degrading, murderous and unspeakable acts become routine and are accepted as "the way things are done"…It is the function of the defense intellectuals and other experts and the mainstream media to normalise the unthinkable for the general public (Herman 1992: 67).

TOUCHSTONE OF THE ENLIGHTENMENT

The abolition of torture as part of the legal process is generally regarded as one of the touchstones of the Enlightenment.[1] Michael Ignatieff observes that "liberal democracy's very history and identity is tied up in an absolute prohibition of torture" (Ignatieff 2005: 136). Torture was a key issue in the Enlightenment critique of ancien regimes acquiring "a universally pejorative association…[as] the supreme enemy of humanitarian jurisprudence and of liberalism" (Peters 1996: 75).

Although the comforting narrative of moral progress, which was the founding myth of 19th century liberalism, has long been smashed, explicit support for the use of torture to gain information from terrorism suspects is still comparatively rare in the British press and tends to be confined to the letters page, humorous columns, and occasional opinion pieces by outside contributors.[2] Even conservative British commentators have not tended to support the high profile position of the American Alan Dershowitz, the Harvard law professor who has notoriously argued for the limited use of torture, and its incorporation within the US legal system, on the grounds that terrorist attacks represent a mortal threat to democratic states.[3]

This is an understandable reticence, as the most routine invocation of torture in British editorial columns has been associated with descriptions of "non-democratic", "totalitarian" states. Discussions in the press usually present its use as a barbarous aberration alien to an imagined British and Anglo-Saxon tradition. Indeed, the case made for the 2003 invasion of Iraq was not only based on the alleged existence of weapons of mass destruction but the appalling human rights record of the regime – as, for example, described by President Bush in February 2003: "Bringing stability and unity to a free Iraq will not be easy, yet that is no excuse to leave the Iraqi regime's torture chambers and poison labs in operation" (quoted by Blumner 2003). Of course, the demonisation of Saddam Hussein in the run-up to the invasion of Iraq in 2003, allowed a large scope for moral manoeuvre in terms of the tactics that the West might adopt. Setting a standard of absolute evil allows lesser evils "wiggle room" to be condoned. As the *Independent* war correspondent Robert Fisk observes: "If Saddam's immorality and wickedness had to be the yardstick against which all our own iniquities were judged, what did that say about us? If Saddam's regime was to be the moral compass to define our actions, how bad – how iniquitous – did that allow us to be?' (Fisk 2005: 1,262).

But on torture, as on slavery, British national identity is formed on the basis that historically "our" hands are clean. This position has a firm basis of support in the British judiciary and in English and Scottish legal tradition – as Lord Bingham asserted forcefully in December 2005 when the Law Lords pronounced against the use of evidence obtained by torture in British courts: "The English Common law has regarded torture and its fruits with abhorrence for over 500 years"(*Economist* 2005). In the Scottish *Daily Express*, the MSP and Shadow Justice Minister Kenny MacAskill declared: "Torture has put all our laws under threat" (MacAskill 2005).

This comforting notion that torture has always been alien to the operations of the British state (although certainly not alien to English trials involving crimes against the state, and some witch trials – see Thomas 1973: 615-618) buttresses what Mark Curtis describes as an overarching concept of the "basic benevolence" of British foreign policy and Britain's historic role as a champion of human rights (Curtis 2003: 380). This complex of moral sentiment, liberal myth and wish-fulfilment still broadly informs the press coverage of torture.

THE DOMINANT MYTH

The long form of the comforting myth dominating mainstream British press coverage of the torture controversy runs as follows, with some variations: torture is alien to British traditions but Britain can be infected by less morally enlightened cultures. Where we discover an abuse we correct it. Torture is the invention and the fault of "the other" – whether it be the KGB or the CIA. For example, one frequently cited source for the imagined reintroduction of torture techniques in the twentieth century is Nazi Germany or the Soviet Union. But, as Malise Ruthven argues "in this...the Nazis have been made scapegoats for other European powers. The British...did not learn the techniques of torture that were employed in Cyprus, Kenya and Aden from the Nazis or the Russians. Torture was widely used by the native police in India during the first half of the nineteenth century – in fact, it became the subject of a major row between the reformists and the supporters of the old East India Company in 1854" (Ruthven 1976).

In fact, torture was integral to the operations of the Victorian empire. The 1855 Report of the Commissioners for the Investigation of Alleged Cases of

Torture in the Madras Presidency described the torturing activities of native police, allegedly against the commands of superior British officers. According to the historian of India's premier daily newspaper, the *Hindu*, the earliest popular association formed in the Madras Presidency, the Madras Native Association, in July 1852 "became a focal point for an agitation against torture for collecting government dues" (Parthasarathy 1978: 2). But native police were an easy target, and the commissioners were reluctant to ascribe blame to the colonial authorities (Peters 1996: 137).

Torture was possible in a colonial setting because of the twin tyrannies of distance from the imperial heartland and racism – at the level of policing, colonial subject peoples were not regarded as worthy of the consideration of white citizens and possessed no "natural" rights, while the colonial setting lacked the structures of convention, legal authority, and media surveillance that offered protection. In pre-1947 colonial India, observes Tapan Raychaudhuri, "All Indians, whatever their status, shared the experience of being treated as racial inferiors...British people reacted violently against proposals that would make them subject to the authority of Indian judges. The Viceroy Lord Curzon commented that the British in India got away with murder because no white jury would find a white man guilty of killing a native. As late as 1930 British officers were advised in a secret army memorandum that they should not kick Indians" (Raychaudhuri 1996: 367).

George Orwell, as a young policeman in Burma, experienced this reality at first hand. "In a job like that you see the dirty work of the Empire at close quarters. The wretched prisoners huddling in the stinking cages of the lock-ups, the grey, cowed faces of the long-term convicts, the scarred buttocks of the men who have been flogged with bamboos – all these oppressed me with an intolerable sense of guilt" (Orwell and Angus 1968: 236).

This reality was that the potential for torture was inherent in the power relations, between coloniser and subject people, as Peters reflects: "The colonial experience indeed seems to have contributed to the reappearance of torture, but not because colonial administrators and police learned such practices from the populations they governed; rather, the very circumstances in which they governed populations which became increasingly restive during the twentieth century led to the abuse of authority that included torture and later became routine in places like Algeria" (Peters op cit: 138).

Since 1945, Britain has been involved in a bewildering series of overlapping colonial and post-colonial operations including: East Indies (1945-46), Indo-China (1945-46), Palestine (1945-48), Malaya (1948-60), Korea (1950-53), Kenya (1952-60), Suez (1951-52, 1956), Greece (1944-48), Cyprus (1954-59), Jordan (1958), British Guiana (1962-66), Borneo (1963-66), Brunei (1962), Muscat (1963), Aden (1962-67), Northern Ireland (1969-), the Falklands (1982), the Gulf (1961, 1990-91, 2003-), Bosnia (1992-92) and Kosovo (1999). In Malaya and Kenya, "coercion tended to be the first resort of policy" (Cain and Hopkins 2002: 631). Malaya, "part of the triple engine of British economic development in the post-war colonial world" (Brown and Louis 1999: 35) provided the initial testing ground where the techniques of "low intensity operations" were pioneered – a holistic approach to anti-insurgent warfare which prioritised small group, low level military operations, intelligence operations, intensive interrogation of suspects and propaganda campaigns. This came to be seen "as a model for the suppression of communist insurgency" (Grey 2002: 73; see also Stubbs 1989).

THE BRITISH TRADITION OF TORTURE

Malaya and many of these subsequent operations – notably Kenya, Aden, Cyprus, and Ireland – have involved allegations of torture by British forces. If there is a British torture tradition it appears to be intimately associated with these late imperial activities – and as India was the largest operation in the global racket, India "hands" appear to have had an intriguing role in the transfer of torture techniques. For example: recent investigative journalism has begun to uncover details of the systematic abuse of Nazi prisoners in immediate post-war British internment camps and prisons (Cobain 2005, BBC Radio 4, 9 January 2006) operated by the Combined Services Detailed Interrogation Centre, a division of the War Office. Its centres included the celebrated London Cage, and documents unearthed in November 2005 "show [it] was a secret torture centre where German prisoners who had been concealed from the Red Cross were beaten, deprived of sleep, and threatened with execution or with unnecessary surgery" (Cobain op.cit). Foreign Office files also detail allegations of appalling treatment at the Bad Nenndorf prison in Austria, overseen by a former Colonel in the Indian army, transferred to military intelligence (ibid).

   In Cyprus, the British authorities fought a bitter campaign against fierce resistance by insurgents seeking union with Greece. "Increasingly, intelligence was extracted from interrogations, which degenerated into torture, with prisoners thrashed with a metal chain. Even the *Daily Express* noted in passing that 'every known method had been tried except electric shock'" (Dorril 2000: 553-4). Kenya was also a counter-insurgency campaign that gave extensive scope to official and systematic brutality, and the creation of a British "gulag" (Elkins 2005) despite quite extensive publicity in the UK deriving from the testimony of police officers, former officials and Christian activists. The *Daily Mirror* funded a high-profile visit by the Labour MP, Barbara Castle, (Perkins 2003: 140) in which she unearthed examples of unlawful detention and beatings to extract information, and published a series of campaigning articles on her return. As well as the *Mirror*, the *Manchester Guardian*, *Observer*, *Daily Worker* and *News Statesman* all published stories alleging torture (Elkins op cit: 286-7).

   But the campaign made little headway in the face of the lack of interest of senior figures in the Labour opposition, and a dominant narrative, orchestrated through the conservative press, of courageous white settlers, threatened with massacre, going about their lawful business of building a prosperous country for all races, with Britain as their benevolent guardian. In fact, 32 white settlers were killed during the emergency – 1,090 Kikuyu were hanged for Mau Mau crimes, probably 20,000 rebels died in combat and perhaps 150,000 Kikuyu were detained in British camps (Anderson 2005: 4-7).

No accurate figures exist for the number of deaths as a result of detention, but estimates range from 130,000 to 300,000. (Elkins op cit: 366 and 429). But until recently, this record has attracted little attention. As Anderson observes: "The Algerian war was just as notoriously dirty as the British campaign in Kenya, with several allegations of state torture and atrocity being published at the time and never seriously disputed; but whereas in Britain allegations of this kind have been left to slip into the forgotten litter of history, in France…public confessions to the institutional use of torture…have sparked a reexamination of the French experience in Algeria, and a national reckoning" (Anderson op cit: 293-4).

BRITAIN'S NATIONAL RECKONING: NORTHERN IRELAND

The closest to a national reckoning came when an emergency erupted on Britain's own doorstep in Northern Ireland. With the introduction of internment in 1971, and initial swoops on 342 republicans, eleven suspects were chosen for interrogation at secret centres as guinea-pigs for the use of the "five techniques" of interrogation (hooding, noise bombardment, food and sleep deprivation, forced standing) pioneered in the previous colonial emergencies, notably Malaya and Aden (Taylor 2002: 68; English 2003: 142; Moloney 2002: 102). In response to widespread allegations of torture, the Compton inquiry was set up by Heath government in August 1971 and concluded there had been no torture or brutality but "a measure of ill-treatment". The Irish journalist and historian Tim Pat Coogan observes that "the name Compton became a synonym for 'whitewash' in the minds of many Irish people" (Coogan 1995: 129).

A further inquiry produced a stringent minority report from Lord Gardiner, who concluded the techniques were morally unjustifiable and illegal. Prime Minister Edward Heath announced that his government would discontinue the use of the techniques. In September 1976 Britain was found by the European Commission of Human Rights in Strasbourg of breaching the European Convention on Human Rights and employing not only "inhuman and degrading treatment" but also torture. The "torture" part of the judgment was withdrawn by the European Court of Human Rights in a subsequent verdict in January 1978 (Taylor op cit: 73-74).

Twelve out of seventeen judges "seemed to have agreed with the position laid out by Sir Gerald Fitzmaurice, the British judge on the court, who argued that if having one's fingernails torn out, being impaled on a stake through the rectum, or being roasted on an electric grid is torture, then the five techniques were something less" (Conroy 2000: 187). The continuing controversy during the 70s about the use of the five techniques probably constitutes the longest and most detailed public debate about torture in the British media, and saw the full deployment by the mainstream press of the limited number of rhetorical strategies available to defend a state against allegations of torture – roughly, they come down to an overlapping set of fourteen or so propositions (see Conroy 2000: 244):

1. outright denial that events happened or what was done constituted torture
2. treatment was not torture but tough, standard practice
3. treatment was really to safeguard welfare of suspect – e.g.hooding protected identity
4. acts complained of were isolated mistakes in heat of action
5. acts were perpetrated by a minority of 'bad apples'
6. terrorists commit worse atrocities
7. dealing with fanatics precludes kid gloves
8. what we do is more humane than what is practised in other countries – torture alien to our traditions
9. information could not be got any other way
10. information was time sensitive – the 'ticking bomb' scenario
11. no permanent damage to subjects
12. attacks/criticism of security forces are part of a propaganda war
13. need to move on / no point raking up past
14. we must practise a "lesser evil" to guard against a greater – moral dilemmas inevitable

In terms of Britain's trade, it is reasonable to conclude that the five techniques, even if discontinued in the land of their invention, and updated beyond recognition by the latest in medical research, remain among the most enduring and successful of our invisible exports.

RENDITION AND THE BRITISH PRESS

British national press coverage of the rendition issue in November-December 2005 was overwhelmingly hostile to the practice, but the level of criticism of the United States varied considerably, from outright condemnation of the US political system to a more-in-sorrow-than-in-anger reproachfulness. Most newspapers attacked the term "extraordinary rendition" as a piece of sinister bureaucratese or "weasel words". Some explored its etymology more deeply. One example was George Kerevan in the *Scotsman*, who argued: "The phrase is not meant to hide anything from you or me…rather, it is meant to allow the users to hide from their own conscience." The volume of coverage also varied markedly (see Table 1). Items using the term "rendition" and/or "extraordinary rendition" were highest in the *Independent*, closely followed by the *Guardian*, with *The Times* and *Daily Mail* affording substantial coverage in third and fourth place respectively.

Most striking was the lack of coverage in popular News Corporation newspapers (owned by Rupert Murdoch) – notably the *Sun* and the *News of the World*, with both papers only notching up one reference to "torture flights" and none to "rendition", compared to the *Daily Mirror* (17 references to "rendition", 5 "torture flights") and the *Express* (11 references to "rendition", 7 to "torture flights").

Of the papers surveyed none explicitly argued for the use of torture against terrorist suspects, although the *Sun*, *News of the World*, and the *Daily Express*, in varying ways, gave some support to the argument that the "war on terror" required exceptional methods. Within the broadly consensual approach of the rest

Table 1 Incidence of items using terms relating to rendition in UK national periodicals and 2 US newspapers, December 1-31, 2005

TFs = "torture flights(s)"
Rs ="rendition(s)"
ERs ="extraordinary rendition(s)"
CIAFs = "CIA flights(s)"

Publication	'TFs'	'Rs'	'ERs'	'CIAFs'
Times 7	28	15	6	
Telegraph/ST	1	13	5	7
Guardian	9	45	16	10
Independent	5	57	19	14
Scotsman/SoS	5	11	9	5
Mail/MoS	6	25	14	9
Express/SE	7	11	4	5
Mirror/SM	5	17	10	2
Sun	1	0	0	0
Standard	2	3	2	0
Sunday Times	0	3	3	1
Observer	0	4	3	0
Economist	2	4	1	0
News of World	1	1	0	0
People	0	0	0	0
New York Times	0	23	7	0
Washington Post	0	9	2	3

Source: count based on NewsBank Newspapers UK Ltd database of all items in selected UK and US periodicals, British Newspaper Library, 2-5 January 2006

of the press, there were a number of distinct positions – ranging from a stand on the absolute human rights enshrined in the UN Convention Against Torture and a total condemnation of torture under any circumstances, to a more nuanced, equivocal, utilitarian position – implying that, in certain circumstances, and in a changed world, it might be understandable, if regrettable, as a lesser evil to prevent a greater evil.

The *Independent*'s editorial comment for 2 December 2005 is a good illustration of the absolutist human rights position:

Britain and Europe must stand by their principles
The British political establishment has been demonstrating a *disgracefully equivocal attitude* on the subject of torture for some time…now we learn that our government has *sunk even lower into this immoral quagmire* than we previously imagined…Torture "no matter how light" cannot be justified on any grounds. It is not too late for Britain to stand up to its ally and refuse to have any part in *this vile practice* whatsoever (*Independent* 2005 my italics).

'THE TREACHEROUS TERRITORY OF MORAL UNCERTAINTY'

Imagery associated with swamps – the treacherous territory of moral uncertainty, summoning up entrapment, dirt, and contamination – recurs frequently in discussion by leader writers. The animating idea is of the reduction of all moral certainties to a relativist morass in which all states, no matter what their human rights records, become equivalent.

In a similar vein, leaders in the *Scotsman* also condemned the use of torture as absolutely wrong, although a substantial comment piece by George Kerevan detailed the case of Wolfgang Daschner, deputy head of Frankfurt am Main police, who, in October 2002, threatened a kidnapper with torture unless he revealed where his victim was. Daschner was prosecuted for "aggravated coercion", fined and put on probation.

> "I have to admit I'd probably have done what [he] did in the circumstances – and accept the legal consequences as did Mr Daschner. So anyone who thinks the torture debate is an open-and-shut moral case is being naïve. But that said, we can't leave the torture question in some relativist limbo where the state – any state – can turn physical coercion in to a global industry" (Kerevan 2005).

The perils of naivety and the need for alertness to moral ambiguity also characterises *The Times*'s David Aaronovitch comment piece, which adopts an uneasy, ambivalent rhetorical posture that moves confusingly between condemning torture and hinting that, in some circumstances, it is understandable:

All right it can work – but let's keep the thumbscrews under lock and key...

...*Good old-fashioned disastrous* realpolitik would suggest that we turn aside when torture happens. If, in the short term, we have a chance of extracting a few key names, places and plans, then lives may be saved and *we should let the renderers rend*. It is precisely the same logic that led us to trade smiles and Sandhurst places with Middle Eastern dictators for years (Aaronovitch 2005 my italics).

GRABBING THE MORAL HIGH GROUND

In this faux-jocular rhetoric, "realpolitik" is both "good" and "disastrous". Lives 'may be saved' if we let rendition continue and perhaps "torture works" if a ticking bomb is involved.[4] However, because "we" are enlisted in a "war of ideas" in which it is assumed "we" have the moral high ground, "we" must not become like the "Middle Eastern" dictators who, of course, represent everything "we" must not become. Torture itself is characterised in a jokey way as "thumbscrews", summoning up Pythonesque early modern images of the Spanish Inquisition, rather than the sophisticated repertoire of 21st century assaults on the nervous system and the integrity of the personality. As Peters observes: "Not only the traditional institutions, but the traditional methods of torture have been generally discarded; the strappado, the rack, thumbscrews, legsplints and fire now below to an age whose technology...has been surpassed by modernity' (Peters 1996: 163).

This may be to subject a columnist's linguistic play to a more demanding interrogation than routine, diurnal wordsmithery should be asked to withstand. But Aaronovitch represents a key distinction within the anti-torture consensus between papers taking a broadly pro-American stance, and those more critical of US policy. The *Sunday Times*, which provided the longest and most detailed analysis of rendition published by the weeklies (see December 11, 2005) ran a more-in-sorrow-than-in-anger leader which was both critical of torture but supportive of the US:

A noble vision lost
...There are of course moral dilemmas here. The White House is *understandably irritated* by a *holier than thou attitude of Europeans* who would be the first to complain if suspects had knowledge of impending terrorist attacks in their cities which was not extracted from them. But we are *rarely if ever* talking about the 'ticking time bomb' threat beloved of apologists for brutality. Information obtained by 'enhanced interrogation' is also *quite likely to be so unreliable* as to be of no use...The [US] was built on the enlightenment rejection of arbitrary justice. To tolerate torture betrays that

great republic's founding fathers' (*Sunday Times*, 11 December 2005 my italics).

In its appeal to the myth of the founding fathers and the purity of their Enlightenment project – airbrushing slavery and the arbitrary justice meted out to native people from the picture (e.g. see Rose 2004: 138), this accepts the main charge whilst being supportive of the US. In a similar fashion, the *Economist* reduces issues to presentational ones – Messrs. Cheney and Rumsfeld, in their eagerness to pursue "military efficacy", have forgotten the importance of "America's good name". It then argues that the allegations are unproven, the "alleged transgressions pale when set beside those of the enemies both it and Europe are fighting" and that US intelligence has helped save European lives "– so far unproven".

UNCRITICAL SUPPORT FOR US

In striking contrast to the *Sunday Times*, News Corporation's popular stablemate, the *News of the World*, uneasily rubbishes the charges completely and demands uncritical support of the US:

> **Abuse claims refuted**
> Human rights groups allege the CIA is using Shannon Airport to transport Al Qaeda suspects for interrogation by torture. They say these *so-called* torture flights have landed at Shannon no less than 50 times. But we should treat these *wild* claims with a pinch of salt. The unequivocal denial today from James Kenny, the US ambassador to Ireland, leaves absolutely no doubt that this is untrue. Both he and US Secretary of State Condoleezza Rice state quite clearly that the US does not condone, or use, torture any any circumstances. We are tied to the USA by blood and history. And when our friends deny these claims we must believe them. (*News of the World*, 11 December 2005, Eire edition).[5]

The *Observer*, along with the *Guardian*, also stood on an absolutist human rights position in rejecting torture and took a more explicitly anti-American line. A leader of 4 December declared "the fact that this repugnant practice exists shames an administration...cavalier approach to human rights...undermine the very values that the War against Terror was supposed to encourage" (*Observer* 2005). The following Sunday, Henry Porter's long comment piece condemned US policy for sinking "to the moral level of Saddam" and invoked World War 11 as a touchstone of civilisation:

> Are we Europeans content as long as the torture is not going on in our

backyard? It would seem so, but in Britain we should remember that during the war, when we faced a greater threat than the one posed by al-Qaeda, we did not resort to torture. The late Colonel T.A. Robertson, a friend of my family's, was known as TAR in MI5, where for much of the Second World War he directed the B1(a) section responsible for tracking down Abwehr agents. He would no more have contemplated torture than amputating his own right hand. No doubt this charming man was as hard as nails but he was also *civilised* and, like the rest of his generation, fought for civilisation (Porter 2005).[6]

Like Porter, most British people born between the 1940s and the 1960s were swaddled in the comfort blanket of the essential decency of "our" forces and the integrity of the British human rights record. But a gathering volume of research is ripping this blanket away.

CONCLUSIONS: THE DIRTY WORK OF EMPIRE

The short form of the comforting myth for the British and their leader writers is essentially that torture was and is something done by other people. This myth is alive and well and routinely re-presented in leader columns as a given. The rendition controversy did nothing to shake those basic assumptions. The culprits were reassuringly foreign – American, Egyptian etc – and the agencies involved were an administration, regarded by liberals as outlandishly right-wing even by US standards, and the CIA. The most newsworthy and scandalous factor of the continuing coverage was the interesting possibility of British and European connivance – a helpful club for the *Daily Mail* and others with which to beat the Blair government.

A reflex anti-Americanism, accompanied by a patronising attitude to US culture, institutions and values is, of course, a familiar default position for sections of the British press – in conservative newspapers such as the *Daily Telegraph* and the *Daily Mail* it surfaces in the argument that if only Americans would behave properly and live up to their founding fathers, their constitution, their imperial responsibilities, and the English language and so on all would be well. Many comments also utilised the imagery of infection and moral contamination involved in an alliance with a serial human rights abuser and the damage to British standing in the world.

Although the explicit advocacy of torture still remains largely outside the pale, many editorial discussions alluded to moral ambiguity, and implicitly entertained the possibility that, in an imperfect world, there were circumstances in which torture was understandable, even if not condonable, and something that should be done by morally inferior others. In this very British assumption of moral superiority, the dirty work of empire continues.

NOTES

1. Torture is defined in Article 1 of the UN Convention Against Torture and Other Cruel, Inhuman or Degrading Treatment or Punishment as follows: "an act by which severe pain or suffering, whether physical or mental, is intentionally inflicted on a person for such purposes as obtaining from him or a third person information or a confession, punishing him for an act he or a third person has committed or is suspected of having committed, or intimidating or coercing him or a third person, or for any reason based on discrimination of any kind, when such pain or suffering is inflicted by or at the instigation of or with the consent or acquiescence of a public official or other person acting in an official capacity. It does not include pain or suffering arising only from, inherent in or incidental to lawful sanctions". Article 2 states: "No exceptional circumstances whatsoever, whether a state of war or a threat of war, internal political instability or any other public emergency, may be invoked as a justification for torture." Article 3 states: "1. No State Party shall expel, return or extradite a person to another State where there are substantial grounds for believing that he would be in danger of being subjected to torture. 2. For the purpose of determining whether there are such grounds, the competent authorities shall take into account all relevant considerations including, where applicable, the existence in the State concerned of a consistent pattern of gross, flagrant or mass violations of human rights." Extract from UN General Assembly Resolution 39/46, UN GAOR Supp. (No 51), adopted 10 December 1984 (reprinted in Peters op cit: 273-285). The Convention does not define cruel, inhuman nor degrading treatment.

2. See for example this example from the *Daily Express*, 21 December 2005: letter: "What is the fuss about these so-called torture flights? If they do exist, and terrorist suspects are being transported around the world for interrogation, the information gleaned will undoubtedly prevent more attacks such as 9/11, Madrid, Bali, or 7/7." For humour see another example from the *Daily Express* Hickey column 15 December 2005: "A busy time at Hickey Towers. I have had the staff up all night clearing a landing strip on the north pastures, the use of which I plan to offer my old chums at the CIA. If the shrieking liberals force our brave allies away from Prestwick, Glasgow, Edinburgh and Wick etc with their complaints about 'torture' flights, then the least I can do is offer to step in and help…"

3. Although Melanie Phillips (of the *Daily Mail*) on BBC Radio 4's Moral Maze ethics discussion programme of 8 December 2005 argued in cross-questioning a "witness" that torture was an acceptable evil in averting a major terrorist atrocity – the so-called "ticking bomb" hypothesis. A representative statement of the ticking bomb hypothetical is Michael J. Perry's: "Is it really the case that there are no imaginable conditions under which it would be morally permissible to subject a person to torture? An affirmative answer is counter-intuitive. Imagine that the person, a terrorist, has placed a nuclear bomb in the middle of a large city, that the bomb has been set to go off in a few hours, and that the terrorist, just captured in another city,

will disclose the location of the bomb, which can be defused, only if he is tortured." Perry describes the point of his "thought experiment" as to suggest the difficulty many people face in a claim that the moral right not to be tortured is absolute (Perry 1998: 94).

4.   Slavoj Zizek, discussing the US espionage series *24 Hours*, observes the following "Such a sense of urgency has an ethical dimension. The pressure of events is so overwhelming, the stakes so high, that they necessitate a kind of suspension of ordinary moral concerns; displaying such concerns when the lives of millions are at stake means playing into the hands of the enemy. The CTU [counter terrorism unit] agents, as well as their terrorist opponents, live and act in a shadowy space not covered by the law, doing things that 'simply have to be done' to save our societies from the threat of destruction' (Zizek 2006).

5.   To justify sending detainees to these countries, the Administration appears to be relying on a very fine reading of an imprecise clause in the United Nations Convention Against Torture (which the U.S. ratified in 1994), requiring "substantial grounds for believing" that a detainee will be tortured abroad. Martin Lederman, a lawyer who left the Justice Department's Office of Legal Counsel in 2002, after eight years, says: "The Convention only applies when you know a suspect is more likely than not to be tortured, but what if you kind of know? That's not enough. So there are ways to get around it" (Mayer 2005).

6.   Jane Mayer in the *New Yorker* also observes: "Perhaps surprisingly, the fiercest internal resistance to this thinking has come from people who have been directly involved in interrogation, including veteran F.B.I. and C.I.A. agents. Their concerns are as much practical as ideological. Years of experience in interrogation have led them to doubt the effectiveness of physical coercion as a means of extracting reliable information. They also warn that the Bush Administration, having taken so many prisoners outside the realm of the law, may not be able to bring them back in. 'It's a big problem,' Jamie Gorelick, a former deputy attorney general and a member of the 9/11 Commission, says. 'In criminal justice, you either prosecute the suspects or let them go. But if you've treated them in ways that won't allow you to prosecute them you're in this no man's land. What do you do with these people?'" (ibid).

REFERENCES

Aaronovitch, David (2005) "All right it can work – but let's keep the thumbscrews under lock and key", *The Times*, Features section, 6 December p 24

Anderson, David (2005) *Histories of the Hanged. Britain's Dirty War in Kenya and the End of Empire*, London, Weidenfeld and Nicolson

BBC Radio 4 (2006) "Document", 9 January.

Blumner, Robyn E. (2003) Perspective Column, *New York Times*, 16 November

Bright, Martin (2006) "Rendition: the Cover-Up", *New Statesman*, 23 January pp 12-13

Brown, Judith M, and Louis, W. Roger (eds) (1999) *Introduction to The Oxford History of the British Empire. The Twentieth Century*, Oxford, Oxford University Press

Cain, P.J. and Hopkins, A.G. (2002) *British Imperialism 1688-2000*, London, Longman second edition

Cobain, Ian (2005) "Britain's Secret Torture Centre. The interrogation camp that turned prisoners into living skeletons", *Guardian*, 17 December pp 8-9

Conroy, John (2000) *Unspeakable Acts, Ordinary People*. Berkeley and Los Angeles, University of California Press

Coogan, Tim, Pat (1995) *The Troubles*, London, Hutchinson

Curtis, Mark (2003) *Web of Deceit. Britain's Real Role in the World*, London, Vintage

Curtis, Mark (2004) *Unpeople*, London, Vintage

Daily Mail (1971a) "Army cleared of torture. Just rough stuff says Ulster report", 15 November, p.2

Daily Mail (1971b) Comment. "Nothing to be ashamed of", 17 November p.6

Dorril, Stephen (2000) *MI6. Fifty Years of Special Operations*, London, Fourth Estate

Economist (2005a) "Minced Words" 11 December

Economist (2005b) "The fruit of a poisoned tree. When evidence obtained by torture can and cannot be used," 17 December

Elkins, Caroline (2005) *Britain's Gulag. The Brutal End of Empire in Kenya*, London, Jonathan Cape

English, Richard (2003) *Armed Struggle. A history of the IRA*, London, Macmillan

Fisk, Robert (2005) *The Great War for Civilisation. The Conquest of the Middle East*, London, Fourth Estate

Grey, Jeffrey (2002) Malaya, 1948-1960. Defeating communist insurgency, Thompson, Julian (ed.) *The Imperial War Museum Book of Modern Warfare*, London, Sidgwick and Jackson

Herman, Edward (1992) *Beyond Hypocrisy: Decoding the News in an Age of Propaganda*, Boston, MA, South End Press

Hilton, Isabel (2004) "Alleged terror suspects are held incommunicado all over the world", *Guardian* 28 July 2004

Ignatieff, Michael (2005) *The Lesser Evil. Political Ethics in an Age of Terror*, Edinburgh, Edinburgh University Press

Independent (2005) "Britain and Europe must stand by their principles", 2 December p. 42

Kitson, Frank (1991) *Low Intensity Operations: Subversion, Insurgency and Peacekeeping*, London, Faber and Faber

Kerevan, George (2005) "When torture becomes an intelligence tool", *Scotsman*, 9 December

MacAskill, Kenny (2005) "Torture has put all our laws under threat", *Daily Express*, 11 December

Mayer, Jane (2005) "Outsourcing Torture: The secret history of America's 'extraordinary rendition' program", *New Yorker*, 14 February

Moloney, Ed (2002) *A Secret History of the IRA*. London, Allen Lane the Penguin Press

Observer (2005) "Torture must stop. US 'rendition' shames its allies", 4 December p. 28

Orwell, George (1968) Shooting an Elephant, Orwell, Sonia and Angus, Ian (eds) *The*

Collected Essays, Journalism and Letters of George Orwell, Vol. 1 "An Age Like This" 1920-1940, London, Secker and Warburg

Parthasarathy, Rangaswami (1978) *A Hundred Years of the Hindu*, Madras, Kasturi and Sons

Perry, Michael J. (1998) *The Idea of Human Rights. Four Inquiries*, Oxford, Oxford University Press

Perkins, Anne (2003) *Red Queen: The Authorized Biography of Barbara Castle*, London, Macmillan

Peters, Edward (1996) *Torture*, Philadelphia, University of Pennsylvania Press, second edition

Porter, Henry (2005) "Into harm's way. By 'rendering' suspects to torturers America sinks to the moral level of Saddam", *Observer*, 11 December p.29

Priest, Dana and Barton, Adam (2002) "US Decries Abuse but Defends Interrogations", *Washington Post*, 26 December, Section A p.1

Raychaudhuri, Tapan (1996) "British Rule in India: An Assessment", Marshall, P.J. (1996) *The Cambridge Illustrated History of the British Empire*, Cambridge, Cambridge University Press

Rose, David (2004) *Guantanamo: America's War on Human Rights*, London, Faber and Faber

Russell, Alec (2005) "Condoleeza Rice has a lot of explaining to do to Europe", *Daily Telegraph*, 7 December

Russell, Bertrand (1950) *Unpopular Essays*, London: Routledge reprinted 1995

Ruthven, Malise (1976) "The extraordinary revival of torture to make people 'tell' ", *The Times*, 26 January p.12

Stubbs, Richard (1989) *Hearts and Minds in Guerrilla Warfare: The Malayan Emergency 1948-1960*, Oxford, Oxford University Press

Sunday Times (2005) "A noble vision lost", leading article 11 December, Section: Features p.16

Taylor, Peter (2002) *Brits: The war against the IRA*, London, Bloomsbury

Thomas, Keith (1973) *Religion and the Decline of Magic*, London, Penguin University Books

Zizek, Slavoj (2006) "The depraved heroes of 24 are the Himmlers of Hollywood", *Guardian*, 10 January p.27

NOTE ON AUTHOR

John Tulloch is Professor of Journalism and Head of the School of Journalism, University of Lincoln. Previously he was chair of the Department of Journalism and Mass Communication at the University of Westminster. Recent work includes jointly editing, with Colin Sparks, *Tabloid Tales* (Maryland: Rowman and Littlefield 2000) to which he contributed the essay The Eternal Recurrence of the New Journalism. He has written on press regulation, official news management, popular television and the press's coverage of the "war on terror". He has also had a chapter on the journalism of Charles Dickens in *The Journalistic Imagination: Literary Journalists from Defoe to Capote and Carter* (edited by Richard Keeble and Sharon Wheeler; Routledge 2007). Contact details: Lincoln School of Journalism, Faculty of Media and Humanities, University of Lincoln, Brayford Pool, Lincoln LN6 7TS, UK. Tel: +44 (0) 1522 882000. Fax: +44 (0) 1522 886021 Email: jtulloch@lincoln.ac.uk.

2

Human writes: The media's role in war propaganda

Liz Harrop

War propaganda is illegal under international human rights law. Liz Harrop argues here that by filtering communications, distorting facts and compromising access to contrary views, war propaganda is capable of violating human rights, including freedom of information, freedom of expression and freedom from discrimination. This chapter uses examples from the United States of America and the United Kingdom, particularly in relation to the 2003 conflict in Iraq. It concludes by stressing that media professionals should consider their role – not just in exposing human rights violations – but in perpetuating their own.

States wage war in the name of peace and democracy. Yet war propaganda can violate human rights and undermine the democratic principles it seeks to champion. Despite this it is rarely acknowledged, by the media, governments, or even anti-war campaigners, that war propaganda is illegal under international human rights law.

To date there is no legal precedent accusing government officials or media professionals of disseminating war propaganda. However, media workers have been tried by the International Criminal Tribunal for Rwanda (ICTR), which has provided important precedents for incitement to genocide. In the case of Georges Ruggiu, a journalist and broadcaster with Radio Television Libre des Milles Collines, the judgment found Ruggiu "played a crucial role in the incitement of ethnic hatred and violence, which RTLM vigorously pursued".[1]

According to the International Council on Human Rights Policy, "The central questions in (the ICTR) are these: Can journalism kill? And at what point does political propaganda become criminal?"[2]

These questions also apply to the role of media professionals in war time. The media's packaging of information may not always be as extreme as Rwanda's radio broadcasts, but may still undermine human rights principles including the right to freedom of information, the right to freedom of expression, the right to freedom from discrimination and the freedom of the media themselves.

PROPAGANDA NEEDS A MEDIUM

Governments are not obliged to reveal every detail of their military operations. Indeed the UN human rights treaty, the International Covenant on Civil and Political Rights 1966 (ICCPR)[3] allows governments to restrict many rights including freedom of information during a declared "State of Emergency".

However, the guidelines for governments operating within a state of emergency can be unclear in international law. In communication terms, this results in a blurry division between appropriate censorship and unjustifiable withholding of information; between appropriate restrictions of freedom of expression and the unsanctioned silencing of dissenting voices.

It is not just governments which are responsible for the machinery of propaganda. Effective war propaganda selects which voices and messages to legitimise and undermines contrary views and information. Successful war propaganda, therefore, requires a media which are unwittingly manipulated by governments, or which are a willing party to its propaganda.

HOW PROPAGANDA VIOLATES HUMAN RIGHTS

Through its prohibition in Article 20 of the ICCPR,[4] war propaganda is an acknowledged opponent of human rights. Ironically, many wars, including the 2003 Iraq conflict, are based on an agenda of combating human rights abuses or diffusing a threat to global peace and security.

The ICHRP (2002) has expressed concern over the misuse of human rights concerns in war propaganda, stating: 'Governments and other authorities have often used human rights to manipulate or inflame public opinion, particularly when they are involved in wars.'[5]

FREEDOM OF INFORMATION AND EXPRESSION

The most obvious human rights which war propaganda erodes are those to freedom of information and freedom of expression. Inextricably connected, without the freedom to express information, there can be no access to a diversity of information sources. Likewise, without the freedom to access information, creative thought and the formulation of an informed opinion are undermined.

Freedom of information and expression are also a vital component for the realisation of other rights. Access to information is a prerequisite of the right to education outlined in Article 13 of the International Covenant on Economic, Social and Cultural Rights (ICESCR).[6] In addition, without access to information on political parties, and the ability of political parties to express their opinions, a democratic voting system can not operate. Article 25 of the ICCPR therefore talks about "guaranteeing the free expression of the will of the electors".

As Denis McQuail (1991: 71) summarises: "…democratic political process…requires the services of public channels of communication; the full concept of citizenship presupposes an informed and participant body of citizen." War propaganda limits the availability of facts, context and transparency of political motivation. Such information, were it available, would allow objective judgments to be made. For example, in allowing citizens to answer the question: "Is the desire of our government to go to war valid and necessary?"

The media, therefore, have a crucial role in refusing to parrot the government line without further investigation and in uncovering hidden facts. Article 1 of the 1978 Declaration on Fundamental Principles concerning the Contribution of the Mass Media to Strengthening Peace and International Understanding, to the Promotion of Human Rights and to Countering Racialism, Apartheid and Incitement to War (Declaration on Mass Media) reinforces this point:

> The strengthening of peace and international understanding, the promotion of human rights and the countering of racialism, apartheid and incitement to war demand a free flow and a wider and better balanced dissemination of information. To this end, the mass media have a leading contribution to make.[7]

FREEDOM FROM DISCRIMINATION

Article 2, paragraph 1 of the ICCPR protects an individual's freedom from discrimination "without distinction of any kind, such as race, colour, sex, language, religion, political or other opinion, national or social origin, property, birth or other status". The effects of war propaganda, however, are inherently discriminatory. In order to "make the enemy thoroughly hated" (Williams 1992: 157) and predispose the public to war, the enemy must be characterised as worthy of destruction.

War propaganda, therefore, fosters ignorance and creates a climate of prejudice and fear. Violations of the human rights of the enemy state may be tolerated as necessary to the war effort, for example targeting civilians and the torture of prisoners of war. Meanwhile racial prejudice, discrimination and suspicion on home soil thrive, for example, in the treatment of detainees under British anti-terrorism legislation, which the UK Special Immigration Appeals Commission found to be unlawful and discriminatory.[8]

Peoples and their leaders are polarised as "good" and "evil", which pre-supposes a moral right to wage war on (or "liberate") the enemy, and which attempts to establish the crusade of civilising goodness as a higher norm than respecting the rights of alleged "evil-doers". For example, Tony Blair's comment on the Kosovo war of 1999 that it was not just a military campaign "it is a battle between Good and Evil; between civilisation and barbarity" (see Knightley op cit: 507).

Lee Wigle Artz and Mark Pollock (1997: 121) analysed the caricatures that accompanied the 1991 Gulf War, commenting:

> The singular demonisation of Hussein was accompanied by commonplace images of other Arabs – including US allies – as incompetent, weak, self-centred and incapable of diplomacy in their own region…The corollary, of course, was another powerful commonplace: the righteousness of a civilized Western world courageously defended by US soldiers. These images had little subtlety or variation.

MARGINALISING THE VOICE OF DISSENT

Violations of freedom of expression and freedom from discrimination combine in branding dissenters, among both the domestic population and international community as traitors who are unworthy of being heard. For example, in the US, Pulitzer Prize winner Seymour Hersh was labelled a media terrorist by Pentagon advisor Richard Perle for opposing the 2003 Iraq war.[9] Meanwhile Defense Secretary Donald Rumsfeld categorised France and Germany as "old Europe"[10] for their unwillingness to support a war with Iraq and according to the US Administration, the UN "risked irrelevance".[11]

The disapproval and silencing of dissenting voices is therefore officially sanctioned and encouraged. As a result, dissenters may be less willing or able to air their views due to factors including popular opinion, being publicly discredited or having media unwilling to carry their views. This applies equally to members of the public, journalists, academics and politicians.

As Edward Herman (1992: 11) explains a "greatly underrated constraint on freedom of speech is dissenters' lack of access to the mass media, and thus to the general public. Their freedom is in an important sense only a personal freedom with limited public and social significance".

Even where two opposing views are given, this may still be unsatisfactory.

David Detmer (1995: 96-100) outlines the "both sides" ideology whereby journalists invite debate by illustrating two sides of a story. Detmer comments: "Members of the audience…are not encouraged to consider the possibility that both sides might share important points in common and that these points might be precisely those standing most in need of being challenged."

FREEDOM OF THE PRESS

Under the various UN Human Rights treaties, states carry the responsibility for ensuring freedom of the press. This has a legal basis in for example Article 19 of the ICCPR on freedom of opinion and expression and Article 15 of the ICESCR which concerns the right to take part in cultural life including steps necessary for "the diffusion of science and culture".

Supporting the right to freedom of the press is often in conflict with the aims of the state, which may wish to dominate media output to protect state power. Government control is of paramount importance in time of war, and it is at exactly this time when the media can be dependent on government for access to information. The dilemma facing media is played out in the roles of unilateral versus embedded reporters, whereby the embedded reporters exchange their independence for access to information and army protection, while unilateral reporters enjoy both the benefits and disadvantages of going solo.

One of the most famous unilateral reporters, Robert Fisk, has been criticised by embedded journalists for jeopardising media access through disobeying army instructions. For example in the first Gulf War of 1991, Fisk discovered that fighting remained in the Iraqi town of Khafji long after the US-led forces claimed it was liberated. He was harshly criticised by an NBC-TV pool reporter of whom Fisk said: "For the NBC reporter, however, the privileges of the pool and the military rules attached to it were more important than the right of journalists to do their job" (Knightley op cit: 492).

Some journalists are explicit in their support for the government. In the Iraq war 2003 for example, Fox News took an openly pro-war stance in its new output, despite its seemingly ironic strapline of "We report, You decide". During the conflict, Oliver North, infamous for his role in the Iran/Contra affair of 1987-88 and an embedded commentator for Fox News, said: "You're an American before you're a journalist."[12]

For media reporters who do not comply, government pressure attempts to force cooperation. Paul McMasters, of the Freedom Forum, comments: "Federal officials, after all, have what journalists need: the news. A journalist's usefulness to her news organization flames out if she burns a source by complaining about the ground rules, let alone resists abiding by them."[13]

MEDIA DEATHS

The most devastating blow to freedom of the press is the deaths of the many media who have lost their lives reporting war. There have been allegations that media "murders" on the battlefield are used, in the words of the BBC's John Simpson, as "the ultimate act of censorship"[14] in the war propaganda process.

The International Press Institute (2003) reported that "some observers claim that they had been targeted as media workers"[15] and journalist Robert Fisk said "I suspect they were killed because the US...decided to try to 'close down' the press".[16] This amounts to an extremely grave charge, which would violate both international human rights law and international humanitarian law under the Geneva Conventions. Protocol 1 of the Geneva Conventions relating to the Protection of Victims of International Armed Conflicts contains measures for the protection of journalists in Article 79. This considers journalists to be civilians and therefore affords them special protection including "general protection against dangers arising from military operations" and that they "shall not be the object of attack".[17]

The Iraq war has had tragic consequences for the media. According to Reporters Without Borders, by October 2007, 205 journalists and media assistants had been killed since the start of fighting in Iraq in March 2003, two were still missing and 14 had been kidnapped.[18]

CONTEXT

In order to avoid subjectivity and the presentation of a narrow viewpoint, the media, it could be argued, should provide context and analysis over and above simple news briefings. However, contextualising news is an important but often missing part of contemporary news reporting. In terms of reporting around a war, this could include how power balances have shifted over the years so that once allied regimes are now branded as enemies. Likewise, valuable political context, about what a state has to gain from war, over and above the righteousness of the moral and political high-ground would provide valuable background.

John MacArthur, publisher of *Harper's Magazine*, identifies a particular problem for the United States. He explains: "Americans live in a perpetual present. This is the country with the shortest attention span in the civil world, and it is a cultural problem. We don't know anything that happened six months ago much less 20 years ago when we supported the Afghan resistance and Bin Laden against the Soviet Union. No one remembers that we were Saddam's ally and supporter during the Iran-Iraq war."[19]

The continual flow of short news pieces, although large in quantity can be short on quality and are unable to relay deeper meaning and context. As Philip

Taylor comments on TV coverage of the 2003 Iraq war: "Discerning the truth is complicated, if anything, by the incessant television coverage from Iraq; news comes in so fast that we barely have time to evaluate its wider meaning before the next images fire in."[20]

Noam Chomsky argues that the very structure of the media is designed to induce conformity to established doctrine. Chomsky says (1989: 10): "In a three-minute stretch between commercials, or in seven hundred words, it is impossible to present unfamiliar thoughts or surprising conclusions with the argument and evidence required to afford them some credibility. Regurgitation of welcome pieties faces no such problem."

These welcome pieties, form what Chomsky calls "the basic presuppositions of discourse". In the case of the US, these include the assumption that foreign policy is guided by a benevolent "yearning for democracy" in the face of aggressors (ibid: 59). These presuppositions allow the media to gloss over uncomfortable facts and to paint out grey areas which require deeper explanations and risk boring or unsettling viewers, seeking an instant news summary and confirmation of their belief system.

News segments are designed to be short, sharp and sexy and to educate the audience instantaneously. To help meet this objective, news reporting may be sensationalised so that its messages are more obvious and immediately digestible. In any number of news items, the public is given a black and white version of grey reality, where selected facts paint a morally simplistic picture. This applies whether it is a celebrity divorce or a war.

ACTS OF OMISSION

Context, or lack of it, is therefore a key factor in media bias. However, bias and distortion in media reports is not just about the presence of false information, it is also about the absence of information. A 2001 report by media watchdog, Fairness and Accuracy in Reporting,[21] found that the evening newscasts of the three commercial broadcast networks in the US (ABC, CBS and NBC) had deliberately avoided discussing the effects of bombings of civilians in the 2001 Afghanistan war. The study claimed that network journalists failed to inquire about the numbers of casualties, nor did they discuss the legal implications of these bombings. Instead, they communicated the civilian casualties as a regrettable but justifiable consequence of America's military retaliation or as unverifiable Afghan propaganda.

The media's attribution of the source of stories is also problematic because as long as the media attribute their story to a source and quote that source accurately, they are being "truthful". It could be argued that a journalist or media outlet does not have the resources to cross-check every single report or quote given to them by an official spokesperson, and that to do so would hinder the news-making process so much as to make it commercially uncompetitive.

According to David Gordon, attribution is not an acceptable media practice without verification of the facts. Says Gordon (1999: 86): "The media…have the responsibility to assess the validity or truth of the information they disseminate…(to) allow readers, listeners and viewers to reach their own conclusions."

However, Daniel Hallin sees attribution not as a violation of duty, but as a positive norm of media ethics. Talking of the Vietnam war, he comments (1994: 50): "It was not simply the use of official sources which gave officials so much influence over news content. It was the fact that the norms of objective journalism required the journalist to pass on official information without comment on its accuracy or relevance."

CENSORSHIP OF MEDIA BY MEDIA

Who carries the responsibility for fair and accurate reporting? Is it the journalists themselves, their editors or media owners and what is the impact of stakeholders such as consumers and advertisers? The different motivations and pressures applied to the media in censorship of wartime news is a complex one, involving different actors and ethical frameworks.

The interplay between all these groups means that the final media output has been influenced by a manifold of different sources. Therefore holding the individual author to moral or legal account for an act of omission or commission may not be realistic.

John MacArthur believes the Iraq War 2003 was "the most self-censored war in history", arguing: 95 per cent of the "war" coverage had nothing to do with the war. "It was trucks rolling down the highway…boxes being loaded and unloaded, GIs talking about feeling lonely."[22]

Journalists may opt for self-censorship for a variety of reasons including personal loyalty as an embedded reporter, patriotism, to best ensure promotion, or simply from a weight of official pressure. CNN's top war correspondent, Christiane Amanpour, commented on the 2003 Iraq war: "My station was intimidated by the administration and its foot soldiers at Fox News. And it did, in fact, put a climate of fear and self-censorship, in my view, in terms of the kind of broadcast work we did."[23]

Media proprietors are certainly guilty of censoring their journalist's work and opinions. For example, in the Iraq war 2003, MSNBC's Ashleigh Banfield was openly critical of the war's sanitised media coverage. The *Hollywood Reporter* noted that NBC News president Neal Shapiro "has taken correspondent Ashleigh Banfield to the woodshed" for a speech in which she criticised the networks for portraying the Iraq war as "glorious and wonderful". An official NBC spokesperson later told the press: "She and we both agreed that she didn't intend to demean the work of her colleagues, and she will choose her words more carefully in the future."[24]

Meanwhile pro-government media apply pressure by rallying against media displaying rebel tendencies. For example, the *Sun* newspaper in the UK turned on the *BBC*, *Guardian* and *Mirror* during the 1982 Falklands conflict, accusing the *Mirror* and *BBC* of treason because of their war reporting. Speaking also of the Falklands, Phillip Knightley (op cit: 481), comments: "Some newspapers contributed as a matter of policy. They supported the government all the way, even to the extent of attacking other newspapers or television programmes that expressed the slightest reservation about Britain's actions. This helped create a climate in which to dissent was little short of treason."

The flip side to the resistance of censorship is the desire for censorship, with some journalists preferring to be explicitly censored, rather than use self-censorship at their own discretion. Kevin Williams (op cit: 161) discusses the Vietnam war, in which it is widely argued there was less formal censorship than in other wars. An increase in self-censorship during the war, he says, proved that many journalists preferred official censorship, being "uncomfortable with taking the responsibility for what they wrote".

COMMERCIAL CONCERNS

The unattractiveness of "un-newsworthy" information and the short, sharp format of news coverage, prohibit the contextualising of news output and are largely governed by commercial concerns. The need to satisfy an audience with a short attention span and to maximise audience numbers and advertising revenue can therefore be barriers to accurate reporting. With commercial factors taking prevalence, Kevin Williams (ibid: 166) comments that in a competitive mass media market "truth must take second place to the swift production of copy".

The ICHRP (2002) has expressed its concern over the influence of commercial factors in journalism, saying: "Driven by new technologies and the lure of lucrative mass markets, media owners are themselves guilty of upsetting the balance of interest between journalism as an instrument of democracy and its exploitation as a tradable commodity."[25]

With exactly this kind of situation in mind, the Vienna Declaration on Public Broadcasting 1993, outlined a range of measures to ensure media freedom, including in paragraph 10: "...the abolition of monopolies and...of all forms of discrimination in broadcasting and frequency allocation, as well as the abolition of all barriers to the launching of new private media outlets".

CONCLUSIONS

The issues surrounding the prohibition of war propaganda are complex. From a legal perspective they involve problematic arguments about the legality of war, the declaration of states of emergency, the ratification, reservations and reporting on the ICCPR and the domestic codification of war propaganda as an internationally illegal practice.

The media, meanwhile, at the behest of commercial, governmental, ethical and legal influences and responsibilities, attempt to find a balance (or not) between them. A whole range of rights, including freedom to information and expression, freedom from discrimination, academic freedom, freedom of the press and even the right to life, are interwoven with the prohibition of war propaganda in an intricate web of mutually supporting human rights.

One of the roles of a free press could be to educate the public about its role, particularly in a state of emergency, when freedom of information is threatened. In this way it may be possible to confront the prejudice encountered by the "voice of dissent" discussed above. War reporter, Peter Arnett, believes this is a valid role for the press. Arnett reported from the Iraqi side during the 1991 Gulf War and was heavily criticised. Phillip Knightley (op cit: 493) recounts: "On his return to the United States Arnett defended his role, saying that the media was partly to blame for the negative reaction because it had not educated the pubic about the function of a free press in wartime."

The importance of freedom of the press can not be underestimated as a moderator of social injustice, including war propaganda. As Denis McQuail (1997: 70) concludes: "The most practical instruments for protecting freedom and combating tyranny have involved using the means of communication to claim rights, criticise power-holders, advance alternatives."

NOTES

1. Paragraph 50 of the judgment of International Criminal Tribunal for Rwanda, The Prosecutor versus Georges Ruggiu, 2000. Available online at http://www.ictr.org/default.htm, accessed on 30 October 2007

2. International Council on Human Rights Policy (2002) *Journalism, Media and the Challenge of Human Rights Reporting,* Switzerland, p16 quoting Marlise Simons, *Internatinal Herald Tribune,* "Trial examines war crimes free speech and journalism", 5 March 2002

3. The ICCPR has 156 State Parties as at 14 July 2006. Available online at http://www.ohchr.org/english/bodies/docs/status.pdf, accessed on 30 October 2007

4. "1. Any propaganda for war shall be prohibited by law. 2. Any advocacy of national, racial or religious hatred that constitutes incitement to discrimination, hostility or

violence shall be prohibited by law."

5.   International Council on Human Rights Policy, *Journalism, Media and the Challenge of Human Rights Reporting* p 90

6.   The ICESCR has 153 State Parties as at 14 July 2006. Available online at http://www.ohchr.org/english/bodies/docs/status.pdf, accessed on 30 October 2007

7.   Article 1 Declaration on Fundamental Principles concerning the Contribution of the Mass Media to Strengthening Peace and International Understanding, to the Promotion of Human Rights and to Countering Racialism, Apartheid and Incitement to War 1978. Available online at http://www.unhchr.ch/html/menu3/b/d_media.htm, accessed on 30 October 2007

8.   In 2002, the UK Special Immigration Appeals Commission judges found there was a public emergency justifying the derogation from Article 5 of the ECHR – allowing people to be detained without charge or trial – but found that the derogation was unlawful and discriminatory because the new powers only concerned foreign nationals. The judgment means a core part of the Anti-Terrorism, Crime and Security Act is contrary to the ECHR. See http://www.liberty-human-rights.org.uk/issues/2-terrorism/index.shtml, accessed on 30 October 2007

9.   Danny Schechter, The Media Channel, The Link Between The Media, The War, And Our Right To Know, 1 May 2003. Available online at http://www.mediachannel.org/views/dissector/moveon.shtml, accessed on 30 October 2007

10. BBC News Online, Plain-speaking Rumsfeld strikes again, 12th March 2003. Available online at http://news.bbc.co.uk/2/hi/americas/2843311.stm, accessed 30 October 2007

11. Tarik Kafala, BBC News Online Analysis: Does the UN risk irrelevance? 5 March, 2003. Available online at http://news.bbc.co.uk/2/hi/middle_east/ 2823149.stm, accessed on 30 October 2007

12. How Fox is Winning the War, *Chicago Tribune*, 17 November 2003

13. Quoted by Robert Jensen, CommonDreams.org, News Media Industry's Criticism of Iraq Coverage Reveals Deeper Problems with Mainstream Journalists' Conception of News, 4 August 2003

14. Quoted by Ciar Byrne, *Media Guardian*, "US soldiers were main danger to journalists, says Simpson", 27 June 2003. Available online at http://media.guardian.co.uk/iraqandthemedia/story/0,12823,986601,00.html, accessed on 30 October 2007

15. International Press Institute, *Caught in the Crossfire: The Iraq War and the Media*. Available online at http://www.freemedia.at/cms/ipi/attachments/8/6/2/ CH0057/CMS1141820686901/the_iraq_war_&_the_media.pdf, accessed on 30 October 2007

16. Robert Fisk, CounterPunch, Did the US Murder Journalists? 29 April, 2003. Available online at http://www.counterpunch.org/fisk04292003.html, accessed on 30 October 200

17   Article 51 of Geneva Convention relating to the Protection of Victims of International Armed Conflicts

18. Reporters Without Borders. Available online at http://www.rsf.org/

special_iraq_en.php3, accessed on 30 October 2007

19. John MacArthur, Censorship And The War On Terrorism, 27 September 2001. Available online at http://www.mediachannel.org/views/interviews/macarthur. shtml, accessed on 30 October 2007

20. Philip M Taylor, *Washington Post*, Credibility: Can't Win Hearts and Minds Without It, 30 March, 2003. Avaliable online at http://ics.leeds.ac.uk/papers/vp01. cfm?outfit=pmt&requesttimeout=500&folder=40&paper=45, accessed on 30 October 2007

21. How Many Dead? Major networks aren't counting, 12 December 2001. Available online at http://www.fair.org/activism/afghanistan-casualties.html, accessed on 30 October 2007

22. Interviewed in Channel 4 Television, "The War we Never Saw", 5 June 2003

23. *USA Today* Amanpour: CNN practised self-censorship, 14 September 2003

24. As quoted by Danny Schechter, The Media Channel, The Link Between The Media, The War, And Our Right To Know. Available online at http://www.mediachannel.org/views/dissector/moveon.shtml, accessed on 30 October 2007

25. International Council on Human Rights Policy, *Journalism, Media and the Challenge of Human Rights Reporting* p. xv

REFERENCES

Chomsky, Noam (1989) *Necessary Illusions: Thought Control in a Democratic Societies*, New York, South End Press

Detmer, David (1995) "Covering Up Iran: Why Vital Information is Routinely Excluded from US Mass Media News Accounts", Kamalipour, Yahya (ed.) *The US Media and the Middle East: Image and Perception*. Westport, CT, Greenwood Press pp 91-101

Gordon, David (1999) "Manipulation by the Media: Truth, Fairness and Objectivity", Gordon, David and Kittross, John Michael (eds) *Controversies in Media Ethics*, White Plains, Longman pp 72-91

Hallin, Daniel (1994) *We Keep America On Top of the World: Television Journalism and the Public Sphere*, London, Routledge

Herman, Edward (1992) *Beyond Hyprocrisy: Decoding the News in an Age of Propaganda*, Boston, MA, South End Press

Knightley, Phillip (2002) *The First Casualty: The War Correspondent as Hero and Myth-Maker From the Crimea to Kosovo*, London, Prion.

McQuail, Denis (1991) "Mass Media in the Public Interest: Towards a Framework of Norms for Media Performance", Curran, James and Gurevitch, Michael (ed.), *Mass Media and Society*, London, New York, Edward Arnold pp 68-8

Wigle Artz, Lee and Pollock, Mark (1995) "Limiting the Options: Anti-Arab Images in US Media Coverage of the Persian Gulf Crisis", Kamalipour, Yahya (ed.) *The US Media*

*and the Middle East: Image and Perception.*Westport, CT, Greenwood Press pp 119-135
Williams, Kevin (1992) "Something more important than truth: Ethical issues in war reporting", *Ethical Issues in Journalism and the Media*, Belsey, Andrew and Chadwick, Ruth, London, Routledge pp 154-169

NOTE ON AUTHOR

Liz Harrop is a writer and public relations consultant with 16 years' experience managing communications campaigns in the corporate, non-governmental and inter-governmental sectors. With a Masters Degree in Human Rights, she specialises in public awareness activity for human rights campaigning organisations and humanitarian projects. Her publications include Propaganda's War on Human Rights (*Peace Review Journal*, Fall 2004); and a detailed online report of the same name www.tiger-tail.org/propaganda.htm. Contact details: Tel: +64 33 888 022; email: www.tiger-tail.org/contact.htm; website: www.tiger-tail.org.

3

'A senior British official said...' The media's use of anonymous sources

Julie-ann Davies

On 29 May 2003, BBC defence correspondent Andrew Gilligan reported on Radio 4's *Today* programme that a "senior British official" had told him the British government's dossier on Iraq had been "transformed in the week before it was published to make it sexier" and build a stronger case for war. The unnamed source was Dr David Kelly and Gilligan's report nearly brought the BBC and the British government to their knees.

In a post-Hutton environment the media's use of anonymous sources has come under increasing scrutiny. Anonymity gives sources the ability to distance themselves from a story if necessary. But should journalists differentiate between the demands of Whitehall officials and those of genuine whistleblowers?

The public editor of *The New York Times*, Daniel Okrent, told *LA Weekly*: "I hate unattributed sources and think they're absolutely necessary to journalism. I know that sounds like a terrible contradiction, but I have no other way of addressing it. They are used too much. They undermine the credibility of journalists and publications. On the other hand, if you did not have any unattributed sources, you would have very few whistleblowers."

Journalist, author and film-maker John Pilger says anonymous sources are essential to investigative journalism but recognises an ethical difference between granting anonymity to officials and allowing whistleblowers the same privilege. He says: "Politicians are elected to be accountable – at least they should be – and have no right to engage in undemocratic, secretive manipulation. Whistleblowers often reveal something that is vital to the public interest: the sort of thing that politicians conceal. They have the right to be protected. But I think it is a 100 per cent true that the public want names when politicians are being quoted without attribution."

THE RUSH TO GET EXCLUSIVES

Author and former BBC political correspondent Nicholas Jones believes unattributed quotes are appearing more frequently in hard news stories. Jones says: "The Blair government has brought in a large number of special advisers, many of whom are spin doctors. They have always traded information on an anonymous basis. The same thing happens with officials who like to use anonymity to get information out which may, or may not, be true. I started as a journalist in the 1960s and it was very difficult to get a story into a local or national paper unless you had attributed people speaking.

"Competition has increased phenomenally now and today's journalists are judged on their ability to deliver exclusive stories. This has led to a change in culture where journalists think it is nothing exceptional to make up quotes to brighten their stories and I think that is a significant change. The trend has gone too far and it is worrying that in the rush to get exclusives this is what journalists are prepared to do."

Jones raises a valid point. In March 2004 it was revealed that Jack Kelley, a Pulitzer Prize-nominated journalist for *USA Today*, had fabricated and embellished several of his stories. His case finds an echo in that of Jayson Blair. In May 2003 Blair, a star reporter on *The New York Times*, resigned after admitting to faking quotes and even entire interviews. *The New York Times* now demands that its reporters reveal an unnamed source's identity to a ranking editor. However, exceptions can be made in cases that involve "crucial issues of law or national security in which sources face dire consequences if exposed".

David Shayler, a former member of MI5, the British security service, was prosecuted and convicted under the Official Secrets Act for passing classified information and documents to the *Mail on Sunday* in 1997. Shayler sees the use of unattributed quotes and anonymous sources as part of a decline in journalistic practices due to commercial pressures. He says: "This is part of a bigger picture. It is part of the whole issue of ethics in journalism. I worked on *The Sunday Times* and I've worked with newspapers covering my story. I don't think there are any ethics in British journalism."

Shayler argues that, wherever possible, whistleblowers should stand up and be counted but he is aware that many do fear the consequences of being identified. "I think the ideal is to have people on the record all the time. But the problem in Britain is that we have draconian secrecy laws. Any official who talks to the press could be breaking the law. From that point of view we do need to protect whistleblowers.'

LACK OF LEGAL PROTECTION FOR WHISTLEBLOWERS

Katharine Gun worked as a translator for GCHQ, the British Government's eavesdropping centre. In 2003, in the weeks leading up to the Iraq War, she revealed that the American National Security Agency had asked the British Government to assist in the illegal surveillance of the UN Security Council. Gun was arrested and charged under the Official Secrets Act with disclosing secret information. The case against her was dropped in February 2004. She believes the lack of legal protection offered to whistleblowers lies at the heart of the anonymity issue.

Gun says: "I was deliberately anonymous when I made my leak, even the *Observer* didn't know who I was. The issue of whistleblower protection is important here. If whistleblowers felt they were not putting themselves at disproportionate risk, then protection might not be such a necessity. In a truly open and responsible democracy whistleblowers would not have to fear retaliation. There is a distinction between a whistleblower and an off the record briefing. If civil servants are in the habit of briefing misleadingly then it is up to the journalist to judge accordingly. It is the same with intelligence gathering; how much can you trust your source? To the public if the source is hidden, there is no way to judge their validity and journalists must reflect this in their reporting."

Robert Fisk, Middle Eastern correspondent for the *Independent*, says dealing with off the record stories from government officials or ministers can present its own difficulties. The decision not to publish an unattributed quote could mean concealing an important story from the public. According to Fisk part of the problem is that journalists encounter many kinds of anonymous sources from terrified dissidents living in repressive regimes to self-serving government officials. "You have to be judicious about this. Some people will die if you name them but government officials will not die if you name them. There is no perfect answer to this is there? You have to trust your source don't you? You have to know who he is. If your source is some psychological operations general then, frankly, I think you should dump him. If your source is a frightened family living under a dictatorship telling you about torture then you have to take into account what they say. They are taking a risk to tell you in the first place so they are probably telling you the truth."

PRESERVING THE FOURTH ESTATE ROLE

In 1971 Daniel Ellsberg leaked the Pentagon Papers – a collection of classified documents detailing US military activities in Vietnam – to the American media. Their publication contributed to the erosion of public support for the Vietnam War and led to a campaign by Nixon's White House to discredit assault or assassinate Ellsberg. For Ellsberg the defining characteristic of a whistleblower is that they are speaking without authorisation. He argues that as sources they offer stories or perspectives their superiors or agencies would never willingly release. "In these cases the disclosure is unauthorised and that means it is dangerous for the subordinate who will be punished if their disclosure is discovered. To get their information and a perspective of how things are seen on the inside, or what the real facts are, journalists must ensure that whistleblowers' identities can be concealed."

Ellsberg believes whistleblowers are essential to journalistic freedom and the preservation of the media's fourth estate role. In 2004 he set up The Truth-Telling Project, which encourages US officials to blow the whistle on government wrongdoing. He says: "Without unauthorised disclosures you are just reprinting official handouts and that is nothing but propaganda. If a journalist is content with that then they are simply acknowledging they are a willing and conscious part of a propaganda apparatus."

Sheila Gunn is a former political correspondent for *The Times*. In 1995 she was appointed as personal press adviser to the then Prime Minister John Major. She is currently a political affairs consultant, Camden councillor and the Conservative Party's candidate for Slough in the forthcoming general election. Gunn says stories based upon anonymous sources increase public cynicism as they create an impression of a cosy relationship between journalists and politicians. She also believes journalists could do more to minimise the risk of being misled by officials.

"Too many journalists don't bother to check out stories or do a bit more digging and hence risk being 'used' by informants – often party spin doctors – or presenting slanted stories. I have always warned politicians, including John Major, never to say anything to a journalist that they don't want to see splashed across the front page of the *Sun*. However, I can't say I kept to that rule myself. Journalists should report for their audience rather than for their news desks.

"Producers and editors should monitor their journalists' output of stories with little or no attribution and trust them a little more when they refuse to play the spin doctors' games. The media should refuse to betray genuine whistleblowers who are prepared to risk their careers in the greater public interest even if it means the journalists or editor risking a jail sentence. After all, that's a great scoop in itself!"

JOURNALISTS FACING JAIL

In July 2003 US syndicated columnist Robert Novak, citing unnamed sources, broke the story that Valerie Plame, wife of former US diplomat Joseph Wilson, was a CIA operative. Novak's sources relayed the same information to Judith Miller, of *The New York Times*, and Matthew Cooper, of *Time* magazine and both journalists investigated the story. In June 2005, US Federal Judge Thomas F. Hogan gave Miller and Cooper a stark ultimatum. If they did not comply with a Grand Jury order to reveal the identities of their sources they faced prison sentences of up to 18 months.

After discussions with the source of his published story Cooper testified and avoided jail. Miller still refused to co-operate and was incarcerated for 85 days for a story she investigated – but never published. She was released on 29 September 2005 when, after her source waived their right to confidentiality she agreed to testify. Miller's source was Lewis "Scooter" Libby, the then Chief of Staff for Vice-President Dick Cheney. Libby had also briefed Novak and Cooper on the story but was not the sole source of the leak.

Cooper later named former Deputy Secretary of State Richard Armitage as the primary source and claimed the story was also verified by President Bush's senior policy advisor Karl Rove. Novak did not comment on the case until July 2006. Writing in *Human Events* he denied he had ever been a target for prosecution and said: "I have co-operated with the investigation while trying to protect journalistic privileges under the First Amendment and shield sources who have not revealed themselves."

Eason Jordan, a former CNN chief news executive, was less fortunate than the Plame source. In January 2007, at the World Economic Forum (WEF) in Davos, Switzerland, he said he believed it was official US military policy to target journalists. It is WEF policy that all sessions are off the record but a blogger, Rony Abovitz, posted Jordan's comments on the Internet and a website was launched to petition for a full transcript of the session. Jordan resigned in February to spare CNN's blushes.

COMPLEX DILEMMAS FACING JOURNALISTS

In some instances it can be argued there is a definite and pressing need for anonymity. But there can be little doubt that a growing army of Whitehall officials, agencies and politicians now insist on off the record press briefings. The dilemmas facing journalists in these cases are complex. Refusing to publish without attribution could mean hiding an important story from readers, but naming a source would mean never using them again.

But is journalism's first duty to its sources or to its audience? There are no easy answers. Studies have shown that readers find unattributed quotes less credible but it may be difficult for journalists to gain a higher level of public trust unless they address their use of anonymous sources and unattributed quotes.

NOTE ON AUTHOR

Julie-ann Davies is a PhD candidate at the Department of Geographical and Earth Sciences at the University of Glasgow. Contact details: jadavies2007@gmail.com.

4

New militarism, massacrespeak and the language of silence

Richard Lance Keeble

This chapter explores the links between George Orwell's concept of newspeak as outlined in his novel Nineteen Eighty Four *and Paul Chilton's notion of nukespeak. This, Chilton argued, was a specialised vocabulary for talking about nuclear weapons which was neither neutral nor purely descriptive but ideologically loaded in favour of the nuclear culture. The chapter goes on to trace the evolution through nukespeak to massacrespeak. It argues that with the demise of the Cold War a New Militarism has emerged in the US and UK, with the dominant vocabulary, best described as massacrespeak, now serving ideologically to silence critical perspectives and the horrors of "humanitarian" conflicts.*

THE PERSONAL AND THE POLITICAL

I've always been interested in silence. The first pamphlet I ever wrote was for the Peace Pledge Union back in May 1983 and I called it *A language of silence*. I looked at the way in which our culture, individual thought processes and language were dominated by militarism. Militarism had become a core defining reality of our society. And our language, in preparing us for the possibility of the ultimate horror – the destruction of the globe in a nuclear confrontation – was moving in a process of self destruction towards silence. Or so I argued.

Significantly, I called my book on the coverage of the 1991 Gulf conflict in the US and UK press *Secret State, Silent Press: New militarism, the Gulf and the Modern Image of Warfare*. Why silent press? I liked the alliteration with secret state to be frank. But my essential thesis was that the mainstream press had silenced what in reality was a series of US-led massacres beneath the fiction of heroic warfare.

Colin Powell (1995), in his account of the conflict, estimated that 250,000 Iraqi soldiers had perished. The reality of that horrific explosion of hi-tech barbarism was silenced in the British and American press which represented the conflict as largely bloodless: a triumph of clean, precise, surgical weaponry. In the book I call the US/UK military media system – with its pools and self censoring journalists – along with the complex workings of ideology the apparatus of silence (Keeble 1997: 109-126).

NEWSPEAK AND THE DESTRUCTION OF LANGUAGE

Significantly, George Orwell was preoccupied with the potential shift of language towards silence. In his novel *Nineteen Eighty Four* (1976/1949), Orwell described a Big Brother state in which the authorities controlled thought and language by inventing a new one – newspeak. In the Appendix titled "The principles of newspeak" he wrote: "The purpose of newspeak was not only to provide a medium of expression for the world-view and mental habits proper to the devotees of Ingsoc but to make all other modes of thought impossible" (ibid: 917). In other words the dominant language served above all to silence all dissident modes of thought. And newspeak was inherently moving towards silence. Syme, Winston Smith's colleague, admonishes him like this: "You don't grasp the beauty of the destruction of words. Do you know that Newspeak is the only language in the world whose vocabulary gets smaller every year?" (ibid: 773).

NEWSPEAK'S CLONE: NUKESPEAK

During the Cold War, Paul Chilton, currently of the School of Linguistics at the University of East Anglia but then a senior lecturer at Warwick University, coined the term nukespeak. The seminal text (of 1985) he edited was titled *Language and the Nuclear Arms Debate: Nukespeak Today*. He had earlier provided a chapter "Nukespeak: nuclear language and propaganda" to a text *Nukespeak: The Media and the Bomb* (Aubrey 1982).

In coining the term nukespeak, Chilton was making three main claims. Firstly there existed a specialised vocabulary for talking about nuclear weapons together with habitual metaphors. Secondly that this variety of English was neither neutral nor purely descriptive but ideologically loaded in favour of the nuclear culture. And finally that nukespeak was massively important since it affected how people thought about the subject and largely determined the ideas they exchanged about it (ibid: 95).

But there was no massive conspiracy to inject this vocabulary into the culture: there were no Orwellian grammarians munching their sandwiches at the Ministry of Truth and rewriting the English language. The atomic bombs which fell on Hiroshima and Nagasaki in August 1945 were, indeed, weapons of mass destruction. Their deployment represented according to Chilton a revolutionary jump in military strategy. And inevitably it heralded a new order of experience in science, politics and the everyday. Chilton commented: "The language used to talk about the new weapons of mass extermination was partly an attempt to slot the new reality into the old paradigms of our culture. It was also no doubt a language that served the purpose of those who were concerned to perpetuate nuclear weapons development and deployment" (ibid: 95).

Nukespeak then, as a specific linguistic register, drew on deep patterns of symbolic thought, on myths, religious beliefs, symbols, stereotypes and metaphors which we use to organise and normalise our everyday experiences. In August 1945 politicians together with the mainstream press spoke of the bomb mainly in terms of religious awe. For instance while Truman was meeting Churchill and Stalin at Potsdam an official report on the Hiroshima explosion was rushed to him. It said: "It was the beauty the great poets dream about....Then came the strong, sustained, awesome roar which warned of doomsday and made us feel that we puny things were blasphemous to dare to tamper with the forces heretofore reserved to the Almighty" (ibid: 97). *The Times* reported eye-witnesses: "The whole thing was tremendous and awe-inspiring," said a Captain Parsons of the US Navy.

The names given to these horrific bombs are also very telling. They are strangely humanised. They become familiar parts of our normal everyday lives. The Hiroshima bomb was called "Little Boy", the plutonium bomb dropped on Nagasaki "Fat Man". Edward Teller is known as the father of the H-Bomb.

Brian Easlea in his seminal, feminist history *Fathering the Unthinkable* (1983) highlights the creation of nuclear weapons in the context of the masculinity of science. He sees the development of science as a process of domination over both nature and women. According to Easlea, men create science and weapons to compensate for their lack of the "magical power" of mothering. In other words, the distorted psyche at the heart of masculinity and the "technical, phallic rationality" it promotes gives birth not to life but death. Easlea quotes a note slipped to Truman at the Potsdam conference on 17 July 1945 after a successful test of the plutonium bomb that said simply: "Babies successfully born." And the President knew precisely what it meant (ibid: 103).

Later generations, note that word, of nuclear weapons were given military status and a patriotic role. They were called "Corporal" and "Sergeant". "Honest John" appeared later in the European theatre (another nukespeak term). The devastating "Minuteman" missile drew on the name of the heroic militiamen of the American Revolutionary war who were trained to turn out at a minute's notice. So in this way the missile takes its proud place in national folklore. Or they have been given names of classical gods: such as Polaris, Skybolt, Jupiter, Titan,

Poseidon, Trident (Chilton 1982: 104-105). In these various ways weapons of mass destruction have been assimilated into our culture to appear "natural" and "civilised".

THE MAKING OF NEW MILITARISM

Jean Baudrillard, the French post modernist, has controversially claimed that the Gulf War never existed (1991). Indeed, it is possible to draw on different perspectives to arrive at the same conclusion. There was no war, rather a series of massacres silenced beneath the fiction of a necessary, heroic "war" against a manufactured "enemy".

Here's a list of recent US/UK adventures – manifestations of a distinctly new form of militarism.

1982 The Falklands
1983 Grenada
1986 Libya
1989 Panama
1991, 1993, 1998, 2001, 2003 Iraq
1992-1993 Somalia
1999 Kosovo
2001 Afghanistan

NEW MILITARISM'S DEFINING CHARACTERISTICS

These new militarist adventures (with the exception of Somalia where US troops suffered humiliating defeats and so rapidly withdrew leaving the impoverished country to its fate) all bore certain crucial hallmarks.

Most importantly, all the invasions were mediacentric: overt warfare becomes essentially a media event, an entertainment, a spectacle. Baudrillard, in his more recent writings, talks of the necessity of the "spectacular set-piece" (2002: 12). It's like a Hollywood blockbuster: warfare is transmuted into a symbolic assertion of US and to a lesser degree UK global media and military power. The main concern of the military is to control and manipulate the image of warfare.

In the traditional, militarist wars of 1914–18 and 1939-45 people felt they were fighting wars of national survival. And they engaged in the war efforts through active participation. Similarly there was mass participation through conscription during the long Vietnam war but it brought massive casualties and massive social dislocation. In these post-1982 manufactured, spectacular wars people neither participate en masse nor feel the survival of their societies are at stake – so they have to be mobilised through their consumption of the heavily censored media (much of the censorship being self-imposed by journalists).

They were all quickie attacks. And in the fast moving events, the military become the primary definers of the "war" narrative. The Libya bombings lasted just 11 minutes. All the others were over within days. For instance, the Gulf conflict of 1991 lasted 42 days; the 2003 "war" lasted just 21 days.

They were all (until 2003) relatively risk-free and fought in secret mainly from the air.

The massive displays of US force bore little relation to the threats posed. At the same time, the threats posed to US/Western interests were grossly exaggerated – with media coverage focusing on the hyper-demonisation of the enemy leader.

WHAT ARE THE UNDERLYING FACTORS DRIVING NEW MILITARISM?

Firstly, since the collapse of the Soviet Union there has been a significant mellowing (though not complete elimination) of the nuclear confrontation between the superpowers. The language of nukespeak has been marginalised. But at the same time, the US/UK have been desperate in their search for new enemies – if only to provide a raison d'être for their massively over-resourced military industrial complexes.

In the UK, the arms industry is worth more than £5bn a year, amounting to 20 per cent of global weapons sales. It employs up to 150,000 people, the UK standing as the world's second largest manufacturer after the US with 32 per cent of the market. Over in America, its budget plans for 2004 incorporated defence spending of more than $400 bn (alongside a record White House deficit of $455 bn) – with many extra billions expected for the occupation of Iraq. All this represents more than the military spending of the rest of the world and more than twice the spending of the next 15 of the world's powers.

Moreover, the US has military bases in three quarters of the countries of the world and 31 per cent of all wealth. In contrast to its investment in warfare, the US government spent just 2 per cent of the $18.4 bn (£10bn) it had obtained from Congress for the urgent reconstruction of Iraq before the end of June 2004 (Goldenberg 2004). According to economist J.K Galbraith (2004), half the total US government discretionary expenditure is used for military purposes. The military budget is, in fact, 30 times the size of its aid budget. As Michael Mann comments (2003: 53): "Imperial priorities are clear – guns over butter. But guns are also hiding in the butter. Just a quarter of the aid budget actually goes to military assistance and training programs and a further quarter goes to 'security aid' which means providing US weapons." This is a military colossus (backed by the UK) of a kind never before seen since the Roman empire – and it is running out of control. Enemies have had to be manufactured; mythical wars have been fought.

SECRET STATE: SECRET WARS

The second important feature of New Militarism is the growth of the secret state (Keeble op cit). Alongside the "democratic" state there exists a secret and highly centralised state occupied by the massively over-resourced intelligence and security services such as MI5, MI6 and GCHQ, the Cheltenham-based signals spying centre, secret armies and undercover police units. Since the 1980s a raft of legislation – such as the Official Secrets Act 1989, the Intelligence Services Act 1994 (which protects MI6 officers carrying out acts abroad which if they took place in this country would be illegal) the Regulation of Investigatory Powers Act 2000, the Anti-Terrorism, Crime and Security Act 2001 – has reinforced their growing powers (Morgan 2003; Todd and Bloch 2003).

Mark Almond (2003) has highlighted the way in which intelligence has reached into the heart of the Blair government: "More than any predecessor, Blair has relied on a kitchen cabinet in Downing Street but one made up of a cabal of diplomats and intelligence officials rather than ambitious, if unelected party apparatchiks. Hence the focus on globalisation rather than domestic issues. Blair has liberated British politics from the influence of politicians." Professor David Beetham (2003) has similarly highlighted the "secret, warfare" state which has totally undermined the democratic system.

Indeed, the fabrication of the lies by a clique of politicians and spooks over Iraq's supposed weapons of mass destruction to legitimise the invasion culminated a process in which the secret state has now actually taken over the democratic state. By March 2003 this clique (their meetings un-minuted) comprised Prime Minister Tony Blair, communications director Alastair Campbell, chief of staff Jonathan Powell, chair of the Joint Intelligence Committee (where the CIA is represented) John Scarlett and head of MI6 Sir Richard Dearlove (see Plesch 2004; Owen 2004). Even prominent Cabinet members, such as Defence Secretary Geoff Hoon, were excluded. As a result, the public sphere is now dominated by unattributed leaks and disinformation from competing political and intelligence service factions (Keeble 2004).

And secret states fight secret wars. Indeed, the US and UK have deployed forces virtually every year since 1945 mostly in covert actions far away from the glare of the media (Peak 1982; Hussain 1988; Collins 1991; Vidal 2002; Newsinger 2002; Curtis 2003). Significantly during that series of new militarist adventures against manufactured enemies highlighted above, links between the compliant mainstream media and military grew in the US and UK so that by 1991 necessary, spectacular overt conflict in the glare of 24-hour television could be conducted in as much secrecy as covert warfare.

FLEET STREET'S NEW MILITARIST CONSENSUS

All of the adventures were backed by the mainstream media. In 1991 all Fleet Street and 95 per cent of columnists backed the military option. During the Kosovo war, not only did all Fleet Street back the attacks but called for a ground assault on Serbia – a strategy that not even the generals dared implement. There was one exception – the *Independent on Sunday* and its editor was forced to quit just days after the end of the assault (Keeble 2002; 2001). By 2003 the elite consensus over new militarism had broken down and massive global protests were growing against US/UK imperialistic aggression. But still the bulk of Fleet Street backed the "war" – and dominant ideological frames and discourses appeared in all Fleet Street papers whether they backed or opposed the invasion.

As Curtis argues "...there exists an ideological system that prevents the public seeing the reality of Britain's role in the world". He continues: "It is not a conspiracy: rather, it works by journalists and academics internalising values, accepted wisdom and styles of reporting. Neither is the system monolithic. There is some space for dissent and there are several outstanding, independent journalists in the mainstream. But major criticism of government policy and dissent is infrequent and tends to occur only at the margins and within narrow limits. It amounts to a system because it works across the mainstream media (and academia) in very visible ways" (op cit: 356).

HIDING THE HORROR OF WAR

And all of the New Militarist adventures resulted in massive civilian casualties – though the media represent them as largely "heroic", "clean", "precise" and "humanitarian". Thousands died during the Kosovo attacks; many more were traumatised and military sites, broadcast stations, hospitals, homes were bombed (Knightley 2000: 514; Keeble 2000: 93-95). Hundreds of thousands were left jobless. Michael Mann (op cit: 130) calculates that up to 10,000 civilians died during the US-led attacks on Afghanistan from October 2001 to July 2002 – triple the deaths inflicted by 9/11. He adds: "This looks like state terrorism committed as revenge for terrorism and like most revenge it exacted much more blood than the original provocation." Up to 10,000 civilians died during the Iraq invasion of 2003 (Pilger 2004: xxiii). As J.K Galbraith comments (op cit): "We are accepting programmed death for the young and random slaughter for men and women of all ages. So it was in the first and second world wars and is still so in Iraq. Civilised life, as it is called, is a great white tower celebrating human achievement, but at the top there is permanently a large black cloud. Human progress dominated by unimaginable cruelty and death."

Thus the essential function of the mainstream media in New Militarist wars is no longer to naturalise and humanise the possibility of nuclear holocaust as during the Cold War but to acclimatise the public to the acceptability of mass slaughters of the nameless "enemy". In place of nukespeak we have the massacrespeak. *New York Times* reporter Chris Hedges writes (2004): "War is made palatable. It is sanitised. We are allowed to taste war's perverse thrill but usually spared from seeing its consequences. The wounded and dead are swiftly carted offstage. The maimed are carefully hidden in the wings while the band plays the majestic march."

MASSACRESPEAK AND PROPAGANDA OF HUMANITARIAN WARFARE

Central to the manufacture of the myth of warfare has been the constant propaganda focus on precise, clean weapons. War is a civilised, humanitarian business – that's the essential message. As Edward Herman comments (1992: 67): "Doing terrible things in an organised and systematic way rests on 'normalisation'. This is the process whereby ugly, degrading, murderous and unspeakable acts become routine and are accepted as 'the way things are done'…It is the function of the defense intellectuals and other experts and the mainstream media to normalise the unthinkable for the general public." And people don't die in New Militarist "wars", massacres never happen – unless through mistakes or through the fault of the "enemy". During the 1991 massacres descriptions applied to the weapons of the US-led forces were always positive: sophisticated, super, spectacular, awesome, stunning, brilliant, smart, precise, accurate, amazing, incredible.

For the enemy the descriptions were the opposite: dirty, crude, primitive (the Iraqi supergun was an exception – but that was being constructed by British firms). Allied onslaughts always provoked superlatives – such as the "greatest aerial bombardment in history" – behind which all the terrible human suffering was hidden, silenced. Throughout the Iraqi crisis from the invasion of Kuwait in August 1990 until the formal start of Desert Storm onslaught on January 17 the military monopolised the agenda and the language in which it was articulated – the glorification of military technology was the inevitable consequence (Keeble 1997: 139–159). Let's take an example from *The Sun* of 18 January 1991:

> The Allied blitz on Baghdad and other Iraqi targets – the biggest air raid in history – was also a victory for the state-of-the-art technology packed into the Tornados and American F15E bombers. The cruisers aimed at

Saddam Hussein's key installations are believed to have landed exactly where intended. Again sophisticated technology gave the missiles their fantastic precision.

Notice how that word "Allied" nostalgically draws on Second World War rhetoric. Like all the Hitler analogies directed at Saddam Hussein, it represents an ideologically motivated use of history by the US-led powers and their propaganda media to silence many other histories – in particular the imperial roles of the US and UK in the Middle East and more globally (Curtis 1998). And it seeks to legitimise the massacres by drawing a parallel between the Allied fight against evil Hitler with the current war against Saddam.

"Targets" is that impersonal word behind which hides the deaths and suffering and trauma of how many people? With the "enemy" depersonalised in this way the perpetrators of the atrocities manage to avoid any moral responsibility or feelings of guilt. Soldiers kept on telling the press they were simply doing their job.

"The biggest raid in history" manages to extract a soundbite superlative from the horror of the massacres all the more horrific since there was never any credible enemy. The Iraqi army was constantly represented in the run up to the massacres as 1 million strong, the fourth largest army in the world, battle-hardened after the eight year war with Iran. When in January and February 1991 Iraqi soldiers were deserting in droves and succumbing to one massacre after another, Fleet Street still predicted the largest ground battle since the Second World War. In the end there was nothing more than a walkover, a rout (Knightley op cit: 483; 500).

"Blitz on Baghdad" reduces the slaughter to a game of alliteration, while "state of the art technology" symbolises the glorification of military hardware that became such a prominent feature of the coverage. New militarist wars are essentially manufactured to provide narratives in which armies win "victories". Hence the necessary stress here on "victory". Tornado, like Desert Storm, evokes the inevitable onrush and power of nature while that F15E acronym is so typical of militaryspeak – it's a fetishistic celebration of jargon that shifts from the language of myths and metaphors into the amoral landscape of numbers and letters.

Death delivering Cruise missiles are here referred to as "cruisers" – an intimate sounding nickname while the reference to Saddam Hussein continues the hyper personalisation which was such a central feature of all the coverage (Keeble 1998). Significantly, during the Iraq-Iran war (1980–1988) Iraq was, in general, referred to simply in Fleet Street as Iraq or Baghdad. Even following the chemical bombing of Kurds in Halabja on 16 March 1988 little blame was levelled personally at Saddam Hussein. Instead, Iran was blamed.

But then, after the Iraq invasion of Kuwait the personality of Saddam Hussein became the prime focus of sensationalist press coverage. Hussein, in effect, became Iraq. In this way the human interest bias, so deeply embedded in journalists' culture, served a crucial propaganda function simplifying an enormously complex history and directing all blame on the one man. Thus, when on 14 February 1991 a Stealth jet bombed the Almeriyya shelter in central Baghdad killing up to 1,600 people, mainly women and children, there was one simple, predictable response: it was all Saddam's fault. On the responsibility of the US-led forces for the atrocity – simply silence.

And notice the celebration of the "fantastic precision" of the weapons. They landed exactly where intended. People are spared in this "surgical", new non-war; only buildings, installations are destroyed in humanitarian wars. Edward Herman, drawing on Orwell's concept of "newspeak", highlights the use of "warspeak" during the 1991 attacks on Iraq (op cit: 62–63). "The aim is to soften language that might suggest unpleasant happenings and to lend support to our claims of benevolence and decency." He continues: "The concept of a surgical strike was developed during the Vietnam War to assert that we were aiming accurately at military targets, and implying that we were able to avoid killing civilians. In reality, massive firepower was used to reduce US casualties…Vast numbers of Indochinese peasants were killed in 'surgical strikes'." And following the 42-day round-the-clock bombardment of Iraq the devastation caused what a March 1991 UN survey described as a "near apocalyptic" tragedy. The survey warned that it threatened to "reduce a highly urbanised and mechanised society to a pre-industrial age". The massacres created 1.8 million refugees of whom 30,000 were estimated to have died.

HOW BARBARISM BECOMES A BIG JOKE

Another way in which the press hid the horror of the massacres was to hype them into a fun event. Barbarism became a big joke. With the absence of any credible enemy and the dull repetitiveness of the US-led air attacks, the war rapidly became boring to Fleet Street. So the patriotic pops solved the problem of the dull war by concentrating on celebrities and human interest angles, making it all a bit of a giggle. Roy Greenslade, editor of the *Mirror* at the time and now professor of journalism at City University, London, commented: "People have turned their backs on the political system and industrial organisation and sought a kind of leisure. Thus a serious subject if it is not to lose their attention has to be covered in a way to feed their diet of fun. This even includes war" (Keeble 1997: 152).

Accordingly the *Sun* tried to encourage its women readers to "Flash your knickers for our brave boys. Go give 'em a frill." Accompanying the story was a picture of a woman bending over and showing her knickers. "Who bares wins", the paper added. Pushing puns to the limit, it said: "Our boys know all about military briefings but if you look racy in lacies we want you to give 'em a cheeky low-down briefing of your own." Later the paper reported: "Wives say knickers to Iraq." Lovesick army wives were supposedly bombarding fellas with their favourite lingerie.

On 29 January, the *Sun* carried Gulf war jokes under the headline "Giggle at the Gulf". For example, Iraqi soldiers are changing their socks every day – because they smell de-feet." On 2 February, the paper invited its readers to learn the "hilarious new slang used by US troops in the Saudi desert". For instance, BAM (Big Assed Marine: women officers); BMD (Black Moving Object: Iraqi woman dressed in Arabic robes). Even the military hardware was transformed into a merry massacring machine. A "profile" of the B52 bombers (famed for its "carpet bombing" of Iraqi conscripts) described them as "Jolly Green Giants".

MASSACRESPEAK CELEBRATES THE 2003 INVASION

Now let's take an example from the 2003 Iraq invasion. Again the US/UK's weapons of mass destruction were seen (like the Hiroshima bomb) as awesome. All the mainstream media highlighted the use of 2,000 precision missiles in the US's "shock and awe" opening attacks on Baghdad. Notice how the *Guardian* highlighted the precision claims on 19 March, just before the launch of the "shock and awe" attacks. Under the headline: "US microwave bomb to make debut in most hi-tech battlefield campaign ever" the new bomb is celebrated as "new and devastatingly effective". Reporter Stuart Millar continues:

> The so-called high-powered microwave (HPW) weapon, or ebomb, will be the most sophisticated new weapon to get its operational debut in Iraq during a campaign that promises to be the most hi-tech ever fought. The last Gulf war may have marked the introduction of space age weapons – from laser guided bombs to cruise missiles 'smart' enough to know which set of traffic lights to turn left at but as collateral damage figures later proved, the technologies were still in their infancy.

Let's examine closely this text since it shows how the *Guardian*, one of the most outspoken in its criticisms of the US/UK rush to conflict, still promotes various dominant discourses that ultimately serve to legitimise the attack on Iraq. Note the use of the phrase "most sophisticated" in relation to the weapon – with all its positive associations of intelligence and efficiency. And the reference to turning left at the traffic lights is such an extraordinary phrase reducing the horror of mass slaughter to the level of the familiar, ordinary discourse of the urban everyday. "Collateral damage" is that heartless militaryspeak euphemism for civilian deaths while the reference to the "infant technologies" of mass slaughter again reduce the horror of military power to the innocence of a baby.

MASSACRESPEAK AND THE DESTRUCTION OF WAR

Or let's take this story in the *Sun* of 20 March as US jets began their attacks on Baghdad. Under the headlines: "The first 'clean' war" and "Civilian deaths could be zero, MoD claims", it reported: "The war in Iraq could have almost no civilian casualties, defence chiefs claimed last night." It continued: "A senior defence source said last night: 'Great attention to precision-guided weapons means we could have a war with zero casualties. We are a lot closer towards that ideal. We may be entering an era where it is possible to prosecute a humanitarian war.'"

How extraordinary. Just as US/UK imperialism is reaching new levels of unnecessary aggression so the language used to legitimise it is reaching new heights of exaggeration. In effect, could not the military's rhetoric about precision and smart weapons have betrayed its ultimate ambition – to destroy war itself?

MERRY MASSACRES 2003-STYLE

And as for the merry massacres 2003-style, let's take this story from the *News of the World* of 6 April. For them it's not shock and awe but Shock and Phwoarr. And the story reads "The Desert rats are rolling towards victory in Iraq equipped with the ultimate secret weapon…Nell McAndrew's pink knickers." It goes on: "Fun-loving Nell, 29, immediately sent off a pink pair of knickers she wore for a magazine shoot." She doesn't speak. She laughs. Two pilots are shown smiling with a painting of Nell on the side of their Tornado. This killing business sure is fun!

THE CRUCIAL TASK: CHALLENGING THE LIES OF NEW MILITARISM

It is possible to conclude on an optimistic note. Certain important trends are now apparent. In its desperate search for enemies, the hegemon appears to have over-reached. New militarism was built around the strategy of short, risk-free conflicts against manufactured enemies and conducted largely in secret from the air. After 20 days, with the symbolic toppling of the Saddam statue, Bush and Blair had their "war victory" to celebrate. But in Iraq today, as a result of policy decisions based on intelligence lies and dutifully reported in the mainstream press, America and Britain are trapped in an appalling quagmire and facing massive global opposition. The lies and fictions on which new militarism has always been based are being exposed and challenged.

REFERENCES

Almond, M. (2003) "So how will he be judged?" the *Guardian*, 15 May

Aubrey, C. (ed.) (1982) *Nukespeak: The Media and the Bomb*, London, Comedia Publishing Group

Baudrillard, J. (1991) "The reality gulf", the *Guardian*, 11 January

Beetham, D. (2003) "The warfare state", *Red Pepper*, June

Chilton, P. (198 2) "Nukespeak: nuclear language, culture and propaganda", *Nukespeak: The media and the bomb*, Aubrey, C. et al, London, Comedia pp 94–112

Curtis, M. (1998) *The Great Deception: Anglo American Power and World Order*, London, Pluto Press

Curtis, M. (2003) *Web of Deceit: Britain's Real Role in the World*, London, Vintage Easlea, B. (1983) *Fathering the Unthinkable: Masculinity and the Nuclear Arms Race*, London, Pluto Press

Galbraith, J.K. (2004) "A cloud over civilisation", the *Guardian*, 15 July

Goldenberg, S. (2004) "Iraq gets fraction of US aid billions", the *Guardian*, 5 July

Hedges, C. (2004) "Evidence of things not seen", the *Nation*, 24 May

Herman, E. (1992) *Beyond Hyprocrisy: Decoding the News in an Age of Propaganda*, Boston, MA, South End Press

Hussain, A. (1988) *Political terrorism and the state in the Middle East*, London/New York, Mansell Publishing

Keeble, R. (1997) *Secret State, Silent Press: New Militarism, the Gulf and the Modern Image of warfare*, Luton, John Libbey

Keeble, R. (1998) "The myth of Saddam Hussein: new militarism and the propaganda function of the human interest story", *Media Ethics*, Kieran, M. (ed), London, Routledge pp 66-81

Keeble, R. (2000) "Hiding the horror of 'humanitarian' warfare", the *Public*, Vol. 7, No. 2 pp 87–98

Keeble, R. (2001) "The media's battle cry", *Press Gazette*, October 5

Keeble, R. (2004) "Agents of the press", *Press Gazette*, 27 August

Knightley, P. (2000) *The First Casualty: The War Correspondent as Hero and Myth Maker from the Crimea to Kosovo*, London, Prion Books

Mann, M. (2003) *Incoherent Empire*, London/New York, Verso

Morgan, D. (2003) "Climate of Fear"; *Morning Star*, 12 June

Newsinger, J. (2002) *British counter-insurgency: From Palestine to Northern Ireland*, Houndmills, Basingstoke, Hampshire, Palgrave

Orwell, G. (1976/1949) *Nineteen Eighty-Four*, London, Secker and Warburg pp 741–925

Owen, D. (2004) "How to read the Butler report: start with the vital annexe", *The Times*, 16 July

Peak, S. (1982) "Britain's military adventures", London, the *Pacifist*, Vol. 20. No. 10

Plesch, D. (2004) "Missing link", the *Guardian*, 16 July

Pilger, J. (2004) *Tell Me No Lies: Investigative Journalism and its Triumphs*, London, Jonathan Cape

Powell, C. (1995) *Soldier's Way*, London, Hutchinson (with Joseph Persico)

Todd, P. and Bloch, J. (2003) *Global Intelligence: The World's Secret Services Today*, London, Zed Books

Vidal, G. (2002) *Perpetual War for Perpetual Peace: How We Got to Be So Hated*, Thunder's Mouth Press/Nation Books, New York

NOTE ON AUTHOR

Richard Lance Keeble is professor of journalism at the University of Lincoln. He previously taught in the journalism department at City University, London, for 19 years. His publications include *The Newspapers Handbook* (London, Routledge 2005 fourth edition) and *Ethics for Journalists* (London, Routledge 2001) He has recently co-edited *The Journalistic Imagination: Literary Journalists from Defoe to Capote and Carter* (Routledge 2007) and *Communicating War: Memory, Media and Military* (Arima 2007). He is also the joint editor of *Ethical Space: The International Journal of Communication Ethics* and he edited the first volume of the journal which was published in book form as *Communication Ethics Today* (Troubador, 2006). Contact details: University of Lincoln, School of Journalism, MHAC Building, Brayford Pool, Lincoln LN6 7TS. Tel: 01522 886940. Email: rkeeble@lincoln.ac.uk.

6

Hippoglossus hippoglossus and chips: Twice please love? Adventures in the underbelly of Euromyths

Simon Cross

The British are proud to have given the world the English language. After the painful shedding of an empire, English, a global lingua franca, is all that Great Britain has left to remind its people of its former status as a world superpower. Imagine, then, the horror experienced a few years ago by more than three million readers of the *Sun* (Britain's biggest-selling daily tabloid newspaper) as they read of a so-called "chip shop plot" so dastardly in its linguistic (indeed *culinary*) implications, that it could only have been conceived by a profoundly disturbed and dangerous mind:

> Chippies [i.e. fish and chip shops] could be forced to sell fish by their ancient Latin names – thanks to the craziest European ruling so far. If barmy Brussels bureaucrats get their way, baffled Brits will have to ask for hippoglossus hippoglossus instead of plain halibut. ... Takeaways, restaurants, fishmongers and supermarkets are all set to be BANNED from using names that have been around for centuries. (*Sun*, 5 September 2001: 3)

Being forced to speak Latin is no joke (as thousands of scarred British grammar school survivors can testify). Not only is it linguistically complex (how *do* you pronounce "hippoglossus"?), it is also a reminder of a time when a foreign occupying power (think Romanesque soldiers sporting swarthy, continental complexions) forced Latin verses on Britannia's plucky inhabitants without so much as a Italian-English dictionary to compensate for the loss of sovereignty). Leaving aside the Latin influences that resonate through modern English (since that only hinders my point) one can scarcely imagine a more sacrilegious assault on the British psyche than to attack the English language – and through the sacred domain of the "chippie" no less!

This unprovoked attack on a core symbol of Britishness (think of it as the bureaucratic equivalent of a group of illegal immigrants beating up a Chelsea pensioner) appears not to be an isolated incident, however. Poke beneath the surface of European involvement in British *affaires des coeurs* (note to reader: see how easily foreign influences can creep into the English language!) and one discovers a panoply of apparent intrusions in the "British way of life". Consider the following:

- EU to outlaw Britain's unique double-decker buses (*The Times*, 9 April 1998, supplement: 3)
- Britain no longer appears on EU maps (*Sun*,15 April 1999: 2)
- Standardised Euro-condoms that ignore the "large requirements" of the virile British male (*Independent on Sunday*, 12 March 2000: 25)
- British farmers forced to give toys to pigs and pat them for at least ten minutes to stop them from getting bored (*The Times*, 29 January 2003: 1)
- Homemade cake makers such as Britain's Women's Institute forced to list their ingredients (*Daily Express*, 9 July 2004: 9)
- Brussels ban barmaids from baring too much cleavage (*Sun*, 4 August 2005: 5)
- EU rules GM food can be labelled as "organic" (*Daily Mail*, 5 January 2006: 3).

ASSAULTS ON OUR GREEN AND PLEASANT LAND

These examples, taken from UK newspaper reports of EU policy proposals, hint at the array of Brussels-based bureaucratic (always referred to in UK newspaper discourse as 'Eurocratic') assaults on our green and pleasant land. What unites these and similar newspaper reports of policy pronouncements from Brussels (the administrative home of the EU and symbol *par excellence* of European vindictiveness towards Britain) are that they contain hardly a shred of truth. They are in fact "Euromyths".

Euromyths are lies and distortions perpetrated by journalists concerning EU-related issues, and dressed up as "facts". As can be seen in the list above, Euromyths are not the exclusive fare of tabloids, concerned only with trivia, gossip and "non-news". Here, the traditional view of the "serious" press, informing readers on important "public affairs" with its measured and rational discourse, is thrown into question. "In a manner that highlights how the tabloid press in Britain often sets the journalistic pace that the broadsheets follow, the latter too, revel in the pleasure of mobilising Euromythology according to their own particular criteria and partisan interests."[1]

The origin of Euromyths lies in harmonisation policies (now ended) which were intended to make the Single Market in Europe viable. But they attracted the ire of UK newspapers determined to protect the "British way of life" (whatever that means). While not a uniquely British newspaper phenomenon (the Greeks apparently have a similar problem), they appear with such regularity in the UK press that the London headquarters of the EU in 2004 introduced a "rapid rebuttal service" that identifies and counters inaccurate and misleading EU-related news reports (see: www.cec.org.uk/press/myths/index.htm). The site ("Get Your Facts Straight") employs "information workers" to update everyday examples of Euromyths alongside an accompanying rebuttal – but this suggests they are fighting a losing battle.

GOOD CLEAN FUN TO ENTERTAIN AND TITILLATE

This is because Euromyths are beloved by British journalists (90 per cent of Euromyths appearing on the European Commission's web site originate in the British press) for at least three reasons. Firstly, they offer deliverance from the journalists' day-to-day problem of not letting the facts get in the way of a good story (no doubt encouraged by the no-lose situation in which no right of reply exists that might discourage newspaper editors from printing blatant lies and untruths about the EU). Secondly, journalists delight in good clean fun to entertain and titillate readers (for example, what could be more fun than barmaid's cleavages – jokes about "banning jugs" were perhaps inevitable). Thirdly, Euromyths are ideological shorthand for imagining how European "Others" are destroying our "thousand year old island heritage". In this sense Euromyths constitute a banal form of xenophobia that is often not recognised as such precisely because of its dressage as journalistic "fact".

EU attempts to counter Euromyths is a lost cause, however. This is not only because the number of Euromyths appearing in the British press have reached national epidemic proportions (and are beginning to circulate internationally – for example, the pigs and toys story was reproduced in German and Czech Republic newspapers). It is also because Euromyths are an outcome of lost understanding about Britain's role and place in the world. The loss of Britain's pre-eminent status as the last great European empire has resulted in Britain's newspapers reporting *affaires de Europe* with detachment, as through a telescope (though a looking glass is perhaps more apt): "as reminders of British hopelessness, challenges to British ingenuity, as irritating stimulants of a repetitive fin-de-siècle obsessiveness with 'British-could-be best'".[2]

This has resulted in Britain's special contribution to Europe being one of our *detachment* from it. The result is a complex and precise cultural relationship with that continent where our particular set of telescopes enable us to put Europeans "in their place" based on the following template: "Let them meddling Eurocrats try to implement their ludicrous red-tape legislation here, they'll get a bloody nose!" (At this juncture, those who imagine Euromyths are of no serious political consequence might like to bear in mind the extent to which the UK tabloid press set the agenda on EU-related issues; whether Britain eventually rejects or accepts the Euro as its currency may well come down to the "drip-drip" effect of daily xenophobia manifest in Euromyth-type news stories.[3])

Not far below the surface of the Euromyth, then, is a symbolic hate-figure: the EU official. Let us call him (they tend to have a gendered appearance) by his newspaper *nom de plume*: the Barmy Brussels Bureaucrat (hereafter BBB). Here, the *Sun's* infamous 1991 two-fingered gesture to the then EU Commission President Jacques Delors (replete with its headline "Up Yours Delors!" 8 June 1991: 1) constitutes a classic journalistic defence of British sovereignty against incursions by the unelected BBB. That Delors is French only added to the pleasure of inviting the paper's readers to make their own two-fingered salute to Delors. (It published a selection of two-fingered reader photographs the following day including one taken on the symbolic quintessence of the British homeland: the white cliffs of Dover.)

The BBB is the ghost at the feast of every Euromyth. Politicians from EU countries come and go (how the British press love to see them go!) but the BBB remains an *idée fixe* (just how many more of these foreign language-infractions can my English-heart take?) at the centre of UK newspaper coverage of the EU affairs (especially when it concerns stories of EU fraud and corruption). They are, in fact, common newspaper currency traded by journalists mindful that they are writing for a generally "Eurosceptic" UK readership (incidentally, one that they have shaped and nurtured). In this context, journalists have little or no inclination to challenge their readership's opinion (nor their own for that matter) about any aspect of European life.

NIGHTMARE OF ORWELLIAN BUREAUCRACY GONE MAD

The newspaper image of the BBB is anchored in a nightmare world of Orwellian bureaucracy gone mad. They appear as the quintessence of pasty-faced, besuited, Big Brother officialdom; a subterranean cabal producing half-baked policies to stave off boredom and justify their own highly paid existence (why else would BBB's require EU fishing vessels to carry a minimum of 200 condoms? – see *Daily Mail*, 8 August 1999: 18). But can we emerge from under the symbolic weight of the Euromyth Mountain to understand not only the real world of BBB's, but also the murky world of media spin and lobby group interests in which Euromythology is produced?

Perhaps we can. In January 2002 a spate of stories appeared in the UK press that briefly cast light on how Euromyths are manufactured and for what sort of purpose. The story in question concerned how BBBs were intent on discovering whether commercially produced cooking sauces are actually vegetables in disguise (yes, you read that sentence correctly!). It appeared to confirm our worst fears about Brussels and EU intrusion replete with images of BBBs passing sauce through metal sieves with an aperture of five millimetres! Such a heaven sent storyline – one actually based on fact, unusual for a Euromyth-type story – picked up the ludicrous/trivial nature of such enquiry and mobilised inevitable headlines (e.g. *The Times*' "Brussels can like it or lump it", 8 January 2002: 8). The story is far from heaven sent, however.

Close inspection by the *Guardian* (11 January 2002: 4) revealed the source of the story (no pun intended!) to be a well known sauce manufacturer that had retained a commercial lobby group with a remit to find a way around EU rules governing sauce thickness (current EU rules apparently mean that the lumpier the sauce, the higher the import/export vegetable tariff sauce manufacturers must pay). EU officials had also recently deferred a decision as to whether to raise the lump threshold from 20 per cent to 30 per cent as a sop to sauce manufacturers who apparently want to produce "textually interesting" – hence lumpier – sauces to meet changing consumer demands. Sauce producers would, therefore, be hit by EU rules governing high vegetable tariffs. In short, profit margins were at stake.

With its lucrative consultancy fee pending the lobby company hit on the Euromyth angle as a way of embarrassing the EU into dropping lumpy sauce testing. They cast the "ludicrous Eurocrat" angle and journalists took the bait. The EU was apparently dismayed and angered by the "inaccuracy" of the story, not least because it undermined the work of the customs committee responsible for implementing vegetable size/quality across the EU (a necessary job given the number of member states: then fifteen, now twenty three). However, a senior EU spokesman put his own particular spin on the issue by pointing up one minor journalistic error in *The Times'* coverage as evidence that UK news reports were entirely fabricated.

MURKY TALE OF EURO-MYTHOLOGY

At the heart of this brief but murky tale of Euro-mythology is the politics (and profits) of spin in which the line between truth and half-truth is blurred. What is lost from view is how powerful commercial interests of lobby groups and their clients coincide with journalistic impulse to titillate rather than "inform" readers. Writing in the *Guardian*, a rare journalistic acknowledgment of this mutually beneficial arrangement was offered by Andrew Osborn: "… the perfectly legal yet stealthy way in which multinationals fight their lobbying battles through the press leaves a rather sour taste, even if corporate interests do happen to coincide with media ones" (*Guardian*, 11 January 2002: 4).

Herein lies the rub. Euromyths are the tip of an iceberg of commercially produced spin (remember that journalists, too, work in commercially-minded environments) such that the effect is a dilution of public knowledge and understanding about what EU officialdom does on behalf of the people of Europe. BBBs do serve on obscure committees, and make powerful decisions that do not sit easily with national and cultural differences, but the contribution they make to the organisational life of Europe – how they actually oil the wheels of EU institutions – remains consistently hidden from view.

Exploring the dark underbelly of Euromyths reminds us how easily images (in this case, stereotypes of EU officialdom) can be mobilised for spurious commercial and/or political interests. And it reminds us how too many journalists are complicit in serving corporate rather than public interests.

NOTES

1. Cross, S. and Golding, P. (1996) "United Kingdom: Europe through the looking glass", *The European Union in the Media 1996*, Madrid, Fundesco/AEJ Annual Report
2. Smith, A. (1995) "United Kingdom: 'Bent and twisted journalism' – The British press of the 1990s", *The European Union in the Media 1995*, Madrid, Fundesco/AEJ Annual Report
3. Anderson, P.J. and Weymouth, A. (1999) *Insulting the Public? The British Press and the European Union*, Harlow, Addison Wesley Longman

NOTE ON AUTHOR

Dr Simon Cross is lecturer in media and cultural studies at Nottingham Trent University. He is the author a forthcoming book *Mediating Madness: Mental Distress and Cultural Representation* for Palgrave Macmillan. Email: s.cross53@ntlworld.com.

7

From bad to good: An exploration of binary oppositions in the representation of Carole Caplin in the *Daily Mail* and the *Mail on Sunday*

Jane Taylor

Over less than eight weeks at the turn of 2002/2003, Carole Caplin was plucked out of obscurity by the Daily Mail *and the* Mail on Sunday *and handled in two contradictory ways. She was first demonised as a woman of alleged bad influence close to the Prime Minister's wife, only to be given the approval of an insider by the* Mail on Sunday *in an apparent volte face when it promptly employed her as a columnist. Did this take place in an ethical vacuum? What does it say about the relationship between news and commentary, journalists and their subjects, a newspaper and the expectations of its readers? To explore these questions, this chapter draws upon Richard Rorty's ideas about language and identity, since his notions of pragmatism and contingency offer particularly relevant insights.*

Rorty does not speak specifically of the media, nor of media language as such – in fact, he contests language as a *medium* of either representation or expression. "If we stick with language as a medium, something standing between the self and nonhuman reality with which the self seeks to be in touch, we have made no progress," he argues. "We are still using a subject-object picture, and we are still stuck with issues about scepticism, idealism and realism" (Rorty 1989: 11). Instead, he focuses on the *contingency* of language. This provides a useful context, given the extraordinary but ultimately strategic placing by the *Mail on Sunday* of Carole Caplin in symbolically different parts of the newspaper while at the same time inviting readers to interpret her as both a "good" and a "bad" person.

Rorty treats the demands of individual self-creation, on the one hand, and collective solidarity on the other, as equally valid, though forever incommensurable; rather, he suggests, these essential world views are based on the idea of truth as made, rather than found. For Rorty, only *descriptions* of the world can be true or false, rather than aspects of the world itself: "The world does not speak. Only we do ... Europe did not decide to accept the idiom of Romantic poetry, or of socialist politics ... Rather, Europe gradually lost the habit of using certain words and gradually acquired the habit of using others" (ibid: 6). In a world of alternative vocabularies rather than essential truths, then, this view of language, which also extends to conscience, leads us towards "a picture of intellectual and moral progress as a history of increasingly useful *metaphors* rather than of increasing understanding of how things *really are*" (ibid: 9). I want to begin by suggesting that one problem for newspapers occurs when values are applied to stories that are predicated on utopian ideals of "right" and "wrongs", rather than on alternative *descriptions*, and that this typically reaches a degree of false intensity in certain aspects of the rolling political news agenda, particularly in the popular press.

CAROLE CAPLIN AS NEWS

The "Cheriegate" story broke with an allegation of dubious practice. Peter Foster, an Australian with a string of previous convictions for fraud, was in a relationship with Carole Caplin (who was in turn a confidante of Cherie Blair) and through this association he brokered Cherie Blair's purchase of two flats in Bristol where her son was an undergraduate, prompting questions about the ethics of such a relationship. It is worth recording that British Prime Minister Tony Blair, deeply unpopular as he was to the *Daily Mail* (*DM*) and the *Mail on Sunday* (*MoS*) – and arguably the ultimate target of the running story – was, nevertheless, treated with rather less verbal vitriol than his wife, a working barrister as opposed to a traditional consort, whose independent success and socialist views seemed at odds with these newspapers' rather ambivalent construction of its female readership. One chilling headline captures the tenor of Cherie Blair's coverage as a dangerous and demented woman: "But beneath the veneer lay obsessive secrecy and a craving to control" (*DM*: 6/12/02).

    Concurrently, Carole Caplin, the friend, the single woman pursuing her own career, was portrayed as a dangerous influence (as well as an especially irritating one, since she steadfastly refused to talk directly to the media): "Lifestyle guru's liking for topless sunbathing and see-through clothes" scorned one strangely tangential headline, with a crosshead: "Worming her way in" (*DM*: 07/12/02). Cherie Blair eventually attempted to deflate the story by making an impassioned plea for some understanding of her multiple roles as a mother, professional woman, and wife of the Prime Minister (BBC TV news, 10/12/02). Contrary to indications thus far, in January, 2003, the *Mail on Sunday* took Caplin into the fold as a weekly named columnist on its *Night & Day* magazine.

THE SCANDAL

As a mark of the significance they attached to this story, these two newspapers labelled their exclusive "Cheriegate". "Cheriegate scoop is immortalised" boasted the *Mail on Sunday* (30/11/03) confirming its place in the pantheon of apocryphal news stories. As such, it seemed to exemplify principles laid down in the early 20th century by Lord Northcliffe, the *Daily Mail's* founder, whereby his new "product" would attract a loyal mass readership through its campaigning journalism, creating what he called "talking points" to create a powerful coalition of readers' overlapping interests in order to ensure their brand loyalty (Tulloch 2000: 144).

The "-gate" suffix placed it alongside other major political scandals, for example the original Watergate, and Irangate (in the 1970s and 1990s respectively), though in Cheriegate it was the *wife* who was the protagonist, rather than active players in a high level engagement with matters of political power. That this was possible while maintaining the credibility of the story draws our attention to the root association of "-gate" in the press, reminding us that such stories are made when people are *breaking in*, violating legitimate barriers, as opposed to being *allowed* access to privileged knowledge. In Rortian terms, the term "Cheriegate" is a good example of the *progress* of such an emerging metaphor, heralding the articulation of something newly conceptualised. He writes:

> Old metaphors are constantly dying off into literalness, and then serving as a platform and foil for new metaphors. This analogy lets us think of "our language" – that is, of the science and culture of twentieth century Europe – as something that took shape as a result of a great number of sheer contingencies (ibid: 16).

With this in mind, the Caplin story may also be read as a *lieux de memoire* of current popular newspaper culture, the "-gate" in this case an example of a type of popular journalism determined to weaken the distinction between private and public information/knowledge, raising further epistemological questions about the role of the exposure story as well as its purported aim, the establishment of "the truth".

IN SEARCH OF CAROLE CAPLIN AND HER ALTER EGO, THE COLUMNIST "CAROLE CAPLIN"

Immediately post-Cheriegate, the emphasis moves to the construction of a newly formed duality: Carole Caplin, much-reported private person, and "Carole Caplin", an eponymous column, leading to a number of questions about *identity* as well as *identification* – about the construction of journalists (as well as their subjects) on the public stage offered by the *Mail* and the *Mail on Sunday* for the negotiation of these different roles. This leads to the idea of a constituency of readers whose perceptions of the news they read is in constant negotiation of social, political and economic changes in the global marketplace. As Zygmunt Bauman observes:

> We seek and construct and keep together the communal references of our identities while on the move – struggling to match the similarly mobile, fast moving groups we seek and construct and try to keep alive for a moment but not much longer … switching on the mobile, we switch off the street. Physical proximity no longer collides with spiritual remoteness (Bauman 2004: 26–27).

This prompts us to ask: to what extent does Carole Caplin, through the extraordinarily powerful self-legitimation of the column, personify this sense of mobility, and in doing so endow it, somewhat paradoxically, with the illusion of intellectual anchorage each Sunday? Equally, how does the *Mail on Sunday* perform such a seamlessly unchallenged shift in values in its representation of the Carole Caplin it lately *devalued* to the institutionally *valued* "Carole Caplin" of the column? What does this abrupt and unexplained turn say about the nature of the covenant between the popular press and their constructed readers? What exactly is the implicit, intersubjective agreement between journalists and readers regarding the validity and appropriateness of these two Carole Caplins? As a starting point, the Rortian view more broadly circumnavigates orthodox dualities:

> Positivist history of culture … sees language as gradually shaping itself around the contours of the physical world. Romantic history of culture sees language as gradually bringing Spirit to self-consciousness. Nietzschean history of culture [sees] language as we now see evolution, as new forms of life constantly killing off old forms – not to accomplish a higher purpose, but blindly (ibid: 20).

That is, by hitting upon a language tool which *happened* to work at a certain time better for certain purposes than any previous tool. For example, in our multivocal society, a journalism has arisen which makes its own contribution to an idea of progress Rorty defines as "the history of successive metaphors" (ibid: 20) to produce the constant *illusion* of individuality while at the same time celebrating diversity, the *illusion* of a cluster of public freedoms. We can follow the metaphorising of Carole Caplin in the following example, when the journalist A. A. Gill – twice in one edition of the *Sunday Times* (05/07/04) – alluded to the kind of collective narcolepsy which tends to govern the reception of habitual grazing on lifestyle matters, while invoking what has clearly become an embedded, received idea of the composite, metonymic Carole Caplin.

On the opening of Princess Diana's memorial he wrote: "It is stylish: Carole

Caplin, Habitat, sleeping policeman symbol-lite. It doesn't so much as make you think and feel as ask you what you'd like to think and feel." Then, reviewing the Channel 4 programme *You are What You Eat*, he mused: "And it's still true: obesity and bad diet are class and wealth definitions. In essence, this programme offers you a new-Labour, new-age, Notting Hill loft-living, nouveau-Establishment Carole Caplin … to patronise and make fun of a trailer-trashy, old-world, flabby *untermensch*.' This is entirely compatible with Rorty's notion of an expanding repertoire of alternative descriptions as opposed to The One Right Description (ibid: 40), through perpetually emerging *ways of describing*, or redescriptions, which will in turn strike the next generation as inevitable, bearing the "blind impresses" (those contingencies which make each of us an "I") of something whose time has come (ibid: 20).

Enter Carole Caplin and her *MoS* column, whose concerns about "healthy" modes of living follow what has become the orthodoxy of the alternative: anti-junk food (12/11/03), anti-binge drinking (04/01/04), anti-smoking (08/02/04, 13/06/04), anti-the use of carcinogens in food (18/01/04), pro-music therapy, concerned about a shortage of midwives (22/02/04), pro-vitamins and food supplements (08/02/04) and anti-sunbeds (28/03/04). It is worth noting that this is the orthodoxy of the person variously characterised during the reporting fury of Cheriegate by the *Daily Mail*'s own columnists and writers as: "mystic's daughter" and "Cherie's Rasputin" (Paul Harris 03/12/02); "former soft porn actress" (Linda McDougall 06/12/02); "former model" (Peter McKay 02/12/02); "Former topless model" (Stephen Glover 03/12/02); "Mrs Blair's personal dresser" (with salacious undertones) (Gordon Rayner 07/12/02); and many, many references to a "lifestyle" or "style guru" – both terms used pejoratively, the first to suggest shallowness, the second, exotic pretension rather than wisdom.

If, as P. David Marshall argues, the celebrity is a "negotiated 'terrain' of significance" and, as such, "a production of the dominant culture", then at the same time and in a kind of symbiotic relationship, we must concede that "the celebrity's meaning is constructed by the audience". Not surprisingly, then, "an exact 'ideological fit' between production of the cultural icon and consumption is rare" (Marshall 2001: 47). He argues:

> These conceptions of the celebrity, those arising from below (the audience) and those emerging from above (the cultural and political producers), never entirely merge into one coherent form of celebrity identity. They do converge – in a very material sense – on the person who *is* the celebrity. He or she represents therefore a site for processes of hegemony. To use a New Age formulation, the celebrity is a "channelling" device for the negotiation of cultural space and position for the entire culture (ibid: 49).

The interesting point here is that Caplin's public persona (both as self and column) has apparently achieved a position that is at the same time *of* the crowd while being detached *from* it, since her core message via the column is a populist one, whilst her refusal to co-operate with a spurious parallel news agenda in defence of her own personal privacy gives her an aura of authenticity and immunity, particularly since identity-formation is, essentially, her chosen subject matter. Caplin's appeal in the public identity-formation market may be that both pre- and post-Cheriegate she represents to a greater or lesser degree the critical tensions between subjective-modernist as against objective-rationalist conceptions of public performance, her "journalism" encapsulating the shift described by the authors of *Media and the Restyling of Politics* towards:

> ... a variety of "romantic", "aesthetic" or "performative" views which elaborate matters of representational style in order to level the traditional hierarchy with "low" popular culture and more "ordinary" practices and skills of world-making ... (Corner and Pels 2003: 16).

These writers are keen to emphasise:

> ... a shift from predominantly discursive or textual view of performativity and performance towards a more "tacit", material, or "practical" view which focuses upon aesthetic display, bodily encounters and "libidinal" attachments to objects and spaces (ibid: 16).

Thus, the material, the topicality and the range of the Carole Caplin column as it picks up on sensitive lifestyle issues controversial enough to also find a place in the news agenda, all starts to coalesce, giving her the added veneer and tacit approval attached to the role of "expert". This is, indeed, a powerful position to be in, one which the newspaper which has made it possible is no doubt aware, since, as an employee she now serves *it*, as well as herself.

IDENTITY

That we are experiencing a crisis of identity-formation as one of the off-shoots of globalism is another way of explaining the heightened appeal of the informed "lifestyle" column that focuses on relations between the self and other as a reflection and articulation of inner truth-seeking about the self, reflecting the passage of cultural forms from their solid, traditional development over time to their current fluid state.

Zygmunt Bauman describes the temporary "cloakroom communities" that come into being as a result of this, one form of which may be imagined each Sunday as the Carole Caplin column is briefly consumed. This fluctuating community of readers tends to be:

... conjured into being, if in apparition only, by hanging up individual troubles, as theatregoers do with their coats, in one room [which are] patched together for the duration of the spectacle and promptly dismantled again once the spectators collect their coats from the hooks in the cloakroom ... Any hyped or shocking event may provide an occasion to do so (Bauman 2004: 30–31).

Including, we may add, the original misfortune of Carole Caplin when she was catapulted into the limelight and therefore ripe (in a particular moment of time, and for a limited period only) for redefinition. Even the "guru" status which has stuck, post Cheriegate, signifies, however subliminally, a period of accelerated change sympathetic to remnants of shamanic guidance drawn from ancient practices. Although this remains tacitly at odds with the rational and rather paternalistic scepticism of the newspapers in question towards alternative, healing, detoxifying and generally therapeutic means of negotiating self-identity through attention to the private sphere of mind and body, the Caplin column itself clearly rejects any crude notion of women as stained, wounded, flawed and in need of mending. Rather, it implies that the self-consciously fit are destined to be life's winners. And so Caplin's "guru" instead gives rise to a complex set of images, through which her Medusa gaze radiates woman-as-nature – but who, if cast as one of the "flotsam and jetsam lifestyle gurus" dismissed by Suzanne Moore (*MoS*: 30/05/04) becomes an impostor; or, racy and implausible: "colourful lifestyle guru, Carole Caplin" (*MoS*: 01/02/04).

Another way of interpreting the almost instant shift in output between Caplin-of-the-news and Caplin-of-the-column is through the paradigm shift from "news you can use ..." to the homelier and less ambitious "news that you can feel" (Harrington 1997: xix, xx). This sort of "intimate journalism" has as its goal "to describe and evoke how people live and what they value" (ibid: xx) and may also be a manifestation of Rorty's unhierarchised languages when he comments: " ... the world does not provide us with any criterion of choice between alternative metaphors ... we can only compare languages or metaphors with one another, not with something beyond language called 'fact'" (Rorty op cit: 20). This may be the Carole Caplin column's central achievement, then, according to Harrington:

...to understand other people's world from the inside out, to understand and portray people as they understand themselves. Not the way they say they understand themselves but the way they really understand themselves ...It is the motivation of the anthropologist and the novelist, not the judgemental journalist or the self-righteous crusader (ibid: xxv).

And this necessarily implies "a hybrid ethical outlook" (ibid: xxiv) rendering flat and over-simplified the all-embracing certainties of Cheriegate, a version of journalism whose emphasis on public life has missed, or misjudged, what private meanings might be made of it. In this case, the Carole Caplin column wholly vindicates the adverse coverage of the news story, since its continuing popularity demonstrates that it is she who is able to engage readers' many-faceted subjectivity. The genre of the column is certainly a sympathetic backdrop against which readers' identities can be developed since, through her weekly testimony there, a journalism with the hallmarks of intimacy has:

> ... the capacity to open up hackneyed issues to fresh debate, to establish uncomfortable connections between the personal and the political, to confront us with the limits of our own preconceptions, and then scratch away at the gloss of official discourses (Macdonald 2000: 264).

In this case, accepting its parameters, it can be read as providing readers with a space in which to consider no less a thing than the bifurcated nature of their own selves: firstly, as the self is continually and *publicly* brought to recognition through the whole gamut of "lifestyle" statements contributing to that aspect of it concerned to interact with others; secondly, *privately*, through the complex of beliefs and attitudes activated by the column that reveal to the self its engagement with wider issues. By throwing out these weekly shards of affective/objective material, it qualifies as a journalism of cultural interpretation and therefore, to an extent, as an epistemology of social inclusion.

AUTHOR-SUBJECT RELATIONS

Despite Caplin's refusal to be drawn into Cheriegate reportage directly, by her very existence as the one who introduced the conman to the Prime Minister's wife she must be described as a key source. In this case, her *silence* during the news phase is an eloquent response in itself, and "speaks" of a conscious or unconscious acknowledgement of the power of such personal testimony. I would contend that an engagement is, in fact, taking place precisely in the space where the story is being performed: on the page and beyond her, where innuendo, supposition and the carefully worded amplification of scant information about her tells its own story. There is a certain eloquence about her silence, because, as Macdonald argues:

> Unlike other aspects of evidence, testimony is most potent and acute when it opens up more questions than it can resolve. Paradoxically, the gap between the articulated and the lived, between official rhetoric and experience can be more knowledge-enabling than the smooth thesis emerging from ... commentary and structure. These facets of testimony are crucial guarantors of critical space, acting as a defence against sweeping emotionalism that might absorb us ... (ibid: 261)

The eloquence of Caplin's silence may have played a part in her vindication through the column, then, because it captured the public imagination to the extent that she was confidently given a public voice as a result, reclaiming the right to her own story and how (and whether) to tell it.

If those who wrote about her during Cheriegate were, in effect, performing an invasive act in search of pinpointing her identity as a news-subject, then it is easy to see how journalism itself enacts "… the dire theme of Promethean theft, of transgression in the service of creativity, of stealing as the foundation of making" (Malcolm 2004: 14). Janet Malcolm describes what *usually* happens in the course of this author-subject relationship (based on an unspoken collaboration: the journalist's desire to get "inside" the subject, and the subject's desire to be written about) in this way when she observes: "Something seems to happen to people when they meet a journalist, and what happens is exactly the opposite of what one would expect." Malcolm explains:

> One would think that extreme wariness and caution would be the order of the day, but in fact childish trust and impetuosity are far more common. The journalistic encounter seems to have the same regressive effect on a subject as the psychoanalytic encounter. The subject becomes a kind of child of the writer, regarding him as a permissive, all-accepting, all-forgiving mother, and expecting that the book will be written by her. Of course, the book is written by the all-noticing, unforgiving father (ibid: 32).

That Caplin's news-silence is contrary to this expectation is, I believe, an indication not of her naïveté but her sophistication in relation to publicity, and the unpredictability of the public-private interface being played out in newspapers. Janet Malcolm proposes an intriguing addendum to this, reflecting Rorty's privileging of the dialectic over demonstration in the process of change towards self definition (Rorty op cit: 20). Malcolm writes:

> There are people (psychoanalysts among them) who think that the action of psychoanalysis is, as it were, to transfer the patient from one novel to another – from a gothic romance, say, to a domestic comedy – but most analysts and most people who have undergone the therapy know that this is not so, and that the Freudian program is a far more radical one … It is the denovelisation of their lives, and their glimpse into the abyss of unmediated individuality and idiosyncrasy that is the Freudian unconscious, which causes them to feel this way (op cit: 123).

On the assumption that material never "speaks for itself" – because different readings are continually being made of it (ibid: 127) – we may then interpret Caplin's transformation as being drawn, firstly, into a political intrigue/detective story over which she had little control, then, through a "denovelising" process, into the functional camouflage of her own column. This, too, demonstrates an astute pragmatism by which personal identity is always "in character," in the theatre of the public domain, and the column does indeed attempt to create its own discursive terms. By denying interviews during Cheriegate, Caplin unwittingly gave licence for a particular version of her "self" to be created instead. But the "I" of the column is just as much a construction as the "lifestyle guru" character invented for her by the *Daily Mail* and the *Mail on Sunday*. Such a role will be, according to Malcolm:

> … almost pure invention … connected to the writer only in a tenuous way – the way, say, that Superman is connected to Clark Kent. The journalistic "I" is an over reliable narrator, a functionary to whom crucial tasks of narration and argument and tone have been entrusted, an ad hoc creation, like the chorus of a Greek tragedy. He is an emblematic figure, an embodiment of the idea of the dispassionate observer of life (ibid: 160).

This, we could say, is precisely what gives the column its authority. But it still leaves in an ethical limbo for journalism the fact that without the scandal the column would not have existed; and that it rests on the residual notoriety attached to the writer and the slightly unstable truce between Caplin and the two newspapers that were the agents of contradictory facets of her public persona. The first Caplin has not been entirely replaced but – as we have seen and continue to see from time to time – actually remains latent in the column, surfacing into the news proper when it is newsworthy to resuscitate Cheriegate on the back of a current story it is running. At times like this, Caplin is once again instantly re-cast back into scapegoat mode for Cherie Blair's inconsistencies. "The moral ambiguity of journalism lies not in its texts," suggests Janet Malcolm, "but in the relationships out of which they arise – relationships that are invariably and inescapably lopsided" (ibid: 162).

Ultimately, through the insistent loudness of the convention of sensationalism, we cannot but fail to read "power" as a legitimate and dominating frame for this story of crisis of identity with its references to competing realities involving: the Prime Minister (pure, political power); his wife (her professional power and her imputed influence over her husband); and the "insider" friend with no power at all but imputed influence over both (i.e. *illegitimate* power). We can then read in the coda that is the Carole Caplin column the feeding back of any tangential personal influence into legitimate power (that of the fourth estate, personified by her column).

CONCLUSION

Undeniably, both Cheriegate, and Carole Caplin the column, have been responsible for selling newspapers, confirming that at a basic level there is room for a multiplicity of appeal to readers through the different conventions of the news and personal commentary. According to Julian Baggini, scandal is each era's conditioned response to this signifier of moral decline, the gloomy tendency of every age to see its own as degenerate. However, he also suggests:

> An alternative view is that we have shifted our view of what the proper subject matter of morality is. This debate reflects a fundamental difference in thinking on ethics, between those who see the centre of moral gravity in the conduct of our private lives and those who see morality as being centered in the public realm, where our acts affect others (Baggini 2002: 52-53).

This is exactly the tension that I believe is being worked out through first Cheriegate, then Carole Caplin's acquisition and acquittal of her column, though not in a contest *between* the relevance of public/private rhetorics, but in their *dialogue*. In readily activating a moral panic questioning the trustworthiness of public figures, there is something in news coverage which runs counter to the approach of the column in its softer and more variegated approach to the construction of the self, and public opinion; but ultimately there is ample room for both. Always, the big prize in terms of news journalism is that in their mobilisaton of hierarchies of discourses, such stories may "achieve hegemony by constructing a single, incontestable discourse" (Chritcher 2003: 177). This is perhaps how such newspapers as the *Daily Mail* and the *Mail on Sunday* vindicate the illusion of moral certainty they purport to represent. Caplin's column, on the other hand, presents an equally attractive illusion of solidarity. "You have the power to stop GM food – use it!" she demands on one occasion (7/03/04) In this alternative way, moral certainty is also mobilised – but then it is diffused and returned, ultimately and quite correctly, to the ownership of those who read her.

In this way, the reportage of ethical impropriety in a political context does not interfere with the reportage of ethical considerations relating to the emergence of self. Instead, the linguistic tools applied to each may be described, *pace* Rorty, as merely appropriate, its purpose easily distinguishable by being positioned either as news, or as informed commentary. Carole Caplin's story does not illustrate a moment when a new language is being formed – necessarily. However, it is through the commerce of daily newspapers – which, by their nature, are in the business of "gradual trial and error" with language (Rorty op cit: 12) that we find a prime site for the rehearsal of such things – of progress, in the broadest sense, exemplified by changing language. They are nurseries for the emergence of thoughts that one day, in other forums, may be talked of in genuinely new terms.

REFERENCES

Baggini, J. (2002) *Making Sense: Philosophy Behind the Headlines*, Oxford, Oxford University Press

Bauman, Z. (2004) *Identity: Conversations with Benedetto Vecchi*, Cambridge, Polity

Chritcher, C. (2003) *Moral Panics and the Media*, Maidenhead, Open University Press

Corner, J. and Pels, D. (eds) (2003) *Media and the Restyling of Politics*, London, Sage

Harrington, W. (1997) *Intimate Journalism: The Art and Craft of Reporting Everyday Life*, London, Sage

Lule, J. (2001) *Daily News, Eternal Stories: The Mythological Role of Journalism*, New York, the Guildford Press

Macdonald, M. (2000) "Rethinking Personalisaton in Current Affairs", Sparks, C. and Tulloch, J. (eds) *Tabloid Tales: Global Debates over Media Standards*, London, Rowman and Littlefield pp 251-266

Malcolm, J. (2004) *The Journalist and the Murderer*, London, Granta Books

Marshall, P. D. (2001) *Celebrity and Power: Fame in Contemporary Culture*, University of Minnesota Press

Rivers, C. (1996) *Slick Spins and Fractured Facts: How Cultural Myths Distort the News*, New York, Columbia University Press

Rorty, R. (1989) *Contingency, irony, and solidarity*, Cambridge, Cambridge University Press.

Tulloch, J. (2000) "The Eternal Recurrance of New Journalism", Sparks, C. and Tulloch, J. (eds) *Tabloid Tales: Global Debates over Media Standards*, London, Rowman and Littlefield

NOTE ON AUTHOR

Jane Taylor was programme leader of the BA(Hons) Journalism at the Surrey Institute of Art and Design University College and is now a visiting lecturer at Roehampton University. Contact details: jtjanet@aol.com

7

Africanness in the British press: Splicing the news or the right to tell?

Kate Azuka Omenugha

Objectivity in news reports aims at getting to the "truth". It anchors on the need to separate facts from opinion, news from views. The interplay of a number of factors (including the ideological) in the production of news continues to raise significant doubts about the notion of "objective news reports". This chapter discusses noticeable presentation styles of news stories on Africa in two mainstream British newspapers, examining how these are probably informed by notions of otherness and racial myths, accentuated by the constraints of journalism practice. These formative dynamics in the British press produce news about Africa which seems to fan the notion of news as a construction rather than a reflection of reality/truth. These news (re)presentations, though probably benign in intent, raise a principal question: Is Africanness in the British press a result of the "right of journalism to tell" or merely a "spiced" product of an ideological news structure?

INTRODUCTION

This chapter is the outcome of my three years as a PhD student in Britain. It is, therefore, shaped by a number of factors closely linked with those years. In the first instance, while I was immersing myself in the British press, I noted the preponderance of negative news about Africa. I found stories about Africa all very captivating and moving. This is not surprising as the graphic nature of the stories and the dominating images make such an effect inevitable. But one question that persistently nagged me was: why do the British press categorise Africa by specific images to such a great extent? This question no doubt needs a lot of unpacking and I will start by discussing scholarly views about representations of Africa within Western news discourses.

REPORTING AFRICA: NEWS, RACE AND IDEOLOGY

It has been argued (Philo et al 1999; Van Dijk 2000) that news about Africa in the Western press is structured by a discernible racialisation of news discourses by journalists, suggesting "racial bias" in the ritualised practices of "objective" news reporting. It is also argued that the news from the "Third World" has low priority in the Western news agenda. Often there is scant representation and the range of explorations offered in the news reports is limited (Philo et al op cit). However, this argument may be challenged somewhat when positioned within the ideology of news values that privileges geographical proximity (Fowler 1991).

Africa is far away from the West and thus issues affecting Africa are low on the ladder of Western news values. Interestingly, there has been a suggested relationship between the way continental Africa is reported in the Western media and the position and status of diasporic Africans within multicultural Western states. Parekh (1988: 117) and (Badawi 1988: 139) signpost this when they argue that how the home countries of the immigrants are portrayed in the press goes a long way to influencing the respect they command within the British society.

Scholars have examined a number of potential reasons for the dominant negative images of Africa in the British press. Two principal explanations have emerged:

1. the "fire-brigade" or "parachute journalism" (Moeller 1999: 26) approach according to which journalists are sent to Africa for short periods to cover the "big" story. Such journalists are ill-equipped to report Africa, lacking proper knowledge of the politics or language of the areas they are sent to cover (Philo et al op cit; Egwu 2001). One effect of this approach is the tendency to rely on clichés about Africa and on images that are culturally meaningful to the majority of the audiences (O'Reilly 2003);
2. the "racial knowledge" of Africa, traceable to colonial and slave discourses and sustained in "modern" re-worked and updated images (Hall 1999).

GATHERING THE DATA

The data I used in this research was generated with the assistance of the LexisNexis search engine. I conducted an online search for one year (2002) of news articles on Africa in the British press (the *Daily Telegraph* and *Guardian*). I deliberately chose these newspapers because they represent the polarised ends of mainstream British politics – the conservative and the liberal (the British Council

1999). The *Daily Telegraph* has for a long time been closely associated with the Conservative Party; a trend consolidated during the 1930s by its owner Lord Hartnell (Michael Berry), while the *Guardian* promotes a "liberal" stance (the British Council ibid). Together with *The Times*, the *Independent* and the *Financial Times*, these newspapers form Britain's major daily "quality" newspapers. Through a systematic random choice, I keyed into LexisNexis some countries in Africa for news of those countries. This yielded more than 400 news stories. Faced with such kaleidoscopic of data, what I needed was an uncomplicated way to analyse the data and make discoveries about the content. McQuail (2000: 306) asserts that:

> There is no coherent theory of media content and no consensus on the best method of analysis, since alternative methods are needed for different purposes and for different kinds of content and different media genres.

Strengthened by McQuail's view, I decided to adopt a symptomatic approach to my data. By using a symptomatic analysis, I decided not to concern myself with a quantitative study but look out for news items about Africa and attempt, through a qualitative approach, to identify recognisable themes, patterns and trends in the reporting of black African people in the newspapers chosen. The strength of a symptomatic analysis is in its ability to provide clues and to use such clues to tease out the "secrets" of representation (Goring et al. 2001). Such themes, patterns and trends might be considered more or less the overt messages about African people in the newspapers. They provide the clues to the covert and uncertain meanings imbued in the texts.

In line with the cultural studies tradition that challenges transparency of meanings (Hall et al 1980; During 1999), while emphasising linguistic and ideological structuring of media messages (Hall 1997), I considered another question: What do these themes, patterns and trends in the reporting of black African people in the key British newspapers say about the construction of Africa in British cultures? I now examine the presentation styles of news on Africa in British press using the dominant stories about Africa in the British press: for example, the story of AIDS, hunger, rape, famine and under- development.

CONSTRUCTING AFRICANNESS: STYLES AND PRESENTATION TECHNIQUES IN REPORTS OF AFRICA

Journalists have been called "professional story tellers" (Bell 1999: 236). This is in recognition that there is a story underpinning every news item. McQuail, reading Morin's (1976) analysis of news form, argues: "…an event has to be rendered into a 'story about an event'" (2000: 347). It is this *rendering into a story* that constitutes news. Thus, it is popular to say that "news is not an event but the account of an event", that is, an event rendered into a story. News and story, therefore, share a similarity; they both have *telling* quality. Both recount or narrate an event. This *telling* makes it difficult to distinguish what precisely constitutes news and story or what is the nature of these two terms.

A *story* has been defined as the telling of a happening or connected series of happenings, whether, true or fictitious[1]. News, however, is considered a reliable, truthful account of an event. Perplexingly, news is often thought of as stories. Reah (2002: 5) writes:

> We talk about 'news stories'. Other texts that deliver information are not referred to as 'stories'. We don't talk about 'report stories' or 'lecture stories' or 'textbook stories'. A story is an 'account of imaginary or past events, narrative tale, anecdote ....*colloquial* fib'. Why are news stories referred to in any way that gives them the status of fictional accounts? The definition 'account of past events' may to some extent relate to a factual account, but carries the implication of interpretation, elaboration and the creation of a narrative.

It is possible that this loophole allows journalists to use words imaginatively, employ fictional devices and use personalised anecdotes. These devices are prominent in the stories of Africa in the British press. They have some positive uses, but could possibly challenge the veracity of the news accounts. Writing specifically about eyewitness accounts (one of the devices employed in telling a story) Macdonald (2003: 69) notes:

> In newspaper news and features, eye-witness account and personal experience also provide affect, varying from titillation (in the 'kiss and tell' story) to celebration of human spirit (in the 'triumph over adversity' story) to vicarious grieving (in the 'tragedy/victim' story). In each case, the personalised account invites reading *as if it were fiction*. Its 'repetition with difference' mimics the generic structure of popular narratives, which also elicit basic emotional responses through crafting scenarios and characters that offer familiar modes of identification (emphasis added).

I will illustrate how these are applied within stories of Africa in the British press.

THE USE OF PERSONALISED ACCOUNTS

Evident in the stories on Africa is the use of personal and individual accounts. These obviously have the aim of holding the reader's attention. But how do we know that the news accounts go beyond merely holding readers captive? Let us look at AIDS story (for clarity called AIDS story 1). Reporting from Mbale,

Uganda, on a charity plan to help victims of the epidemic, the Neil Darbyshire reports:

> It is impossible with words and cold statistics fully to convey the distress and alienation of a generation of African children orphaned by Aids. Already traumatised by the untimely deaths of their parents and struggling to cope with their own pain and confusion, children, as young as 14 or 15 frequently find themselves heading a family driven to the margins of society by a combination of poverty, stigma and exploitation.... At a small settlement in the Sironko district of Uganda, Beatrice Namutosi begins to weep as she contemplates the future of five children, four of them under 13. Beatrice, who lost her husband to Aids in 1998, is clearly in the advanced stages of the disease herself. Her face is gaunt, her skin is becoming translucent, her limbs are stick-thin and she suffers from persistent fever and coughing fits. "I want to teach the children to look after themselves but I just don't have enough strength," she said. "I don't see how they can live with their grandmother for very long. She can't take care of them because she is weak and needy and old. My husband's family are poor and my children can't live with my sister because she already has eight children of her own".... A few miles away in Mbale district, Rose Amunat has been pushed into the role of mother and main breadwinner many years before her time. Rose was 15 when her mother died of Aids, leaving her to look after five younger brothers and sisters, the youngest a baby of 18 months (*Daily Telegraph*, 30 November 2002: 22).

There are clearly well-intentioned thoughts in the AIDS story reported above. First, it creates a vivid image of the agony of AIDS through the recounting of individual experiences. One cannot but be moved by Beatrice who "weeps" as she obviously realises she was going to die of AIDS and will be leaving her children orphans (having lost the husband to AIDS) or by Rose who at the age of 15 is left to look after five young brothers and sisters, one of whom is just 18 months. Yet, it is significant that the stories offer no further analysis than human miseries and fail to address political and economic differences between the West and Africa.

It would be an avenue to offer positive and constructive suggestions about how the AIDS problems in Africa might be solved (for example, if these individuals were in richer countries, they would have more access to drugs. Also, how would richer countries aid the people to combat the disease?). This is one of the difficulties signposted by Macdonald (2000: 255) about the use of individual accounts in the media as it may offer "opportunities for constructing polemic rather than analysis or for promoting voyeurism rather than understanding". This seems to be the case in the story of AIDS as in constructing the vivid accounts without providing any analysis; it feeds a style of reporting capable of intensifying the stigmatisation of those already stigmatised.

One of the dominant myths circulating in British society about Africans concerns their sexuality. Within colonial discourses, Africans have been constructed as strongly sexed and sexually irrepressible (Walvin 1982). In Africa at least, AIDS is claimed to be largely transmitted through heterosexual sex. These stories thus seem to fan the myth of Africans as highly sexed with an unbridled sexuality. The issue is not whether AIDS is a problem in African societies. Statistics show that it is. However, we need to keep our antenna tuned to the possibility that rather than reporting AIDS as a problem that needs to be addressed, the construction of the stories merely feed on the circulating myths about Africa to give them legitimacy.

> One of the ways in which these myths are legitimised is by *Africanising* AIDS. The disease seems to be given an African face and, indeed, so have all kinds of other ills or adversities – violence, sickness, corruption, poverty. The stature of a UK child abuse victim Ainlee Labonte is likened to "an African famine victim" (*Independent*, 7 September 2002: 11}. Malnourished Afghanistan children spotting matchsticks legs, wrinkled, limp and hanging buttocks and swollen tummy are described as "image out of Africa, so it seems fitting that the two nurse nutritionists looking {them} in a feeding centre run by charity World vision should be Africans" (*Guardian*, 4 April 2002: 17).

I have cited these two instances to show how Africa has become a general metaphor for many ills and discursively circulated in the media. It would not be surprising, therefore, if these personalised reports simply feed from pre-exiting myths about Africa discursively circulated within the society. Moreover, as Macdonald (2003: 61) notes, personalisation sometimes results from lazy journalism and inadequate research.

FIGURATIVE DEVICES

An obvious observation in the language of the stories on Africa is the use of many literary devices to illuminate and embellish stories. Literary devices used in the stories about Africa range from metaphors, personification, hyperbole, euphemism, to literary allusions. The title of Tim Butcher's report on AIDS in South Africa (AIDS story 2 for the purpose of clarity), "Cry for AIDS orphans of the beloved country" (*Daily Telegraph*, 30 March 2002: 20) carries a clear literary allusion playing on Alan Paton's novel *Cry the Beloved Country* (1952). Set against the turmoil of apartheid during the 1940s and early 1950s, it tells of South Africa – the beloved country fractured with racial hatred.

The novel paints a picture of fear, gloom and disillusionment. However, Paton offers some hope – through love and forgiveness. The allusion to this literary text in the story about AIDS in South Africa seems to suggest that South Africa has hardly changed, even with the apparent outlawing of apartheid and the assumption of power by the majority blacks. It seems to have traded one form of ill for another: racism for AIDS. While Paton offered hope for the country through love and forgiveness, AIDS as presented in the news closes up all hopes. This is seen in the fatalistic end to the story:

> There comes a time when we call the ambulance and they do not return. Outside the voices of the school choir practice could be heard. The AIDS tragedy in South Africa is sad beyond any singing of it.

Such endings, which are expressive and extremely moving, are routinely used stories on AIDS in Africa.[2]

EUPHEMISM

Another literary device consistently used in the news of Africa in the British newspapers is euphemism. For example, in AIDS story 2, describing the death of Vuma's parents, the news reports that they "became ill, lost their appetite, refused to leave their beds and finally disappeared in an ambulance to the local hospital 40 miles away, never to return". This is a euphemistic way of expressing the pains of death by AIDS, refusing to leave their beds referring to being bed-ridden. This form of expression jars with the Western belief of the language of the news. Keeble writes:

> Journalists stress their commitment to plain English and so it is not surprising that euphemisms (bland expressions) are considered out. Thus never write so-and-so 'passed away' or 'slipped away calmly' – they died (2001: 85).

Like other figurative languages used in the news, euphemism is for a special effect. For such similar effect too, the *Guardian*, writing in a headline "Starving Zambia spurns GM food aid" begins the story thus: "In the woodlands of southern Zambia hunger arrives with the rhythmic clack of stone against stone as villagers pound open the hard mungongo nuts, a food of last resort…" (*Guardian*, 17 October 2002: 19).

PERSONIFICATION AND THE VOYEURISTIC GAZE

Hunger here is personified. Personification is a figure of speech that gives human qualities to abstract ideas, animals, and inanimate objects. By giving the human quality *arrives* to an abstract thing like *hunger*, the story creates a special image in the reader's minds. This effect is heightened by the alliterative use of words that follow: "the rhythmic clack of stone against stone as villagers pound open…"

However, we need to address the issue raised by Macdonald (2003: 66): does the affective quality of stories take us into a developed understanding of the complexity of an issue, or is merely being used to stir strong emotions? The similarity in the use of devices in the stories makes the latter option a possibility. The use of fictional devices, which call up emotion, turn "real life" into spectacle; and invites the reader's voyeuristic gaze. Voyeurism is used in this sense, not as "sexualised form of gazing, but to the *frisson* of the emotional excitement that comes in part from knowing that we are safe from a returning look" (ibid: 70).

As the camera provides the means of scrutiny and engaging in voyeurism, so also do the literary devices, which paint cinematic pictures, provide opportunities for scrutiny while at the same time they create a distance between the reader and the objectified Africans. This distance is a prerequisite for the voyeuristic gaze. As Moeller (op cit: 25) notes: "Too much harping on the same set of images, too much strident coverage with insufficient background and context, exhaust the public." The public, however, are safe in the knowledge that "we" are not like "them" – increasing both the distance and the voyeurism.

THE USE OF ATTRIBUTION

Attribution takes place when journalists credit their knowledge to some source. This usually increases the believability and credibility of the stories. Unattributed or anonymous sources lessen a story's credibility. Attribution serves an important function in the telling of news stories.

> It reminds the audience that this is an account that originated with certain persons and organisations…. In theory, a news story should be regarded as embedded under a stack of attributions, each consisting of source, time and place (Bell 1991 in Harcup 2004: 109).

By using attribution therefore, the journalist detaches *self* from the story and projects a sense of neutrality and balance. Keeble writes (op cit: 44):

> Reporters use sources to distance themselves from the issues explored. Rather than express their views on a subject, reporters use sources to present a range of views over which they can appear to remain objective and neutral.

Newspaper practice requires also that people in the news are accompanied by a title or description since the reader needs to know on what authority or on what basis they are speaking. In most cases, such people are identifiable people. There are occasions, however, when the people in the news are not expected to be named or identified. One of such is in reporting rape and indecency stories. The code of practice of the Press Complaints Commission explicitly requires that "the press should not identify victims of sexual assault or publish material likely to contribute to such identification unless, by law, it is free to do so".[3] As I argue subsequently using the story of rape, the use of attribution in the news on Africa in British press seems to be a codified method of reporting that hides an ideological preoccupation.

Stories of rape seem to support one of the dominant ideologies about African men in British society that have circulated since times of slavery (African/Black men as rapists) (Hooks 1982). Explaining 17th century European construction of polygamy in Africa, Van Den Boogart (1982: 48) writes: "African men had few restrictions in the gratification of their sexual desires ... the size of their penises also demonstrates their great libido...."

Incidences of rape are frequently reported in most newspapers. As "bad" news, rape obviously meets key news values. There are, however, racial connotations discernible in the reports of the rape in Africa as reported in the British press. My starting point is to comment briefly on how the British press reports rape incidents in Britain to create a point of reference to how incidences of rapes in Africa are constructed within British news. The *Guardian* (7 December 2002: 2) carries a typical rape incident in Britain. Titled "Man charged with nine rapes". Rebecca Allison reports of "a married railway worker [who] was last night charged in connection with a string of sex attacks on girls and women across the south-east of England".

Here the story focuses on one subject: rape. The lead aptly summarises the story. The story then moves forward quoting sources and attributing the quotes to named persons.

> Antoni, Imiela, 48, from Appledore, Kent, was charged with nine offences of rape, Detective superintendent Mark Warwick, of Thames Valley Police, the acting head of Operation Orb, confirmed. "This is a complex investigation which has involved five police forces working together in close co-operation. The co-operation and close working continue," he said.

In the news item also, victims of rape cannot, by law, be named. The language, also, is distanced, telling the story in a unobtrusive style that simply gives the "kernel" of the story. We may need to compare this type of presentation with that seen in the story of rape in Africa as reported in British press

The *Daily Telegraph* (6 August 2002: 12) began its story in this dramatic style: "In the past years Neema Mushobora has been raped by soldiers from two armies, has watched as her uncle and grandmother were hacked to death and seen her friends die of hunger."

The question one could ask is who is Neema Mushobora? The answer is provided in the third paragraph of the story: Neema is a victim of the Congolese war. The story describes how she was been kept prisoner and raped by several militiamen. In her own words: "Everyday I would be raped, sometimes by many men," she said. "Some of the other women were raped 20 or 30 times, one soldier after the other. Then they just bled to death." The use of attribution here works to factualise and validate the story as news, but also raises some ethical questions. In rape cases, journalism ethics as well as the law require that the victims are not identified. Why, then, is Neema or Heeshima Tupatie (raped as a 13-year-old and gave birth to a child called Chance) named? Or are these people constructed not as the subjects of the news, but as merely narrative objects, simply to move the tales of horror along and substantiate racial beliefs and knowledge?

As van Dijk (2000) points out, racist discourses rarely appear blatantly in media texts, but operate via forms of "discursive" signification. First, we address the lead of the story, which ostensibly addresses the issue of rape (has been raped by soldiers from two armies) but, in fact, addresses other ills: brutality (has watched as her uncle and grandmother were hacked to death), and hunger (seen her friends die of hunger). Within the single sentence, a cinematic picture of barbarism and death is created.[4]. This device increases the suspicion that the stories on rape in Africa as reported in British press may have been crafted to bring Africa under a voyeuristic stare to sustain racial myths and beliefs. Part of the story further reads:

> Neema escaped in October when the Mayi Mayi went on another pillaging spree. She fled to an ill-equipped hospital in Panzi, outside the town of Bukavu. In May she gave birth to a girl, Rebecca, the product of rape.

Note the emphasis on the dysfunctional nature of the society: "Mai Mai went on another pillaging spree", "…an ill-equipped hospital in Panzi", and "Rebecca, the product of rape". Why is the emphasis on Rebecca as "the product of rape"? Rape is considered an act of a dysfunctional mind. Rebecca may possibly be a symbol of African children in the narrative whose dysfunctional production is symbolically transferred on to African children. This seems to be the preferred reading as the news stresses: "Rebecca and Chance are the Congo's future…."

THE USE OF IMAGERY

Spatial under-development

In many stories about Africa in the British press, the emphasis is often put on constructing images of under-development and deprivation by calling up disparaging spatial distinctions (see Akurang-Parry 2001). As Goldberg notes:

> The category of space is discursively produced and ordered. Just as spatial distinctions like "West" and "East" are racialized in their conception and application, so racial categories have been variously spatialized more or less since their inception into continental divides, national localities, and geographic regions (Goldberg 1993: 185).

Thus the *Guardian* reports:

> In the woodlands of southern Zambia hunger arrives ... as villagers pound open the hard mungongo nuts, a food of last resort for which they compete with monkeys and elephants. The pounding is the only sound in hamlets such as Siatumbu where families slump in front of thatched huts ... We go further into the bush to find nuts and berries... (*Guardian*, 17 October 2002: 19).

Words such as "woodlands", "hamlets", "thatched huts" and "bush", construct Zambians as living in a jungle and suggest backwardness and underdevelopment. More significantly, the image of the Zambia as a jungle where animals roam is sustained in this phrase: "...food of last resort for which they compete with monkeys and elephants". This further reduces the Zambians to the level of animals as well. A similar imagery is evident when the *Guardian* reports "the bleached shantytowns of Southern Africa ...a shack dustier than most...a sprawling shantytown in northern Zambia..." (30 October 2002: 20). Similarly, during Prime Minister Tony Blair's visit to Ghana in 2002, the *Guardian* reported: "He saw the women and children carrying huge burdens on their heads; the corrugated-iron roof, the abandoned cars, the mud huts" (9 February 2002: 13).

Over-population

Another dominant theme in the reporting of Africa is that of over-population – suggesting a link between that and under-development. Marshall (1996: 16) stresses the relationship between such a construction and the denial of certain benefits to black Africans in Britain: "It is claimed that instead of contributing to the British economy we have too many children and are social scroungers."

The following extract from the *Daily Telegraph's* report on the Ivory Coast illustrates a possible "panic" about Africa's population:

> There was a sense of terror in the Ivorian city of Bouake yesterday as its

civilians fled in panic. By the thousands they streamed south, an endless line of men, women and children, clutching a few bags and balancing bundles on their heads, snaking through the dense African bush for mile after mile....(28 September 2002: 20).[5]

The use of numbers – "by the thousands" – encourages readers to guess the "real" numbers and heightens the hyperbolic nature of the phrase (van Dijk op cit). This device associates Africa with problems of over-population. The graphic description of the exodus reminds one of ants moving in lines in millions. The same animal imagery continues as the story further describes them as "snaking" through the "African bush".

Images of dependency: Behold Father Christmas

Often the news of Africa is constructed in ways that represent the continent as dependent while celebrating the superiority of Europe. For example, while Africa is projected as corrupt, incapable of self-government, passive, uncivilised, Europe is constructed as always there to pick up the pieces, to be benevolent and to save Africa from itself (Goldberg 1993).

Stereotypes of dependency, passivity and unruliness in relation to Africa are constantly repeated in press reports about Africa, while Europe is depicted as the kind "Father Christmas" *par excellence*. For instance, the *Guardian* reported:

The delicious irony is that in those African countries where there is a semblance of hope, it is because of a canny, enlightened neo-colonialism from the charities, bi-lateral donors and UN organisations (7 February 2002: 4).

In racist ideologies (Biddis 1970), conquering the "inferior races" was considered both a necessity and a duty for Europeans. Today, it could be argued that this continues in the "positive self representation" and "negative other- representation" (Van Dijk op cit) that is prevalent in Western dominant news discourse about Africans. Writing about the New Partnership for Africa's Development, a government-led initiative to improve development in Africa, the *Daily Telegraph* reported:

The much-hyped initiative to rebuild Africa elicited little enthusiasm from Mercy Mugai as she clutched her two underfed children and glanced wistfully at the fast-food café in central Nairobi. "All these people do is talk, talk, talk," she said. "If our leaders do get any money from the Wazungu (white men), they steal it for themselves. We have no food, no schools, no future. We are just left to die." New Partnership for

Africa's Development (Nepad) requires the West to pump in billions in annual investments in exchange for good political and economic governance (28 June 2002: 14).

The story above juxtaposes African corruption ("If our leaders do get any money from the Wazungu (white men), they steal it for themselves") with white generosity (requires the West to pump in money). A similar theme of European generosity and African dependency is sustained in the following headline: "Britons urged to help avert African catastrophe" (*Guardian* 26 July 2002: 20), which represents Africa as passive and incapable of any informed decision. It is left to the magnanimity of Britons to avert the catastrophe in Africa.

Uncivilised behaviour and primordial discourses about Africa

The visit of Tony Blair to Africa provides images associated with uncivilised behaviour and disorder, drawn from primordial discourses about Africa. For instance, the image of the horde and the mob were resurrected in this report on his 2002 visit to Ghana:

> Tony Blair saw rural Africa where the bulk of the continent's population live for the first time yesterday.... In Nankasi, he was mobbed by hundreds of villagers. "It moved his heart", a colleague travelling with him said. "He could not be other than affected by the dignity of the Ghanaian villagers" (*Guardian*, 9 February 2002: 13).

The use of the words "mobbed by hundreds of villagers" to describe the Ghanaians' enthusiastic welcome to Blair echo the image of an unruly crowd. Blair is also represented as the messiah whose presence the villagers wanted desperately to behold. As in the days when Christ "saw a great crowd and had compassion for them for they were like sheep without a shepherd" (as the Gospel of Mark records), Tony Blair's heart was moved by the mob of villagers and could not but be affected by their "dignity". Ghanaians are thus constructed as "objects to be pitied" by the benevolent white man. This type of representation of Westerners when they visit Africa has been previously noted (see Badawi op cit, Akurang-Parry op cit). In the representation of Nigeria during Blair's 2002 visit, the unruly imagery is also sustained. The speaker of the National Assembly was described as "giggling", National Assembly members "sat in comfy airport armchairs when they are not milling about, the speaker's request that mobile phones be switched off was answered by repeated electronic thrilling" (*Daily Telegraph*, 8 February 2002: 17). Nigerians' unruly and uncivilised behaviour is contrasted with Tony Blair, who is represented as deeply restrained. The story on Nigeria continues:

The Prime Minister was welcomed by a brass band that pumped out waltzes and tangos with vigour. Its rendition of the national anthem rather collapsed in the last bars, somewhere around "long to reign over us", but Mr Blair did not flinch *(Daily Telegraph* 8 February 2002: 17).

This extract significantly emphasises the "disorderliness" of Nigerians. In contrast, the fact that, in spite of the 'confusion', Blair did not flinch, portrays him as the quintessential signifier of Western civilised order.

CONCLUSION

News reports of Africa in the British press are too complex to be explained away as simply racially biased. Various factors dialectically function to create the dominant images of Africa prevalent in the British press. Constrained by time, resources and logistics, mainstream journalists continuously resort to myths and stereotypes as a gateway to meeting deadlines. As a result, Africa is consistently reported within narrow repertoires of understanding, which are dominated by mostly negative images. In personalised reports using individual accounts, in the prominent use of "human interest" stories, in the emphasis on negative stereotypes and through the conventions of attribution, Africa's "otherness" is emphasised. In conclusion, news about Africa in the British press serves to reinforce long-held ideologies and myths of race.

NOTES

1. Webster's *New World Dictionary of the American Language*
2. See "Ray of hope for the orphan generation" *Daily Telegraph*, 30 November 2002: 22; "Africa's ugly sisters leave trail of death"; *Guardian*, 30 October 2002: 20 and "Land where only coffin makers thrive", *Daily Telegraph*, 24 June 2002: 11 for similar endings
3. See the UK Press Complaints Commission's Code of Practice (esp. clause 12) www.pcc.org.uk/index2.html
4. For similar device, see "Just talk talk talk and we are left to die", *Daily Telegraph*, 28 June 2002: 14; "Since I was born, I've never seen such hunger", *Guardian* 7, November 2002 p. 21
5. See also for more reference on population: Adrian Blomfield "Thousand pack Nairobi as poll campaign opens". *Daily Telegraph,* 19 November 2002 p. 18

REFERENCES

Akurang-Parry, Kwabena (2001) "Otherizing space and cultures: the American media's coverage of President Bill Clinton's visit to Ghana in 1998", *Journal of Cultural Studies*, Vol 1, No 3 pp 74-89

Badawi, Zeinab (1988) "Reflections on TV coverage of Africa", *The black and white media book*, Twitchin, John (ed.) Stoke-on-Trent, England, Trentham Books pp 133-139

Bell, Allan (1999) "News stories as narratives", *The discourse reader*, Jaworski, Adam and Coupland, Nikolas (eds) London, Routledge pp 236-251

Biddis, Michael D. (1970) *Father of racist ideology: the social and political thought of Count Gobineau*, London, Weidenfeld and Nicholson

During, Simon (ed.) (1999) *The cultural studies reader*, London, Routledge, second edition

Egwu, E.U. (2001) "Foreign media projection of Africa: The role of African communicators", the *Nigerian Journal of Communications,* Vol 1, No 1 pp 1-13

Fowler, Roger (1991) *Language in the news discourse and ideology in the press*, London and New York, Routledge

Goldberg, Davis T. (1993) *Racist culture: Philosophy and the politics of meaning*, Cambridge, Mass, Blackwell

Goring, Paul et al (2001) *Studying literature: the essential companion*, London, Arnold

Hall, Stuart et al (eds) (1980) *Culture, media and language: Working Papers in Cultural Studies 1972-79*, London, Routledge

Hall, Stuart (ed) (1997) *Representation, cultural representations and signifying practices*, London, Sage

Hall, Stuart (1999) "Racist ideologies and the media", *Media studies: A reader*, Marris, Paul and Thornham, Sue (eds) Edinburgh, Edinburgh University Press pp 271-282

Harcup, Tony (2004) *Journalism: Principle and Practice*, London, Sage

Harris, Geoffrey and Spark, David (1997) *Practical newspaper reporting*, Oxford, Focal Press, third edition

Keeble, Richard (2001) *The Newspapers Handbook*, London, Routledge, third edition

Macdonald, Myra (2000) "Rethinking personalisation in current affairs journalism", *Tabloid tales: global debates over media standards*, Sparks, Colin and Tulloch, John (eds) Lanham, Rowman and Littlefield pp 251-266

Macdonald, Myra (2003) *Exploring Media Discourse*, London, Arnold.

Marshall, Annecka. (1996) "From sexual denigration to self-respect: resisting images of black female sexuality", *Reconstructing womanhood: Reconstructing feminism writings on black women*, Jarret-Macauley, Delia (ed.) London and New York, Routledge pp 5-35

McQuail, Denis (2000) *McQuail's Mass Communication Theory*, London, Sage, fourth edition

Moeller, Susan D. (1999) *Compassion fatigue: How the media sell disease, famine, war and death*, New York and London, Routledge

O'Reilly, Carole (2003) "Unreliable representations: Ethnicity and Irishness in British television fiction", *Identity politics and media*, Ross, Karen and Derman, Deniz. (eds) Cresskill, New Jersey, Hampton Press pp 11-24

Parekh, Bhikhu (1988) "Reflections on the language of racism; the legacy of colonialism; prejudice and the press", *The black and white media book*, Twitchin, John (ed.) Stoke-on-Trent, England, Trentham Books pp 111-123

Philo, Greg *et al* (1999) "The media and Rwanda crisis: Effects on the audiences and public policy", *Message received,* Philo, Greg (ed.), New York, Longman pp 213-228

Reah, Danuta (2002) *The language of newspapers,* London and New York, Routledge, second edition

The British Council (1999) *Newspapers in Britain: British Studies Resources.* Available online at http://www.britishcouncil.org.tr/education/bcs/background/index.ht, accessed 11 February 2002

Uche, Luke U. (2003) Nature of news, structural and institutional bias in reporting Africa, paper presented at the 13th biennial conference of the African Council for Communication Education (ACCE), Abuja, Nigeria, August

Van Dijk, Teun. A. (2000) "New(s) racism: A discourse analytical approach", *Ethnic minorities and the media,* Cottle, Simon (ed.), Buckingham, Philadelphia, Open University Press pp 33-49

NEWSPAPER REFERENCES

Allison, Rebecca (2002) "Man charged with nine rapes". *Guardian,* 7 December p. 2

Blomfield, Adrian (2002) "Just talk talk talk and we are left to die", *Daily Telegraph,* 28 June p. 14

Brogan, Benedict (2002) "Blair left wilting by a warm welcome; Brass, sweat and cheers for the Prime Minister at Nigeria's National Assembly", writes Benedict Brogan, *Daily Telegraph,* 8 February p. 17

Butcher, Tim (2002a) "Cry for AIDS orphans of the beloved country", *Daily Telegraph,* 30 March p. 20

Butcher, Tim (2002b) "Inside the city of fear rebel troops await attack", *Daily Telegraph,* 28 September p. 20

Carroll, Rory (2002a) "Starving Zambia spurns GM food aid", *Guardian,* 17 October p. 19

Carroll Rory (2002b) "Africa's ugly sisters leave trail of death", *Guardian,* 30 October p. 20.

Darbyshire, Neil (2002a) "Ray of hope for the orphan generation: On the eve of UN world Aids day", *Daily Telegraph,* 30 November p. 22

Darbyshire, Neil (2002b) "Land where only coffin makers thrive", *Daily Telegraph,* 24 June p. 10

La Guardia, Anton (2002) "Straw finds the 'healing Africa' is a tough task", *Daily Telegraph,* 24 January p. 20

Liddle, Rod (2002) "Inside story: Mr Blair says that we should feel guilty about this. Sorry, but I don't", *Guardian,* 7 February p. 4

MacAskill, Ewen. (2002) "Blair gets first sight of African poverty", *Guardian,* 9 February p. 13

McGreal, Chris (2002a) "Blair confronts 'scar on world's conscience'", *Guardian,* 7 February p. 16

McGreal, Chris (2002b) "Britons urged to help avert African catastrophe", *Guardian,* 26

July p. 20

Meldrum, Andrew (2002) "Since I was born, I've never seen such hunger", *Guardian*, 7 November p. 21

Raif, S. (2002) "Girl, 2, looked like famine victim". *Independent*, September 7 p. 11

Steele, Jonathan (2002) "Going home to hunger and death: Aid agencies fear for families persuaded to leave refugee camps", *Guardian*, 4 April p. 17

Wilson, Margaret (2002) "Will their protests leave her hungry?" *Daily Telegraph*, 20 November p. 26

NOTE ON AUTHOR

Kate Azuka Omenugha, PhD, teaches gender and communication studies in the Department of Mass Communication, Nnamdi Azikiwe University, Awka, Nigeria. Her research interests focus on gender, race, representation and ethics of communication. She has published in many academic journals such as *Media Development, Feminist Media Studies* and *Humanitas*. She belongs to many professional and academic bodies including the African Council for Communication Education (ACCE), the World Association for Christian Communication (WACC), the Nigerian Institute of Public Relations (NIPR) and the Institute of Communication Ethics (ICE). Contact details: Department of Mass Communications, Nnamdi Azikiwe University, Awka, P.M.B. 5025, Anambra State, Nigeria. Email: komenugha@gmail.com. Telephone 00 234 (0) 8057960830.

8

Media standards slump in Germany's beastly year

Susanne Fengler and Stephan Russ-Mohl

With the media in crisis, German journalists like to think of themselves as victims of "profit maximisation". They turn a blind eye, however, to the fact that they, too, do not always contribute to the greater good but also act out of self-interest. Trade-offs with executives and politicians are therefore widespread. A real debate within the media and editorial departments over declining standards is overdue.

Looking back at the events of 2005 we can conclude it truly was a beastly year for the German media – in more ways than one. Bird flu with its associated perils dominated newspapers and broadcast channels, even though the disease had not claimed a single victim for weeks. Even the parrot imported from Brazil, which dropped dead in the UK, has now been exonerated.

In the months before that, a locust invasion was all the rage. Adroitly, the then head of Germany's Social Democrats, Franz Müntefering, took advantage of journalists' weakness for colourful language and started a fake debate, mainly to please his own party loyalists, over the detrimental effect of Anglo–Saxon investors on the German economy. And then there was the unforgettable so-called "Elephants' round table", the post-election television talk show where the soon-to-resign Chancellor Schröder spoke of a conspiracy against his government in an interview conducted by Nikolaus Brender, the editor-in-chief of Germany's second public television station ZDF. According to Schröder, almost everybody who had a say in German journalism was involved in the conspiracy.

THE FOURTH ESTATE'S TARNISHED REPUTATION

Bird flu, locust alarm, elephants' round table: three topics which not only represent the fundamental changes taking place in politics, business and society, but are also emblematic of a gradual change in journalism. The myth of the "fourth estate" that has long nurtured Western journalism, particularly after Watergate, has lost part of its magic.

It was in the 1990s when the buzzword "economisation" (*Ökonomisierung*) made its first appearance. Media observers and people working in the media sector were debating the damaging consequences of a changing economic environment on journalism. In light of soaring corporate earnings, publicly-listed media companies and media executives driven by profit maximisation bore the brunt of the criticism. With the new millennium, newspapers suddenly faced stiff competition from the internet and free-sheets and, in addition to a decline in advertising revenue, had to cope increasingly with a generation that seemed less inclined to read. The business model of publishing high-brow journalism was – and continues to be – called into question. In both boom and bust, journalists miraculously succeeded in assuming the role of the victims of "economisation", rather than being actors driven by self-interest. This misconception becomes evident if one takes a closer look at the issues which dominated the media in 2005.

ARE JOURNALISTS LOCUSTS TOO?

The reason why the "locust invasion" of the German capital markets received such intense media coverage was because of Müntefering's unique ability to reduce to a single powerful image a complex issue, which, in fact, would normally seem rather dull to the general public. From the Bible to Nazi parlance: the expression left ample room for journalistic debate. For weeks, the issue was hotly contested in editorials and talk shows but, in the end, the pithy words were not followed by any political action.

Although it seems blindingly obvious, it occurred to no one, however, that we might have actually been facing a locust plague in journalism for a long time. In huge, buzzing swarms, journalists descend on individual topics and gnaw everything which can be printed or broadcast down to the root. After that, they take to the skies almost simultaneously in their search for a new potential field to feast on. We will later return to the most recent example of this: bird flu.

PACK JOURNALISM

In this context, economists like to use the expression "Tragedy of the Commons": a public good is exploited until it is of no use anymore. In German, the expression used is the term "Allmende" (common land). The land can be used for grazing by anybody free of charge, but only until the livestock has eaten away every last blade of grass. Roughly the same picture emerges in journalism: When it is published, even the most exclusive piece of news turns from a "private" into a "public" good. The journalist who uncovered the scoop and the corresponding media outlet may get something out of it. But the moment it is published, the piece of news becomes a common good from which all editors can profit.

The people working in the media who participate in this pack journalism behave almost identically to the peasants on the common land – or to cunning investors, for that matter, who calculate the risks and want to make money with as little an effort as possible, thus surfing the waves as far as their free ride will take them. And far indeed it can be. Probably all of us have watched the New York Twin Towers collapse dozens of times. SARS, BSE, anthrax, the donation scandal battering Germany's Christian Democrats kept us on our toes for weeks before they were finally dealt with *ad nauseam*. Even more, the Clinton-Lewinsky scandal absorbed Washington's attention for several months in 1998. Media hypes are not unlike the much-cited "bubbles" on the stock market; not least because they may burst overnight.

LOW-COST INVESTIGATION

Despite their apparent herd instinct, many journalists still like to think of themselves as sleuths in the midst of an investigation. Frank Denton, editor of the *Tampa* (Florida) *Tribune*, once sarcastically remarked that he and his colleagues are still "using as a measure of success how many heads we can hang on the wall, either for being thrown out of office or into jail". The fact is, however, that time for investigation is in increasingly short supply – not least because most media companies have cut back on their editorial spending. Hence, journalists must make do with limited resources, which means economise. Which topic deserves time and money for investigation? Will it generate a return, i.e. higher ratings or an increase in circulation? Might it not be smarter, in the end, to avoid the hassle of investigating and let the reporters of the national papers do the job? Eventually, the free rider will get a nice headline anyway – for nothing, of course.

Looking at the bird flu frenzy reveals the self-interested thinking behind many headlines, statesmanlike commentaries and fear-mongering TV reports. Bird flu has obvious news value and fills countless pages because it appeals to the primal fear of millions of an invisible and fast-spreading disease. At the same time, investigative efforts are limited. Consumer advocates and health experts are ideal interview partners; news agencies provide the numbers on dead and killed animals in far away lands. The bulk of the investigation is limited to enquiring at the local pharmacy about the sales and availability of "Tamiflu", apparently the sole effective treatment against the virus infection. Explicit or implicit thinking in clear-cut cost and benefit categories is thus not limited to investors (anymore), but is also prevalent among journalists.

CAPITALISM'S NECESSITIES

In light of this, the open letter published on page three by Uwe Vorkötter, editor of the *Berliner Zeitung*, seems all the more brave. In the letter, he railed against the unprecedented acquisition of the Berlin publishing house by a British consortium of investors led by David Montgomery. He wrote that "maximising profits is not the aim of our work. Our editorial ambitions are on a par with the financial success of the company". Thinking about their profession, many of those working in the media would, fortunately, subscribe to Vorkötter's point of view. Despite all that, a bitter aftertaste remains. Talking in a variety of different media outlets to young journalists who haven't yet been given the key to the editorial room and are not cushioned by collective wage agreements, you hear a lot about short-term contracts and meagre pay per line. This is probably much more closely linked to "locust capitalism" than their established, fixed-contract colleagues may like to admit; a capitalism they relish attacking on other occasions.

No wonder then, that many of those often outsourced freelance journalists are looking elsewhere for employers that allow them to make ends meet – and find them in the PR sector, where journalists can earn extra income. This, however, triggers a vicious circle which threatens to undermine journalism's resource basis. The more PR agencies and departments produce professional content, which they then offer free of charge to newspapers, the greater the temptation for the papers to include such content without having to pay for costly investigative journalism. Cost-conscious publishing executives may use this as an excuse to cut back on other journalistic positions.

On top of that, the successful publishing of PR material may well lead many corporations, authorities and non-profit organisations to reflect on their own practices. To them it seems logical to scan their own advertising budgets for content that might better be published using PR channels. If this catches on, it will leave publishing executives with even less ad revenue and money to pay for journalists and editors.

THE ODD PROXIMITY BETWEEN JOURNALISTS AND POLITICIANS

But it is not only the line separating PR and journalism that is becoming increasingly blurry. One reason why the post-election round table was such a sobering experience was that it put the spotlight on the odd proximity between journalists and politicians. The omnipresent, if usually more clandestine, trade-offs suddenly became apparent. To those watching Schröder and Brender arguing on live television the whole scene seemed like an embarrassing family row.

Later that night, Schröder apparently reprimanded a journalist working for Germany's *Spiegel*, which is odd given the fact that the chancellor only last year openly admitted that, if he wants to take something public, he tells it to this very news magazine. It is no surprise, therefore, that *Spiegel*'s editor-in-chief Stefan Aust was furious about Schröder's comment, since the "political animal" and media-savvy Chancellor thus laid bare the inner workings of the market for information which has developed in the grey zone between politics and journalism.

Exclusive, if often not really exclusive, information is traded by politicians and spin doctors in exchange for attention and is leaked to a select group of journalists who preferably work for one of the leading papers or channels to ensure that the "pack" will pick up on the story. The lucky beneficiaries show their thanks by publishing headlines which might be a tad bigger or more positive than appropriate.

INFORMATION ABOUT DISINFORMATION

Bird flu, locust invasion, elephants' round table: all three examples show that, contrary to popular perception, journalists can, and indeed have to, bear economic considerations in mind. There are, however, implications of their own work that many in the sector would like to forget about. There is no doubt that the media are exceedingly beneficial to the public if they report fairly and without fear and fervour. Not enough attention is paid in public discourse to the costs of external effects imposed on society as a whole or on sectors or individuals by sensational reporting, the distorting of facts or insufficient investigation – which is ultimately disinformation. It is time, therefore, for a more serious debate about "Corporate Governance" and "Corporate Social Responsibility" among editors and in the boardrooms of media companies.

NOTES

An earlier version of this article was first published in *Neue Zürcher Zeitung*, 3 December 2005

NOTES ON AUTHORS

Dr. Susanne Fengler is a communications researcher with focus on journalism, PR and political communication. She is based in Berlin, teaching at the Universities of Lucerne and Zurich in Switzerland.

Stephan Russ-Mohl is Director of the European Journalism Observatory (www.ejo.ch) and Professor of Journalism and Media Management at the Università della Svizzera italiana in Lugano/Switzerland. As a freelance, he contributes frequently to *Neue Zürcher Zeitung* and other print media.

9

Journalistic standards and democratisation of the mass media in Poland, Hungary and the Czech Republic[1]

Angelika W. Wyka

The mass media are often considered one of the most influential "tools" in the process of transformation from an authoritarian regime to democracy. In 1989, when communism started to collapse in East Central Europe, the mass media were challenged both politically (being freed from state control) and economically (as they entered a new competitive environment). This chapter examines the positive and negative elements of this process and, in paarticular, the impacts on journalistic standards and professionalism.

As an integral force of civil society, the mass media are expected to play a central role in reporting the activities of parliament, the government and the judiciary, in investigating whether private companies and financial interests respect the law, sounding the alarm if the environment is polluted, and engaging in conflict prevention and resolution (Leigh 2003: 2). It is argued they have a dual responsibility for: giving a full and fair account of the news and passing critical comment and thoughtful judgment on public affairs (Budge, Newton et al. 1997: 14).

Without free and balanced political communication, democratic institutions will become corrupt; without the provision of relevant business information, the free economy will collapse; without information about new trends in art, fashion and music, the world of culture will not progress (Reljic 2003: 1).

It is difficult to be specific about the extent of indirect or direct impact of the media on political behaviour and the decision-making process (especially in post-communist countries undergoing transition). However, it is certain that the mass media make a contribution of vital importance to the field of social communication. These opportunities for the media have obviously emerged as a result of the collapsing role of political parties as intermediaries between state elites and the citizens.

The political transformation in the late 1980s and at the beginning of the 1990s in East Central Europe brought about the liberation of the mass media, both print and broadcast, from the control and the information monopoly of the communist parties. There was a significant shift from the overwhelming presence of the state (or rather communist party) in the media, and its interventions became more limited. It is essential to note that during the communist period the media were considered dependent upon the authoritarian state in terms of content, access, ownership, financing, production and distribution (Gulyas 2001:2).

PROBLEMS OF MEDIA REGULATION

Dismantling the old system is one matter, but setting up a framework for a new media system is another. It is not enough to leave the media to the mercy of either free market or political forces and hope that these will produce the desired effect. The problem of regulation of the media in Poland, Hungary and the Czech Republic has thrown up a number of vital questions (a lot of them still remain open) concerning the safeguarding the independence of the media against the control and power held both by politicians and by private industry. For instance:

- What are the rights and duties of the free media?
- How should they be regulated and by whom?
- What steps should be taken to prevent private media monopolies and oligopolies?
- Should commercial and public radio and television exist?
- Should newspapers be subsidised by the state?
- What should be the limits of foreign ownership?
- Should the old leaders/managers of the communist media be prevented by means of the so-called vetting process (Wyka: 2003: 64) from playing a role in the new mass media (Budge, Newton et al. op cit: 148)?

The post-communist elites in Poland, Hungary and the Czech Republic were aware of the significance of these challenges. However, they have been reluctant to provide the new criteria needed to create independent means of mass communication. Moreover, it was difficult for them to shake off entrenched standards whereby rulers (members of the communist parties) were publicly untouchable, and propaganda was considered a major and legitimate force of social transformation (Bajomi-Lazar and Sukosd 2003: 13). Even though censorship has been abolished and new media laws have been introduced in the countries in question, they still have loopholes that offer governments the opportunity to put pressure and limits on the media (Dragomir 2003: 19; see also Jakubowicz 2005: 7-8).

The first years of democratic consolidation in East Central Europe showed that the new political elites could be highly creative when it came to exerting pressure on the media (ibid: 13). For example, some heads of state and other prominent political leaders in the region have very often used their position of authority and their influence, over both public and commercial media, to present themselves as uncorrupted and as standing above the political institutions and other political elites (Andreev 2002: 5).

SPREAD OF FOREIGN OWNERSHIP

Although the situation relating to freedom of the media in East Central Europe has seemed to be rapidly improving, because of the need to harmonise media law with that of the European Union (this was one of the conditions for Poland, Hungary and the Czech Republic to become full members on 1 May 2004) as well as the political influence exercised by a large number of international monitoring agencies, a high percentage of the printed and broadcast media are in the hands of foreign owners (see, for instance, Gross 2002).

This affects the independence of the mass media. Nevertheless, some political rulers, having received a democratic mandate from the nation, have increasingly supported different authoritarian tendencies and practices, especially in the public broadcast media. When preparing new bills concerning the mass media, legislators responsible for them very often used "the public service television" and "the state television" as equivalent terms, in particular in Poland. They have tended to assume that the public media should continue to act as their mouthpiece, or that they could appoint politically friendly personalities to media boards.

For instance, in Poland the president had the right to appoint the National Broadcasting Council (Krajowa Rada Radiofonii i Telewizji) chairman until 1995 when the law was amended. Political pressure is also exercised against the commercial media: for example, legal actions against inconvenient journalists and publishers, special taxes and regulations (the so-called Rywingate in Poland, concerning media concentration). Selective state-sponsored advertising has been among government actions aimed at ensuring pro-government coverage in newspapers and creating pro-government segments in some countries' press markets (Bajomi-Lazar and Sukosd op cit: 14).

However, legislators were forced to pass their respective broadcasting acts to encourage foreign investment – a precondition for the modernisation of the media sector. In addition, the newly passed broadcasting act, at least according to their preambles, also aimed at protecting media freedom and improving the plurality of views; for instance, the Hungarian Act I of 1996 on Radio and Television Broadcasting was created "in the interest of free and independent radio and television broadcasting, the freedom of expressing opinion" (www.net.jogtar.hu/jr/gen/getdoc.cgi).

REFORMING THE MEDIA

The media regulation passed in the first part of the 1990s, in fact, created a new legal and institutional structure to regulate the media in the new democracies. This, the so-called first wave of media reform (Bajomi-Lazar and Sukosd op cit: 14), had two major effects: firstly, the previously state controlled media were transformed into public services and funds to finance public service broadcasting were established. Second, it became possible to demonopolise the sector by introducing commercial broadcasting. The first country that passed a new media law, in 1991, was Czechoslovakia. This remained in force until 2001, when the Czech parliament adopted the new Broadcasting Act 2001 on Radio and Television Broadcasting Operation following a national protest against the dependence of the mass media on the political elite.

The Polish Broadcasting Act was passed in 1992 and modified three years later. Since 1995 there have been a number of the attempts to change the law. Of the countries discussed in this paper, Hungary was the last one – it passed the new media law in 1996 (Act No.1 of 1996 on Radio and Television Service). The 1996 media law was modified in 2002.

It would be no exaggeration to say that the first wave of broadcasting reform played a historic role in media democratisation (ibid: 14) and indirectly contributed to the political democratisation of East Central Europe. At the same time, a discrepancy emerged between the declared objectives of the laws and the actual achievements during their implementation.[2]

THE EMERGENCE OF MEDIA AUTONOMY

According to what K. Jakubowicz of Poland (1995) has described as the fundamental prerequisites of media change (a process of gathering autonomy), the cumulative effects of the development of a free market in the mass media in terms of the political, economic, social, mediatic, technological and professional dimensions in Central and Eastern Europe should be: "demonopolisation, differentiation, professionalisation of journalists and democratisation". In turn, S. Splichal of Slovenia (2001) has argued that the processes (he termed them "imitative tendencies") that are actually taking place are the following: (1) *renationalisation,*(2) *denationalisation and privatisation,* (3) *commercialisation,* (4) *inter- and transnationalisation,* (5) *nationalistic and religious exclusivism,* (6) *italianisation or cross-fertilisation* (Splichal 2001: 72). These "imitative tendencies" are accordingly clustered by the scholar into two broader groups, namely: those imitating external environment, primarily Western Europe and the USA (2-4 and 6), and those imitating the past (1 and 5) (ibid).

Demonopolisation (denationalisation) − this process safely assumes the existence of a private media sector operating in the public interest and respecting the law, with journalistic ethics set out by independent broadcasting authorities. The so-called European way of organising the new media system postulates the existence of the public service media as "autonomous state organisations" (World Development Report 2002: 186). Privatisation was perceived as the only strategy that could significantly reduce, and even abolish, state intervention in the media (Splichal 2001: 44). True, the presence of foreign investors makes state control of the media at least virtually impossible. However, it is also worth mentioning at this point that foreign ownership influences media autonomy and subsequently the quality of journalism.[3]

Parts of the broadcasting systems were, at least at the beginning, renationalised and put under the control of the leading political parties. S. Spilchal, taking his ideas from P. Mancini, called this process the "Italianisation" of the media[4] (Spilchal 1994) because it is a mirror image of what happened in Italy during the 1980s and 1990s. The most important characteristics of this system are:

• The media are under strong state control, either directly as in the case of state-owned television or indirectly as in the case "of various forms of state-owned and/or economically supported press".

• The degree of mass media partisanship is strong; "the political parties have always been involved in editorial choices and the structure of mass media".

• Equally strong is the degree of integration of the media and political elites; for example, there is a strong professional mobility between the worlds of politics and journalism.

• There is no consolidated and shared professional ethic among media professionals (Mancini 1991: 138).

THE NEW DANGER OF 'ITALIANISATION'

Reljic goes further and identifies the next stage of Italianisation as a new danger for the countries of Eastern Europe, namely "the Berlusconisation" of the media.[5] The negative phenomenon of Berlusconisation is largely characterised by providing the audience with mainly sensational information and low-quality programs such as obscene soap operas, talk shows, private monopolies in the broadcasting industry, as well as permanent control over the media and blatant partisanship in the media (Reljic 2003: 14). More to the point, the Berlusconisation[6] process of the media means that the mass media are monopolized by politicians and businessmen and used for their personal, political or business purposes exclusively.

The worst examples of political fighting over television took place both in Hungary and the Czech Republic, as well as in Poland (but on a smaller scale). For instance, the struggle for control of radio and television in Hungary led to the so-called "media war" (see, for instance: Downing 1995; Spilchal op cit; Ociepka 2003; Sukosd 2003) at two levels (Bajomi-Lazar 2002: 14).

The first level related to the political warfare about the power over the free mass media. The nationalist and conservative Hungarian Democratic Forum – Magyar Demokrata Forum – claimed that most means of mass communication, in particular the national broadcasting media, were under the control of the previous regime elites. In turn, the liberal Alliance of Free Democrats – Szabad Demokratak Szovetsege – accused the MDF of wanting to use the media for the election campaigns. The second level related to the debate on maintaining the Hungarian national identity in the media, in order to protect Hungarian culture against foreign investments (this was supported by the MDF and criticised by the SzDSz).

In December 2000, the director of the national TV station (Ceska televize) was fired and replaced with new one with political connections. The nomination of Jiri Hodac provoked a strike amongst the journalists who barricaded themselves in the newsroom and broadcast their own unauthorised news programmes. In addition, they demanded guarantees against political interferences and the de-politisation of the Czech public broadcasters. The journalists and the media, enjoying the high level of the public trust, were supported by hundreds of thousands of Czechs who took in the streets of Prague. The demonstrations, protests and public pressure led to the amendment of the media law passed in 1991. Significantly the new Broadcasting Act 2001 guarantees wide autonomy for journalists, as well as diminishing the power of the political elites over the media (see Ociepka 2003; Dobek-Ostrowska 2002).

The second aspect of denationalisation of the communication sphere is represented by privatisation and mainly by the setting up of new, privately owned and commercially oriented radio and television. As Spilchal notes, the licensing process for a new broadcasting station was more often a party-political decision than the result of identifying the needs and interests of the public.

The third tendency in the denationalisation process is transnationalism (Spilchal op cit). This tendency can be described in the following way. The transnational corporations (e.g. Murdoch, Time-Warner, Bertelsmann, Springer) have tried to force state broadcasting authorities to make more channels available and give way to private and foreign broadcasters. The goal is to ensure high profits from broadcasting entertainment programming and thereby make more and more dependent on the influence of the big global media networks.

THE NEED FOR PROFESSIONALISATION[7]

In addition to the already presented stages (demonopolisation, decentralisation and internationalisation/transnationalism) of media autonomisation, the next stage of Jakubowicz's suggestions for changing the media scenery of East Central Europe includes new media legislation and signs of journalistic professionalisation in new private media. The third stage assumes not only the consolidation of media legislation, professionalisation and democratisation, but also the beginnings of media concentration and the influence of foreign media capital (Jakubowicz 1995, 2001; Downing 1996).

Usually, the ideal of professionalism has been defined by fairness, impartiality, non-partisanship, a lack of bias, balance and a lack of distortion, accuracy, truthfulness, decency and good taste (Skolkay 1998: 312; Bennett 2001: 181-210). J. Corner, in order to describe the prime goal that guides journalistic reporting uses terms such as impartiality, fairness and accuracy (Corner 1995 as cited in Skolkay ibid.).[8] In connection with this East Central Europe's journalists were expected to transform themselves from party-affiliated, propaganda-oriented journalists to good and reliable watchdogs of democracy, and from market-oriented "providers" of mass culture to responsible advisors on democratic decision-making (Jakubowicz 1999; 2001).

The level of professionalisation of the East Central Europe's journalists varies greatly. The media laws have attempted to establish such norms of journalistic performance as impartiality, objectivity and balance. However, widely known and approved professional norms have not crystallised so far (Bajomi-Lazar and Sukosd op cit: 18). There is a lack of professional ethos within the journalistic environment in Poland, Hungary and the Czech Republic. There are no formal nor informal rules regulating the relationship between journalists and politicians to safeguard the former from interference in their work. This has a negative influence on the media sector, especially when the politicians serve as a major source of information (Andreev op cit: 4).

The journalists themselves, of course, are aware of their role in creating a democracy. However, they consider the existing conditions of journalistic performance poor. While some journalists believe that it is their job to provide critical coverage of the politicians, others are convinced they should be loyal to democratically elected governments. Self-censorship is still practised; it is driven by political considerations in public service broadcasters and by economic interests in the private media. A large proportion of the journalistic community is politicised and divided along political cleavages. The tradition of partisan, involved journalism remains strong, especially in the formerly government controlled electronic media and in the press. They act as "teachers, prophets, interpreters of reality" (Davidoff as cited in Pehe 1996: 90).

Indeed, as the internationally renowned media scholar P. Gross wrote, Polish journalists are still fundamentally deficient in terms of their comprehensiveness, objectivity and professionalism and – he further writes – to this day, when they try to separate news and opinion, they... continue to perform an "advocate function" (Gross op cit: 104). Journalists practise double standards and cover reality in a very selective way – they use only information that fits their messages (Bajomi-Lazar 2005: 120; see also Gross 2002).

Some media make no secret of their political orientation. In their book *The second wave of media in East Central Europe*, M. Sukosd and P. Bajomi-Lazar of Hungary write that in the news coverage of the commercial broadcasting media, objectivity as well as balanced journalism have become the norm (op cit: 18). However, I cannot quite agree with that statement, because their objectivity and independence are hugely limited. Nowadays, the mass media, especially the private broadcasters, are educating so-called mediots (idiots of the media or more colloquially, couch potatoes).

In order to increase their profits, the privately-owned media carry programmes with the highest viewing ratings, for instance, talk-shows, reality shows, and sensational information, but these programmes are not necessarily of high quality. Consequently, minor dangers are blown out of proportion, whereas much more serious dangers in societies go un-remarked on (Wyka op cit). As a result, the entertainment function of the media has become dominant. Some journalists employed in the commercial media are paid "by piece", which makes them focus on quantity instead of quality. There is a great deal of so-called "waiter journalism"(Wyka 2003) or "disc jockey journalism"(Bajka 2000: 47).

In essence, waiter or disc jockey journalism aims to provide information (mainly sensational) and low quality entertainment and to serve the political elites (Sonczyk 2001: 41). In most cases, professional standards have been hurt by corruption amongst the media professionals. It should be stressed that because of not being paid well enough, journalists have, increasingly, become corruptible. This so-called "soft corruption" involves a variety of gifts, such as trips abroad, high quality equipment and so on being awarded to journalists by influential political or business groups. This is particularly dangerous at local and regional levels, where the commercial market remains relatively narrow, and the mass media suffer from a lack of sponsors (Wyka 2005: 3).

Many media experts writing about the media industry in CEE have observed with much truth that investigative reporting,[9] where journalists are watchdogs of democracy and keep an eye on the government of the day, has been rarely seen[10] (see, for instance: Gross 2004; Jakubowicz 2005; Bajomi-Lazar and Sukosd 2003; Television Across Europe 2005). The exception is Poland (Ociepka 2003; Wyka 2005; Mocek 2006), where high quality newspapers such as *Rzeczpospolita* (*Republic*) and *Gazeta Wyborcza* (*Election Gazette*) as well as published *Nie* (*No*) by Jerzy Urban, the former spokesperson for the Communist Party during martial law have been performing this kind of journalism.[11] Nevertheless, ironically, Tomasz Patora, one of the leading Polish investigative reporters who works at *Gazeta*, describes the situation in the following terms:

> Investigative journalism is very weak for a number of reasons. First and foremost, the functioning media are absolutely not interested in doing serious journalism, because it requires tremendous financial outlays. Of course, not only the money, but also a huge amount of time is required. No one is actually keen to invest in the future, and at the same time, uncertain things. It basically means that every time I start writing about a new subject, I am never 100 per cent sure if it, in fact, works. From my experience, just one out of three or even five subjects works. In point of fact, instead of investigative journalism, in Poland so-called "mining" journalism [Polish, dziennikarstwo wydobywcze, AW] is being practised on a large scale. A journalist's role is to just verify information that has leaked out of an authority that has been primarily established to reveal corruption, abuse of power, etc. Actually, I have recently been writing more "mining" than investigative pieces. I am not saying that we do not need this kind of journalism. However, one has to keep in mind that investigative reporting is slightly different. A journalist has to "discover" those irregularities on his own and reveals them accordingly (trans. AW).

In turn, in Hungary this kind of investigative journalism has been called by journalists themselves "dossier-journalism" (Galik 2004: 214). There is strong evidence that some of the investigative reporters have been intimidated[12], because neither governments nor businessmen have been willing to tolerate it.

Citizen/public journalism in which citizens play an active role in the process of collecting, reporting, analysing and disseminating news and information (Bowman and Willis 2003) is extremely weak. However, it has been observed that interest in citizen journalism has significantly increased recently. By way of example, Poland's *Gazeta Wyborcza* and Interia.pl, a leading web portal, have recently created their own platforms for journalist-amateurs, where everyone can write blog posts, comment, send a picture or an article (see, for instance

Grzechowiak 2007).

CONCLUSIONS

The general impression is that the media have, at regular intervals, become a target of abuses and stealthy collusion between political and business interests. It seems then that the problem of politicisation is a result of immature political elites and governments' tendency (*inherited from the past*) to control the media. The mass media, in other words, are not the watchdogs of democracy as expected. Rather, they are the tools of the elite few to spread the message (political viewpoints) of those in control of the media outlets. This limits the articulation of various social opinions, and thus weakens the quality of democracy.

The journalistic associations are not sufficiently well developed to protect their members and to ensure media autonomy. Without this support, journalists cannot be good and reliable watchdogs of democracy.

The only way to change the present situation within the community of journalists itself is the reform of editorial and journalistic practices and journalism education. Only well-educated, professionally sound and responsible journalists will be in a position to increase the respect in which the free means of mass communication are held as democratic institutions. All this goes to show that media standards in the East Central European nations have remained poor, and as such, conditions for professionalism and journalistic independence have not yet been truly developed. Thus, as P. Bajomi-Lazar in *The Business of Ethics, the Ethics of Business* observes, the journalistic environment "is only halfway to professionalism" (Bajomi-Lazar 2005: 122).

NOTES

1. This is an expanded and updated version of the original article published in *Ethical Space – The International Journal of Communication Ethics*, 2(2), 2005, pp13-17.Selected excerpts of the article were also presented to the international conference on "Ethics and Journalism" held in Hungary, in March 2005.

2. Legislation that was supposedly to establish such norms of journalistic performance as impartiality and objectivity as well as to democratise the media, has not only ignored cultural and societal differences but also been deliberately used to intimidate independent media (journalists). In other words, these media laws have paved the way for politicians masquerading as disinterested to maintain their control over the so-called "fourth estate". Nevertheless, media legislation has proved to be a major obstacle in the process of media reform in the region. Hopes for more liberal and objective media might well be found in the younger, new generation of journalists.

For more see: P . Bajomi-Lazar and M. Sukosd (2003) "The Second Wave of Media Reform in East Central Europe" [in:] P. Bajomi-Lazar, M. Sukosd (eds), *Reinventing Media: Media Policy Reform in East Central Europe*, Budapest, CPS Books, Central European University Press. See also M. Dragomir (2003) "Fighting Legacy: Media Reform in Post-Communist Europe", the Atlantic Council of the United States, Senior Fellows Publication.

3. Over 80 per cent of the Central European media market belongs to foreign investors (Cashin, 2004; Sukosd, 2003). A Cashin, in her *Reining in free media,* writes: *Editorial meddling seems to be less of a problem than what appears to be publishers' often singular focus on a paper's financial bottom line* (Cashin, 2004: 9). It is obvious then that those foreign investors *want their money back, they want they interest* (ibid.) In consequence, in East Central Europe a kind of *paternal-commercial* media system has been emerging with a tendency to privatisation and commercialisation of the media on the one hand, and the exercise and maximisation of political power over the media (Splichal, 2001:45).

4. S. Splichal in one of his articles on "Imitative Revolutions. Changes in the Media and Journalism in East-Central Europe" (2001, p. 55) explained that naming this tendency after a nation, Italy, as Italianisation was mistaken and calls it now cross-fertilisation.

5. The godfather of Berlusconisation is the former Prime Minister of Italy and media magnate (Mediaset), and the dominant force in Italian broadcasting simultaneously, Silvio Berlusconi. At this point, it seems reasonable to add that Italy is a special case of controversial involvement of politicians in the regulation of broadcasting, and particularly in the state-owned broadcaster RAI (*Radiotelevisione Italiana*). For Berlusconi, ownership of media outlets was clearly of great political value. In the beginning of the 1990s, commercial television helped him move to political power (Berlusconi's party Forza Italia won the 1993 parliamentary elections). He has enjoyed a degree of power over both commercial and public service television in recent years that has no precedent in any developed democracy. The power Berlusconi has had is a result of the duopoly of RAI and Mediaset created by the alliance between politics and the media. For more see, for instance: *Television across Europe: Regulation, policy and independence.* Monitoring Reports 2005 (Open Society Institute and EU Monitoring and Advocacy Program), p.34 and pp 866-954.

6. To learn more on the Berlusconisation process in CEE see: Angelika W. Wyka (2007) Berlusconization of the Mass Media in East Central Europe – The New Danger of Italianisation? available online at http://www.kakanien.ac.at/beitr/emerg/AWyka1.pdf

7. Most of the passages in this section come from my article *Good and reliable watchdogs of democracy? Ethics and journalism: case studies from Poland, Hungary and the Czech Republic* published by the Budapest-based Open Society Institute. Article is available online at http://www.eumap.org/journal/submitted/wyka.pdf.

8. At this point it seems reasonable to mention the view that, although national cultures and patterns of professional education differ as well as various forms of the journalistic organisation, declared professional journalism standards (values) did not differ

significantly from nation to nation (Schudson, 1991: 150; Ruusunkoska, 2004: 83).Yet, as Ruuksunkoska writes, the recent surveys clearly point out that, in spite of general patterns amongst the journalists around the world, there still exist many differences. Actually, in a survey that covered 21 countries, there was more disagreement than agreement over the importance of journalists' roles – such as quick and accurate reporting, providing access for the public and acting as a watchdog of the government of the day – and not noticeably any evidence to support the idea of professional journalism standards (Weaver as cited in Ruusunoksa, 2004:83). See also D. Hallin, P. Mancini (2004) *Comparing MediaSystems.:Three Models of Media and Politics.*

9. The professional organisations define investigative reporting in the following terms: "[R]eporting, through one's own work product and initiative, matters of importance which some persons or organisations wish to keep secret. The three basic elements are that the investigation be the work of the reporter, not the report of an investigation made by someone else; that the subject of the story involves something of reasonable importance to the reader or viewer; and that others are attempting to hide these matters from the public"(DeFleur, and Dennis, 1991, p. 398).

10. In a 1997 study conducted by John Rosenbaum and Heather Duncan of Ithaca College on investigative journalism in the Czech Republic, the informants (reporters, editors and analysts) described seven structural barriers to investigative reporting in the Czech Republic. The situation there is typical for the rest of the region. The barriers are the following: the paradox of objective detachment and active adversarialism, (2) the limits of daily journalism, (3) economic constrains, (4) political partisanship, (5) lack of public understanding, (6) obedience to authority, and (7) lack of investigative skills. For more see J. Rosenbaum, H. Duncan (2001). When the Watchdogs Sleeps: Investigative Journalism in the Czech Republic; *Communications* Vol. 26, No. 2 pp 129-148.

11. It's undeniably true that unique kind of investigative journalism was performed during the communist period in Poland. Yet its role was certainly different since journalism was controlled by the party. First and foremost, the investigative reporting's function was to reveal a social pathology as well as to reveal all abnormalities in the so-called "division of goods". For obvious reasons, media did not keep an eye on politics. More on this in: S. Mocek (2006) Dziennikarze po komunizmie [Journalists After Communism], Wydawnictwo Naukowe SCHOLAR [SCHOLAR Press], Warsaw, pp 199-201.

12. A Hungarian investigative journalist, Iren Karman was brutally assaulted by unknown assailants in the outskirts of capital Budapest, who pushed her into a car, tied her up, severely beat her, and left her on the banks of the Danube river. Karman became famed after a documentary on so-called "oil-bleaching crimes" of the 1990s. Jerzy Jachowicz, a forerunner of Poland's investigative journalism, had been involved in examining the links between organised crime and the former secret service during the communist rule of Poland. At the beginning of the 1990s many attempts were made to threaten him. Ulimately, Jachowicz had his flat set on fire in which his wife

was killed. Jerzy Mac from the political magazine *Wprost* (Right) was abducted and threatened. Also, another famous Polish investigative reporter, Anna Marszałek from *Rzeczpospolita,* received phone threats related to her investigations.

REFERENCES

Andreev, Svetlozar A. (2002) *The Media and Democratic Consolidation in Post-Communist Eastern Europe.* Available online at www.essex.ac.uk/ecpr/events/jointsessions/paperarchive/uppsala/ws18/Andreev.pdf, accessed on 19 September 2004

Bajka, Zbigniew (2000) "Dziennikarze lat dziewi dziesi tych" (Journalists of the 90s), *Zeszyty Prasoznawcze* 3-4 (163-164) pp 42-63

Bajomi-Lazar, Peter (1999) *Press Freedom in Hungary 1988-1998,* Budapest, OSI-IPF Draft Working Papers. Available online at http//www.osi.hu/ipf/pubs.html, accessed on 3 October 2004

Bajomi-Lazar, Peter (2002) "Prasa i media elektroniczne na Wgrzech" (The print and electronic media in Hungary), *Transformacja systemow medialnych w krajach Europy rodkowo-Wschodniej po 1989 roku (The transformation of media systems in East Central Europe after 1989),* Dobek-Ostrowska, Bogusława (ed.) Wrocław, Wydawnictwo Uniwersytetu Wrocławskiego (Wrocław University Press)

Bajomi-Lazar, Peter and Sukosd, Miklos (2003) "The Second Wave of Media Reform in East Central Europe", *Reinventing Media: Media Policy Reform in East Central Europe,* Bajomi-Lazar, Peter and Sukosd, Miklos (eds), Budapest, CPS Books, Central European University Press pp 13-27

Bajomi-Lazar, Peter (2005) *The Business of Ethics, the Ethics of Business.* Available online at www.sajtoszabadsag.hu/publikaciok/files/business_of_ethics.doc, accessed 12 January 2006

Budge, Ian, Newton, Kenneth et al. (1997) *The Politics of the New Europe: Atlantic to Urals,* New York, Longman

Dobek-Ostrowska, Bogusława (2002) "Przej cie do demokracji a transformacja systemów medialnych w Europie rodkowej i Wschodniej po upadku komunizmu" (transition to democracy and the transformation of media systems in the countries of East Central Europe after the collapse of communism), *Transformacja systemów medialnych w krajach Europy rodkowo-wschodniej po 1989 roku (The transformation of media systems in East Central Europe after 1989),* Dobek-Ostrowska, Bogusława (ed.), Wrocław, Wydawnictwo Uniwersytetu Wrocławskiego (Wrocław University Press) pp 13-33

Dobek-Ostrowska, Bogusława (ed) (1998) *Współczesne systemy komunikowania (Modern systems of communication),* Wrocław, Wydawnictwo Uniwersytetu Wrocławskiego (Wrocław University Press)

Dobek-Ostrowska, Bogusława (ed) (2002) *Transformacja systemów medialnych w krajach Europy rodkowo-wschodniej po 1989 roku* (The transformation of media systems in East Central Europe after 1989) Wrocław, Wydawnictwo Uniwersytetu Wrocławskiego

(Wrocław University Press)

Downing, John (1995) *Internationalising Media Theory. Transition, Power, Culture. Reflections on Media in Russia, Poland and Hungary 1980-95*, London, Sage

Galik, Mihaly (2004) *Media Ownership and Its Impact on Media Independence and Pluralism: Hungary*. Available online at http://www.mirovni-institut.si/media_ownership/pdf/hungary.pdf, accessed on 22 October 2005

Goban-Klas, Tomasz. (1997) "Politics versus the Media in Poland: A Game without Rules", *Post-Communism and the Media in Eastern Europe*, O'Neil (ed.), London, Frank Cass pp 24-41

Gociek, Piotr (2007) TVN – stacja, która jest gwiazd (TVN – a Channel That Is a Star), *Rzeczpospolita*, 22 October p.22

Gross, Peter (2002) *Entangled Evolutions: Media Democratization in Eastern Europe*, Washington, D.C., Woodrow Wilson Center Press, Baltimore and London, the John Hopkins University Press

Grzechowiak, Michał (2007) *Alert24 – dziennikarstwo obywatelskie Gazety.pl (Alert24 – citizen journalism of Gazeta Wyborcza)*. Available online at http://www.idg.pl/news/124629.html, accessed on 3 October 2007

Gulyas, Agnes. (2001) *Democratisation and the mass media in post-communist Hungary*. Available online at www.wacc.org.uk, accessed on 17 August 2004

Hribal, Lucie (2003) *Medien und Demokratisierung in Osteuropa. Medien-und politikwissenschaftliche Konzepte der Transformation (The mass media and democratisation in Eastern Europe. The mediatic and political concepts of the transformation)*. Available online at www.medienheft.ch/dossier/bibliothek/d19, accessed on 20 August 2004

Jakubowicz, Karol (1995) "Television: What Kind of Continuity and Change", *Javnost/The Public*, Vol. 2, No. 3 pp 61-80

Jakubowicz, Karol (2001) "Rude Awekening. Social and Media Change in Central and Eastern Europe", *Javnost/The Public*, Vol.8, No.4 pp 59-80

Jakubowicz, Karol (2005) *Post-Communist Media Development in Perspective*. Available online at http://www.fes.de/fes4/publikationen/Jakubowicz.pdf, accessed on 20 May 2006

Leigh, Ian (2003) Civil Society, Democracy and the Law, paper delivered to the the Civil Society Building Project in Russia, Moscow, Russia, May

Mancini, Paolo (1991) "The Public sphere and the Use of the News in a Coalition System of Government", *Communication and Citizenship*, Dahlgren, Peter and Sparks, Colin (eds), London, Routledge pp 137-156

Mocek, Stanisław (2006) *Dziennikarze po komunizmie* [*Journalists After Communism*], Wydawnictwo Naukowe SCHOLAR [SCHOLAR Press], Warsaw

Ociepka, Beata (2003) *Dla kogo telewizja? Model publiczny w postkomunistycznej Europie rodkowej (Who is the television for? The model of public service broadcasters in post-communist Central Europe)*, Wrocław, Wydawnictwo Uniwersytetu Wrocławskiego (Wrocław University Press)

Pehe, Jiri (1996) "Media In Eastern Europe and the Former Soviet Union In a Comparative Perspective", Glenn, P. J. and Soltys, O. (eds) *Media' 95. Experience and*

Expectations – Five Years After, Prague, Karolinum Charles University Press pp 88-92

Reljic, Dusan (2003) Civil Society, Mass Media and Democracy in Post-Communist Countries, paper delivered to the Civil Society Building Project in Russia, Moscow, Russia, September

Rosenbaum John, Duncan Heather (2001) "When the Watchdog Sleeps: Investigative Journalism in the Czech Republic", *Communications,* Vol. 26, No. 2 pp 129-148

Skolkay, Andrej (1998) "Professionalization of Post-Communist Journalists", *Sociologia,* Vol. 30, No. 3 pp 311- 328

Sparks, Colin and Reading, Anna (1998) *Communism, Capitalism and the Mass Media.* Thousand Oaks, London and New Dehli, Sage

Spilchal, Slavko (1998) *Mass Media, Publicity and Civil Society: From Ideals to Practice in Central and Eastern Europe.* Available online at http://www.szignummedia.hu/eng/archiv2.html, accessed 6 January 2006

Splichal, Slavko (2001) "Imitative revolutions. Changes in the Media and Journalism in East-Central Europe", *Javnost/The Public,* Vol. 8, No. 4 pp 31-58

World Development Report 2002, Washington D. C. The World Bank, 2003., Available online at www.worlbank.org/wdr2001/fulltext/fulltext2002.htm, accessed on 16 September 2004

Wyka, Angelika W. (2003) *Społeczny obraz zawodu dziennikarza – rola dziennikarza w społecze stwie (The social picture of the journalistic profession – the role of the journalist in society),* unpublished MA thesis, Wroclaw, Wrocław University

Wyka Angelika W. (2005) *Good and reliable watchdogs of democracy? Ethics and journalism: case studies from Poland, Hungary and the Czech Republic.* Available online at www.eumap.org/journal/submitted/wyka.pdf

WEBSITES

http://www.rrtv.cz/zakony_en/broadcasting_act2001.html
http://www.net.jogar.hu/jr/gen/getdoc.en.html
http://www.ortt.hu/v2004_en.html
http://www.krrit.gov.pl

FURTHER READING

Gross, Peter (2004) "Between Reality and Dream: Eastern European Media Transition, Transformation, Consolidation, and Integration", *East European Politics and Society,* Vol. 18 pp 110-131

Open Society Institute EU Monitoring and Advocacy Program. Network Media Program: Monitoring Reports 2005: *Television across Europe: regulation, policy and independence,* Budapest and New York

Wyka, Angelika W. (2007) *Berlusconization of the Mass Media in East Central Europe – The New Danger of Italianization?* Available online at http://www.kakanien.ac.at/beitr/ emerg/AWyka1.pdf

NOTE ON AUTHOR

Angelika W. Wyka is a Ph.D. candidate in Political Science at the Frankfurt Graduate School, J. W. Goethe University, Germany. While working on her Bachelor's as well as Master's degrees she worked as a freelance journalist for newspapers and radio. In 2002 she was awarded the second place in a prestigious journalistic competition organised by Ruud Lubbers, United Nations High Commissioner for Refugees. She has published and presented extensively in various journals and conferences in the UK, USA, Germany, Poland, Austria, Hungary, Switzerland on, *inter alia*, professionalism of East Central Europe's journalism, the role of journalists, politicisation of the media, Berlusconisation, media transition and the applicability of Hallin and Mancini's three media models to East Central European media. Since April 2007 she has been working for the Lugano-based European Journalism Observatory and for the Berlin-based Institute for Media and Communications Policy. Her recent publications, among others, include "In Search of the East Central European Media Model – The Italianization Model? A Comparative Perspective on the East Central European and South European Media Systems" in *Comparing Media Systems: Central European Media Between Commercialization and Politicization* (forthcoming 2008, Wrocław University Press) and "Good and reliable watchdogs of democracy?"in *Media Ethics: Global Perspectives* (provisional title, forthcoming 2008, the Icfai University Press). Contact details: wykaa@t-online.de or angelikawyka@gazeta.pl.

10

Citizens in the newsroom: Democracy, ethics and journalism

Tony Harcup

The role of alternative media and the role of the National Union of Journalists in promoting more ethical forms of journalistic practice have to date tended to be regarded as relatively discrete areas of study, linked only by the fact that both are rendered invisible in much journalism scholarship. This chapter will argue that they are not discrete at all. Rather, the practices under consideration are informed by a common ethos: that journalists do not have to accept that there is only one way of doing their jobs, which is to carry out unquestioningly the instructions and wishes of an editorial/proprietorial hierarchy. This ethos informs the alternative forms of journalism produced by using more participatory democratic structures within alternative media; and also the way some groups of journalists within mainstream media have, on rare occasions, used their democratic trade union structures to intervene collectively on ethical issues. This chapter synthesises qualitative research in both areas and will discuss the findings within the context of wider arguments about journalism, democracy and citizenship.

"You cannot run a newspaper as a democracy and decide important matters by a vote," argues Andrew Neil (1996: 340) in his autobiography. It cannot be denied that this comment by the former editor of *The Sunday Times* reflects life in the mainstream media where there is precious little democratic ethos about much editorial decision-making.

But what do we mean by democracy? If we mean representative democracy, then it is true that editors and proprietors are, as a rule, unelected. Apart from the editors of some student newspapers, perhaps the only other example of an editor being elected directly by his or her readers is the editor of the *Journalist*, magazine of the National Union of Journalists (NUJ). As for journalists choosing their editors, there is just the example of journalists on the *Guardian* being consulted about the choice of editor; happily, the staff favourite and the employer's choice was one and the same. However, there are other models of democracy.

DIFFERENT MODELS OF DEMOCRACY

Jesper Stromback (2005) identifies four models of democracy: Procedural (free and fair elections); Competitive (competitive elections); Participatory (citizen participation); and Deliberative (discussions among public and their representatives). The key distinction here is between the first two models that are based on the election of representatives and the second two that depend on more direct forms of citizen participation. The representative models require journalists to act as watchdogs on behalf of citizens. Although the participatory models are more likely to allow citizens to speak and to set the agenda, journalists retain a key role as "democracy can never become more deliberative without the active participation of media and journalism" (ibid: 340). Such participatory democracy cannot be divorced from the concept of social justice, argues Iris Young (2000: 17-23), who contrasts the Deliberative model of democracy (participatory and inclusive) with what she terms the Aggregative model (essentially representative). For Young (ibid: 17):

> In the real world some people and groups have significantly greater ability to use democratic processes for their own ends while others are excluded or marginalized. Our democratic policy discussions do not occur under conditions free of coercion and threat, and free of the distorting influence of unequal power and control over resources... [T]here tends to be a reinforcing circle between social and economic inequality and political inequality that enables the powerful to use formally democratic processes to perpetuate injustice or preserve privilege. One means of breaking this circle, I argue, is to widen democratic inclusion...as a means of promoting more just outcomes.

The privileged access to mainstream media enjoyed by more powerful social groupings (Manning 2001) can be seen as one way in which ostensibly democratic processes – a "free press" – can in reality help to preserve privilege. However, as Young (op cit: 3) notes, "more marginalised citizens can sometimes make up for such inequality with organisation and time". One way of breaking this circle is the creation of media structures that are more open, more participatory, than are implied in the Andrew Neil comment above.

For example, I started out as a journalist working on a newspaper that had no editor, on which decisions were taken collectively after debate. Our early editorial meetings were open to contributors and readers, articles were passed around in hard copy, and every article – sometimes every sentence, every word, every punctuation mark – would be discussed collectively before being accepted, rejected or rewritten. It was a form of democracy in action and it was also great training, although obviously it could also be unwieldy, time-consuming and occasionally acrimonious (Harcup 1994).

Not every newsroom is going to operate like that, but nor does every newsroom have to follow the Wapping model of "rule by management diktat" (Neil op cit: 186). Journalists do not have to accept that there is only one way of doing their jobs, which is to carry out – unquestioningly – the instructions and wishes of the editorial/proprietorial hierarchy. This ethos – that there can be another way – informs the alternative forms of journalism that are produced within the more open, more participatory, and more democratic structures that exist within what are labelled alternative, radical, or citizens' media (Atton 2002; Downing 2001; Rodriguez 2001).

This ethos also informs the way that some groups of journalists within mainstream media have, on rare occasions, intervened collectively because of ethical concerns about editorial issues. This paper will draw on research in both areas, based largely on the questioning of practitioners, and will argue that both forms of intervention demonstrate active citizenship.

ALTERNATIVE MEDIA AS ACTIVE CITIZENSHIP

The healthy functioning of a public sphere – space in which informed citizens can engage with one another in reasoned debate and critical reflection (Habermas 1989) – depends on a diversity of people having access to the media. This does not mean access in the form of calling a radio phone-in or being quoted in a newspaper vox pop; it means access on a more equal basis, as James Bohman (2004: 152-153) argues:

> [P]ersons become citizens when they participate in an institutionalised public sphere backed by institutions that make it possible for them to make claims upon each other only if they stand as equals to those who may make the same claims upon them.

Yet the less powerful groups in society face structural obstacles in gaining access to mainstream media (Manning op cit: 137 and 226-227), creating what has been termed a "democratic deficit" within journalism (Hackett 2005: 95). It is precisely such groups, which find themselves excluded or under-represented in mainstream media, that can be given voice via the "democratised media practices" (Atton 2004: 7) of alternative media. In this sense, alternative media can be said to encourage active citizenship, whether among anti-globalisation campaigners who contribute to Indymedia websites, or football supporters who use fanzines to scrutinise the wheeling and dealing of their club's owners. As Chris Atton (ibid: 3) notes, it is "perhaps in addressing radical questions of citizenship in the public sphere that alternative media are most powerful". By encouraging active citizenship and participation in deliberative democratic discussion, therefore, alternative media can be said to help nurture a healthier public sphere than would exist in the absence of such alternatives.

'DEMOCRACY IS DEAD WITHOUT THEM'

The "horizontal communication" between producers and audience in alternative media (Atton 1999: 73) can be seen not only in process but also in content. An internal discussion paper at *Leeds Other Paper* stated this explicitly:

> [P]olitically, a good story for me is one that reinforces the ability of the mass of people to do things for themselves and decreases their reliance on others (especially in work and in the community)... We are committed to doing justice to the subjects we cover. This means well-researched, in-depth articles often and *LOP* stories are longer on average than those in the commercial press... We should be conscious of the need to slow down our readers – to reverse the in-one-ear-out-the-other process – and create lasting impressions... Standard newspaper style tends to trivialise events (often by the very act of sensationalising them, paradoxically). In this, style can reinforce the power of the ruling class (break into *The Internationale*)! (Leeds Alternative Publications 1980s undated.)

Journalists who began working in alternative media and then moved into the mainstream continue to see an important social role for alternative media, according to research I have undertaken with such a group[1]. Some respondents saw society's need for access to alternative perspectives as axiomatic. One said simply that "there has to be an outlet for dissent", whilst another stressed the importance of alternative media in providing "an alternative, unorthodox, and questioning voice" in society. As one put it: "If there's a role for media, there's a role for alternative media." Many respondents felt that alternative media had a role in influencing public debate because, as one argued, some things seem to be "unsayable" until they are said in alternative media. Another said: "There's always a need for alternative viewpoints and diversity if any change is to be made to current conditions."

In this sense, alternative media could be seen as performing a socially useful function, to "puncture the complacency of the established media" and to "disregard conventions, profit margins and other constraints to present a valuable fresh perspective... [It] can also provide a service to a community on a very small scale that would never be commercially viable". As one former alternative journalist put it:

> Democracy is dead without them. The mainstream media is governed by commercial success. Therefore it sticks to safe and popular ideas, tried and tested formulae, and very rarely rocks the boat. The alternative media are governed by ideas, no matter how initially unpopular they may appear to be - that's the whole point of them.

Alternative media were also seen by respondents as giving sections of the population a space within which they could communicate with each other. "[It] is vital that everyone in society has a place they can call theirs," as one respondent put it.

Clemencia Rodriguez (2001) calls this "citizens' media" because the participants become "active citizens". This is a far cry from the way the term "citizen journalist" has been used in the UK recently to describe the phenomenon of non-professional pictures and video (often taken on mobile phones) being supplied to mainstream media by members of the public (Ponsford 2005). This latter use of the term appears to be a misnomer because people who snap a picture of an event and send it in are not being journalists, they are *supplying* journalists who retain their traditional gatekeeping role. And in what way are they acting as citizens? Only if we think of the term citizen as synonymous with civilian, or member of the public, or amateur.

In contrast with sending in mobile phone shots of events we happen to witness, the active citizenship implied in the production of alternative media is concerned more with the creation of conceptual locations in which informed citizens can gather to engage with one another in reasoned and informed discussion and in critical reflection. Sounds good, doesn't it? Alternative media outlets may not necessarily succeed in such high ideals; they may be ugly or boring or hysterical or inept. But, for all its imperfections, the journalism produced in media that are governed more by ideas than by profit has a vitality because it treats people as citizens rather than consumers. That was the case with the radical press that fought so many battles for press freedom over hundreds of years and it is the case with Indymedia which had its web server seized when its London office was raided by police (*Journalist* 2004; *Press Gazette* 2005).

Despite this link with press battles of the past, the role of alternative media tends to be downplayed or ignored within much discussion of journalism (Keeble 2005: 62-63). That is something it shares with the second area of focus within this paper, which is the role of journalists intervening on editorial or ethical issues in a collective rather than individual way, through the vehicle of their trade union the National Union of Journalists. The two areas of study also share a common ethos that rejects the notion that the only one way for journalists to do their jobs is to keep their heads down and carry out the instructions and wishes of an editorial /proprietorial hierarchy.

MAINSTREAM JOURNALISTS SPEAK OUT

Journalists in the UK have only rarely threatened – and even more rarely taken – industrial action in an attempt to influence editorial content. Perhaps the best known example occurred in 1985 when NUJ members in the broadcasting sector staged a one-day strike in protest at censorship of a BBC *Real Lives* television documentary concerning Northern Ireland (Bolton 1990: 166-167; Schlesinger, 1987: xx). *The Times* reported that the 24-hour walkout "represented the most serious industrial action ever undertaken in British television, and attracted more support than has ever been won by a pay claim" (quoted in Curtis 1996: 279). On a much smaller scale, when an *Oxford Mail* photographer was disciplined after refusing to snatch a picture of a child whose mother had requested an end to media attention, members of the NUJ chapel (workplace branch) at the newspaper walked out on strike in protest (McIntyre 2004).

But industrial action should not be seen as the only way of taking a collective stand. During the 1983 general election campaign, for example, the NUJ chapel at the *Daily Mail* passed a motion expressing their concern at one-sided pro-Tory coverage (Hollingsworth 1986: 25). Editor David English responded by informing them: "It is unacceptable for anyone to try to influence the editor" (quoted in Greenslade 2003: 452). Similarly, in the wake of *The Sunday Times'* embarrassing decision to publish the fake "Hitler diaries", the paper's NUJ chapel demanded that editor Frank Giles meet them *en masse*; he declined, arguing that it was not an appropriate matter for a trade union meeting (ibid: 465).

Many journalists have apparently agreed that editorial content is off the union agenda, but the NUJ has a long history of engagement with what we now call ethical issues. It was because of concerns about press standards that the NUJ led calls for a Royal Commission on the Press which resulted in the establishment of what became the Press Council, forerunner of the Press Complaints Commission (Shannon 2001: 8); and it should be remembered that the NUJ was the first body in the UK to establish a code of ethical conduct for journalists, back in 1936 (Bundock 1957: 128-129).

The NUJ created its own Ethics Council in 1986, to promote higher ethical standards through a process of education, and to hear complaints against members who were alleged to have breached the union's code and who could –

in theory, at least – be reprimanded, fined, or even expelled (Frost 2000: 224). There was early suspicion of the Ethics Council among many journalists, with some critics dismissing it as the "thought police" (quoted in NUJ 1988: 32). Its work was made more difficult by the climate of intense employer hostility to trade unions in general and to the NUJ in particular within most of the media during the Thatcher and Major governments of 1979 to 1997 (Gall 1993 and 2004; Gall and McKay 1994; Smith and Morton 1994), and the Ethics Council has focused in recent years more on raising awareness than on acting as a "policing" body (Keeble 2001: 15).

AN ATMOSPHERE OF OBSEQUIOUSNESS

Within many newsrooms from the mid-1980s, an employers' offensive on wages, staffing levels, conditions and union organisation resulted in an atmosphere of fear, obsequiousness and conformity that, according to Paul Foot (cited in Keeble 2001: 6) among others, damaged editorial content by making journalists more compliant and less independent minded. Reflecting on his brief period as editor of the *Independent*, Andrew Marr (2005: 197) describes how he was told by his boss David Montgomery that NUJ activists should be removed from the paper's staff; in the next breath, Montgomery also wanted dreary scenes of poverty or "dead black babies" to be removed from the paper's pages in favour of more stories about fashionable people driving Porsches and wearing Rolex watches. Although proprietors do not usually have to spell out what they want in such an unsubtle manner, their perspectives can become "internalised" by journalists over time (Tracy 2004: 454). Montgomery's exhortations were a far cry from the period just a few years earlier when the *Independent* had been established as a journalism-driven project; a time when, as Marr (op cit: 191) recalls, "editorial lines were discussed among the staff, lolling on sofas or sitting on the floor".

Although most newsrooms never enjoyed the luxury of staff lolling around discussing editorial lines, the harsh wind of Thatcherism that swept through them in the years after the Wapping dispute of 1986 certainly did not produce a climate conducive to the questioning of editorial and ethical decisions. In workplaces where individual journalists felt compelled to keep their heads down, the existence of an active NUJ chapel could, argued Paul Foot (2000: 86), provide a crucial space in which "journalists can collect and discuss their common problems, free from the management hierarchy".

'NOT THE PROPRIETORS' STENOGRAPHERS'

That is precisely what appears to have happened at Express Newspapers in recent years, perhaps helped by the more temperate industrial relations climate that followed the Blair government's Employment Relations Act 1999[2] (Harcup 2002). In 2001 *Express* staff reported their own newspaper to the Press Complaints Commission (PCC) following a series of front-page headlines such as: ASYLUM: WE'RE BEING INVADED. After the *Daily Express* had splashed on asylum seekers for six days in a row, with headlines that often bore little relation to the stories beneath them, journalists' alarm at the "inflammatory" tone of such headlines coalesced with separate claims that the business pages had been used to promote the proprietor's interests, hardly a complaint unique to that newspaper. One *Express* journalist insisted: "We are not the proprietors' stenographers" (Morgan 2001).

Such concerns came to the fore at a chapel meeting that had been called to discuss proposed job cuts. After debating the spate of headlines, the journalists voted to express their disapproval of what they saw as a "sustained campaign against asylum seekers", and their motion continued: "This chapel believes the media has an important role to play in a democratic society and should not distort or whip up confrontational racist hatred, in pursuit of increased circulation" (*Journalist* 2001). The NUJ complained formally to the PCC on behalf of its members at the *Express*, alleging that the asylum stories breached the PCC's own code of practice which says the press should avoid prejudicial references to race. The complaint was rejected (*Journalist* 2002).

Then, in the run-up to the 2004 enlargement of the European Union, the *Daily Express* ran a series of front-page stories attacking Gypsies, with headlines such as 1.6 MILLION GYPSIES READY TO FLOOD IN – BRITAIN HERE WE COME and WE CAN'T COPE WITH HUGE GYPSY INVASION (Ponsford 2004). These and similar stories appeared to many *Express* staff to have been designed not so much to inform public opinion as to chime with existing anti-Gypsy sentiment. This was neither the first nor the last time that the *Express* had published stories that seemed to some of its staff to be pandering to readers' prejudices; and the *Express* was by no means the only newspaper to publish stories attacking Gypsies. But, after a week of such coverage, many *Express* staff were deeply unhappy at their newspaper's apparent obsession with the story of an imminent Gypsy "invasion" of the UK, and several journalists discussed the possibility of resigning.

A representative of the NUJ chapel at the *Express* recalls the mood among staff at the time:

A few involved in those pieces were very upset and were considering whether to resign. Reporters were being bombarded with calls, some of which were critical but the vast majority of which were praising the coverage, with BNP-type people ringing up saying "well done, keep it up". It was very upsetting, there was a great deal of anguish.

Some journalists complained that they had been put under pressure to produce stories to fit a pre-conceived editorial line, and these complaints were added to the agenda of what was to have been a routine meeting of NUJ members at Express Newspapers. A well-attended meeting of *Express* journalists discussed the issue and passed the following motion:

> This chapel is concerned that *Express* journalists are coming under pressure to write anti-Gypsy articles. We call for a letter to be sent to the Press Complaints Commission reminding it of the need to protect journalists who are unwilling to write racist articles which are contrary to the National Union of Journalists' code of conduct. (Ponsford 2004.)

An *Express* journalist told *Press Gazette* at the time: "There's a feeling of resentment that people are being pressured into writing articles which they believe to be racist and inflammatory" (ibid).

Members who spoke at the chapel meeting emphasised that they had no problem with their newspaper covering the story of EU enlargement. Rather, the issue was the *way* the story was being covered, and the feeling that staff were expected to take part in the production of biased, inaccurate and even racist material. It was also argued that *Express* journalists could not be excused from speaking out just because their newspaper was not the only offender. The chapel wrote to the PCC asking it to insert a "conscience clause" into its code of practice, whereby journalists who refused unethical assignments would be protected from disciplinary action or dismissal. The NUJ had called for this when giving evidence to the Commons Select Committee on privacy and media intrusion in 2003. The request was rejected by the PCC, which said there was no evidence that journalists came under such pressure; and even if they did, it was a matter between employers and employees.

The journalists had a different perspective, and they saw the raising of ethical concerns collectively as a viable alternative to the otherwise limited choice between suffering in silence and resigning:

> We didn't see pressure to write anti-Gypsy stories as separate from other workplace issues like job cuts, disciplinaries and so on. It was about sticking up for someone at work, and if we took it to the chapel and stuck together, it would be harder for them to pick on us all than to pick on one. Where does it get us if all the decent people resign? If people leave, who will staff the paper then? People just out of college who will be desperate to do anything to impress?

What, if anything, does the chapel think its stance achieved?

Obviously the company finds it embarrassing to have its staff make complaints about it, and the editor certainly didn't want to be labelled as racist. In the short-term, there was some effect in that there was discussion at editorial conferences about being seen to be more even-handed in the paper's coverage of Gypsy and asylum issues. But I certainly wouldn't claim it as a great success and, in the long-term, who knows? I wouldn't be at all surprised if this is an issue the chapel has to confront again in the future.

STANDING UP TO BE COUNTED

The *Express* journalists were prepared to "stand up and be counted"; a quality that, back in the 1950s, Francis Williams (1959: 226) said should be a fundamental part of being a journalist, although he was talking more in terms of the individual:

> [T]he guardianship of journalistic values rests primarily with the journalist... He [sic] cannot dissociate himself from this responsibility without ceasing, in a fundamental sense, to be a journalist. Nor is there any final excuse for him in the claim that he is, after all, simply a hired man who must do as he is bid. He must be ready, as must all men when issues of principle arise, to stand up and be counted.

This is a recurrent theme in discussion of journalistic ethics. Ian Hargreaves (2003: 167) argues that journalism is a "highly individualistic" job with ethical responsibility resting "as much with the individual journalist as with any institutional framework". John O'Neill (1992: 28) cites "principled resignation" as a form of resistance to the commercial pressures that can compromise a journalist's sense of ethical behaviour. Yet, as Richard Keeble (2005: 58) points out, this emphasis on the individual is problematic:

> In the face of the enormous cultural, ideological and financial power of the dominant media and their hierarchically organised management structures, it is not surprising that isolated journalists (driven by their consciences) feel impotent to effect change.

Some journalists do make individual stands and some journalists do change jobs – quietly or loudly – in search of a more conducive ethical environment. But the journalists at *Express* Newspapers demonstrated that there is another, collective option. Arguably, the one organisation in the UK and Ireland with the potential to empower journalists to stand up and be counted collectively is the NUJ; it is perhaps surprising, then, that the union tends to be written out of most discussions about the ethics of journalism, in which more individualistic perspectives are privileged.

I am not suggesting that individual journalists should not take responsibility for their own actions; nor that collective discussions will always result in unerring wisdom. I am suggesting that journalistic ethics within mainstream media cannot be divorced from everyday economic realities such as understaffing, job insecurity, casualised labour, bullying and unconstrained management prerogative; and that a culture in which journalists do not feel confident enough to challenge editorial decisions is hardly conducive to a journalism that contributes to a well-informed citizenry.

JOURNALISTS ARE CITIZENS TOO

Journalism and democracy are often spoken of in the same breath. One cannot exist without the other, according to James Carey (cited in Stromback 2005: 332). And Bill Kovach and Tom Rosenstiel (2003: 18) point out that it is difficult "to separate the concept of journalism from the concept of creating community and later democracy. Journalism is so fundamental to that purpose that…societies that want to suppress freedom must first suppress the press". They argue (ibid: 12-17) that journalism owes its first loyalty to citizens and has as its primary purpose providing those citizens "with the information they need to be free and self-governing".

Yet we should not forget that journalists are citizens too. Journalists do not cease to be citizens when they enter the newsroom, even if they work for an organisation that is required to adhere to rules of impartiality. Journalists can be active citizens by producing journalistic output that acts as a watchdog on the powerful in society, but their citizenship need not end there. Journalists can also be active citizens by reflecting on journalistic practice itself and by taking part in democratic discussions about – and the questioning of - such practice. One way of doing that has been the production of alternative media – a critique of practice, conducted in practice – and another way has been demonstrated by the collective intervention of *Express* journalists in 2001 and 2004. There may well be other ways. I would be pleased to hear about them.

If there is a connection between democracy and social justice, and if inclusive democratic processes can help society create more just policies (Young op cit: 17), then the actions of the journalists discussed in this paper should be highlighted in discussions about the role of journalism rather than pushed to the margins. Iris Young (ibid: 173) argues that the public sphere should be judged on "how well it functions as a space of opposition and accountability, on the one hand, and policy influence, on the other". Judged by such criteria, the alternative practitioners who produce diverse forms of citizens' media and the mainstream practitioners who spoke up as citizens at the *Express* have both made valid contributions towards the health of the public sphere. If we continue to allow these two areas of activity to be written out of the debate about contemporary journalism, we are in danger of leaving journalistic ethics in the hands of proprietors. History suggests they cannot be trusted to treat either audiences or journalists as citizens. It is time to stand up and be counted.

ACKNOWLEDGEMENTS

This article is based on a paper presented to the annual conference of the Association for Journalism Education (AJE) at Westminster University, London, on 9 September 2005 (http://www.ajeuk.org/conference.html). Thanks to the AJE for allowing publication. Thanks also to the editor and anonymous reviewers of *Ethical Space* for their helpful comments. The arguments in this paper were expanded in the *The Ethical Journalist*, published by Sage in 2007.

NOTES

1. The quotes which follow are taken from questionnaires completed by a sample group of 22 such journalists; see Harcup (2005).
2. The account of events at Express Newspapers is based on an interview with a representative of the NUJ chapel at the Express, in addition to published sources as cited

REFERENCES

Atton, Chris (1999) "A reassessment of the alternative press", *Media, Culture and Society*, Vol. 21 pp 51-76

Atton, Chris (2002) *Alternative Media*. London, Sage

Atton, Chris (2004) *An Alternative Internet: radical media, politics and creativity*. Edinburgh, Edinburgh University Press

Bohman, James (2004) "Expanding dialogue: the internet, the public sphere and the prospects for transnational democracy", Crossley, Nick and Roberts, John Michael (eds), *After Habermas: new perspectives on the public sphere*, Oxford, Blackwell pp 131-155

Bolton, Roger (1990) *Death on the Rock and Other Stories*. London, WH Allen

Bundock, Clement J (1957) *The National Union of Journalists: a jubilee history*, Oxford, Oxford University Press for the NUJ

Curtis, Liz (1996) "A catalogue of censorship 1959-1993", Rolston, Bill and Miller, David (eds), *War and Words: the Northern Ireland Media Reader*, Belfast, Beyond the Pale pp 265-304

Downing, John with Villarreal Ford, Tamara; Gil, Geneve and Stein, Laura (2001) *Radical*

Media: rebellious communication and social movements, London, Sage

Foot, Paul (2000) "The slow death of investigative journalism", Glover, Stephen (ed.) *The Penguin Book of Journalism*, London, Penguin pp 79-89

Frost, Chris (2000) *Media Ethics and Self-Regulation*, Harlow, Longman

Gall, Gregor (1993) "The Employers' Offensive in the Provincial Newspaper Industry", *British Journal of Industrial Relations*, Vol. 31, No. 4 December 1993 pp 615-624

Gall, Gregor and McKay, Sonia (1994) "Trade Union Derecognition in Britain 1988-1994", *British Journal of Industrial Relations*, Vol 32, No 3, September pp 433-448

Gall, Gregor (2004) "State of the union", *British Journalism Review* Vol 15, No 3 pp 34-39

Greenslade, Roy (2003) *Press Gang: how newspapers make profits from propaganda*, London, Macmillan

Habermas, Jurgen (1989) *The Structural Transformation of the Public Sphere: an inquiry into a category of bourgeois society*, Cambridge, Polity Press

Hackett, Robert A (2005) "Is There a Democratic Deficit in US and UK Journalism?", Allan, Stuart (ed) *Journalism: critical issues*, Maidenhead, Open University Press pp 85-97

Harcup, Tony (1994) *A Northern Star: Leeds Other Paper and the alternative press 1974-1994*, London and Pontefract, Campaign for Press and Broadcasting Freedom

Harcup, Tony (2002) "Journalists and ethics: the quest for a collective voice", *Journalism Studies* Vol 3, No 1, February pp 101-114

Harcup, Tony (2005) "'I'm doing this to change the world': Journalism in alternative and mainstream media", *Journalism Studies* Vol. 6, No. 3, August pp 361-374

Hargreaves, Ian (2003) *Journalism: truth or dare?* Oxford, Oxford University Press

Hollingsworth, Mark (1986) *The Press and Political Dissent: a question of censorship*, London, Pluto

Journalist (2001) "Outrage at 'racist' refugee coverage", *Journalist* September

Journalist (2002) "PCC snubs an NUJ complaint", *Journalist* January/February

Journalist (2004) "Mystery surrounds raid on Indymedia servers", *Journalist* November/December

Keeble, Richard (2001) *Ethics for Journalists*, London, Routledge

Keeble, Richard (2005) "Journalism ethics: Towards an Orwellian critique?", Allan, Stuart (ed.) *Journalism: critical issues*, Maidenhead, Open University Press pp 54-66

Kovach, Bill and Rosenstiel, Tom (2003) *The Elements of Journalism*, London, Atlantic

Leeds Alternative Publications (1980s, undated) *Views on the News*, internal discussion paper.

Manning, Paul (2001) *News and News Sources: a critical introduction*, London, Sage

Marr, Andrew (2005) *My Trade: a short history of British journalism*, London, Pan

McIntyre, Peter (2004) "An example to so many", *Journalist*, November/December

Morgan, Jean (2001) "Hellier on sick leave as row over Desmond stance grows", *Press Gazette*, 14 September

Neil, Andrew (1996) *Full Disclosure*, London, Macmillan

NUJ (1988) *NUJ Annual Report 1987-1988*, London, National Union of Journalists

O'Neill, John (1992) "Journalism in the Market Place", Belsey, Andrew and Chadwick, Ruth (eds) *Ethical Issues in Journalism and the Media*, London, Routledge pp 15-32

Ponsford, Dominic (2004) "Express staff call in PCC over anti-gypsy articles", *Press Gazette*, 30 January

Ponsford, Dominic (2005) "'Citizen Journalism' agency signs up 1,200 snappers", *Press Gazette*, 12 August

Press Gazette (2005) "Freedom fears as police seize website server", *Press Gazette*, 8 July

Rodriguez, Clemencia (2001) *Fissures in the Mediascape: an international study of citizens' media*, Creskill, Hampton Press

Schlesinger, Philip (1987) *Putting 'Reality' Together*, London, Routledge

Shannon, Richard (2001) *A Press Free and Responsible: self-regulation and the Press Complaints Commission, 1991-2001*, London, John Murray

Smith, Paul and Morton, Gary (1994) "Union Exclusion – Next Steps", *Industrial Relations Journal*, March

Stromback, Jesper (2005) "In Search of a Standard: four models of democracy and their normative implications for journalism", *Journalism Studies*, Vol. 6, No. 3, August pp 331-345

Tracy, James F (2004) "The News About the Newsmakers: press coverage of the 1965 American Newspaper Guild strike against *The New York Times*", *Journalism Studies*, Vol. 5, No. 4, November pp 451-467

Williams, Francis (1959) *Dangerous Estate: the anatomy of newspapers*, London, Arrow

Young, Iris Marion (2000) *Inclusion and Democracy*, Oxford, Oxford University Press

NOTE ON AUTHOR

Tony Harcup has more than 25 years' experience as a journalist in alternative and mainstream media and is now a senior lecturer in the Department of Journalism Studies at the University of Sheffield in the UK. He is the author of *Journalism: Principles and Practice* (2004, Sage) and has also published research on news values, ethics, and alternative media. His book, *The Ethical Journalist*, was published by Sage in 2007. Contact details: Email: t.harcup@sheffield.ac.uk; telephone: 0114 2222502. Address: Department of Journalism Studies, University of Sheffield, 18-22 Regent Street, Sheffield, South Yorkshire, S1 3NJ.

11

How ethical idealism fades with age

Libby Purves

Broadcaster and novelist Libby Purves criticises the media's daily diet of "unkind intrusions and falsifications" – and traces the alarming growth of cynicism amongst teenagers

Let's start with a couple of stories which might throw a light on the attitude people have to how the media should be, and where their responsibilities lie. They're both about the young.

Starting very young, some years ago I wrote a little book for Puffin, called *Getting the story: How the news is gathered*. The idea was to explain to 7 to 9-year-olds how modern news works – a typical shift in a TV newsroom, and 24 hours in a newspaper office. It had little exercises – for instance they could look at a list of headlines and guess who had fed the story to the paper. "Scouts make £500 for leukaemia fund"....the scouts sent that in; on the other hand "Scout hut causing noise nuisance" was presumably sent in by the neighbours.

One exercise I used to do when I talked about this book in children's libraries was asking these young children to decide which of three headlines to make the main front page story. The examples were: "Cure found for cancer"; "War breaks out between Iran and Iraq" and "Queen chased up tree by escaped gorilla".

Invariably, they argued over whether the most important front page story was the cancer or the war. They brought up good arguments – for instance, how sure are we of the cancer cure? And how important are the warring countries? And I would say: Hold on kids...what about the Queen and the gorilla? And they'd shake their serious little heads and say: No, no...that can go inside. So I'd say: Hey, look, we've got PICTURES....and they'd still say: Hmmm, no, the cancer's more important to more people. And finally I'd say: Look, we've got colour pictures, and the Queen was actually rescued by the Archbishop of Canterbury wearing a personal jetpack and superman tights....and one or two might waver, but quite a few still said: No, we ought to cover the war first. And one or two say: Perhaps the Queen was a bit embarrassed about being chased up a tree and it wouldn't be kind to use the pictures very big.

DILEMMA OVER DUTY OF CARE

OK. So idealism still reigns among the very young. But whip onwards ten years and I'm talking to a group of sixth formers about media careers – which the poor brats all seem to want – and we get into a debate about profile interviews and whether you owe any duty of care to the interviewee as a human being, or just to your readers and your editor.

And I say to them: Suppose you're interviewing a major star and he's had a couple of drinks and is obviously tired, and he says to you, on tape, that he wishes he'd never had children, they're a drag and a nuisance and he doesn't like them. And his children are, say, 12 and 14 years old and still live with him and his wife. Now, are you going to put that in the piece? Or soften it, saying he was laughing ironically? Or ask him later when he's sober whether he minds it being in? Do you have any compassion for those children and how they might feel...or not?

And a couple of bright girls say: Well, it depends. If you were doing the piece for *Heat* magazine, you'd make that the main headline story, you'd go to town on it, it's a scoop. It's his stupid fault for saying it anyway. But I suppose if it was the *Telegraph* you might be a bit more pussyfooting.

So I say: Hang on – are you saying that the morals and ethics of how you treat people are entirely your editor's? Not your own? Or do you think journalists should have private ethical codes of kindness and a desire to avoid doing unnecessary harm? And if so, are there papers you'd have to resign from? And I told them another story, about when a tabloid paper was feuding with a rival journalist and the paper's newsroom rang his parish priest to say: Oy, vicar, you got any dirt you could give us on him from the confessional and that? Some junior reporter was ordered to make that crass call, and his or her job could have hung on it... so what do you do, in your first job?

Most of them said they'd do it.

It is apparent that the 17-year-olds, after 10 more years of consuming media, have got a far, far more cynical attitude than the young children who are still under the impression that an attitude of earnest goodwill to the human race is a Good Thing, and that media are if anything more "serious" in their outlook than their consumers.

HOW THE MEDIA TRAMPLE ON INDIVIDUALS

I have to say that I have watched the way standards of behaviour towards individuals have developed and mainly coarsened during the last decades; largely, I think, because of the proliferation of broadcast media and the fact that print media are desperate for anything which attracts attention and brings more colour. And the thing which brings colour and life to a story is individuals – the risk is that in the pursuit of colour and life, the real individual gets trampled on.

We have, both in terms of photographic intrusion and of the style of reporting, got fatally confused between the use of the word "interest" in the phrase "in the public interest" and the use of it in "Wow, that's interesting, that weather forecaster wears a wig and his first wife left him to be a stripper".

There are thousands of examples of unkind intrusion and falsification every day by feature journalists whose real forte would be writing sentimental fiction. Talk to Victim Support and they will tell you that people feel a real sense of additional pain and outrage when a careless or romantic reporter changes some detail of their real ordeal. For instance, the murdered child is reported as being "on his way to football" when he hated football and was on his way to have his dental brace adjusted...perhaps the reporter thought that football would be more attractive to his readers, perhaps he didn't care... either way, the family feels they have had a little piece of their child's history stolen from them.

And it's wrong. It's never going to attract lawsuits....or the Press Complaints Commission...or questions in parliament...but it's still wrong. Likewise, it's wrong when a whole community gets misrepresented, for the sake of a good headline.

Or else a public couple, actors or models or TV newsreaders or whatever, find their marriage in trouble and split up, without misbehaviour, very sadly; or a newsreader's engagement is broken off – and in search of colour, suddenly a whole pack of saloon-bar psychiatrists, or, shamefully, some real psychiatrists, who ought frankly to be struck off, will think themselves entitled to diagnose the mental problems of these people whom they have never even met.

THE DAY DIANA DIED

I don't think any of us can forget that on the day Princess Diana died, the Sunday paper had a huge feature already on the newsstands called "Diana on the couch", psychoanalysing this complete stranger...written by a professional. These things are intrusive, unjustifiable, and disgusting. But we have grown so used to them now that we hardly notice. Often, a few words of interview will be blown up , mixed with speculation and dishonestly titled "My drugs hell by footballer"....as if he'd written it himself, as a testament.

Sometimes a person gives a quote, or an interview, apparently for one reason but actually for quite another; or a reporter realises that a better story can be made up by taking a few words and inventing a scenario. It happened to me – naive as I am – when Stephen Milligan MP died, in a rather sad and shaming auto-erotic asphyxiation...a huge story. The first reports kept painting him as a bit of a loner, a bit of a weirdo and so when a tabloid paper rang me up and asked what I remembered from being at Oxford with him years before I thought right, here's a chance for the sake of his parents and friends to say look, he wasn't weird, he was a nice guy basically. So I told them that I knew him quite well, we'd once partnered each other at the Magdalen College Ball, as friends, and I'd met his family. They asked, was I his girlfriend and I said no.

Well this turned up in the paper as a grand romance...nights of passion at "uni balls"....you can imagine. So I took them to the Press Complaints Commission, and I won, and they had to print an apology. But it gave me an insight into how angry, how violated, you can feel when something is printed which isn't even damaging, in the legal sense but is a form of identity theft, using you – as thousands of people are used every day – as an accessory in someone's overblown soap opera.

Then, of course, there are the flat lies, which are idly perpetuated not only by news outlets, but by commentators, comedians, whatever. You'll hear BBC commentators and comedians and quite serious people referring casually to "Fergie's toe-sucking episode", whereas anyone with eyes and a memory knows that while her cavorting with the American guy was a bit shocking, he was actually kissing her instep in a jokey, reverent sort of way, not sucking her toes in some mad erotic frenzy. Likewise the made up story – admitted to be made up by Max Clifford, I believe – about David Mellor and his mistress making love in Chelsea strip. That is still cited and joked about even on the BBC as if it was true...and it isn't...but it's not worth suing, is it?

All these small, crude abuses of media power do matter, I think. And they should be noted. People in the public eye get abused this way and editors claim that anyone who uses the media is fair game for any aspect of their life to be laid bare.

ABUSES IN THE VIRTUAL WORLD TOO

And in the virtual world there are obvious abuses of individuals – for instance, gossip websites such as Popbitch appear to be utterly free to publish any rumours they like, while sites (and even print magazines) pay money for camera-phone sightings of celebrities doing their shopping with no make-up on. My instinct is that when a photo privacy law finally comes in and hampers the press, it won't be paparazzi who finally tip a government over, but those creeps with cameraphones who hang about in swimming pool changing rooms.

But in a way, I think the real extra peril of the digital age is not that. It's the sheer volume of stuff we have piped at us, in all media: the information overload, the short attention span, the way stories flare up and fade away....so that it may well be that the only memory we have of a case, or a story, or a family, is an utterly false one. And it never gets corrected. Because once a story has gone, it's gone.

Big truths matter. But spare a thought also for the small truths – the boy who wasn't on his way to football, the woman who was a friend not a girlfriend, the public figure whose psyche gets analysed for money by a venal shrink who's never met him, the family painted as scroungers when they aren't, the decent individual tarred forever with some salacious and untrue rumour about their sex life, never allowed to move on because the jeery comedians and idle reporters like to have a rude tag to put on people. Spare a thought for them. Great evils, after all, often spring from small ones.

This is an edited version of Libby Purves's keynote speech to the conference "Real World, Real People: Communication Ethics in a Virtual World" at Roehampton University, 30-31 August, 2005. The Institute of Communication Ethics joined with a range of other bodies (including the European Ethics Network and the Centre for Applied and Professional Ethics at Surrey University) in promoting the event. Libby Purves's latest novel, Acting up, *is published by Hodder.*

PART 2

**JOURNALISM ETHICS:
HISTORICAL PERSPECTIVES**

12

Republican citizenship, ethics and the French revolutionary press 1789-92

Jane Chapman

This chapter examines the role of the revolutionary press in France in the realisation of the Enlightenment notion of "public opinion". The press, it is argued, saw itself as advancing civic republicanism based on public service as opposed to the liberal, individualistic ethic of today. Exploring the relevance of Habermas's theories of discourse ethics and MacIntyre's notions of "communitarianism", the paper argues that the revolutionary press promoted a "democratisation" of honour. The conclusion draws on the theories of Sandel to argue that newspapers provided the crucial narratives by which people made sense of their condition and interpreted their shared experiences at a time of revolutionary upheaval.

INTRODUCTION

The simultaneous revolutions in politics and communications in France from 1789 to 1792 demonstrate how the press can influence public debate, for newspaper reading was a form of voter participation in politics (Reynolds 1971: 256–263; Wilke 1989: 375-391). The scale of newspaper influence mushroomed temporarily to such an extent that the press was taken seriously as a major force within society. In all, 2,000 titles appeared between 1789 and 1799. Newspapers were used as a vehicle to change society via political campaigns and rival claims to representation by the winning of votes. This was a new feature of the democratic political process (Furet and Ozouf 1989).

Contemporaries grappled with a moral vision of politics concerned with how to construct a genuine democracy through forms of participation that placed duty before rights. Public obligations were the only means of ensuring the very liberty that citizens appeared to be giving up by their discharge of "civic virtue". Under civic republicanism, freedom is incorporated into a polity with protection before the law, making it both social and synonymous with citizenship, which itself is achieved via order and civic virtue. "Republicanism in the eighteenth century is the project of restoring a community of virtue" (MacIntyre 1981: 220).

THE 'ANCIEN REGIME', THE ENLIGHTENMENT AND CHANGING POLITICAL MORALITY

Before the revolution there had been only one official daily paper, the mainly cultural rather than political *Journal de Paris*. Consequently, the printed word became a huge underground industry, largely produced abroad. Despite the harsh environment of censorship, a deluge of clandestine pamphlets against the clergy and the aristocracy helped to encourage a revolutionary mood. Research into the influence of the press has revealed that newspapers still assisted in the general loss of faith in the monarchy before 1789, despite restrictions on them (Censer 1994: 213–214).

> While some pamphlets and exile journals such as the high quality *Annales politiques, et littéraires du dix-huitième siècle* dealt with politically radical and controversial subjects such as the slave trade and colonialism, many of these illegal publications were frequently strident, ribald, defamatory and pornographic (Darnton 1971: 101).

After the outbreak of revolution, the press took every opportunity to decry aristocratic decadence in graphic detail, but morals on the revolutionary side became decidedly puritanical. The term "citizen" was used in preference to the word "subject" from the American and French revolutions onwards. As MacIntyre comments: "It is not difficult to see in this a re-making by societies of democratically inspired craftsmen and tradesmen of the classical ideal" (1985: 238). The role of politics now took on a new moral purpose: "to purify expression (of the collective voice), to correct the multiple forms of aberration" (Bates 2002: 99) as the press began to wrestle with the implications of the new ethics.

The revolution had the effect of bringing the eighteenth century Enlightenment notion of "public opinion" into sharper focus. Indeed, what Habermas has called the "bourgeois public sphere" (1989) was designed to help citizens develop, as public consumption, a form of individual literary rhetoric for a Kantian style use of reason. Conversely, lack of reason, especially when expressed as a lack of political integrity, was considered dishonourable.

Habermas also argued that "public opinion", in its classical bourgeois form, acts as an intermediary between natural law as an abstract principle and the enactment of legislation as a form of practical sovereignty (Habermas 1989: 140, 237–238). Newspapers became brokers in this process within the emerging public sphere. If the principal influence of the revolutionary press was that of communitarian civic republicanism, how did this evolve? Newspapers provide the best record of this change in attitude, for they had "the vocation of measuring the new era and defining its rhythm" (Rétat 1985: 142).

NEWSPAPERS AND THE LANDSCAPE OF PARTICIPATORY DEMOCRACY

According to Alexis de Tocqueville, the previous lack of freedom and practical experience in public affairs meant that "political ferment was canalised into literature, the result being that our writers became the leaders of public opinion and played for a while the part which normally in free countries, falls to the professional politician" (1955: 142).

The aim of newspaper writers was to recreate the drama of debate in the Assembly, as if the reader was there. Good practice in journalistic ethics had been defined in July 1789 by the editor of the *Bulletin nationale*, who maintained that the reader should "follow the progress of opinions, discuss them himself and believe himself to be actually participating". This was essential now that the people were in charge.

As editor Loustallot wrote in *Les Révolutions de Paris* newspaper (of 19-25 September 1789): "Our representatives are not, as in England, the sovereign of the nation. IT IS THE NATION THAT IS SOVEREIGN." Habermas tends to discuss sovereignty in the context of its longer-term relationship with the development of the nation state and not in terms of its manifestation within a potential ethics of citizenship. "The sovereignty of the people was, of course, a diffuse battle cry, which was unfolded in the constitutional debates of the nineteenth century. In its various thought motifs flow together: the sovereign power of the state appears as the expression of a new principle of legitimation, of the domination of the third estate, and of national identity as well" (1979: 192). Admittedly, revolutionaries were still pioneering concepts of sovereignty, described by Cobb as "vague gropings at theories" (1997: 23). But for the press, the importance was crucial. Power invested in the sovereignty of the people was largely ideological: this meant that the responsibility for its definition lay with writers. As Furet says: "Language was substituted for power, for it was the sole guarantee that power would belong to the people, that is, to nobody" (1981: 27).

Since the collapse of the old regime, secrecy was considered counter-revolutionary, so the French insisted that all politics had to be carried out in public to be legitimate. From 1789 through to 1799 when Napoleon made himself dictator, law-making was conducted in public assemblies open to the people. Most contemporary journalists were also leading politicians, such as Robespierre, Marat, and Hébert. All were propagandists who knew what was going on within parliamentary circles because they mixed in them. Stylistically, the political rhetoric of newspaper articles was oratorical, intended for reading aloud and therefore almost indistinguishable from the discourse of parliamentary speeches.

Attempts at participatory debate in politics are given a theoretical role model by Habermas in his "discourse ethics". Discourse ethics expresses our moral intuitions in so far as these impinge on the process of discursive justification of norms. Furthermore, the emphasis on normative consensus rather than on abstract universalism means than a discourse ethic can include the more universal structural aspects of ways of life relating to communicative action itself (1990: 116). As Held points out: "Habermas would argue that he is less concerned with particular theoretical and value positions which are relative to social and historical contexts, and more with the conditions for the possibility of argument as such" (1980: 397).

Nevertheless, in *Moral Consciousness and Communicative Action*, Habermas places his theory of discourse ethics into a theoretical context of the historical development and evolution of human societies, reconstructing it as a learning process influenced by Piaget's theory of cognitive development (1971) and Kohlberg's theory of moral development (1981; Habermas op.cit: 8, 33-42), along with historical materialism adapted from Marx. This procedural model for language provides "transcendental" guarantees of the rules of speech which assume people will make a rational choice about how to operate when, in fact, the existence of culture means there are always elements of irrationality that still remain. (McMylor 1994: 171; Held 1980: 331).

THE COMMUNITARIAN APPROACH AND THE REVOLUTIONARY PRESS

Thus discourse ethics has provoked considerable debate between those who favour a Kantian concept of universalisability and "contextualists" or "communitarians" who argue for the embedding of moral principles in cultures and ways of life where these become both objects and sources of moral value (Outhwaite 1996: 178; Benhabib and Dallmayr 1990; Baynes 1992). In terms of its historical specificity, it is probably more appropriate to measure the French revolutionary press against the latter communitarian approach. This is defined by Sandel: "For a society to be a community in the strong sense, community must be constitutive of the shared self-understandings of the participants and embodied in their institutional arrangements, not simply an attribute of certain of the participants' plans of life" (1996: 173).

MacIntyre's work has similarly has been called "communitarian", although it is a label that he himself rejects (MacIntyre 1994: 265). Although his communitarianism is specifically neo-classical and anti-liberal, thus not linked to liberal pluralism, the kind of community envisaged by MacIntyre in later writings encourages a discourse comparable to the ones that took place in the pages of the French press, presupposing deliberation, argument and insisting that citizens can put into doubt "what has hitherto by custom or tradition been taken for granted" (MacIntyre 1998: 241).

Part of the reason that ethical models are difficult to apply is that the revolutionary mentality, as Cobb points out, was never a body of doctrine or a carefully reasoned philosophy of life (1997: 7). There were political and moral standards, but these were soon put under pressure by the speed of events, foreign invasion and intolerance of dissent, all of which are all dealt with later. The most dramatic change that took place was in the power of print media to influence events as they were happening – by being part of them. Newspapers in that period provided a "feedback mechanism that stimulated and intensified the rising level of revolutionary fervour" (Wilke op cit: 387). Therefore newspapers were not only the "child" but also the "father" of the revolution (Gilchrist and Murray 1971; Popkin 1990).

The press also helped form a new revolutionary culture: a Declaration of the Rights of Man and a constitution, new administrative systems, the defeat of the Church, a different currency, map, calendar, weights and measures, even new forms of address, including revolutionary celebrations or fêtes. Through their language and symbolism such events were experienced as communications events aimed at encouraging like-minded feelings amongst the participants (Wilke op cit: 388; Ozouf 1988).

During this era of active street culture newspapers were often pasted up as bills in public places, then pasted over by rival newspapers. Ideas were disseminated via handbills and posters, via public reading sessions which helped the illiterate to develop political awareness, and through fierce discussion in the streets, in clubs and in other public places. Within this climate, the press helped to encourage and co-ordinate the emergence of a democratic movement in many Paris districts. Detailed historical research on the march of the market women from Paris to Versailles to fetch the royal family back to Paris, for instance, concludes that the press "not only prepared the disturbances and made them possible, but also gave them their shape and purpose" (Rudé 1958: 22; see also Mathiez 1998: 41-3). Thus newspapers "reflected the diverse strands of public opinion and, at the same time, helped to form them" (Gough 1988: 235).

By 1792, political societies were overtaking the press as the main forums for policy formation. Although the majority of journals were pro-revolutionary, perhaps it was inevitable that, like the clubs, they too would become a forum for disputes between rival groups and tendencies seeking to influence the people.

TOWARDS AN ETHICS OF CITIZENSHIP

Journalistic progress was linked to the difficult evolution of the political process and the moral vision of politics that it traded in was concerned with how to construct a genuine democracy through forms of participation that placed duty before rights. The emphasis of civic republicanism on virtuous public service differentiates it from modern liberal individualism. The press saw itself as a moral agent dedicated to the distinct normative end of civic virtue. "The revolutionaries were optimists; they were convinced that they were in the process of creating not only a new form of society, but also a new revolutionary man, virtuous, serious, patriotic" (Cobb op cit:18).

THE UNWRITTEN JOURNALISTIC CODE OF REVOLUTIONARY HONOUR

Citizenship and public probity came to acquire the highest value. Influence over the formulation of public opinion carried responsibility, but, as William Reddy has demonstrated, it revolved around an invisible code of civic "honour" (1997). According to Brissot, who was influenced by the British and American informational style, journalists should retain their independence by never dining with dignitaries and people in power or being dependent on information from just one person or source. People should be judged by facts and opinions, not by gossip and speculation. Journalists should have knowledge of the good political practices of ancient democracy (for the Greek city states were a model) and should seek to expose the way that the aristocracy in France undermined the new system by their corruption (1791).

Classical analogies abounded as part of the republican ideal. In 1789 journalist Camille Desmoulins had waxed: "Here I am a journalist, and it is a rather fine role. No longer is it a wretched and mercenary profession, enslaved by the government. Today in France it is the journalist who holds the tablets, the album of the censor, and who inspects the senate, the consuls and the dictator himself" (*Révolutions de France et de Brabant 1789*). A few years later, Brissot was to berate Desmoulins publicly for his lack of journalistic ethics in a three-part series of articles (1791: 656, 657, 659) yet Desmoulins' prose is the most eloquent of the period.

In 1789 writing was considered to be a vocation not a business, so there was a scepticism about the ethical implications of writing for hire. The concern was that a writer would lose public honour if his (or sometimes her) work was not consistent. Increased demand for newspapers led to an increase in demand for prose, but the "democratisation" of honour made even the lowliest hacks anxious about the consistency of their political positions. The sudden growth in the newspaper industry had only exacerbated the problem. For example, Marat noted that any person who had managed to get one article in the *Gazette* and wanted to "make it" could then proceed to "try and make a fortune by launching a newspaper. Empty headed, with no contacts, ideas or views, he goes in to a café to pick up gossip, the allegations of public enemies, people's moans and the complaints of the underdog, then goes home with his head full of this mishmash that he puts on to paper and hands to his printer for circulation the following day to the idiots who are stupid enough to buy it. That's the output of 99 per cent of these people" (*L'Ami du Peuple* No.382, 25 February 1791).

Journalists could face public shame, yet the nature of basic honour was never defined. For instance, Marat's commentaries on the assembly were aimed at exposing certain deputies' treasonous intentions, and also at mobilising the people against them. Unwritten ethical codes, however, clearly did not extend to literary method, truth or accuracy. For instance, the writer Hébert, euphemistically dubbed the "Homer of Filth", was originally against the execution of the King but eventually called for the "monster's blood" in his satirical journal *Le Père Duchesne*, which stretched to 368 editions.

Hébert complained that it was such a long and complicated business to "knock off a tyrant's head: yes, damn it! The traitor Louis, shut up like an owl in the Temple tower, would not be so complacent there, if he did not have a strong following in Paris. Already, damn it, they have tried more than one surprise attack to release him.....It must not happen that the greatest scoundrel that has ever been should remain unpunished. It is good that the sovereign people become used to judging kings" (*Le Père Duchesne*: Hatin 1859:V1, 516-517). He believed that "you must swear with those who swear", admitting that he did not write for the ladies: "anyone who appreciates frankness and probity will not blush at the 'foutres' and 'bougres' that I insert here and there with my joys and my angers". The style had instant appeal to "sans culottes" readers because it was well suited to reading aloud for those who were illiterate.

THE PROBLEMS OF PLURALISM AND DISSENT

From 1789 to 1799 newspapers with their libel, sedition and insults, form a record of one of the most passionate periods ever (de Monseignat 1853: 235, 239). During this period there was no distinction between "comment" and the factual reporting of events so the latter could easily become self indulgent slander or support for a faction. Every editor wanted to influence both the assembly and the people, but their political opinions as stated in their journals, differed. Hence as press freedom evolved in France, it became a double edged sword at the same time as its educative role was overtaken by a less restrained and uncontrolled war of ideas. As François Furet commented: "It [the revolutionary press] strove for power, yet denounced the corruption power inevitably entailed" (1981: 49).

If the price of democracy is eternal vigilance, then the price of newspaper freedom was inevitably a critical and damaging press. In particular, the counter revolutionary press had a number of the most talented journalists as well as substantial financial backing and, in some cases, subsidy from the King's Civil List (Murray 1986). The royalist newspapers fought their battle ruthlessly on the revolutionaries' territory. Royalist papers such as the *Ami du roi* portrayed the assembly as divided and disorderly, whilst the satirical *Actes des apôtres* thought it mad. The continuous slander of the newspapers, the venting of grievances and the publicity in support of various factions, all had the disconcerting effect of keeping France, and especially Paris, in a state of permanent unrest and incipient revolt (Popkin 1980).

The overthrow and arrest of the King heralded a new phase of radicalisation of the revolution, but during 1792 complete newspaper autonomy became threatened by the Terror and the victory of the Montagnards factions over the Girondins. Across the political spectrum journalistic nationalism induced by war became evident, tending to clash with the intrinsic universalism and egalitarianism of the Revolution. The enormity of the problem helps to explain the decline of democracy: by the spring of 1793 France was faced with the combined forces of Austria, Prussia, Britain, Holland, Spain, Naples, Rome, Venice and Sardinia. The Revolutionary Wars destroyed many of the earlier progressive measures passed by the Assembly and imposed an unbearable pressure on the new republic.

The problem in retrospect seems to be that Europe had not yet embraced the modern day democratic concept of plurality of expression. Instead, diversity was seen as a threat. Unlike America and Britain, constitutional initiatives in France had not created any formal space for dissent, although revolutionary leaders tried to create one. "Absolute, the sovereignty of the people excluded pluralism of representation because it assumed the unity of the nation" (Bates 2002: 110).

The process then entailed creating a series of enemies: aristocrats, the monarchy, counter revolutionaries, which in turn facilitated the creation of a sense of national unity in opposition. Thus, in the eyes of contemporaries stability was associated with unity, which was threatened by dissent. Dissent had to be eliminated because it divided society into hostile factions, represented and articulating their views in diverse newspapers. Therefore, the Terror could be interpreted as an erroneous attempt to reestablish this unity. "Criticism and dissent are always paramount, the indicators of a healthy society, but when unlimited they destroy the virtues and end all chance of securing the good.....when political authority...goes beyond its limits and tries to initiate an unrestrained politics of virtue, the outcome is invariably oppression, what (sic) poisons the well-spring of legitimacy and destroys unity" (Breen 2000: 8).

CONCLUSIONS

In theory, civic republicanism is a relatively neutral idea around which we can organise the politics of a pluralist society, even if this challenge was not totally successful in 1789–92. In the early years of the French Revolution, political morals approximated to this perspective of liberty, but ironically the journalism practice that was underpinned by it eventually conspired, along with events, to undermine the ethic. Yet French revolutionary newspapers were essential as a forum for discourse. As Sandel argues: "Political community depends on the narratives by which people make sense of their condition and interpret the common life they share; at its best, political deliberation is not only about competing policies but also about competing interpretations of the character of a community, of its purposes and ends. The loss of the capacity for narrative would amount to the ultimate disempowerment of the human subject, for without narrative there is no continuity between past and present, and therefore no responsibility, and therefore no possibility of acting together to govern ourselves" (op cit: 351).

REFERENCES

Translations of all French language sources cited in the text are the author's own, with the exception of de Tocqueville.

Primary sources

Archives Gironde (A.G. 1794) 11 L 27, Club national de Bordeaux. Archives Nationales (A.N.1794) F7 4669 d3, Dennevers. Brissot, J.P. (1791) *le Patriote français*, nos 656, 657, 659, June Bulletin nationale, July 1789. Desmoulins, C. (1789). *Révolutions de France et de Brabant*, second edition. Hébert, J.-R. (1791) *Le Père Duchesne*, juillet, Hatin Vol. V1, 516–517. Loustallot, E. (1789) *Les Révolutions de Paris 11*, 19-25 September. Marat, J.-P. (1791) *L'Ami du peuple*, 25 February

Secondary sources

Bates, D. W. (2002) *Enlightenment Aberrations: Error and Revolution in France*, Ithaca and London, Cornell University Press

Baynes, K. (1992) *The Normative Grounds of Social Criticism: Kant, Rawls, and Habermas*, Albany, New York, State University of New York

Benhabib, S. and Dallmayr, F. (eds) (1990) *The Communicative Ethics Controversy*, Cambridge, Mass. MIT Press

Breen, K. (2000) *Alasdair MacIntyre, Virtue, and the Alternative Politics of Local Communities*, New Waverley Papers, Edinburgh, University of Edinburgh

Censer, J. R. (1994) *The French Press in the Age of Enlightenment*, London and New York, Routledge

Cobb, R. (1997) "The Revolutionary Mentality in France", The French and Their Revolution, selected writings edited and introduced by Gilmour, D., London, John Murray

Darnton, R. (1971) "The High Enlightenment and the Low-Life of Literature in Pre-revolutionary France", *Past and Present*, Vol. 51 pp 81–115

Furet, F. (1981) *Interpreting the French Revolution*, Cambridge, Cambridge University Press

Furet, F. and Ozouf, M. (1989) *The French Revolution and the Creation of Modern Political Culture*, Vol. 3. Oxford, Pergamon Press

Gilchrist, J. and Murray, W.J. (1971) *The Press and the French Revolution: a selection of documents taken from the press of the Revolution for the years 1789–1794*, London, Ginn

Gough, H. (1988) The Newspaper Press in the French Revolution, London, Routledge

Habermas, J. (1979) *Communication and the Evolution of Society*, London, Heinemann

Habermas, J. (1989) *The Structural Transformation of the Public Sphere: An Enquiry into a Category of Bourgeois Society* (trans.Burger, T.), Cambridge, Polity Press

Habermas, J. (1990) *Moral Consciousness and Communicative Action*, Cambridge, Polity Press

Hatin, E. (1860) *Histoire politique et littéraire de la presse en France avec une introduction sur les origins* (Vols 4 and 6), Paris, Poulet-Malassis et de Broise

Held, D. (1980) *Introduction to Critical Theory: Horkheimer to Habermas*, London, Hutchinson

Kohlberg, L. (1981) *Essays on Moral Development, Vol.1 "The Philosophy of Moral Development"*, San Francisco and London, Harper Row

MacIntyre, A. (1981, 1985) *After Virtue: a study in moral theory*, London, Duckworth

MacIntyre, A. (1994) "An Interview with Giovanni Borradori", Knight, K. (ed.) *The MacIntyre Reader*, Cambridge, Polity Press pp 255–266

MacIntyre, A. (1998) "Politics, Philosophy and the Common Good", Kelvin, K. (ed.) *The MacIntyre Reader*, Cambridge, Polity Press pp 235–252

Mathiez, A. (1998) "Les journées des 5 et 6 octobre 1789", *Revue Historique. LXVII*

McMylor, P. (1994) *Alasdair MacIntyre: Critic of Modernity*, New York and London, Routledge

de Monseignat, C. (1853) *Un Chapitre de la Révolution Française ou histoire des journaux en France*, Paris, Librairie de L. Hachette

Murray, W. J. (1986) *The Right Wing Press in the French Revolution, 1789–1792*, London, the Royal Historical Society

Outhwaite, W. (ed.) (1996) *The Habermas Reader*, Cambridge, Polity

Ozouf, M. (1988) *Festivals and the French Revolution*, Cambridge, Mass., Harvard University Press

Piaget, J. (1971) *Biology and Knowledge* (trans. Walsh, B.), Edinburgh, Edinburgh University Press

Pocock, J. G. A. (1975) *The Machiavellian Moment: Florentine Political Thought and the Atlantic Republican Tradition*, Princeton and London, Princeton University Press

Popkin, J.D. (1980) *The Right-Wing Press in France, 1792–1800*, Chapel Hill, University of North Carolina Press

Popkin, J. D. (1990) *Revolutionary News: The Press in France 1791-1799*, Durham, NC, Duke University Press

Reddy, W. (1997) *The Invisible Code: Honor and Sentiment in Post-Revolutionary France 1814–1848*, Berkeley, University of California Press

Rétat, P. (1985) "Forme et discours d'un journal revolutionnaire", *L'Instrument periodique*,

Labrosse, C. and Retat, P., Lyon (eds), Presses Universitaires de Lyon

Reynolds , B. K. (1971) "Context of Girondist rhetoric", *Western Speech* , 4, Fall pp 256–263

Rudé, G. (1958) *The Crowd in the French Revolution*, Oxford, Oxford University Press

Sandel, M. J. (1996) *Democracy's Discontent: America in Search of a Public Philosophy*, Cambridge MA and London, The Belknap Press of Harvard University Press

de Tocqueville, A. (1955) *The Old Regime and the French Revolution* (trans. Gilbert, S.) Garden City, New York, Doubleday/Anchor Books

Wilke, J. (1989) "History as a communication event: The example of the French Revolution", *European Journal of Communication*, Vol. 4, No 4 December pp 375–391

NOTE ON AUTHOR

Dr. Jane Chapman is Reader in Journalism Studies at Lincoln University School of Journalism, U.K. She is the author of several recent articles on the journalism of George Sand, also the literary activist role of Arundhati Roy, as well as *Comparative Media History: 1789 to the Present* (2005) and *Documentary in Practice* (2007), both published by Polity Press. Contact details: School of Journalism, University of Lincoln, Brayford Pool, Main Campus, Lincoln LN6 7TS. Email: jachapman@lincoln.ac.uk.

13

Expanding ethical discourse in Wooler's *Black Dwarf*

Martin Conboy

Ethical concerns about journalism are most often associated with the professionalisation of that practice since the latter half of the nineteenth century. In addition, ethical concerns are consistently rooted within the framing device of capitalist norms of journalism production. This chapter, by focusing on Wooler's Black Dwarf, *seeks to explore some aspects of radical journalism in the early nineteenth century when the central elements of journalism as a discourse were still being formed. This process depended as much on the political economy of journalism as it did on its textual conventions, both of which have clear ethical implications. The chapter also argues that Wooler's journal provided an expanded ethical dimension for radical journalism through its textual experimentation and carnivalesque use of parody and satire.*

JOURNALISM AND THE ENLIGHTENMENT TRADITION

Since the foundation of modernity in the American and French Revolutions, journalism has attempted to engage with the abstract ideals of the Enlightenment on a practical, everyday level and to an increasing number of citizens. This is because two of the most abiding practical demands which emerge from Enlightenment thought – universal suffrage and the right to a free press which allows access to information about the world – are encapsulated within journalism. After the American and French revolutions, informed as they were by the practices of the press, journalism was to continue as one of the main arenas where the expectations and paradoxes of modernity were to be played out. It needed to achieve this within the confines of modernity's dominant economic framework, that of capitalism.

Particularly within that framework, greater access to information for more readers, listeners and viewers does not lead unproblematically to a more enlightened citizenship. As the movement has progressed from conventional, periodical journalism as an elite resource to one where as a popular commodity it comes to supplement and then supersede other popular printed forms such as street literature and ballads, the central issue it faces now appears to be whether it is possible to maintain the ethical ambitions of a journalism committed to those Enlightenment ideals within an intensively populist market. Journalism is located problematically, attempting as it does to foster those Enlightenment ideals at the same time as generating profits.

Yet, of course, journalism has never existed in a rarefied sphere disassociated from the demands of commerce or political pressure. It has always needed to manoeuvre within that complex dialogue of profit and Enlightenment and it is out of this tension that an ethics of journalism emerges. The consideration of ethics within journalism, for the purposes of this paper, is not restricted to the exercise of individual responsibility for the quality of information but also implies the extent to which journalism achieves one of its defining goals, enabling an informed citizenship to play a full part in democratic political processes.

ETHICS ON THE MARGINS – EARLY RADICAL JOURNALISM

Rather than take a look at the more mainstream serious aspects of ethics in journalism, this piece will take a view from the margins of journalistic practice – its satirical and parodic flexibility – to consider whether journalism had, during the political and demographic upheavals of early nineteenth century England, the potential to create an ethical space outside the constraints of the economic and political status quo whence journalism so often derives its norms of behaviour.

We might assert for the purposes of this paper that ethics are a formal range of standards and interventions which seek to maintain or improve levels of human conduct. Ethics within journalism which are concerned with standards of reliability, impartiality and even truthfulness are particularly complex when its informational function comes into conflict with journalism's role within a set of profit-driven criteria. This chapter will examine briefly one attempt to produce a radical form of journalism at the same time as mainstream journalism was beginning to consolidate itself.

In the early years of the nineteenth century in England, there emerged a radical version of journalism centred on the reform of political representation and particularly on the role of working men in politics. This new popular radicalism in print generated a variety of approaches to popular ethics in journalism. They were all dependent on the promotion of a journalism in the interests of ordinary readers as opposed to one which sought to safeguard the social and financial interests of the owners of respectable newspapers and journals. Previously, most debates on the responsibilities and freedoms of the press had been principally concerned with securing more autonomy for privileged sections of the bourgeoisie despite frequent rhetorical claims invoking the people (Conboy 2002). At the start of the nineteenth century, newspapers were becoming lucrative enough in business terms. Their owners wanted that translated into political influence to substantiate a standing with readers which was becoming less dependent on the financial and informational support of government factions (Conboy 2004: 109-116).

However, on the margins of journalism we can see in the early years of the nineteenth century an alternative ethical dimension which is completely disassociated from the mainstream economic and political consolidation of newspapers such as *The Times*. The radical journals and pamphlets of this era attempted to provide an ethical space outside of and contesting the economic and political status quo by representing the voice and aspirations of disenfranchised people. The radical movement demanded a democracy of representation and a democracy of expression (Calhoun 1982: 89). Writers such as William Cobbett, Richard Carlile and John and Leigh Hunt provided a range of radical, unstamped journals and newspapers which provided what Thompson has called the "heroic age of popular radicalism" (1979).

The perceived threat of the radical movement and its papers was captured unequivocally in *Blackwood's*, an essentially conservative barometer of these turbulent times. "Radicalism is subversion, total excision and overthrow, the substitution, not of one order of polity for another, but an utter destruction of the present state of things" (*Blackwood's Edinburgh Magazine*, 8, 1820: 329).

Yet the Radical movement, popular though it was in drawing on the genuine anxieties of ordinary people was Quixotic in that demanding resistance and overthrow of the emerging industrial economy which had brought these radical communities into existence, it was literally demanding the impossible. Patricia Hollis has summarised the main thrust of this radicalism as being based on a critique of "old corruption" (1970). This analysis demonstrates that despite its passion, there was little of a political programme beyond resistance to and retreat from the forces of capitalist modernity in this journalism. It concentrated on the abuse of power and the abuse of working people and trusted that an entitlement to vote would enable the system to be rectified.

Yet no systematic analysis of the deficiencies of industrial capitalism was available before the proto-socialist critiques of the 1830s. Nevertheless, these deficiencies did not detract from the high levels of ethical intent in the journalism of the radical movement. This journalism had an impact on a wider popular audience than at any time since the English Civil War.

WOOLER'S BLACK DWARF

A very different contribution to radical journalism from the sustained and serious critical polemic of Carlile, Cobbett and the Hunts came in Thomas Wooler's *Black Dwarf* (1817–24). It started as a four pence a week production until after the Six Acts brought in by the Government to suppress radical unrest when it was forced to increase its price to six pence. It had a strong enough readership, estimated to be in the region of 12,000 (Altick 1957: 326), to survive the effects of post-Peterloo repression and price increase. In 1819 it had gained such notoriety that Castelreagh, the Foreign Secretary, announced in Parliament that Wooler had become the "fugleman of the Radicals" and that his *Black Dwarf* could be found in northern mining areas "in the hatcrown of almost every pitman you meet" (Wickwar 1928: 57).

The *Black Dwarf* was a provocative contribution not only in its content but more especially in its style. It contained a strong blend of satire, parody and humorous intervention of all sorts in support of Reform and the interests of the labouring classes. Drawing on the popular culture of the working poor, poetry, ballads, songs were all published in support of radical ideas and the culture they supported. It blended with the oral nature of popular culture also in its use of reported speeches, quotations, questions, answers and most interestingly for the purposes of this paper, parodies.

Wooler's satire was very much of the "old corruption" school – iconoclastic and populist. It built on traditions of oral popular culture and developed an anti-authoritarianism with a contemporary flavour in its mockery of those in power. In other ways his iconoclasm, channelled through parody and satire, played a part in destabilising lower class deference to the political classes and brought a level of literary sophistication to popular working class culture and one which thrived for a period. It offered little in explicit analysis but it provided a style, an ethical engagement with journalism as a tool which could go beyond reporting and set the tone for political debate among a new audience, a tone which was based on the "expanded use of public satire…" (Hendrix 1976: 128).

This was a rich combination of political engagement and satirical, textual experimentation in advancing both conventional and parodic arguments in favour of Reform and against the corruption of politicians. Its motto made this explicit:

Satire's my weapon; but I'm too discreet,
To run a-muck and tilt at all I meet:
POPE

Although it announced itself in this motto as following in the tradition of the satirical model of Pope's imitation of Horace's satires, Wooler was not interested in some polite critique of the foibles of society and indeed did tilt at almost everything that he met. Despite the stated oblique mode of attack, Wooler identified himself as the editor and had to take the consequences of this like the other radical journalists of the time acting as editor-proprietor. He was prosecuted in 1817 shortly after the first appearance of the paper. On this occasion, he successfully fought against a charge of seditious libel. Later, in 1819, he was imprisoned in Warwick Gaol for 18 months though he continued to edit the journal. The paper's sub-title, the "Address to the Unrepresented Part of the Community" makes clear both the constituency his paper was aimed at, as well as stressing that, in order to change society, this community had to become more actively aware of their current situation:

> …You are *something*, you are indeed; and although few dare tell you what you are, you must perceive yourselves to be *"slaves, on whose chains are inscribed the words liberty and freedom!"* SLAVES? Englishmen Slaves? You are startled, and well you may be, but it should be at your *condition*, and not at the proclamation of it. Look around you. Do, I beseech you, make use of your eyes (*BD*: 8 July 1818).

As in the example above, Wooler often employed devices based on an approximation of oral rhetoric to appeal to readers and, no doubt, illiterate listeners who would have had the paper read to them with all its visual clues for intended delivery.

Wooler did additionally provide a more traditional range of journalism in the printed news of meetings of the Reform movement and he printed signed letters, long a staple of the respectable press, but ones which suited his radical agenda such as those protesting against ARBITRARY IMPRISONMENTS. These included provocative accounts of miscarriages of justice:

> INSTANCE OF WANTON AND EXCESSIVE
> PUNISHMENT
> SIR … two individuals of the "Lower Orders",
> for carrying coals ashore, which appears to

Yet despite its evident service to the radical movement and the informational content of its journalism, the most significant aspect of Wooler's project was the way in which he used his paper to play humorously with the conventional forms of journalism. It was this parodic and satirical approach which was to push at the boundaries of the ethical contours of journalism. In doing so, it was challenging journalism's generic variety which had been established with some coherence for more than 150 years, especially with regard to political reporting (Frank 1961: 54. Mendle 2001: 58).

TEXTUAL INVENTIVENESS

The novelty of the *Black Dwarf*'s humorous engagement with politics from a radical stance was that it highlighted the instability of established (and the Establishment's) forms of journalism as public information, thus providing an alternative and multiple set of ethical perspectives for popular consideration. In doing so it also made the most of the instability of contemporary readerships. Klancher has observed that during these years it was the English Romantics, sensing the turbulence of these times, who first became radically uncertain of their readership and faced the task Wordsworth referred to as "creating the taste" by which the writer is comprehended (Klancher 1987: 3). During this period, the English reading public was passing through the social and demographic turmoil of the industrial revolution, a new social and political consciousness was being created in the working class and Wooler attempted to exploit this in providing a complex range of voices and textual experiments to articulate that sense of movement and instability. The taste which Wooler was attempting to create was a multiple one which played with clear political intent on the established patterns of journalism in a humorous and disruptive way.

Even his protagonist, the Black Dwarf himself, was a symbol of the mutability and radical unpredictability of shape and form which could be used in this radical venture. The Black Dwarf is described in the first edition by Wooler as "secure from his invisibility, and dangerous from his power of division, (for like the polypus, he can divide and redivide himself, and each division remain a perfect animal" (*BD*: 29 January 1817).

The instability of the "polymorph" is reflected in the highly volatile mixture of voices (heteroglossia) which Wooler uses to destabilise and critique the ruling classes and the institutions and customs of their repression. One of the chief targets of his comic strategies is the Establishment's conventional journalism which was continuing on its own way towards an economically and politically acceptable truce with the status quo in their own engagement with reform politics. Wooler seems to be providing a range within which his new readership can locate itself as the consciousness of an oppressed class begins to take shape against the grain of the patterns and articulations of the Establishment. He does that by encouraging his readers to consider the range of choices from which they must begin to compose their own language so over-determined by the interests of others. Bakhtin has stressed the importance of orientating one's language in opposition to the dominant discourse of the time, highlighting the dynamic nature of this process:

> Language is not a neutral medium that passes freely and easily into the private property of the speaker's intentions; it is populated – overpopulated – with the intentions of others... Consciousness finds itself inevitably facing the necessity of having to choose a language. With each literary-verbal performance, consciousness must actively orient itself amidst heteroglossia, it must move in and occupy a position for itself within it, it chooses in other words, a "language" (1996: 294-95).

Wooler uses this carnival of language and voice to demonstrate the complexity of linguistic choice. The Black Dwarf, the Yellow Bonze, the Green Goblin, the Black Neb and the Blue Devil all provide different voices and perspectives within which Wooler can confront and ridicule the corruption of the status quo. This multiplicity of voices, a literal heteroglossia, allows Wooler to take up a whole spectrum of satirical and parodic positions which would have been closed to the more traditional and serious writing of Cobbett or Carlile.

The continuation of such radical ventures, particularly after 1819, meant that these journals needed to be able to be flexible and responsive to threats and to the loyalty of readers in order to survive. "The survival of a paper through constant mutation became in every sense its plot. Even where this plot assumed a certain continuity, as in Wooler's linked series narrative suspense hinged on a threat to the very capacity to narrate" (Gilmartin 1996: 82).

RADICAL ETHICS THROUGH SATIRE AND PARODY

It was not only through narrative and discursive variety that the *Black Dwarf* enabled a novel variety of ethical critique to be turned on the corruption of the contemporary ruling classes. Parody played an important part. Parody can briefly be described as a wide range of textual borrowing and echoing for critical/humorous purposes and meshes easily with a further stylistic method, that of satire. The *Black Dwarf* deployed a potent combination of these two devices to increase its popular and radical following and to enhance the Black Dwarf's connections with ordinary people's causes and thus have a real impact within radical politics.

These forms of textual play created an ethics which drew on a series of textual interventions and subversions which contested the conventional placement of journalism within a capitalist socio-political framework. Wooler used the whole range of journalism's repertoire for comic/disruptive effect: "reporting" "foreign correspondents" "political discourse", "reports of trials", "poetry" and "readers' letters" were all used to destabilise and force reflection on the conventions of journalism and its relationship to those in power.

In such a volatile social environment, prior relationships between speech acts and status could more readily be fractured. Parody, according to Wood, could be deployed by radical propagandists as an act of linguistic acquisition and by the same token, subversion:

> Parody was knocking away continually and uncontrollably at the notion that language reflected class and social position, that polite and literary forms of language could be set up above, and separate from…the literature of the multitude (Wood 1994: 13).

Nowhere is this clearer than at the moment when the *Black Dwarf* parodies the advice of the King James Bible in a vituperative piece whose climax is:

> The LORD giveth, and the LORDS taketh away.
> Blessed be the way of the Lords
> (*BD*: 27 January 1817).

Most regular features of conventional newspapers were inverted in a set of parodies which were designed to entertain but at the same time undercut the credibility of his political enemies. For instance, he had regular sections of news narrated from a mischievous and subversive perspective such as: "NEWS FROM THE CITY..." which signed off: "Your's, A CITY IMP".

His most renowned exercise in textual disruption was his "Cross Readings in a Newspaper". These were a political version of an old game of reading across rather than down columns of print to produce unexpected juxtapositions:

CROSS READINGS The Ministers are quite shocked to hear –

> Turn'd pale amid his high command,
> And trembled at the press!...

> Rise, Britain, rise! withstand their power,
> Now is the dread, the fated hour,
> To curse mankind or bless.
> The wolves, to make their sheep their prey
> Would lure the guardian dogs away,
> Whose barking kept the thieves at bay,
> O! guard the sacred Press!
> R GILMOUR
> (*BD*: 24 December 1817)

The Queen Caroline affair (1820–21) was a source of huge delight to radical satirists such as Wooler who used it to denounce the corruption of the monarchy and surely, the most sardonic example of news reporting and commentary on current events comes in one of the *Black Dwarf*'s poems on the death of Queen Caroline:

ON HEARING OF THE DEATH OF HER MAJESTY
Ah Me! what news is this I hear?
Alas? They say the *Queen* is dead!
Bless me! the *onions* will be dear;
For *tears* of *fashion* must be shed!
(*BD*: 2 December 1818)

Most often Wooler saved his most withering satire for the exchanges between the Black Dwarf himself and his correspondent, the Yellow Bonze in Japan. In a high parody of the exchanges common in the respectable press and journals of the time, we are offered a radical satire based on cross-cultural commentary between the two:

> LETTERS OF THE BLACK DWARF *From the* Black Dwarf *in London, to the Yellow Bonze at Japan*
> DANGER OF REASON TO THE POOR AND MIDDLING CLASSES ....But alas! high birth is no security for reason. That uncertain gift is not always *found* where it is *most wanted*; kings often lack it; and princes and princesses go without. We can but lament that heaven should so often have suffered common sense to wander among the *lower orders*, where it can be comparatively of no value. Why should the poor possess so *dangerous a quality as reason*? They were not born to *reason*, but to *labour*! Why then has providence given them reason to discern the faults and follies of those who were born above them?....Were I a senator, I would endeavour to remedy this evil. I would enact that no peasant should be born with the power of thought. I would levy a severe penalty upon every rational expression, uttered by one who had not at least five hundred a year, or a sinecure place (*BD*: 18 February 1818).

Parodies of trials had been popular and effective in radical terms between 1817 and 1819 but with the Six Acts there was even more scope to challenge the seditious and blasphemous prosecutions which filled the courts:

> The Trial of Mr Parliament for various acts of
> High Treason, Sedition and Swindling, and
> other Misdemeanours committed against the
> Majesty of the People (*BD*: 29 July 1818).

A parody of the well-known rhyme The House that Jack Built was published in the *Black Dwarf* in January 1818 on the acquittal of the radical pamphleteer Hone who had himself used the rhyme for satirical purposes:

> This is the verdict recorded and found,
> By the Jury unbiass'd, unpack'd and *unfrowned*
> That frighten'd the Judge so choleric and old,
> Who swore 'by the oath of his office' so bold,
> 'Twas an impious, blasphemous libel, and so,
> The man should be ruined ex-oficio,
> By the servant of servants who blustered so big,

With his ears in his hand and his wits in his wig;
To please the Ministers
Who hated the truth
That was told by the man
Who published the parodies.'

THE END OF THE DWARF

Even the heroic efforts of Wooler to invigorate the cause of Reform was exhausted by the declining fortune of radical papers in the wake of the increased taxes on and surveillance of the radical press after 1819 (Wood 1994: 13). He is writing from an apparent trough of despondency in the last copy of his paper in 1824 in his "Final Address":

> In ceasing his political labours, the Black Dwarf has to regret one mistake, and that a serious one. He commenced writing under the idea that there was a PUBLIC in Britain, and that public devotedly attached to the cause of parliamentary reform. This, it is but candid to admit, was an error (*BD*: 12 1824).

His despair is based on a recognition that, in order to succeed, any radical journalism needs to be able to depend on the support and political conviction of a radical readership. Without this political commitment of the people, radical journalism is an inadequate weapon.

The *Black Dwarf*'s radicalism lay as much in the disruptions and distortions of the textual conventions of journalism as in its radical commitment to popular causes. In this it demonstrates the ethical potential of textual play as a radical weapon and reminds us how the style and conventions of journalism can carry political and ethical weight as much as its content. Parody and satire are used to mock both the abuses of authority and the emptiness of much conventional journalism of the time. The *Black Dwarf* disrupts and plays with the Establishment's forms of journalism and in doing so invites a readership in formation to identify itself in this contestation and disruption of the established order as well as indicating ways of constructing a radical alternative constituency. Indeed, the pages of the *Black Dwarf* managed to link a range of radical constituencies: radical meetings, fundraising, information and public speaking found an expression amidst poetry, ballads, contributions from readers and the more dramatic carnival from the pen of Wooler himself.

The mixture of high and low culture characteristic of Wooler's periodical has been seen as intrinsic to the birth of modern journalism (Campbell, 2000: 40–53) but it was a commercially acceptable version of that hybrid which was to emerge over the nineteenth century as popular journalism (Conboy 2002). In the *Black Dwarf* we see a glimpse of a possible utopian alternative to the mainstream journalisic tradition which emerges with its ethical traditions in the nineteenth century.

Thompson was not as kind in his judgment of its political contribution to the emergence of an identifiable English working class, categorising it as a "mixture of heavy-handed satire and libertarian rhetoric" (Thompson 1963: 674–675). But despite this perspective on its limitations, Wooler's journal did provide an expanded ethical dimension for radical journalism through its textual experimentation. It gives a glimpse of a brief flowering of a utopian alternative engagement between journalism and popular ethics.

CONCLUSIONS

Parody and satire were nothing new in the English literary landscape but their deployment as part of a radical journalism was a powerful and provocative intervention. It may serve as a reminder that there are political questions to be asked of journalism's formats as well as of its content and that ethical concerns need to be addressed to both aspects of its output. It may also serve as a reminder of the potential of humour to reformulate certain established traditions within journalism and that entertainment need not be of the hollow and populist variety but might serve genuine political ends. At the start of the nineteenth century, the formats embodying the perspectives of propertied media ownership were becoming ever more sophisticated. The *Black Dwarf* exposed the limitations of journalism fixed within a capitalist system and offered a more radical and popular engagement through its textual experimentation.

REFERENCES

Altick, R. D. (1957) *The English Common Reader*, Chicago, Chicago University Press

Bakhtin, M. M. (1996) *The Dialogic Imagination*, (ed.) Holquist, M. (trans. Emerson C. and Holquist, M.), University of Texas Press

Calhoun, C. (1982) *The Question of Class Struggle: Social Foundations of Popular Radicalism During the Industrial Revolution*, Oxford, Basil Blackwell

Campbell K. (2000) "Journalistic Discourses and Constructions of Modern Knowledge", Brake, L., Bell, B. and Finkelstein, D. (eds) *Nineteenth Century Media and the Construction of Identities*, London, Palgrave pp 40-53

Conboy, M. (2002) *The Press and Popular Culture*, London, Sage

Conboy, M. (2004) *Journalism: A Critical History*, London, Sage

Frank, J. (1961) *The Beginnings of the English Newspaper*, Cambridge Mass., Harvard

University Press

Gilmartin, K. (1996) *Print Politics: The Press and Radical Opposition in Early Nineteenth Century England*, Cambridge, Cambridge University Press

Hendrix, R. (1976) "Popular Humour in the Black Dwarf", *Journal of British Studies*, Fall, Vol. 16 pp 108–128

Hollis, P. (1970) *The Pauper Press*, Oxford, Oxford University Press

Jones, S. (1997) "The Black Dwarf as Satiric Performance; or, the instabilities of the 'Public Square'", Behrendt, S.C. (ed) *Radicalism, Romanticism and the Press*, Wayne State University Press

Klancher, J.P. (1987) *The Making of English Reading Audiences 1790-1832*, Madison, University of Wisconsin Press

Mendle, M. (2001) "News and the pamphlet culture of mid-seventeenth century England", Dolley, B. and Baron, S. (eds) *The Politics of Information in Early Modern Europe*, London, Routledge

Thompson, E.P. (1979) *The Making of the English Working Class*, London, Penguin.

Wickwar, W. H. (1928) *The Struggle for the Freedom of the Press*, London, Allen and Unwin,

Wood, M. (1994) *Radical Satire and Print Culture 1790–1822*, Oxford, Clarendon Press

NOTE ON AUTHOR

Dr Martin Conboy is a Reader in Journalism Studies at the University of Sheffield. He is the author of numerous books and articles on the history of journalism including *The Press and Popular Culture* (2002) and *Journalism: A Critical History* (2004) and books on the analysis of the language of news media such as *Tabloid Britain: Constructing a Community Through Language* (2006) and *The Language of the News* (2007). He is on the editorial board of *Media History*, *Journalism Studies* and *Journalism: Theory, Practice and Criticism* and is the co-editor of a series of books entitled *Journalism*. Contact details: the Department of Journalism Studies, University of Sheffield, Minalloy House, Regent Street, Sheffield S1 3NJ. Email: martin.conboy@virgin.net.

PART 3

COMMUNICATION ETHICS
AND PEDAGOGY

14

Compromise and ethics in teaching abortion: A personal experience

Raphael Cohen-Almagor

The aim of this chapter is to analyse the concept of compromise through a discussion of teaching ethics in class. The discussion opens with some reflection on compromise. Next the complexity of abortion is addressed and I discuss my personal experience in teaching this issue in the United States. Some ideas are offered on strategies to teach complex ethical issues in class and the chapter ends with some question marks for further debate.

ON COMPROMISE

According to the *Oxford English Dictionary* "compromise" is a "settlement of a dispute by which each side gives up something it has asked for and neither side gets all it has asked for". The settlement may be achieved by consent reached by mutual concessions. It can be reached without any external interference or assistance, or by arbitration. In arbitration, the parties take their conflict to a third party, conceived by them as impartial, who tries to resolve the conflict through agreement. Here we may distinguish between *voluntary* and *compulsory* arbitration. Sometimes parties in conflict will decide to seek arbitration on their own initiative, e.g., a couple who wishes to separate outside the courts and seek arbitration to settle their dispute. In other times parties may commit themselves to arbitrate certain categories of issues. It fits into a previously established framework, and the parties may not choose whether or not to be included. They automatically find their case in arbitration (Schellenberg 1996: 195). This is the case, for instance, when a person buys a property with the obligations and the arbitration framework of the previous owner.

Compromise has preconditions. The discussion presupposes that some forms of communication and cooperation take place between the involved parties (notice that compromise requires some kind of cooperation, but not all forms of cooperation require compromise), and that the parties speak the same language, in the sense that they share some basic norms which form the grounds for potential understanding. Here I refer to the underpinning foundations of every democracy: the norms of respecting others and of not harming others. When divergences become so fundamental that they can no longer be compounded, then no compromise can be reached (Sabatier and Jenkins-Smith 1993). There is simply nothing to talk about.

FUNDAMENTAL BACKGROUND RIGHTS

A favourable condition for compromise is mutual respect. In compromise, interests are accommodated rather than regulated, and this accommodation should be inspired by the respect we feel for the autonomy of the other. When we are sensitive to the rights of the other, then we will prefer settlement to coercion, and we will be more willing to acknowledge the need for concessions in order to reach an agreement. Different types of conflict will generate different sorts of compromise, according to the nature of the diversity at issue, the content and context of the dispute, and the complexion of the groups involved. Whereas splitting the difference entails mutual concession, compromises over ideological and identity issues prove more challenging and require constructing a distinctive position to accommodate the various claims, values and ideals at stake (Bellamy 1999: 103-104).

The norm of respecting others is derived from the Kantian-deontological school, while the norm of not harming others is derived from the Millian school. Both were largely adopted by liberal democracies. Respect for a person means conceiving of the other as an end, rather than as a means to something. As Kant explains, rational beings are designated "persons" (to be distinguished from "things") because their nature indicates that they are ends in themselves. Such beings are thus objects of respect and, so far, restrict all arbitrary choice. Such beings are not merely subjective ends whose existence as a result of our action has a worth for us, but are objective ends, that is, beings whose existence in itself is an end. No other end can be substituted for such an end (Kant 1969: 52-53).

The Kantian ethics is based upon reflexive self-consciousness. It speaks of respecting people as rational beings, and of autonomy in terms of self-legislation. The ability to be motivated by reason alone is called by Kant the autonomy of the will, to be contrasted with the "heteronomy" of the action whose will is subject to external causes. An autonomous agent is someone who is able to overcome the promptings of all heteronomous counsels, such as those of self-interest, emotion and desire, should they be in conflict with reason. Only an autonomous being perceives genuine ends of action (as opposed to mere objects of desire), and only such a being deserves our esteem, as the embodiment of rational choice. The autonomy of the will, Kant argues, "is the sole principle of all moral laws, and of all duties which conform to them; on the other hand, heteronomy of the will not only cannot be the basis of any obligation, but is, on the contrary, opposed to the principle thereof, and to the morality of will". (Kant 1883: 169; Scruton 1982: 65).

The notion of obligation instructs us how to behave. According to Kant, an action has moral worth only if it is performed from a sense of duty (see Brandt 1964: 374-93). Duty rather than purpose is the fundamental concept of ethics. It is the practical unconditional necessity of action and, therefore, it holds for all rational beings. For that reason it can be a law for all human wills. Duty commands us to accept moral codes because they are just, regardless of the other's attitude toward them. This deontological ethics proscribes a set of actions, with the effect of constraining our range of options, not because the results will be useful, but because this set of actions is incompatible with the concept of justice. Transgression of the rights of others intends to make use of them merely as means, without considering that, as rational beings, they must always be esteemed at the same time as ends (Kant 1969: 54-55).

RESPECT FOR AUTONOMOUS HUMAN BEINGS

Thus the defence of personal liberties is founded on the assertion that we ought to respect others as autonomous human beings who exercise self-determination to live according to their life plans; we respect people as self-developing beings who are able to develop their inherent faculties as they choose, that is, to develop the capability they wish to develop, not every capability that they are blessed with. A person, for instance, may have the faculties to become someone like Florence Nightingale, but it is against her interest to develop them (Cohen-Almagor 1994: 40). A talented teacher who is married to a successful businessman with three children may decide to compromise and give up her job, and becomes a housewife upon realising that for various reasons she better stay at home for the sake of her family. She is knowingly sacrificing her job, realising that raising her children is more important to her than keeping her teaching interest.

In turn we respect people in order to help them realise what they want to be. Each individual is conceived as a source of claims against other persons, just because the resolution of the others is theirs, made by them as free agents. If we pursue the idea to its logical extreme, then to regard others with respect is to respect their decisions, because they are their decisions, regardless of our opinions of them. We simply assume that each of us holds that our own course of life has intrinsic value, at least for the individual, and we respect the individual's reasoning. This recognition may lead us to compromise when conflicting interests are at stake.

Ronald Dworkin regards the entire political morality, as resting on the single fundamental background right of everyone to human dignity and to equal concern and respect. By background rights, Dworkin means rights that provide a justification for political decisions by society in the abstract, without connecting them to any specific political institution. Dworkin implies that some rights are better viewed as universal, as applicable to every political framework, because they are essentially derived from the conception of people as human beings. Such is the right for equal concern and respect (Dworkin 1975: 1069-1071). This right may be morally applicable to any society, but Dworkin would agree that this right may not necessarily be morally convincing. That is, it may not necessarily be one that every society would wish to adopt. Indeed, the Respect for Others Argument can be said to underlie a liberal–democratic society and not just any society.[1]

TREATING PEOPLE WITH RESPECT

Treating people with concern means to treat them as human beings who may be furious and frustrated, who are capable of smiling and crying, while to treat them with respect is to treat them as human beings who are capable of forming and acting on intelligent conceptions of how their lives should be lived.[2] That is, respect for human beings involves the presupposition that others should be allowed to make their own decisions, based on their conception of what is good and just. Respecting a person results when you give credit to the other's ability for self-direction, acknowledging the other's competence to exercise discretion when deciding between available options. Accordingly, each person is viewed as speaking from that person's point of view, having perceived interests in his or her own way. We may be asked to give our opinion, or decide to express our view anyway; nevertheless, we recognise the other's right to make choices. We recognise that the final decision rests with the agent. This so long as persons operate within the area of tolerance, so long as they do not harm others. We accept the idea that every person should be respected and treated as a moral agent whose views can be discussed and disputed, as a person who is capable of changing opinions if rational grounds are provided.

The Harm Principle which qualifies the Respect for Others Argument holds that every person should be able to pursue that person's conception of the good as long as the person does not harm others. Liberals often accept this principle and see it as necessary for prescribing limitations on tolerance. Here they follow J. S. Mill's theory as formulated in his *On Liberty* (Mill 1948).

Mill argued that, as human beings should be free to form opinions and to voice them without reserve, so freedom of action is a precondition for the development of individuality. Without liberty of action we are not able to choose between different paths of action, nor can we experiment with different plans of life: 'As it is useful that while mankind are imperfect there should be different opinions, so it is that there should be different experiments of living' (Mill 1948: 114-115).

Mill assumed that we can evaluate the rightness and wrongness of an action by considering its consequences, believing that the morality of an action depends on the consequences it is likely to produce (Mill 1973: 386; Cohen-Almagor 1997a: 141-176; Cohen-Almagor 1997b: 131-152). Since we are to judge before acting, then we must weigh the probable results of our doing, given the conditions of the situation. The general usage of 'harm' includes in its reference any or all of a miscellany of disliked mental states (disgust, shame, hurt, anxiety etc.) (Feinberg 1985: 1-26). Individuals should not harm one another unless they do it for a justified reason: self-defence.

INDIVIDUAL AT THE CENTRE OF LIBERAL IDEOLOGY

Liberal ideology places the individual as the centre: all liberal reasoning derives from seeing the individual as the focus of analysis, and all its reasoning is aimed at the advancement and development of the individual which, in turn, would result in the progress of society. The tradition evolving from the philosophical thought of John Locke (1632-1704), Thomas Paine (1737-1809), Alexis de Tocqueville (1805-1859), John Stuart Mill (1806-1873) and, in our time, John Rawls and Ronald Dworkin, places the individual, in contrast to the collective, in the centre of analysis, viewing the state as a mere instrument to serve the interests of the individual. The liberal state is conceptualised as a means of protecting society from external attacks, a framework regulating the implementation of the law for the prosperity of the citizens, a sophisticated tool to ensure individual rights.

Thus my concern is with liberal democracies which perceive human beings as ends and which respect autonomy and variety. The arguments are relevant to other countries, but because non-democratic countries do not accept the basic liberal principles, because their principles do not encourage autonomy, individualism, pluralism, and openness, and their behaviour is alien to the concepts of human dignity and caring, one can assume that the discussion will fall on deaf ears. Non-liberal societies, based on authoritative conceptions and principles, deserve a separate analysis. Their willingness to compromise is highly constricted. If at all they opt for tactical compromises, without giving up their real ends (Cohen-Almagor 1994: 37-38).

It should be further noted that a fundamental question of moral legitimacy precedes the act of compromise. The issue is whether compromise is compatible or incompatible with integrity and with justice in some sense. Compromise should be considered and reached according to the content of the demands, with regard to their substance and meaning. One contested and heated issue for which some people in the United States are even willing to kill is abortion.

ABORTION: THE ISSUES

When the United States Supreme Court grappled with the highly intricate issue of abortion, it seems the justices wished to make a genuine compromise between the pro-life camp and the pro-choice camp. Writing for the court, Justice Blackmun argued that the right of personal privacy includes the abortion decision, but this right is not unqualified and must be considered against important state interests in regulation. The court's decision leaves the state free to place increasing restrictions on abortion as the period of pregnancy lengthens. For the stage prior to approximately the end of the first trimester, the abortion decision must be left to the medical judgment of the pregnant woman's attending physician. For the stage subsequent to approximately the end of the first trimester, the state, in promoting its interest in the health of the mother, may, if it chooses, regulate the abortion procedure in ways that are reasonably related to maternal health. Finally, the court argued, for the stage subsequent to viability, the state in promoting its interest in the potentiality of human life may, if it chooses, regulate, and even proscribe, abortion except where it is necessary, in appropriate medical judgment, for the preservation of the life or health of the mother (*Roe v. Wade* 1973).

However, abortion is one of those issues on which it might be extremely difficult, even impossible, to reach a compromise. *Roe v. Wade* attracted criticisms from both pro-life and pro-choice activists. The former argue that the decision effectively allows the murdering of innocent children, while the latter assert that the decision does not give due weight to wishes of the woman who is solely responsible for what is inside her body. The state should not interfere. Indeed, a person who believes in the sanctity of life no matter what would principally object to abortion, euthanasia and capital punishment. People who take issue with this position may seek a compromise, trying to persuade the opponent to recognise some considerations that, to their mind, play a major part in such grave decisions. For instance, with regard to abortion they would try to persuade that abortion might be available if conducted at an early stage of pregnancy and when the reason is compelling, say rape.

With regard to euthanasia they would insist that it should be available when the patient voluntarily asks for that, without any pressure, the prognosis for some recovery is nil, and the patient is suffering miserably. And regarding capital punishment they may argue, quite persuasively so they think, that when vicious serial killers are concerned, and where ample and unmistaken evidence from different sources is available to prove the killer's guilt beyond a reasonable doubt, then capital punishment may be considered as an option. To push the point further, they would ask the sanctity-of-life believer to consider the case of S.S. officers who brutally murdered Jews and gypsies during World War Two. Would you then see that even your staunch principle has exceptions?

Yet it might be the case that all arguments would fail to persuade the sanctity-of-life believer. Sanctity of life is conceived in absolutist terms, i.e., it means for her exactly that: sanctity of life, period. This viewpoint upholds an unqualified ban on all forms of life termination. This issue is taken outside the realm of politics. The only power who may take life is the almighty, he and he alone (vitalists will speak of nature instead of God). People should not decide for themselves such issues, and no considerations are ever compelling enough to persuade otherwise.

To explicate this further, suppose that a suffering patient asks her doctor to terminate her life; however, the doctor belongs to those who believe in the sanctity of life and is unable to comply. All he can offer is palliative care. Again, no compromise is possible in this case. The patient will continue to live and will not see palliation as a solution, certainly not as some form of compromise, but as something that is imposed on her, for she feels life as such is imposing on her (Cohen-Almagor 2002: 111-126). Therefore, we need to recognise that not on all issues it is possible to reach a compromise. Some issues for some people are black and white, or in computer language 1 and 0, and there is nothing in between, no bridges, no scales, no meeting grounds.

PERSONAL EXPERIENCE

A few years ago I taught a graduate seminar titled "The right to live in dignity and the right to die in dignity" at an American school of law. The first part of the seminar dealt with beginning of life issues, mainly with abortion. The second part dealt with end of life issues, mainly with euthanasia. At that point of time I have been teaching this course for eight years at two Israeli law schools. I was well aware of the sensitivity of the issues, and of the possibility that one or more of the students in the class might have personal experience that might obscure their ability for careful reasoning. A student who had to undergo abortion can be expected to have strong feelings about the issue, and justifiably so.

Teaching abortion in that specific American law school was different from any previous experience I had. Reading included the following: *Roe v. Wade,* op. cit.; Thomson (1971: 47-66); Dworkin (1993); Finnis (1973: 117-145); Sumner (1974: 163-181); Wertheimer (1973: 67-95). But despite my candid efforts to present the complexities of the issue, the atmosphere in class was one-sided as five strong-minded, articulate feminist women dominated the conversations (there were 16 students in the seminar). They advanced pro-choice reasoning and dismissed all counter-arguments as "fundamentalist", "religious" and/or "illiberal".

For them, abortion was a woman's right and any reason was good for the act even at advanced stage of pregnancy. Thus having a Caribbean cruise overrides pregnancy and if a woman is determined to go on a scheduled cruise she has the right to terminate unexpected pregnancy that interferes with the joyful plan. Interestingly, the men in the class took a silent backseat position and hardly contributed to the discussions. To somewhat balance this one-sided voice in class I assigned a couple of students to present the main controversies. A female student (I shall call her Judy) was supposed to present John Finnis's conservative arguments in class, and a male student (Rick) to present Judith Jarvis Thomson's feminist arguments.

When the presentation time came, Judy rose to speak and to my surprise she began to explain what Thomson had argued. I thought at first that Judy was using Thomson as a point of departure, to better understand the context in which Finnis's arguments were made. But no, this was not the case. Judy started with Thomson and finished with Thomson. When I realised that Judy had no intention to present Finnis it was too late to stop her, so I had to let her complete her presentation. Then Rick rose to speak and he presented Finnis. This switch was done without consulting with me, without my prior knowledge or consent.

After class, I called Judy and Rick and asked for some explanation; maybe they did not understand my instruction. Well, they perfectly understood but, as Judy explained: "I began to read Finnis and could not stand him. Therefore, I phoned Rick and suggested that we switch the reading. Rick did not mind." Indeed, Rick confirmed that he did not mind. Well, I did, a great deal. The entire purpose of the assignment was for Judy to at least comprehend Finnis's arguments and not simply to dismiss the other side as "chauvinist" or "ridiculous". Judy did not have the mental energies or the will to deal with views that were contradictory to hers. Should have I insisted that Judy assume upon herself another assignment in which she had to present pro-life stance? I did not wish to enter into even more troubled water and decided to avoid such a confrontation. Rick, I should say, was very passive also in this exchange, like most, if not all, men in class when abortion was at stake.

PRESENTING PROPAGANDA

I then decided to present my students a film called *Silent Scream*, a propagandist plea prepared by a pro-life organisation.[3] This film is highly tainted, does not pretend to present both sides of the controversy and consequently it attracts lots of critique. But it shows an actual abortion and I thought that people who advocate abortion so easily should at least know what it involves. I asked the Law School Library to order the film but to my complete astonishment the head librarian declined my request on the ground that the film lacks educational merit. I contested this ruling and provided counter arguments regarding the importance of the First Amendment and academic freedom, to no avail. The scope of tolerance does not extend to a pro-life ideological film at this school of law. I should clarify that limitation of resources was not an issue. In my orientation tour of the library I was told the memorable sentence, which I have never heard before (and hope to hear in the future): "We don't have any shortage of resources."

Some time later I told of this exchange with the head librarian to two prominent First Amendment scholars, Ken Karst and Robert Post. Both could not believe that an American law school library refused to order a film for class instruction on such grounds. In Israel, a country that does not have First Amendment, Bill of Rights or even a special law that protects free expression, this had never happened to me. Since 1985 I have been teaching in several universities and none to date had ever refused to order an item to the library because it lacked educational merit. The assumption always is that I have valid reasons behind my requests.

I was able to find a copy of *Silent Scream* and to show it in class after providing a warning about its highly tainted content and allowing students who wished not to watch it to exit the classroom. All students chose to remain in the room and most of them did not appreciate my efforts to counterbalance the discussion with this film, and subsequently asked me to show a pro-choice film in class. I said that the class was pro-choice anyway, and I did not see any point showing such a film, given that we had a tight schedule and the pro-choice stance had been presented in elaborate fashion for several weeks. A compromise was reached that I would organise for those who are still interested to see the film a room with the necessary equipment (TV and VCR) immediately after the seminar. As expected, the wide majority of those who remained to watch the film appreciated, even enjoyed, the pro-choice message.

When the semester was over, I told my host at the law school of my experience in teaching bioethics in his institution. He caught his head and said: "I should have warned you. There are three issues that a white male professor should not teach in American law schools: abortion, pornography and race." A female professor may teach the first two; an African-American may teach the third.

CONCLUSION

Compromise is not only a matter of two or more parties dealing with a common subject of concern or resources. Sometimes a compromise is made by one side with regard to its aims, in deciding how to allocate the available means and in determining priorities. Compromise, then, often is required between the different demands, needs, and ideas that are to be pursued and satisfied, and between what is believed in and the circumstances. In short, people compromise between the "ought" and the "is", between what they aspire to, and what is given in reality. In this connection the given circumstances, conflicting goals, scarcity of resources, uncertainty, complexity of the subject involved, availability of means, and pressure precipitated by time may induce a party to compromise in making a decision.

If conducted in the genuine sense of the word, compromise yields two winners, i.e. the two sides to the dispute. Compromise lasts as long as the parties communicate and maintain trust and good will between them. They need not feel that they sacrificed part of their autonomy. I compromised by showing the pro-choice film after class. Was it a satisfactory compromise? Should I had shown it as part of class to satisfy my students' wishes? Was it a good idea to insist on showing *Silent Scream*, knowing that the film might spark negative reactions? Maybe I should have compromised more with my pedagogic conscience and leave the contentious film outside the class.

Yet I am still convinced that liberal democracies should enhance and promote civic education – which includes discussions on the merits of tolerance, based on respect for others, and of compromise, based on mutual genuine concessions between different groups of society.

This chapter formed part of a large-scale, multi-disciplinary research project on The Scope of Tolerance that began in 1997 and was carried out in the United States, Canada, the United Kingdom and Israel. Grant support came from Johns Hopkins University, the Fulbright Foundation, the Rockefeller Foundation, the British Council and the Canadian Government.

NOTES

1. I am not suggesting that currently widespread agreement exists in constitutional democracies that all people should be accorded the same rights and opportunities. Unfortunately this is not the case. I think, however, that this is one of the major ideas of liberalism and that liberal–democracies should strive to apply it. I add, sharing Jean Hampton's view, that we have an obligation as philosophers committed to arguing with, and thus respecting, our fellow human beings to persuade opponents of this idea and thus to change their minds: c.f. Hampton (1989: 813)
2. Dworkin's terms "concern" and "respect" signal the values of well-being and autonomy, respectively: we ought to show equal concern for each individual's good and equal respect for the individual's autonomy: c.f. Buchanan (1989: 879).
3. http://www.silentscream.org/, accessed on 29 May 2005

REFERENCES

Bellamy, R. (1999) *Liberalism and Pluralism*, London and New York, Routledge

Brandt, R.B. (1964) "The Concepts of Obligation and Duty", *Mind*, LXXIII pp 374-393

Buchanan, Allen E. (1989) "Assessing the Communitarian Critique of Liberalism", *Ethics*, Vol. 99

Cohen-Almagor, R. (1994) *The Boundaries of Liberty and Tolerance: The Struggle Against Kahanism in Israel*, Gainesville, FL, the University Press of Florida

Cohen-Almagor, R. (1997a) "Ends and Means in J.S. Mill's Utilitarian Theory", *The Anglo-American Law Review*, Vol. 26 (2) pp141-174

Cohen-Almagor, R. (1997b) "Why Tolerate? Reflections on the Millian Truth Principle", *Philosophia,* Vol. 25, Nos 1-4 pp131-152

Cohen-Almagor, R. (2002) "Dutch Perspectives on Palliative Care in the Netherlands", *Issues in Law and Medicine*, Vol. 18, No1 pp111-126

Dworkin, R. (1975) "Hard Cases", *Harvard Law Review*, Vol. 88 pp 1069-1071

Dworkin, R.(1993) *Life's Dominion*, New York, Knopf

Feinberg, J. (1985) *Offense to Others*, New York, Oxford University Press

Finnis, J. (1973) "The Rights and Wrongs of Abortion", *Philosophy & Public Affairs*, Vol. 2, No.2 pp 117-145

Hampton, J. (1989) "Should Political Philosophy Be Done without Metaphysics?", *Ethics*, Vol. 99

Kant, I. (1883) *Critique of Practical Reason* (trans. Abbott, T.K.), London, Longmans, Green and Co

Kant, I. (1969) *Foundations of the Metaphysics of Morals*, (trans: Beck, Lewis White), Indianapolis, Ind, Bobbs-Merrill

Mill, J.S. (1948) *Utilitarianism, Liberty, and Representative Government*, London, J. M. Dent (Everyman's edition)

Mill, J.S. (1973) Bentham, in *Dissertations and Discussions*, New York: Haskell House Publishers, Vol. 1

Roe v. Wade 410 U.S. 113, 93 S. Ct. 705 (1973)

Sabatier, Paul A. and Jenkins-Smith, Hank C. (eds) (1993) *Policy Change and Learning*, Boulder, Co., Westview Press

Schellenberg, James A. (1996) *Conflict Resolution,* Albany, NY, State University of New York Press

Scruton, R. (1982) *Kant*, Oxford, Oxford University Press

Sumner, L.W. (1974) "Toward a Credible View of Abortion", *Canadian Journal of Philosophy,* Vol. 4, No. 1 pp 163-181

Thomson, Judith J. (1971) "A Defense of Abortion", *Philosophy and Public Affairs*, Vol. 1, No. 1 pp 47-66

Wertheimer, R. (1973) "Understanding the Abortion Argument", *Philosophy and Public Affairs*, Vol. 2, No. 2 pp 67-95

NOTE ON AUTHOR

Raphael Cohen-Almagor is Professor and Chair in Politics, The University of Hull. Presently he is a Fellow at The Woodrow Wilson Center for Scholars,

Washington DC. Author of *The Boundaries of Liberty and Tolerance* (1994; Hebrew 1994, 1999), *The Right to Die in Dignity* (2001), *Speech, Media and Ethics* (2001, 2005; Turkish 2002), *Euthanasia in the Netherlands* (2004), *The Scope of Tolerance* (2006), and *The Democratic Catch* (2007, Hebrew). Editor of several other books, among them *Liberal Democracy and the Limits of Tolerance: Essays in Honor and Memory of Yitzhak Rabin* (2000), and *Challenges to Democracy: Essays in Honour and Memory of Isaiah Berlin* (2000). He also wrote two poetry books (in Hebrew): *Middle Eastern Shores* (1993), and *Voyages* (2007). Phone (USA): 202-691-4004; fax (USA): 202-691-4001. Email: R.Cohen-Almagor@hull.ac.uk; Web: http://www.hull.ac.uk/rca.

15

The importance of caring: Ethics, communication and higher education

John Strain

The current debate over professional ethics in the curriculum points towards two important questions for higher education. The first is whether and why the teaching of professional ethics is important across all disciplines in higher education, not just communication studies. Secondly, it raises the question of what is common and what is distinctive about professional ethics across different professions and disciplines. Both of these questions are considered in this chapter which highlights the importance of communication in the ethics of all professions and identifies the scope for collaboration across the different professions.

INTRODUCTION – ETHICS AND COMMUNICATION

In launching the Great Curriculum Debate, Rogerson (2004) drew our attention to the need to include communication ethics in the undergraduate curriculum in Higher Education. Providing qualifications to support communication as an ethical discipline is one of ICE's four aims, one which includes the teaching of communication ethics to students in higher education.

Interestingly, many of the issues highlighted by Rogerson are important issues for professional ethics in many other disciplines. Getting the balance right between the generic core, common to all disciplines, and the discipline-specific contexts and practices is a challenge common to many disciplines and professions. Steering a course between the need for a well founded theoretical and philosophical base and the need to engage with the practical questions that arise in each discipline is another common challenge. Again, finding the delicate balance between universalism and relativism is another common task.

Alisdair MacIntyre (1981) pointed out that a set of universal ethical principles that is no particular people's principles is not a set of principles at all. Claims to universal principles can easily be a mask to excuse one particular group imposing their ethics on another. But on the other hand, ethics is a different quest from the pursuit of personal whims or even aesthetic judgement. We are called on to account for our actions and our ethical justification of them in ways that make sense to others. Finding answers to these difficult but important questions might benefit from bringing people interested in teaching applied and professional ethics together.

Teaching communication ethics can be seen as one strand of a bigger story that professional ethics needs to be a core component in the higher education curriculum more generally. Doctors, nurses and psychologists have included ethics within their curricula for many years. More recently, engineers, computing professionals, bio-scientists have all taken steps to include ethics in the curricula, frequently encouraged by professional associations who insist on ethics in the curricula as a condition of accreditation. The various learning and teaching support networks of the Higher Education Funding Council's Higher Education Academy all provide support for the teaching of professional ethics.

But communication ethics has an importance in this bigger story, an importance beyond simply being a single discipline component of ethics in higher education. Ethics, more generally, is about the communication of ourselves to others, the communication of our whole selves with all we bring along with it: our sincerity, our most deeply held assumptions and beliefs, our inclinations and our actions. The communication of ourselves as professional people to clients, customers or a readership is an activity that figures in every domain of professional ethics and is critically related to a proper understanding of communication.

Language provides another special link between communication and ethics. The articulation of ethics is not just about the content of what is communicated but about the manner in which it is said. How we say it makes a difference. This is not to give justification to spin rather than substance. It is to recognise that very often we only discover what is ethically important through conversations in which the quality of human relationships needs to be sufficient to sustain a particular quality of the conversation.

Communication ethics and the teaching of ethics more generally in higher education have important contributions to make to each other. This chapter describes a rationale for teaching ethics in higher education and an agenda for collaboration by those involved in teaching ethics within different disciplines.

WHY STUDY ETHICS IN HIGHER EDUCATION?
SMALLER ORGANISATIONS NEED ETHICALLY 'SAVVY' PEOPLE

Increasingly graduates enter an employment market where the large organisations of the past form a much smaller part of the total. Downsizing, business process engineering, supply chain re-organisation have all had, for good or ill, traumatic effects on the pattern of employing organisations. As Handy (1996) reminds us, people are no longer likely to spend their careers in the large organisations of the past; and they have responded by being less prepared to commit themselves to organisations for long periods. One consequence of the rise of Small and Medium-sized Enterprises (SMEs) as a proportion of the total number of employers in Britain is that large organisations are no longer there to serve as role models for how people should behave at work. Hence it will be necessary for young employees to develop a "savoir faire" about their employment, about its terms and conditions of employment and to be more able to articulate their own values and principles as they join in the work of new, younger companies.

So one reason why there is a case for ethics being taught in Higher Education is that graduates will need to be empowered as ethically responsible agents in the world of work more quickly than they were hitherto. The changing pattern of emerging technologies, organisations and work makes it ever more pressing to enrich what is taught in Higher Education with an ethical dimension.

BUSINESS NEEDS ETHICS

There is increasing pressure from companies themselves for graduates to be articulate in the issues of business ethics. Recent concern over the sourcing of textiles supplied to large European retailers such as Marks and Spencers highlighted the sensitivity people feel over these issues and the need for companies to respond to it. Sheena Carmichael (2001) reports that in a survey conducted in 2000, three quarters of UK companies had a code of conduct and 62 per cent of respondents from FTSE 350 companies felt that ethical policies were a priority. These are indications of a concern with ethics in business. They do not necessarily indicate that all is well. The same authors points out that bullying and discrimination are frequently tolerated, employees are under pressure to do what they consider wrong to meet targets and safety standards are frequently compromised.

If this is an exaggeration, then it points to the success of having standards. If it understates the problem, it points to the need for standards. Either way, there is a case for ethical frameworks to be considered in the education of our future professionals. But standards alone are insufficient. For ethics is not just about conformance to standards. It is about the criteria by which standards are judged to be good ones or not and about whether or not it would be virtuous to apply a particular standard in a particular circumstance. Students need therefore to be invited to explore the nature of ethics itself.

ETHICS GOES BEYOND THE BOTTOM LINE

The importance of understanding the nature of ethics reminds us of the danger of relying on "utilitarian" type of arguments for why ethics is worth studying in Higher Education – that doing ethics is good because it makes us richer, happier or better organised. There are deeper reasons why it is worth investing in ethics, reasons that go to the heart of Higher Education. The Dearing review of Higher Education defined the aim of HE as that of "sustaining a learning society". Its four main purposes are to:

- inspire and enable individuals to develop their capabilities to the highest potential levels throughout life so that they grow intellectually, are well equipped for work, can contribute effectively to society and achieve personal fulfilment;
- increase knowledge and understanding for their own sake and to foster their application to the benefit of the economy and society;
- serve the needs of an adaptable, sustainable, knowledge-based economy at local, regional and national levels;
- play a major role in shaping a democratic, civilised, inclusive society.

Encouraging and equipping HE students to become ethically responsible agents in their lives and work is valuable because it will contribute to all of these.

John Henry Newman, in his magisterial *The Idea of a University* (1855), lamented the fact that the English language had no word to describe intellectual well-being in the way that "health" is used with reference to physical or mental well being, and virtue is used with reference to our moral well-being. Talent, ability, genius, he suggested, are properties of the raw materials with which intellectual well-being is achieved, rather than descriptions of the achievement itself. When the outcomes of intellectual well-being are considered, wisdom is important but somewhat limited to matters of judgement and conduct.

Knowledge is a product of the process of enquiry, but is still not the end product of education. Somewhat confusingly, Newman used the term "philosophy" to describe what it was that an educated person had, qua being educated. What Newman meant by philosophy was clarity of thought, wisdom to choose well, power to evaluate, the ability to creatively develop and justify the criteria by which to evaluate that which is judged. It included the ability to be logical, to be imaginative, and to make use of memory. Becoming a moral agent is part of this process.

THE POSTMODERN UNIVERSITY

But universities have changed considerably since Newman's time. The monopoly they once enjoyed in knowledge generation and dissemination has now disappeared. New networks of knowledge generation have emerged in which universities are partners rather than sole providers. More than 2,000 books on business management are now published each year, authored by people working in industries and consultancies in which the role of the traditional academic is minimal.

There is a further malaise within the modern university that goes deeper than its loss of monopoly. All our propositions, theories, institutions and practices are now radically contested. This complexity goes beyond the mere extent of the challenges to what is known. These new challenges comprise part of what Delanty (1988) has called "hypercomplexity". It arises in part from the demise of any single set of authoritative institutions in knowledge. Ronald Barnett (2000) goes further and uses the term "supercomplexity" to describe the present condition of universities regarding knowledge. His point is that the very frameworks for making the world intelligible are now in dispute and there is no secure framework by which we can assess truthful propositions. Reality, it would seem, has caught up with the postmodern philosophers.

It is not the intention here to engage philosophically in these claims about the demise of knowledge, except to point out that there seems be a contradiction inherent in the most radical of the postmodern claims. The claim that there can never be any universal yardstick of truth sounds remarkably like the sort of general claim that the radical postmodernists are so eager to condemn in others. But there is a need to face up to the fact of postmodernism in the world we inhabit; particularly perhaps, because universities, in their traditional role of scrutinising all claims to knowledge, have contributed to it. The question that seems important to ask is: What is the responsibility of the university in helping people develop defensible accounts of themselves and their activities in the post–modern world? What responsibility has the university to enable individuals to prosper and grow well amidst this supercomplexity? And what are the implications of these responsibilities for the education of our future graduates?

IMPLICATIONS FOR HIGHER EDUCATION

Much of what teachers might need to do in this new era will be concerned with the development of students as human beings within networks and communities, local, regional and global. Students will prosper in this era if they can understand themselves and if they can understand others and form wholesome relationships with them. There are particular skills that will be needed to cope with the uncertainty of the forms of relationship that will emerge at work. Organisational skills and teamworking skills will be important as will the ability to make good relationships, friendships, with people at work within complex networks.

The term "interpersonal skills" is sometimes used for all these, but the term "skill" can be overworked. Skill suggests a subservience to an intended outcome. It reflects the power of what Habermas (1978) and others have called technical or instrumental reason that we have inherited from the Enlightenment of the eighteenth century. Barnett (1994) has warned of the dangers of this when he writes:

> Higher education is being locked into a Weberian iron cage of prescriptive rationality, of ends and of operationalism....in its various forms – bureaucratic, purposive, strategic and technocratic.... Instrumental reason....[has become]..the dominant mode of reason.....Instead of engaging with each other and with the world in mutual interaction, we end up by always having an eye to the main chance and by getting out of our transactions with each other and with the world what we can get away with.

If the demand of the new era for students to be able to engage with a host of new organisational and personal relationships is to be taken seriously, then our educational endeavours will need to be more explicitly moral than the word "skill" suggests. In his review of UK Higher Education, Lord Dearing pointed out the importance of key skills of communication and "learning to learn" and of cognitive skills such as an understanding of methodologies. But as Blake et al. (1998) point out, if students are really to learn how to listen to others in seminars, to give each other space, neither dominating nor being dominated by others, this would seem to be as much about developing moral qualities and virtues, as skills. Learning to communicate is something to which we bring the whole of ourselves: our sincerity, commitment, personal values and virtues.

It follows that the demands of the new technological era will place a greater, not lesser demand upon us as educators to help develop our students as moral agents. It cannot be reduced to skills. The skilled doctor, as Plato reminded us, also makes an ideal poisoner.

SENSITIVITY TO THE RELIGIOUS CONTEXT

In a society of increasingly diverse ethnic groups, religions and spiritual resources and journeys, it will be important in creating learning opportunities in ethics in HE to be open to the relationships which are important to people between their religious faith and their conduct, whilst at the same time being open to those of no religious faith. Ethics, like politics, is an intrinsically contested activity. So there is a need to tread a careful path between those who would see ethics as so prescripted that no analysis is needed; and those who would exclude all reference to the dependencies that have been claimed between people's beliefs, religious or otherwise, and people's conduct. Ethics in Higher Education needs to draw from all the major religious and intellectual traditions, and serve the learning journeys of people of all religious faiths and none.

AN AGENDA FOR COLLABORATION

Having identified a rationale for teaching ethics in general in HE, the question arises as to how educators might collaborate in the teaching of ethics across different professional disciplines (Strain 2004). One possibility might be to collaborate in identifying what is distinctive about ethics in particular disciplinary practices and what is transferable across different disciplines. This might be addressed by exploring the ways in which common ethical concepts figure slightly differently across the professions and disciplines.

Broadly my thesis here is that three particular concepts: caring for people, knowledge and design, all figure necessarily as common features in the ethics across different professional practices. But the precise way in which these concepts relate together provide for the variety and difference between different professional practices.

CARING FOR PEOPLE, KNOWLEDGE AND DESIGN

Noddings (2003) proposes an ethic of caring in which relationships between people, not individual people themselves, have an ontological primacy. Noddings wrote as an educationalist rather than as a healthcare professional but the ethics of care has been taken up with some enthusiasm within nursing by, amongst others, Benner and Wrubel (1989) and Johnstone (1994). Part of what I want to suggest is that caring for people is common to all professions but the mode in which care for people is expressed is unique to each professional practice.

All professions are concerned with offering some service intended to benefit a client. In less utilitarian terms, we might say that some activity is conducted which the client has good reason to value. For professions are neither about harming people nor acting indifferently towards the interests of clients. To that extent there is some relationship of care between professional and client, a relationship which might be guarded, or not, through various legal embodiments such as duties of care in common law or by contractual obligations of care.

But there is clearly more to being a professional than caring for another in a relationship. What distinguishes a professional relationship from a marriage relationship or a close friendship is that the relationship is bounded by a particular domain of practice and by a body of well-founded knowledge associated with that practice. A nurse, journalist, doctor, architect or school teacher has something to profess in the relationship with a client and the appropriateness of how a professional acts is in part determined by the well-founded-ness of this knowledge. I use the term "well-founded" here to resist any particular purchase into "scientific" or "positivistic" notions of knowledge. But at the same time nurses, doctors, journalists and architects must "know what they are talking about" in a manner beyond that demanded of armchair theorists and people on the Clapham omnibus.

The relationship between a professional's knowledge and the expression of care is often far from straightforward. Frequently, a doctor or nurse will take actions when there is very little knowledge of, or evidence for, the efficacy of the action in the particular circumstance. So care is not expressed simply by the exercise of knowledge. But experience and recognition of the relative risks of acting or taking no action are all deemed to count in the exercise of professional judgement. And they are what frequently distinguishes professional action from the actions of caring people in the community.

The approach to knowledge taken by professionals is not quite the same as the approach taken by scientists or scholars. Scientists or scholars may be content that knowledge adds to (or perhaps replaces) existing theory or adds to the ways in which it is possible for people to comprehend phenomena. But for the professional, there is a more fundamental question: how can this knowledge help this client in this circumstance? There is some artefact, some process that needs to be designed for a client that is somehow "fit for purpose" in relation to the client. This suggests a third key concept in what defines the professional: her or his concern to design something, an event, an artefact or a process which benefits the client and addresses the circumstance in which the client finds her or himself.

As well as identifying care, knowledge and design as key components of professional practice, there can also be identified a number of relationships between caring, knowledge and design which are common to all professionals. If whatever it is that the professional designs for the client is to address the client's circumstances, then some process of communication is necessary. Communication has a bearing on care and on knowledge. If the client is to place adequate trust in the professional to expose sufficient of his or her own vulnerable self for this communication to take place, then a sufficient relationship of care is required. The outcome of this communication for the professional needs to provide some basis for selecting, choosing or deciding upon whatever is to be designed for the client, based on well-founded knowledge. Thus communication, two-way communication, is a link between care and both knowledge and design.

Another relationship between caring and knowledge concerns the process or journey of learning that takes place within the client. A patient's relationship with a nurse is in part a relationship of learning in which the client comes to understand the characteristics of, constraints upon, and opportunities for their own journeys of health, facilitated by the nurse or perhaps a doctor. A client's relationship with a solicitor is in part a learning journey for the client about the characteristics of the client's circumstances in regards to law, the constraints upon these circumstances and opportunities for the future.

The professional is thus an agent of other people's learning. What links the professor with the professional is that knowledge is professed in a way that others learn from it, either in the formal sense of the classroom, in the case of teacher, or through the process of understanding how one's needs and aspirations might be met by an artefact or process, the wisdom of adopting the artefact or process being grounded in knowledge. Both the architect and computing engineer begin with some notion of someone else's needs or aspirations.

The owners of these needs and aspirations, the clients or patients go through some process of learning about how their aspirations can be realised. For a teacher of science, an important aspect of how knowledge figures in his/her professional life is a respect due to the sheer facticity of things, things which are the case regardless of our feelings about, or our perception of them. But for a teacher of poetry an epistemology which stresses and helps articulate a child's response to a poem rather than a set of facts about the poem, may be particularly important.

These three concepts: caring for people, designing something for people and enlightening people through an interaction with knowledge are not altogether independent. The design of a building, process or product in seeking to realise the client's aspirations will often need to respect the laws of physics, mathematics or chemistry. An intrinsic component of caring for people will need to be sensitive to the learning journeys that patients or clients make when they articulate their needs.

VARIATIONS WITHIN THE THEMES

The three themes of care, design and knowledge provide a canvas upon which many variations are possible for different professions. For some professions, particularly in healthcare, to care for persons means to hold them in an "unconditional positive regard", to use Carl Rogers words (1961). It reflects a commitment to the primacy of the perspective of those being cared in a relationship in which the well-being of the person cared for is paramount. This is not an understanding of "caring" which would come naturally to a consulting engineer or a computing engineer. But the codes of conduct of both these professions are quite incompatible with any idea that the client is not cared for or cared about.

Amongst the seventeen rules in the Code of Conduct for Members of the British Computer Society, the first rule specifies the due care and diligence in accordance with the relevant authority's requirements, and the interests of system users that are to be safeguarded in the design of a computing system. Now, within the healthcare profession, and nursing in particular, caring for people has emerged as a defining component of professional identity. But as Hewitt (2002: 434) remarks, drawing too close a link between ethics and caring risks conveying the suggestion that nurses are the only ethically oriented group in contact with patients. Doctors, healthcare professionals outside nursing as much as engineers and teachers all articulate some concept of care for people in their expressions of professional identity.

A clearer understanding of how care, design and knowledge for the professional might be gained by considering some examples of the different ways in which professionals care for clients. A nurse might see caring for a patient as demanding an almost exclusive focus and empathy on a patient's expression of pain. But caring for a patient entails a commitment to finding a remedy, a therapy, a way forward, all of which entail design and all of which must be well founded in knowledge. Where as all three, care, design and knowledge are important there is something natural about regarding a nurse as someone who focuses primarily on care, secondarily on design, and lastly on knowledge. But even here there may be differences across different categories of nursing and across contexts.

Someone working with those approaching the end of their lives in a palliative care context might have little difficulty with the order of priorities of care, design and knowledge, whereas a nursing sister working in an operating theatre might in practice be far more concerned with following the procedures of a particular therapeutic design. But in both cases, the nurses might be seen as practitioners rather than the gatherers and guardians of well-founded knowledge of bodily function and possibility. And medical doctors might be seen as focusing on knowledge, its medical validity and its applicability for the design of processes, but not to the extent that they could be accused of "not caring for patients".

It would hardly be considered ethical for a science teacher not to care about the pupils. But it might not be deemed unprofessional if limits were set to this care, limits set in terms of the safety and security of the child in the learning context and the teacher were then to invest energy in capturing the child's attention and cognition with the sheer wonder of knowledge, of physics or of chemistry. To do this, the teacher's primary activity might be the design of pedagogic steps in the curriculum, steps and devices that engender that sense of "wow" in the child's mind that the world could be as fascinating as this. The teacher's care for the child is put into practice through designing and implementing a curriculum rather than through caring in the sense that a hospice nurse or psychotherapist might understand caring for a person. And the teacher, like the nurse, may be less directly concerned with knowledge.

An architect provides another example of how care, design and knowledge form components of professional practice. A commission begins with a client's brief, followed by a design to meet the requirements of the brief. But the architect is rarely chosen simply on his capability to meet the brief, but to bring a "wow" factor to the design, a wow that stuns the client because the client had no idea a design that met the brief could look or feel quite like that. So the architect does not fail to care for his client's brief but is eager to put energy into aesthetics and design. These examples are intended to illustrate the different ways in which three key concepts of professional ethics, care, design and knowledge figure together in different ways in different professional practices.

So what's the significance of the claim that professional ethics differ across different professions according to the way that care, knowledge and design figure in different ways together? What's the impact on teaching and learning in ethics? One important way of thinking about professional ethics is rooted in the Aristotelian tradition of virtue rather than the more recent, post-Kantian tradition of principles. Virtue theory focuses on the acquisition and development of dispositions in the practitioner, dispositions that enable the practitioner to act with an appropriate emotional response, and which reflect the practitioner's acting with practical wisdom or *phronesis* in any circumstance. Virtuous action is action which can be characterised as lying between two vicious extremes. So acting with appropriate generosity, for example, lies between the vicious extremes of both profligacy and meanness.

But how are these vicious extremes defined? They may, and indeed Aristotle suggests they will, vary in different practices. One possibility is that the meanings of care, knowledge and design help articulate these vicious extremes. In short, we may need to go beyond care in understanding the demands of virtue in different professions.

CONCLUSION

The argument presented here is that care, knowledge and design are common key features of professional ethics, but they figure together in different ways in different professions. Communication is a key factor in all of them, in creating the appropriate relationship between care, knowledge and design for the different professions. There may be scope for considerable collaboration between those working in ethics in different professional disciplines to identify how these concepts work together.

This chapter has identified some specific connections between communications ethics and the teaching of ethics. It has also reviewed a rationale for teaching ethics in higher education more generally. The common features of teaching ethics in higher education point towards some interesting possibilities for collaboration. These might include:

* sharing experiences of learning and teaching methods in applied and professional ethics;

- sharing experience of learning and teaching in ethics in seminars and conferences;
- identifying what is common to all professions in teaching ethics and what is distinctive to different professions and different areas of practice;
- exploring interdisciplinary relationships between philosophical treatments of ethics and ethical claims within each discipline and profession.

REFERENCES

Barnett, Ronald (2000) *Realizing the University in an age of Supercomplexity*, Buckingham, Society for Research in Higher Education and Open University Press

Barnett, Ronald (1984) *The Limits of Competence*, Buckingham, Society for Research in Higher Education and Open University Press

Benner, Patricia and Wrubel, Judith (1989) *The Primacy of Caring: Stress and Coping in Health and Illness*, Boston, Addison Wesley

Blake, Nigel, Smith, Richard and Standish, Paul (1988) *The Universities we need: Higher Education after Dearing*, London, Kogan Page

Carmichael, Sheena (2001) "Accounting for ethical business", *The Moral Universe*, London, Demos

Dearing, Ronald (1997) *National Committee of Inquiry into Higher Education (The Dearing Report)*, London, HMSO

Delanty, Gerard (1988) "Rethinking the University: the autonomy, contestation and reflexivity of knowledge", *Social Epistemology*, Vol. 12, No. 1 pp 103-113

Habermas, Jurgen (1984) *Theory of Communicative Action*, Vol. 1, Cambridge, Polity Press

Handy, Charles (1996) *Beyond Certainty: the Changing Worlds of Organizations*, Harvard, Harvard Business School Publishing

Hewitt, J. (2002) "A critical review of the arguments debating the role of the nurse advocate", *Journal of Advanced Nursing*, Vol. 37, No. 5 pp 439-445

Johnstone, Megan-Jane (1998) *Bioethics: A Nursing Perspective*, Philadephia, W B Saunders

MacIntyre, Alasdair (1981) *After Virtue*, London, Duckworth

Newman, John Henry (1986) *The Idea of a University*, Illinois, University of Notre Dame Press

Noddings, Nell (1984) *Caring: A Feminine Approach to Ethics and Moral Education*, Berkeley, University of California Press

Rogers, Carl (1961) *On Becoming a Person*, Carl London, Constable

Rogerson, Simon (2004) "Launching the Great Curriculum Debate", *Ethical Space: The International Journal of Communication Ethics*, Vol. 1, No. 3 pp 7-8

Scott, Peter (1997) "The Postmodern University?", Smith, Anthony and Webster, Frank (eds) *The Postmodern University: Contested Visions of Higher Education in Society*, Buckingham, Society for Research in Higher Education and Open University Press

Strain, John (2004) "What is distinctive about ethics in particular professional disciplines and what is transferable across them?" *Approaches to Ethics in Higher Education, Ethics across the Curriculum*, Leeds, HEFCE Learning and Teaching Support Network

NOTE ON AUTHOR

John Strain is a chartered organisational psychologist and the Director of the Centre for Applied and Professional Ethics at the University of Surrey and the convenor of the International Conference on teaching applied and professional ethics in higher education. He is a priest in the Church of England with degrees in history, philosophy, theology and psychology. John began his career in the Royal Navy and has a track record of consultancy and research examining relationships between organisational practices and technology across a range of sectors. He teaches professional ethics across a range of disciplines including psychology, healthcare, computing and engineering. He has a particular interest in professional relationships, spirituality and ethics in healthcare. He is currently working on a book on ethics, professions and higher education. Contact details: Centre for Applied and Professional Ethics, University of Surrey, Guildford, Surrey GU2 7TE, UK. Tel: +44 (0)1483 683975; Fax: +44 (0)1483 686736; Email j.strain@surrey.ac.uk. Web address: http://www.intercape.org.uk.

16

Art imitates life: Or how arts tutors can use life coaching to enhance their profesional skills

Brian Hoey

Much of creative arts education is concerned with the tutor enabling and empowering the student. Most tutors treat this as an instinctive, organic, sometimes even, mysterious process. At times this can be ethically problematic. Situations can occur in which the tutor overly influences the student, sometimes having a stronger input to the work being produced than is desirable. Such a situation can be frustrating and counter-productive for both parties. I propose that co-opting systems and processes from the discipline of life coaching can improve this process. This chapter also argues that creative arts academics should consider training in coaching techniques to reduce potential ethical problems and conflicts. And it invites them to enhance their versatility as facilitators and teachers by increasing the techniques at their disposal.

INTRODUCTION

'How do you teach art? How do you teach filmmaking? How do you teach any creative subject? Surely these are gifts, you can't teach a gift!' These are frequent questions and comment from those not involved in the small world of arts education. I am sure many tutors have been buttonholed at some time by these seemingly innocuous questions and felt some degree of discomfort when answering. Not because of a lack confidence in their abilities, but because the process is not readily explicable. Yet, these are genuinely perplexing issues to the questioner.

Obviously, we can begin by talking about the teaching of technical skills; these are evident elements of the discipline. However, if the interrogator is keenly interested they will press beyond into the mysterious territories of creativity, artistry and style, asking how lecturers can profess to teach something so individual to the practitioner. Many people fail to realise that teaching is not a singular skill but a continuum of approaches. At one end of the educational spectrum is the "directive" approach:

> It is the form of education and management that we are most familiar with and which we pick up in our earliest days of schooling. Teacher knows and, like it or not, will tell you; you, on the other hand sit there passively. The assumption is that once you have been told you will know (Downey 1999: 17).

This can be contrasted with the "non-directive" approach:

> Non-directive coaching is, again, just that: you do not direct, instruct or tell. To illustrate what I mean, let me remind you how you learned to walk. You learned to walk through direct experience, a kind of trial and error. You stood up and had a go...I bet that 90 per cent of you are still walking well today and that you have never had any instructions in how to do it (ibid: 19).

At the "directive" end of the spectrum the student, is pushed, they are told, instructed or given advice. At the "non-directive" end of the spectrum the student is "pulled" towards a resolution, the one that is appropriate for them at that point in time. Within creative arts higher education a skilled lecturer will operate across the range using the "directive" approach to teach craft skills: the operation of equipment and manipulation of materials. The same lecturer will then move towards the "non-directive" end of the spectrum to help the student to develop the conceptual framework within which these craft skills will be applied.

I believe that the tutorial is a crucial point of interaction between student and teacher and that "non-directive" techniques are highly appropriate to this process in creative arts education. When a tutorial is highly successful it is a fulcrum that "tips the balance" for the student, providing them with material to think about and a course of action to take. When I am engaged in a tutorial with a student I often question whether "teaching" is a useful way of describing what I do. In a tutorial I am facilitating the development of a student's own innate creativity and individual mode of expression, drawing on the student's innate potential; I am certainly not instructing.

Over time I have often asked myself questions on the nature of learning with particular reference to:

- improving the fidelity of communication between lecturer and student;
- encouraging arts students to develop their own concepts without the form of these concepts being unduly influenced by the lecturer;
- assisting arts students to devise strategies to implement their conceptual basis in ways that are most appropriate to their own skills and situation, as opposed to the lecturer's perception of these;
- achieving these aims within the context of efficiency and widening participation without teaching staff becoming unduly stressed.

WHAT IS COACHING AND HOW CAN IT BE EMPLOYED?

For some time I have been researching strategies that can enhance the lecturer's situation; strategies that provide a greater range of tools to assist teaching staff in dealing with the changes that are a constant in their profession as well as to help them develop and nurture student ability. These strategies can be grouped together under the generic title of "coaching" and I have found models within the fields of Life Coaching and Neuro Linguistic Programming (NLP) that are particularly effective in this arena. NLP is often described as the study and pursuit of excellence.

> Neuro-Linguistic Programming is a revolutionary approach to human communication and development based on the discovery that by changing how you think you can transform what you think. NLP helps modify your thought and behavioural patterns to suit your projected goals. NLP literally "reprograms" your mind and your life for faster learning, better relationships and greater success (Andreas and Faulkner 1996).

NLP has applications in a wide variety of fields including sales, education, creativity, decision-making and can be employed within coaching to enhance the efficiency and elegance of the process. Coaching is a professional and personal relationship between two people, the coach and the client, and is an interactive process where the coach guides and facilitates the client's progress towards defined goals. These may concern any facet of life including relationships, career, self-confidence and financial matters. As each goal or desired outcome is defined, the coach will assist the client to decide on specific actions that will move them ever closer to the desired results. Whilst these actions are important, it is the outcome from those actions that achieve success. A coaching session is very similar to a tutorial in the sense that when both are truly successful the client or student feels that they have moved some significant way towards achieving their goal whilst having played an important, creative role in this achievement.

Within the creative arts we produce work that relies on a symbiotic relationship between craft skills and conceptual development. The student is taught the practical techniques associated with their discipline: how to mix paint, how to correctly expose film etc. This type of teaching uses demonstration and practice to achieve its aims. However, once we move beyond teaching these craft skills, and into the realm of the manner in which these skills can be applied, then a different teaching methodology is required. It has become important to me to develop a structure by which students are drawn towards achieving their goals in ways that are entirely appropriate to their individual skills and attributes and that provides them with a greater sense of investment in the outcome.

The art school system, as we have historically known it in Britain, has been very successful in developing graduates with the ability to analyse problems or desires and design appropriate solutions for their successful resolution. These solutions have often demonstrated original and "lateral" thinking that these graduates have the ability to apply to different facets of business and life, often beyond the world of art. I believe an important factor in these students' enlightenment is that they have been exposed to the original and "lateral" thinking of their tutors. As these tutors are usually products of the same system there is a cyclical process occurring. The system works well but still has some problems. I have often heard creative arts tutors complain that teaching reduces their own creativity as they "give away their ideas" to students leaving themselves bereft.

It often occurs that the student presents the tutor with a situation they have been unable to resolve. The tutor may see a number of potential strategies and offer these to the student who takes the advice and puts it into practice. A successful student will eventually gain insight, begin to emulate the tutor's way of thinking and apply it in the future. On the other hand, I sometimes hear students complain that a tutor "does not like" their idea and they feel pressure to comply with the tutor's viewpoint and change their idea to one that will find more favour. This situation may arise for sound pedagogical reasons; perhaps the idea won't achieve the learning outcomes, however it may be due to bias on the part of the lecturer. At its most extreme this can develop into a "school" or style in which students copy the working methods of a tutor to produce work in a similar vein.

CRITICAL FACTORS

Coaching can be readily adapted to the usual tutorial processes common to creative arts education. It is important to set the right tone for the tutorial so that it is professional yet conducted in an atmosphere of rapport. NLP practitioners have techniques at their disposal that can be used to develop rapport with students and reassure them that it is safe to speculate and exercise their imagination. This is crucial if students are going to derive maximum benefit from the session.

Our emotions impact on our learning. Everyone is familiar with the experience of being in an emotionally overwrought state and being unable to think or process information efficiently. Any kind of learning, therefore, is more likely to occur in a safe, non-threatening environment, otherwise the limbic system in our brains takes over and interferes with our higher cognitive processing (Zeus and Skiffington 2000: 187).

Making effective use of questioning is an important attribute of coaching. The "coaching tutor" must ask questions that orient the student's viewpoint towards the future. In this context there is little use in asking questions that cause the student to ruminate on the past. Instead we must ask questions that stimulate the student into thinking of ways to bring about the desired outcome; we are seeking to assist the student to arrive at their own viewpoint and make their own decisions concerning the direction their work should take.

The "coaching tutor" must also develop their listening skills. Throughout the whole process it is important to listen very carefully. Very often the lecturer may think they can envisage the situation that the student is in, only to find that there are hidden factors affecting the student's thinking and work. These factors may expose major differences between the lecturer's viewpoint and the actual experience of the student.

One important area in which the "coaching tutor" may need to change their behaviour is in the ratio of time spent speaking as compared with listening: well-developed listening skills are essential to the success of the process. The whole process pulls the student towards his or her own optimum learning and the tutor must guard against making too great a vocal input. A brief, but pointed and well-timed, question can have much more impact on the learning process than a long homily from the teacher.

At first the novice "coaching tutor" may feel uneasy about pauses in the conversation. It is crucial to develop the ability to differentiate between a point at which the student has exhausted all that they have to say and a pause while they collect their thoughts. When I initially began to apply these principles I discovered in myself a tendency to fill the silence with thoughts of my own, when it would have been better to allow the student to gather theirs. Once I learnt to keep quiet in these pauses I was astounded at how often students were coming to conclusions that were entirely different to those that I was anticipating.

We tend to think of educators as people who give advice to their students. It may be surprising to discover that there is serious debate within coaching circles as to whether this is a practice to be avoided. Some contend that the best advice is not to give advice. Advice exerts influence and can force the student into behaviour that may not be the most appropriate for them. Occasionally, a gentle suggestion might be useful to keep the process moving but it is important to regulate the scope of this. Advice can also detract from a student's sense of ownership of the ultimate outcome. Instead the process is reliant upon the student making an analysis of his/her own desired outcomes for their work. This is followed by another analysis, that of their particular skills and personal qualities, which then leads to them generating a customised action plan, specific to their own situation. This approach has the benefit of generating a great sense of ownership of the creative process within the student.

CONCLUSION

When I graduated, as a fine artist, I was taken aback by something that my tutor said. He had been wholly supportive throughout our relationship so I was astounded when he told me that he did not really care for my style of work. His point was that it was his job to develop the potential in me regardless of whether he liked my work or not. His professional integrity meant that, once he assured himself that I had serious intentions; he did everything he could to assist me to develop in my own way, despite the fact that it was not to his own taste. I believe that he taught me a very valuable lesson then, one that I have carried throughout my own teaching practice.

Through practice and experimentation I have come to the conclusion that coaching provides a valuable method by which the tutor can enable the student to arrive at their own strategies as appropriate to their own particular circumstances and abilities. It is a set of strategies that can be turned on and off as appropriate to any given situation. Coaching provides the tutor with a systematic process that can provide progress and clarity when normal methods seem ineffective but is conversational and natural for the student. This is not to criticise current teaching methods but I have discovered coaching to be an extremely useful addition to the teaching skills already manifest within the teacher. An extra "set of tools" to be used as, and when, seem fit.

In my own university senior management have been employing coaches to assist them with their own development. Subject heads have also been offered a course in some coaching techniques aimed at giving them a greater facility in managing staff. It is obvious that, in this case, Higher Education management sees the virtues of coaching as a management resource but have yet to grasp its full significance as a teaching tool.

Most importantly, within the tutorial system, the development of coaching skills can increase the effectiveness of helping students to develop their own artistic strengths and direction so that they have a positive focus on their work and a strong sense of self-determination and self-belief.

I propose that creative arts academics consider training in coaching techniques in order to reduce potential ethical problems and conflicts concerning influences within conceptual development and practical production, as well as inviting them to enhance their versatility as communicators, facilitators and teachers by increasing the techniques at their disposal.

REFERENCES

Andreas, S. and Faulkner, C. (1996) *NLP: The Technology of Achievement*, London, Nicholas Brealey

Downey, M. (1999) *Effective Coaching*, London, Orion Business Books

Zeus, P. and Skiffington, S. (2000) *The Complete Guide to Coaching at Work,* Sydney, McGraw Hill

NOTE ON AUTHOR

Brian Hoey teaches within the School of Arts and Social Sciences at Northumbria University; email: brian.hoey@northumbria.ac.uk. He formerly taught at the University of the Arts, London and Hampshire College, Massachusetts. He is also a video artist of long standing and has exhibited internationally since the mid-1970s. His works have been screened in North America, Europe and in the UK and he has presented papers on the application of coaching within HE at international conferences in Brighton, London and Kiev.

17

Blogs, *ba* and care: Virture in virtual world

Brian Morris

The Japanese word ba means a "place that harbours meaning". It may be a virtual place as much as a physical place. Working on the principle of ba, I have added the online diary or weblog as an extra dimension to my students' final year multi-media undergraduate projects – and found that it closes down the distance between the student and supervisor. Much of what follows is a reflection on the philosophy of that practice. The awareness of the power of a safe and trusting environment, or ba, has become for me an ethical imperative for my project supervision exercised under conditions of high-care. With the growth of the Internet it is possible for students to communicate with their supervisors via emails and blogs as well as in face-to-face participation in conversing groups. I argue that this mixture of modes of meeting can create an environment, a ba, in which trust may develop. Once trust is engendered students are able to participate in dialogue (Isaacs 1999), ideas can flow (Csikszentmihalyi 1975) and students become self-organising learners (Thomas and Harri-Augstein 1985). In conclusion, I suggest our models of knowledge need to be adjusted, from a Philosophy of Knowledge to a Philosophy of Wisdom, to deal with real people in our all-too-real world.

INTRODUCTION

Reflecting on my experiences as a lecturer supporting learning on final year computing and multimedia projects over the past twenty years, I realise there were three stages in my thinking and practice that lead to a revolution in my approach. In the first stage, in the 1980s, I followed received wisdom in computing project supervision. During this decade scholars were making a plea for a New Paradigm Research (Heron 1981; Maxwell 1984; Reason 1988). During this period Thomas and Harri-Augstein wrote *Self-Organised Learning* (op cit). In that period these scholars had no impact on my thinking. I was working in technocratic institutions wedded to Technical Rationality and the Empiricist paradigm.

My second stage was during the 1990s. I was responsible for HND Computing and Multimedia courses and so, consequently, was responsible for managing computing projects. This management was administrative and detailed. Students were largely separated from each other, and, as they worked in their communities of one, they tended to struggle to deliver some form of dissertation and working system. Surviving the project was the name of the game. During this period there were a number of crises that caused me concern. Student failure on projects resulting in qualification failure were moments when I started to question the current "hands off" approach. All students had supervisors allocated to them, but supervision as a social activity that promoted learning and progress was more honoured in the breach.

In my concern I turned to the three texts: Thomas and Harri-Augstein (op cit), Harri-Augstein and Thomas (1991) and Harri-Augstein and Webb (1995). Pedagogy interested me, and these three texts had important things to say. And what they had to say made me uneasy for it started to seem as if my communications with students were not ethical: centralised communiqués were not needed. I was not meant to be a module administrator. I was meant to be a module leader. What should I be leading students to, and why? I needed to change, and to make a difference. I formed the view students no longer needed "a sage on the stage, but a guide by their side" – in short students needed a Learning Coach.

Now in the first ten years of the new millennium, I am in the third stage of my thinking. I find my awareness of Learning Coach practice accompanied by extensive reading and reflection on the ongoing practice has created, for me, a new world of academic endeavour and "cooperative inquiry" in supervising student project work. The associated explorations, philosophical deliberations and choices in ethical communications are discussed below.

After an important discussion of philosophy and methodology, I explore the notion of a *ba* – a place that harbours meaning. This is followed by a discussion of the pastoral notion of care. This leads directly to Self-Organised Learning and the ethical decisions involved in the SOL and OOL dichotomy. "Cooperative inquiry" implies participation (Mumford 1997) and building communities of learners. However, groups of learners have different capabilities and degrees of motivation. On motivation, I found Amabile (1998) and Osterloh and Frey (2000) were extremely relevant in emphasising the importance of "intrinsic motivation" and the dangers associated with tainting that intrinsic motivation. A chance comment by a student, followed by an epiphany moment in which I discovered Csikszentmihalyi (1975) and his work on flow, convinced me I was on to something. That led directly in my Action Research to a re-examination of those three books (above) written in the 1980s by Heron (1981), Maxwell (1984) and Reason (1988). As a consequence I have formed the view that we are too constrained by a Philosophy of Knowledge and should turn to a Philosophy of Wisdom, as advocated by Maxwell (1884). This paradigm change is developed in the next section.

PHILOSOPHICAL BASIS FOR A NEW APPROACH: NEW PARADIGM RESEARCH

Heron (op cit) has provided "cooperative inquiry" as a new paradigm for research among people. He poses his "radical question": "To what kind of explanation of the behaviour of my subjects am I committed?" Each researcher must give a personal response. Heron teases out the issues in an examination of research behaviour as it relates to people:

> There is no precise methodology for generating new ideas; new ideas are not the logical product of empirical observations, rather they arise unpredictably to direct it into ever more fruitful channels. Research behaviour is…original creative activity which cannot be contained within an explanatory model of absolute determinism; it is not the sort of event that could be predicted as the outcome of antecedent conditions…What explanatory model can be adopted for such behaviour?…I suggest that central to any such model is the notion of intelligent agency,…the notion of a self-directing person (ibid: 20).

This leads to seeing students as "self-directing persons". It connects with Self-Organised Learning. Students have intentions: they intend to learn. They are human beings. To use Heron's phrase they are "symbolising beings". Heron says of these symbolising beings:

> They find meaning in and give meaning to their world, through symbolizing their experiences in a variety of constructs and actions. This notion of symbolizing activity as an explanatory concept is irreducible to any other, since it is presupposed by and transcends any reductive argument. It points to a determinant and to an explanation of human behaviour *sui generis*. To explain human behaviour you have, among other things, to understand this activity, and fully to understand it involves participating in it through overt dialogue and communication with those who are engaging in it (ibid: 23).

"Participating in it through overt dialogue" leads to the adoption of an action research methodology and, subsequently, to the notions of *ba*, care, SOL, participation, intrinsic motivation and flow. These are developed in the following sections.

ACTION RESEARCH APPROACH

In this study, a participative approach has been adopted from the field of action research. Action Research seeks to "make a difference" in the phenomenon under investigation (Stringer 1999). Participation encourages people when it:

- enables significant levels of active involvement;
- enables people to perform significant tasks;
- provides support for people as they learn to act for themselves;
- encourages plans and activities that people are able to accomplish themselves;
- deals personally with people rather than with their representatives or agents (ibid: 35).

In short, action research seeks to bestow confidence, promote care and improve current practice. It fits well with the spirit of "cooperative inquiry" used in my approach to Self-Organised Learning.

INITIAL PEDAGOGY AND PRACTICE

At the start of the final undergraduate academic year one of my first tasks was to get my supervisees to meet in a group. This was justified on the grounds of expediency. It is not possible to see each student for one hour per week. That would take 10 hours for ten students. With current allocations rising to 18 students per supervisor for project work, it is almost impossible to maintain the "personal touch". However, Vygotsky (1978) maintains significant learning takes place in the Zone of Proximal Development (ZPD). As group members face similar tasks, they often learn from each other. So there are suggested benefits in meeting in a group.

Another important notion in my action research is establishing a "safe place that harbours meaning", or *ba,* to meet each week. At my current university there is a highly centralised and centralising timetable unit. Acquiring a small room, for ten to twenty people to meet, is not easily done. However, the situation is improving with study rooms being built into the library extension. Students may book these rooms for group work. Finally, through adopting a genuinely caring attitude in the learning coach role (see von Krogh 2001) I have found students become interested in what I know. They want to acquire *my* tacit knowledge.

THE NOTION OF *BA*

Nonaka *et al* (2001) describe a *ba* as "a place that harbours meaning". I am surprised at the number of places that harbour meaning. The carpet, in the corner of the room in a primary school, is the place where the class teacher tells the weekly story. The red light in a recording studio gives the message "do not interrupt – a live recording is taking place right now." A *ba* is not like a meeting with an agenda. Rather it is a place without an agenda, it is a place where dialogue takes place and new meanings are created. Nonaka, Kono and Toyama (2001) suggest a *ba* is:

> a Japanese term difficult to translate into English, refers to a physical, virtual, and/or mental space shared by two or more individuals or organisations (ibid: 4).

The nearest we come to it perhaps is a seminar or a tutorial. But in my experience these are often Other-Organised. In contrast, I have been promoting a self-organising activity for dialogue in a *ba*. This *ba* is looked forward to each week: it is both exciting and egalitarian. To quote Isaacs (op cit) dialogue gives priority to the primacy of the whole without sacrificing the primacy of the parts. It is not adversarial, like a debate. It does not involve point-scoring. It is a place that may be both real and virtual, and a way of meeting that is familiar, intimate, safe, holistic, exciting and real.

It is also a place where I can talk of Csikszentmihalyi (1988; 1992; 2003) and his notions of the "autotelic self" and "flow". The "autotelic self" is able to set personal goals, do a task and sustain involvement in that task. In so doing, "flow" is experienced (Csikszentmihalyi 2003) in which the learner finds that

1. goals are clear;
2. feedback is immediate;
3. there is a balance between opportunity and capacity;
4. concentration deepens;
5. the present is what matters;
6. control is no problem;
7. the sense of time is altered;
8. there is a loss of ego (ibid: 42-56).

By reading students' blogs remotely (and conveniently) it soon becomes clear which students are in a state of flow, and which are stuck.

THE NOTION OF CARE

Once we are meeting in a *ba* it seems quite natural to care for my supervisees as learners. The notion of "care" takes thinking beyond the cognitivist notion of the organisation as a machine for information processing and problem solving. The cognitivists maintain that such a "machine" would need to store, manipulate and retrieve knowledge (Kilduff 1992; Morgan 1986). But through the perspective of care, one sees a group of people, not a machine for processing information.

Knowledge may be of a social or individual character, it may be explicit or tacit and, finally, it may be understood or agreed upon in the organisational world. von Krogh, Ichijo and Nonaka (2001) ask: "What characterises organisational relationships that enable effective knowledge development in business organisations?" They then go on to assert that care is the answer:

> Knowledge development, especially social knowledge development of the organisation, cannot be taken for granted, and relationships in organisations must be given more attention. Knowledge development is fraught with emotions, misunderstandings, misconceptions and so on. Care, which involves patience, emotional forbearance, and so forth, is the remedy for such difficulties (ibid: 34).

In my experience, being available and open to students and staff has paid dividends. As Kelly argues (1955):

> The burden of our assumption is that learning is not a special class of psychological processes; it is synonymous with any and all processes. It is not something that happens to a person on occasion; *it is what makes him a person in the first place* (my emphasis) (ibid: 75).

We now find we have a different set of priorities. We are no longer so interested in the metaphor of the organisation as a machine. Rather, we are interested in the metaphor of the organisation as an organism. Here, learning is described as something that is endogenous and that comes from within. We are now dealing with care and learning in a direct sense and with a world of relationships between learners, rather than a world of things in which lists of topics get "covered".

To promote creativity we must address the students' existing construct system, and encourage them to move on from OOL to SOL. My favourite method for doing this is by working as a SOL Learning Coach with groups of students. Is it ethical for me to decide to do this unilaterally? Is it ethical to decide to provide a different form of project supervision experience to that administered by my colleagues? Is it ethical to use the new technologies to read each student's blog remotely? Is it ethical to promote a high care environment in which we dialogue under conditions of high care, while many of my colleagues do not? My answer is yes: I am discharging the duties given to me in the best way possible and I can site the references given here to justify why I think it is a better way of supervising. I am making a virtue of our virtual world. Furthermore, I get the students permission to do this at the outset of each academic year.

von Krogh (1999), in his online interview on care, stresses two important points: (i) care is a gift and (ii) care drives attention. On the first point he says:

Trust is exchange-based; care is voluntary cooperation and voluntary giving. Care is a gift…A person needs care from childhood on in order to develop into a "full" person…Care includes but extends far beyond trust….Tacit knowledge-sharing is impossible without care. Leadership is very strongly affected by caring…

And on the second, he says:

Care is the fundamental concept that drives attention. So if I care for something I pay attention to that particular thing. It's very fundamental, and perhaps it cannot be decomposed – or if you look at the heart of it, care is even the source of love, because it's what drives attention. So if you pay attention to something, you might start to love some aspect of it over time.

von Krogh (2001), in Table 1, illustrates his model of care this way. In a low care environment an individual student will seize a worksheet, or try to grab a lecturer's attention in a corridor. A group of students will transact: they will do their assignment work and expect it to be marked by a lecturer. The relationship between teacher and taught is rather impersonal. (One could mark work by inviting a student to the office where the work is marked. The student may be questioned about certain points made. The marker may be asked "What are you looking for?" But this practice is not usual.) In a high care environment care is bestowed on a group. The group feels cared for and nurtured.

The act of bestowing care seems to me to be similar to the Christian concept of grace. It is freely given, without even being asked for: it is like life itself. An individual in a high care environment finds this sense of care dwells within. It has become a given, like the air we breathe. Its value is in making the individual feel and know he or she is valued. In an organisational setting, it makes the group feel they belong and matter.

Once cared for and freely valued students are invited to consider themselves as self-directed agents or self-organised learners. The next section addresses self-organised learning.

Table 1 Von Krogh's model of care

Range Environment	Individual	Social
High Care	bestowing	indwelling
Low Care	seizing	transacting

SELF-ORGANISED LEARNING (SOL)

In Higher Education there is a near universal requirement for some large individual piece of work in the final stages of a degree or higher diploma. This may be a piece of scholarly work, a dissertation, a project, a constructed artefact or system, or some combination of these. It is uniformly understood learning should be Self-Organised (SOL) in some sense. Harri-Augstein and Webb (op cit) define Self-Organised Learning this way:

> the personal construction of meaning – a system of "personal knowing" – and meaning is the basis for all our actions (ibid: 2).

Yet much of our education system and its processes follow Other-Organised (OOL) approaches (Thomas and Harri-Augstein op cit) according to which "teachers teach, pupils learn; lecturers lecture, students learn". This is essentially an exogenic form of learning, imposed on the learner from the outside. The syllabi are created by others (not the learners) and have the stamp of institutional approval.

So for institutions to embrace an implicit SOL approach is rather confusing for students, if all their experience in earlier levels of study has been of Other-Organised Learning. Is it ethically correct for HE institutions to swing from OOL to SOL in this specific area of assessment? In particular in a largely OOL environment, is it not a contradiction in terms for some supervisors to adopt, as I have done, a Learning Coach approach to promoting Self Organised Learning (Harri-Augstein and Webb op cit)? Indeed, is it right for Harri-Augstein and Webb to characterise most learners as robots, who need to be "challenged", before they can become fully functioning self-aware learners? I think it is right to do this, for without awareness the "autotelic-self", "autotelic learning" and "flow" will not be realised.

THE THREE DIALOGUES IN SOL

All my supervisees are required to attend a weekly, one-hour meeting of "cooperative inquiry" (Heron 1981) for the duration of the project or dissertation. Students freely entered into this agreement. At these weekly meetings I have made extensive use of the Three Dialogues, as outlined by Harri-Augstein and Webb (ibid), at the beginning, middle and end of the project's life. These dialogues are (i) process, (ii) support and (iii) referent. These are shown in Figure 1.

These three dialogues correspond with three dominant forms of student thinking as they progress their projects (see Figure 1).

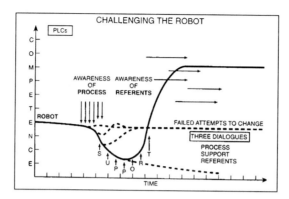

Figure 1 The Three Dialogues used by a Learning Coach with Learners[1]

These dominant forms of student thinking are shown as three phases in Figure 2. In each of these phases, the Learning Coach uses conversation to interact with the student group to promote Self-Organised Learning. Conversation is regarded as the supreme example of interactivity between students (acting as their own project manager) and the supervisor (acting as a Learning Coach). These dialogues help get the tacit knowledge of the Learning Coach across to students. For, in managing themselves and their projects with increasing awareness and confidence, students develop their different project ideas and bring them to fruition. They become more authentic as learners.

In Phase I, *process dialogue* is very important. Students must be fully informed of what has to be done, when and how. This is usually realised by giving out a project handbook and asking students to complete a proposal form. But following Thomas and Harri-Augstein (op cit) the robot (i.e. the unaware student) must be challenged over the difference between Other-Organised and Self-Organised Learning.

In Phase II, *support dialogue* becomes important. Streams of study have emerged and need to be worked on in parallel. A key requirement at this stage, following O'Connell (2001) is: "Know what you are trying to do" (ibid: pp 13-28). Other courseworks have their own requirements, the student begins to worry about the lack of real progress (ideas can come easily, but delivery does not come cheap) and the sense that perhaps they have been over-ambitious. In this phase it is important students realise their personal discipline is paramount. They may need guidance in changing the promised scope in their original proposal. The Learning Coach uses a support dialogue to counteract feelings of wanting to give up.

In Phase III, *referent dialogue* applies as work converges towards the deadline. This is a time for that extra push: for hard editing and, particularly, paying attention to those referents by which the project will be assessed. There is a need to encourage reflection on how work is assessed, even as the deadline gets closer.

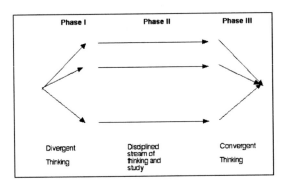

Figure 2 Three phases in student learning

THE NOTION OF A BLOG

A blog is an online journal available for reading from anywhere in the world via the internet. It has great utility in assessing students' progress on projects. It is a virtue in our virtual world. Sites such as www.blogger.com, www.blog.com, wwww.easyblog.com are amongst a number that provide this blogging service for free. Joe Trippi (2004: 141-150), an American political activist, has used blogs extensively on behalf of Democrat politicians and their political campaigns. He used blogs to reinvent political campaigning by giving voters their voice via blogs.

I too wanted to give my project students their voice by promoting the use of blogs. It is a natural move to transfer the traditional log to a blog. Through the means of virtual hyperlinks, a supervisor can read a student's blog remotely. Furthermore, if given permission, a reader can gain access to the blog in order to post comments. I have found useful the combination of reading the blog, writing a comment and emailing the student saying "a comment has been posted" as a permanent record.

I give the example of the blog[2] maintained by Chris Sainsbury, an MPhil student. His blog has been active for some years now. It is a record of all his work and thinking over the past three years or more. On the first page of this blog Chris has posted a comment. In this case it is a more detailed reference to support a point made. A screenshot of the comment posted by the blog's author is shown in Figure 3.

PARTICIPATION V. ALONENESS

Helping students learn better is part of "human welfare". Picking up the theme of cooperation, Enid Mumford, from a systems perspective, has studied the notion of introduced SOL principles to help the organisation, and the thesis is his record of the events. Again, it's very readable and interesting. You can see the people are genuinely interested in and passionate about their subjects. They live it, it *is* them.

Comments on this diary entry:

The PhD by the Post Office manager referred to above was by Andrew Taylor - 'Experimenting with Self-Organised Learning for Organisational Growth: a Person-Centred Approach'

By **Chris**, at **10:10 AM**

1 comments :: **Post a Comment** :: **Request permission to comment** :: **Permanent link to this post**

Figure 3 An example of a comment posted by Chris to his own blog.

participation in relation to systems design over the last twenty-five years. She argues (1997):

> ...participative design, if it is going to be used in industry, must be seen to reduce risk by contributing to organisational stability in ways that are recognised by management. It has to have a purpose and a benefit that pays dividends and increases profits. Few companies will introduce it on the purely ethical grounds that it is beneficial for employees. A reduction of risk and an increase in stability could be seen as worthwhile rewards (ibid: 310).

This stability is a mixture of camaraderie, hanging-together and looking out for each others' interest. "Cooperative inquiry" implies some form of collaboration and participation. Through following the group agenda, students feel they belong. In my pedagogy, being alone managing your project is now a thing of the past.

COUNTERING 'ALONENESS'

Yet becoming aware of aloneness is precisely how my quest came about. Up to 1995, despite being important I had noticed student final year project work was poorly managed. Students were shown little care, help or concern in designing and progressing their projects. They were required to work alone unlike the practice of academics, who co-author papers and attend conferences to give and hear what their colleagues are doing.

This "aloneness" extends through the university system to MPhil and PhD awards. Dissatisfaction with personal higher degree supervision is documented by the National Postgraduate Committee at its website (Staniford 1998). For my part, the supervision of student projects needed to be addressed, simply to avoid Mumford's caveat on failure and administrative inconvenience, and so has led me on an extremely interesting journey into epistemology, ontology and axiology. All of which leads naturally to the question: "Under what circumstances does a participative approach work, and why?" Following Amabile (1998), I will suggest intrinsic motivation is the key.

INTRINSIC MOTIVATION AND UNDERMINING IT

Amabile (1998), in her paper *How to kill creativity,* identifies three components of creativity:

> creative-thinking skills which determine how flexibly and imaginatively people approach problems; expertise: knowledge, and the discipline that goes into mastering intellectual, technical and procedural matters; motivation: an endogenous "inner-passion" leading to creative solutions that are far more effective than those derived from external rewards such as promotion or money. Amabile calls this "inner passion" intrinsic motivation (ibid: 78).

For Amabile intrinsic motivation is the key to excellent work and achievement. For me too, as a Learning Coach, for I seek to unlock this "inner passion" in my supervisees. For once this is done the topic itself, chosen by the student, generates the rewards the learner needs. It is as if a tipping point has been reached, "when everything can change at once" (Gladwell 2001:9). These rewards come from the work itself, from a sense that things are beginning to go well, and that there is *flow* in the work – to use Csikszentmihalyi's term.

When Amabile (op cit: 79) says: "Money doesn't necessarily stop people from being creative, but in many situations, it doesn't help" she is making an important point. Put briefly, external rewards can "taint" intrinsic motivation.

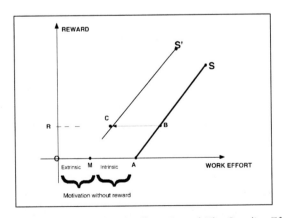

Figure 4   Consequences of Work Effort v Reward: The Crowding Effect

Indeed, there is evidence from the Open Source movement, and its volunteer force of intrinsically motivated computer programmers, that much of its software is robust and of high quality. The Linux Operating System, developed by a volunteer force of decentralised self-selected intrinsically-motivated programmers, under the moderation of Linus Torvald, is now being taken seriously and may become a serious contender to the proprietary Windows operating system.

However, intrinsic motivation can easily be undermined or "tainted" by outside influence. A perspective can be brought to bear on this 'tainting' from crowding theory. Osterloh and Frey (2000), in their paper on motivation, introduce the idea of a crowding-effect. They recognise a person or a team may be motivated, both externally and internally, to do a task. On crowding theory Osterloh and Frey say:

> ...observed behaviour depends on preferences or intrinsic motivation (emphasised by psychologists) and on constraints or relative prices (emphasised by economists). Crowding theory considers both. External interventions, therefore, may have a positive or negative effect on work effort, depending on whether the effect on constraints or on preferences dominates (ibid: 541-542).

Following Deci (1975) and Rotter (1966), Osterloh and Frey argue that intrinsic motivation become tainted "...if the impetus for action is attributed to an external influence, the perceived self-determination is undermined".

With extreme outside pressures the sense of control shifts from inside to outside the person. With extreme inside pressure the sense of control shifts from the outside to the inside. The balance between the two is dependent on the felt intrinsic motivation. Crowding-in, where intrinsic motivation dominates, is a good effect; crowding-out, where extrinsic motivation dominates, is a bad effect. The parallels with the Harri-Augstein dichotomy – Self-Organised Learning and Other-Organised Learning – are clear. This means the Learning Coach, working with his or her group of students on project work, must balance the effects of external interventions.

The diagram in Figure 4 is an adaptation of that found in Osterloh and Frey (op cit: 542). The diagram shows a supply curve (S) for labour effort. Some amount of initial motivation (OA) must exist for someone to start a task even if there is little paid compensation. Now OA is motivation, which is made up of extrinsic motivation (OM) and intrinsic motivation (MA). A reward (R), paid to increase the work effort, raises performance from point A on the supply curve to B. In this situation we must consider the effect of raised external interference. This may have the effect of reducing the locus of control so that responsibility shifts from inside an individual learner to those perceived as pulling the strings.

This destroys the intrinsic motivation effort represented by MA. As a consequence of this destruction of intrinsic work effort, the effort B moves to the point C on the new supply curve S. Figure 4 shows that after the introduction of the reward, and the destruction of the intrinsic motivation (which was free), the benefit is greatly reduced. The literature argues destroying intrinsic motivation can be costly, especially when MA = CB and all initial intrinsic motivation is undermined. As Osterloh and Frey argue: "Managing motivation, especially balancing intrinsic and extrinsic motivation, is an important and hard-to-imitate competitive advantage" (ibid: 544).

PARTICIPATION WITHIN A PHILOSOPHY OF KNOWLEDGE

Buber (1990) has suggested man is born relational. He says there are two main ways in which persons relate: the first is with other persons, the second is with things. He calls these two I Thou and I-It relations. Buber maintains the former relations are more important than the latter. Maxwell (1984), in saying "all rational inquiry…should help us to improve our aims and methods as we live so that we may realize what is of most value to us in life" (ibid: 279-280) goes further to suggest a Philosophy of Wisdom should be adopted in the academe. Rajan (2000) gives a model of knowledge that contrasts with the simpler, three-layer model used from the Enlightenment onwards. For the love of learning associated with the Enlightenment model Maxwell proposes the term a Philosophy of Knowledge.

For the love of learning associated with the Rajan model, Maxwell proposes the term a Philosophy of Wisdom. Wisdom is top of Figure 6. The top layers of Figures 5 and 6 are regarded as the highest forms of knowledge in their respective model. Science gives preference to those theories that simplify and unify. By testing theories against nature, truth is assured, in some sense. This is called "standard empiricism". This commits science to the presupposition that unity exists in nature, often in the form of universal laws. This unity, as expressed in a universal

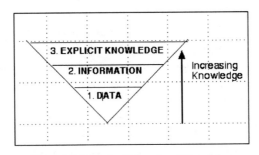

Figure 5 Model of a Philosophy of Knowledge

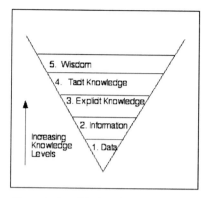

Figure 6 A model of a Philosophy of Wisdom

law, is to be discovered. But what grounds can we have for holding the idea that some kind of unified pattern is implicit in *all* phenomena? Furthermore, how is it possible for us to exist as experiencing, feeling, enjoying and suffering beings?

It seems the pursuit of the Philosophy of Knowledge is indifferent to the aims and purposes of most sentient human beings. It does not allow our personal lives to have meaning. Yet Heron (1981) with his "radical question" invites us to make an ethical choice: humans do have value, and we change our research behaviour accordingly.

In other words if we do not make that choice, science simplifies out the very things that matter – ourselves – and thus a more human form of inquiry is excluded. Maxwell argues that science, in the light of a richer model of knowledge, must seek wisdom in the form of "humanly valuable truth", with "explanatory truth" (i.e. science) being one kind of "valuable truth". He argues not for "pure science" but for curiosity, wonder, knowledge, and understanding achieved by, and shared between, people (1984: 05). He calls this richer model a Philosophy of Wisdom. It fits well with the model of knowledge found in Rajan (2000), and is presented diagrammatically in Figure 6 by this author. In short, Maxwell is arguing for a reassessment of science in the light of human priorities.

CONCLUSIONS: THE COMING 'REVOLUTION' IN UNIVERSITIES

Working with real students in the real world I have found the Learning Coach approach proposed by Harri–Augstein and Webb (op cit) and the interactivity tools, suggested by Harri–Augstein and Thomas (1991) in their book *Learning Conversations*, highly effective. Meeting my supervisees in a group has been efficient and effective. It allows students to enjoy a space (a *ba*) in which their ideas may incubate. Intrinsic motivation has been emphasised and encouraged in our meetings. Through conversation, what were previously insurmountable shared problems often dissolve away. Participation has proved to be invaluable in the first two-thirds of the academic-year in regular democratic meetings. In contrast, in the last three months of the year I have noticed students tend to seek one-on-one appointments with me. This is highly consistent with the Referents Dialogue. Turning to the future, I feel I have made a virtue of our virtual world. The use of new technology in the form of emails (group and individual) and discussion boards has been helpful. But deep thinking about dialogue, motivation and participation has been even more rewarding. I actually enjoy supervising my project students as a Learning Coach and the associated intellectual journey that accompanies it!

Let Drucker (2005) have the last word in his paper *Managing Oneself*:

> Every existing society, even the most individualistic one, takes two things for granted, if only subconsciously: that organisations outlive workers, and that most people stay put. But today the opposite is true. Knowledge workers outlive organisations, and they are mobile. The need to manage oneself is therefore creating a *revolution in human affairs* (my emphasis).

This "revolution in human affairs" will create a revolution in universities, too, as statistics for successful completion rates at MPhil and PhD level are sought. For it is in that arena that Learning Coaches will become greatly prized as assets. For it is they who can bring the Greek idea of the True (what is known about the objective world), the Beautiful (what is appreciated subjectively and aesthetically) and the Good (what we do together with other persons in organisations, teams and families) into focus in an authentic human learning process. The SOL approach outlined here will make a virtue of virtual organisations in the real world, populated by its all-too-real people.

NOTES

1.   This diagram appears in Harri-Augstein and Webb (1995) *Learning to Change*, McGraw Hill, p. 56. Permission to reproduce the diagram has been applied for.
2.   Chris Sainsbury's blog is at http://www.sainsbury.org/assets/html/workbycategory/bitlab.html.

REFERENCES AND FURTHER READING

Amabile, T. (1998) "How to Kill Creativity", *Harvard Business Review*, September–October, p. 79

Amabile, T. (1996) *Creativity in Context*, Boulder, Colorado, Westview Press

Csikszentmihalyi, M. (1975) *Beyond Boredom and Anxiety*, San Francisco, Jossey-Bass

Csikszentmihalyi, M. (1988) *Optimal Experience: Psychological Studies of Flow*, Cambridge, Cambridge University Press

Csikszentmihalyi, M. (1992) *Flow: The Psychology of Happiness*, Rider, London

Csikszentmihalyi, M. (2003) *Good Business: Leadership, Flow and the Making of Meaning*. London, Coronet

Damadaran, L. (2005) "Edemocracy: Challenges for social inclusion", *ITNOW*, British Computer Society, July 2005, Vol. 47, Part 4 pp 10-11

Deci, E., Koestner, R, and Ryan, R. (1999) "A meta-analytic review of experiments examining the effects of extrinsic rewards on intrinsic motivation", *Psych. Bulletin*, Vol. 125 pp 627-668

Drucker, P. (2005) "Managing Oneself", *Harvard Business Review*, January 2005 pp 100-109

Gladwell, M. (2001) *The Tipping Point*, London, Abacus

Harri-Augstein, S. and Thomas, L. (1991) *Learning Conversations*, London, Routledge

Harri-Augstein, S. and Webb, I. (1995) *Learning to Change*. Maidenhead, McGraw Hill

Heron, J. (1981) "Philosophical basis for a new paradigm", Reason, P. and Rowan, J. (eds) *Human Inquiry*, Chichester, Wiley pp 19-3

Isaacs, W. (1999) *Dialogue and the Art of Thinking Together*, New York, Concurrency Press

Johnson, S. (2002) *Emergence*, London, Penguin

Kelly, G. (1955) *Psychology of Personal Constructs, Vol I*, New York, Norton

Kilduff, M. (1992) "Performance and Interactive Routines in Multinational Corporations", *Journal of International Business Studies*, Vol. 23 pp 133-145

Maxwell, N. (1984) *From Knowledge to Wisdom: A Revolution in the Aims & Methods of Science*, Oxford, Blackwell

Morgan, G. (1996) *Images of Organization*, 2nd edn, New York, Sage

Morris, B. (2003) *An Exploration of the Role of the Learning Coach, and Learning Conversations, on Computing Projects in Higher Education*, Brunel University, PhD Thesis, October

Mumford, E. (1997) "The reality of participative systems design: contributing to stability in a rocking boat", *Information Systems Journal*, Vol. 7 pp 309-322

Nonaka, I., Konno, N. and Toyama, R. (2001) "Emergence of *Ba*", Nonaka, 1 and Nishiguchi, T (eds), *Knowledge Emergence*, Oxford, Oxford University Press pp 13-29

Nonaka, I. and Nishiguchi, T. (eds) (2001) *Knowledge Emergence*, Oxford, Oxford University Press

O'Connell, F. (2001) *Simply Brilliant*, London, Prentice Hall

Osterloh, M and Frey, B. (2000) "Motivation, Knowledge Transfer, and Organizational Forms", *Organization Science*, Vol. 11, No. 5, September-October pp 538-550

Polanyi, M. (1958) *Personal Knowledge*, London, Routledge and Kegan Paul

Rajan, A. (2000) "Leadership in the Knowledge Age", *RSA Journal*, Vol. 2, No. 4, 12 January

Raymond, E. (2001) *The Cathedral and The Bazaar*, 2nd edn, London, O'Reilly

Reason, P. (ed.) (1988) *Human Inquiry in Action*, London, Sage

Reason, P. and Rowan, J. (eds) (1981) *Human Inquiry: A sourcebook of new paradigm research*, London, Wiley

Stringer, T. (1999) *Action Research*, 2nd edn, London, Sage

Thomas, L. and Harri-Augstein, S. (1985) *Self Organised Learning*, London, Routledge and Kegan Paul

Trippi, J. (2004) *The Revolution will not be televised: Democracy, the Internet, and the overthrow of Everything*, New York, Regan Books

von Krogh, G., Ichijo, K. and Nonaka, I. (2001) "Bringing Care into Knowledge Development of Business Organizations", Nonaka, I. and Nishiguchi, T (eds), *Knowledge Emergence*, Oxford, Oxford University Press pp 30-52

Vygotsky, L. (1978) *Mind in Society: The development of higher order psychological processes*, Cambridge, MA, Harvard University Press

WEBSITES

Staniford, D. (1 May 1998) Complaints and Codes of Practice, The National Postgraduate Committee. Available online at http://www.npc.org.uk/page/893977200?format= print, accessed on 9 August 2005

Taylor, A. and Crowder, N. (2003) College of Self-Organised Learning. Available online at http://www.selforganisedlearning.com, accessed on 25 July 2005

von Krogh, G. (15 July 1999) "Developing a Knowledge-Based Theory of the Firm", *Dialog on Leadership*, Available online at http://www.dialogonleadership.org/vonKrogh-1999cp.html, accessed on 5 August 2005

NOTE ON AUTHOR

Dr Brian Morris, as a Lecturer in Brunel University, United Kingdom, was involved in the six years 1999-2005 in developing and launching the new BSc Multimedia and, to a lesser extent, the new BSc Marketing in, respectively, the Schools of Engineering and Design, and Brunel Business School. In both situations he explored the use and relevance of Self-Organised Learning approaches in his support of learning. Previous relevant papers and books are *An exploration of the role of the Learning Coach* PhD (Brunel University, 2003) "The role of the learning conversations (and the learning coach) in Computing Projects in Higher Education in the UK", Holcombe, M., Stratton, A., Fincher, S. and Griffiths, G. (eds), *Projects in the Computing Curriculum*, Springer, London, 1998 pp 143-166; and Palmer, D. and Morris, B. *Computing Science*, Edward Arnold, London, 1980. He was Director of the Board of HND Studies at the former West London Institute of Higher Education from 1996-2000 and was a visiting lecturer in information systems at Westminster University, London. Contact details: 25 Alwyn Avenue, London W4 4PA, Telephone +44(0)208 994 2357; email: bd_morris@yahoo.co.uk. He is now retired.

18

PR ethics: forever a will o' the wisp[1]

Simon Goldsworthy

Public relations education can play only a limited role in inculcating ethical practice. However, nourished by the understandable desire of a commonly derided industry to prove itself respectable, plenty of lush moralistic vegetation flourishes. Indeed well-known PR educators have described the role of PR as one of promoting "loving" relations, and given the impression that "Nelson Mandela and Mother Theresa [sic] would have struggled to qualify for admittance to the Institute for Public Relations".

Moral obfuscation is abetted by the fact that a great deal of PR work, including much of what is considered controversial, is conducted behind the scenes and involves deniable conversations and actions. There is no real way of controlling what PR people do, and PR people often make great claims for themselves, knowing their self-proclaimed virtue is hard to challenge. What is important is the practitioner's individual sense of what is wrong – a highly personal matter.

First, let me present the fruits of some qualitative research. Over recent years I have interviewed quite a few of the large number of young people who want to study public relations at university with a view to working in the field. I often ask them to imagine they have just graduated, having accumulated the usual mountain of debt. The job situation is bleak. There is nothing on offer – until a single opportunity comes up. The pay is very good. It involves working for the PR department of a tobacco company. Most of them say they would take the position.

I then explain that, before starting work, they are called in by their future employers. It emerges that the remuneration package is much better than they thought – there's a mouth-watering bonus scheme and a company car to die for. They will leave their peer group from university far behind. Penthouse flats and luxurious holidays beckon. Their actual duties are also spelt out in more detail. The tobacco company is particularly interested in promoting its products in developing countries, and the target market it has in mind comprises school-age children. The PR campaigns would be directed at getting them while they are young.[2] Quite a few will still take the job, although with a bit more umming and ah-ing. These are normally group interviews. Frequently there seems to be a domino effect: whatever the first person says ripples round the room.

I then throw the scenario at would-be journalists (whom we often interview at the same time, in the same room). I ask them to imagine that after graduating they have found short-term work with a TV current affairs programme, but their time there seems to be coming to an end. They are desperately keen to be employed on a permanent basis. Coming up with a big story would make all the difference.

They meet their very good old friend from university, the former PR student who is now working for a tobacco company. Over a drink they hear about the tobacco company's stratagems. They realise that this would make exactly the kind of story they are looking for. They also realise that they could not run the story without destroying their friend's position within the tobacco company – something which their horrified friend makes clear to them in a subsequent, tearful phone call. Almost without exception the would-be journalists say they would run the story.

Can one draw any conclusions from this piece of research? One of my distinguished professorial colleagues, alongside whom I sometimes interview, is horrified. Are "young people these days" more amoral, or just more direct and realistic, and less likely to equivocate and dissemble? I have a feeling that some years ago we may have feigned greater idealism, but have gone on to do the same things: after all, people have always done the sort of things outlined above.

ETHICAL ABSOLUTISM AND PR

However – to me – this little exercise demonstrates the pointlessness of searching for ethical absolutes. Important issues are usually far from one-dimensional. One might refuse to work for a tobacco company because of apprehensions about one's future career, rather than for exalted moral reasons. The reluctance of many PR consultancies to take on such business may also be pragmatic: they may fear that taking on unpopular clients could lead to the loss of valuable staff (although in at least one case of which I'm aware, *junior* staff at a leading PR consultancy were disappointed by their superiors' refusal to take on a cigarette company as a client), or the loss of other clients, existing or potential. Anyone who continues to think it's a black and white case should read Christopher Buckley's brilliant satire, *Thank You for Smoking* (2003), in which he manages to turn a tobacco industry PR, or *smokes*man, into a hero who takes on the po-faced health establishment.

Ethics are ultimately personal, a product of all the factors that make up one's cultural DNA. For my own part, faced by the dilemma I have put to those interviewees, I would not particularly like to work for a tobacco company, but I hope I'd do that rather than betray a friend – so for me, according to the lights by which I try to lead my life, it is the behaviour of the would-be journalists that is most shameful. It makes me glad I'm not a journalist: as Andrew Marr has put it, "the 'honest' journalist must behave like a shit" (Marr 2004: 184).[3]

The basis on which one forms ethical judgments changes over time. Most people would have had few qualms about promoting tobacco until half a century ago, and thereafter doubts lingered for a while. It is hard to deny similar uncertainties when one considers the right course of action on any contemporary bone of contention: mobile phones for kids, SUVs, wind-farms, fast food, GM food, alcopops…Who knows what people will be saying about some of these issues in a few years' time? Other ethical issues are hardy perennials. For some selling meat is unethical, while for many others lending money for interest, the very cornerstone of our financial system, is unethical. What about gambling, pornography, child labour, animal testing, the fur trade?

The head of one large PR consultancy in London has cited his agency's refusal to work for the arms industry as an example of its ethical approach to business.[4] If this is an absolute principle, he would presumably have refused to work for the manufacturers of Spitfires in the late 1930s – yet I for one can think of few more ethical causes. And any such approach fails to recognise the interdependence of business activities: is one to be like some latter-day Quaker businessman, avowing pacifism and making profits from the making of iron, but leaving it to others to beat it into swords and cannon? As these examples and the research cited earlier in this article indicate, it is impossible to overstate how personal and mercurial are the foundations upon which our ethics rest. Saying this does not of course imply that we as individuals are *a*moral, merely that the bases upon which we make moral decisions vary.

PR: A CONVENIENT SCAPEGOAT FOR ANTI-CORPORATISM

Much PR activity is undertaken to serve business interests and if business is seen as the baddy then so is PR. Indeed many attacks on PR are really thinly disguised assaults on the business world, mounted by people who cannot come to terms with the ascendancy of capitalism. For them, PR practitioners are the sinister special forces of the big corporations and their allies in government, operating behind enemy lines and using a variety of unfair, clandestine tricks. As one of the founding fathers of the University of Westminster's distinctive school of media studies wrote:

> The rise of PR [represents] the direct control by private or state interests of the flow of public information in the interest, not of rational discourse, but of manipulation (quoted in L'Etang and Pieczka 1996: 49).

However, beyond raising a litany of complaints about the use of PR it is never clear what such people would do about it.

My starting points are different. It's hard to argue that government is *per se* ethical, and so political PR is forever open to question. Meanwhile business – both in its purposes and the methods it uses – is *a*moral. Business, and hence the PR that serves it, exists to meet human needs and desires, and there are few moral systems which would claim that all human *desires* are ethical (and most moralists would quibble about the ways in which some of the *needs* are met as well). As already suggested, most of us have qualms about some legal forms of business, but these reservations vary. One might argue that where society achieves a consensus then particular forms of business activity are deemed illegal, but even then we sometimes think we have the right to break the law. Does everyone who has ever used cannabis think that he or she has acted unethically?

So much for business and government, but it is perhaps time for critics of the role of PR in contemporary society to subject the not-for-profit sector – non-governmental-organisations or NGOs – to more searching scrutiny. They are the sacred cows of PR and their ethical purity is too readily assumed. They wield great power and influence, but what about *their* accountability and the transparency of *their* decision-making processes? The causes they espouse are just as open to question – and indeed may conflict with those of other NGOs – but they normally remain under-examined, benefiting as they do from the assumption that their intentions are noble. They may eschew the use of the term "public relations", but their PR muscle is extensive, their use of PR techniques just as contentious and, because many of them have no other purpose than to campaign for particular causes, they come much nearer to being pure PR vehicles than either corporations or governments. Indeed it is at least arguable that the large campaigning NGOs are little more than large corporations, trading in the commodity of conscience and competing for funding as they sell the "feel-good" factor to their donors. Is that necessarily ethical?

If one concludes that PR is unethical *per se* then – obviously – it can't be practised ethically. However I happen to believe that public relations is not only an inevitable part of modern life but that any real attempt to curb its activities would involve so many practical difficulties and such gross infringements of human rights as to be beyond both pragmatic and ethical contemplation. I also believe that the desire of people and organisations to put their views forward is perfectly healthy: the important thing, surely, is that others are allowed to put across rival arguments, the hallmark of a free society, and – crucially – that the debates that arise are reported properly. The responsibility for this last duty does not rest with PR but, primarily, with the media. If journalists are inept, lazy, susceptible to pressure, or acting as purveyors of entertainment rather than as dogged watchdogs and intrepid searchers for the truth they should lacerate themselves, not the PR industry. Many of the *causes célébres* used to vilify PR could with greater justice be described as failures of journalism: after all, sensible PR people do not claim to be neutral or objective.

ARE PR PEOPLE SPECIALLY QUALIFIED TO OPINE ON ETHICS?

It has never been clear to me why PR people have any special qualifications to opine on matters ethical. To hear some PR industry panjandrums speak is to enter another world, one where a new religion of business morals is – or soon will be – serviced by a high priesthood of PR people. Such people never deign to explain PR's source of ethical certainty. In practice many contentious issues with moral implications are highly technical, and public relations people cannot expect to be true experts on the full range of problems facing the worlds of business, politics or indeed the not-for-profit sector. What PR people can advise on is how something will play with different audiences (or, to use a current euphemism, with benign suggestions of inclusion and participation, with "stakeholders") and how it will be reported in the media – but I hope we can agree that being popular or getting a good press is not the same thing as acting ethically.

Given the dubious public standing of PR, most outsiders would scoff at the notion that PR people are equipped to act as ethical counsellors, and yet PR's interest in corporate social responsibility (CSR) is a concrete demonstration of the desire of some of its practitioners to act as the conscience of business. Beyond mere importuning for new business I suspect another force is at work here: the PR industry contains its share of erstwhile socialists, those for whom – until recently – big business was anathema. The consumption of so many past words is made more palatable by claiming a fresh dawn for business, a new era in which, after thousands of years, business is no longer immoral, or amoral, but splendidly moral. Such people like to think they are playing a part in achieving this rebirth – and others are quite happy that they should think it.

The notion that one should have a personal belief in what one advocates persists among some PR people and PR educators. One of the few would-be PR students to decline the initial "job offer" in the interview *cum* research exercise that I described above said that she'd been told by an interviewer at another university that you should only do PR work for something in which you really believe. That's a bit sanctimonious for my taste, but if one's students genuinely applied that principle then their career progression rates would, I suspect, be pretty abysmal. Those few students who found work would presumably have to quit their jobs whenever they had to compromise their beliefs in any way. On the other hand someone who prates about genuine belief without really applying it is a mere hypocrite – and that, to my mind, is an ethical problem.

Alternatively, one could argue that there's nothing wrong with promoting any legitimate product – including tobacco. In a free society isn't anyone – or any organisation – entitled to put its views across? Presumably this is the defence that those pioneers of PR, Ivy Lee and Carl Byoir, would have used to justify their work for the Nazi Party. In practice most PR people would jump off the wagon train of this particular argument before it trundles too far: fairly or unfairly, the causes served by PR people leave them guilty by association – they do not share the relative immunity of lawyers. Once again the outcome is usually a highly personal compromise: most PR people cannot afford the luxury of working only for what they really believe in, but perhaps manage to duck out of working for causes which they really detest.

Using the example of tobacco again, one might equally argue that condemning its promotion is a form of hypocrisy – a political fudge – borne of moral cowardice: we don't quite dare ban the product, so let's temporise by shooting the messenger who tells us about it. And, to use the example from my research exercise, doesn't attempting to shield developing countries from the persuasive powers of the free market show a patronising disdain which infantilises them? Isn't it for parents, teachers and other adults to guide children through the maze of persuasive messages they will encounter? In much of the liberal critique of the persuasive industries there is implicit elitist arrogance: we – teachers, would-be intellectuals – can of course see through the messages with which we are bombarded, but other, "ordinary" people cannot, and need to be protected. This comes perilously close to the notion of that founding father of PR, Edward Bernays, that he was by implication part of an "intelligent few", and that PR could be used to exert control over the irrational mass (for example, Bernays 1928: 9-27).

PR EDUCATION: TEACHING THE UNTEACHABLE?[5]

I hope I have demonstrated the difficulty of determining whether any cause or organisation seeking the services of PR is ethical, but what about the nature of the public relations techniques used? Is it permissible to defend the apparently indefensible, provided one's toolkit contains only morally approved implements? And if so, what can educators contribute to this process? I will base some of my observations on experience at the coalface of PR education.

As mentioned, plenty of people want to study PR at university these days, even though whether actually studying the subject confers any advantage upon would-be entrants to the PR industry is hotly debated. But there are many difficulties associated with the teaching of PR as a practical subject. At a simple, basic level PR practice is *necessarily* a social and interactive activity in a way that journalism practice is not. Of course journalism cannot discover its potential until it finds its audience[6], but it is at least theoretically possible for a student journalist to write an article – or prepare an item for broadcast – which is every bit as good as that which we encounter in our newspapers or on our televisions or radios. Even if the text or recording remains in a module box awaiting the government inspector, or gathers dust in a tutor's office, it is potentially exactly the same product, word-for-word and image-for-image, and prepared by the same means, as the work of a fully-fledged professional. In this important, practical sense only the actual act of publication or broadcast separates the best student work from that of the working journalist.

Not so with public relations. True PR work needs a social context not just to realise its potential but to exist at all: it is necessarily socially interactive. Students can certainly present ideas for PR campaigns, but these are not the finished products of public relations. A real PR campaign – or any form of PR work – cannot live in a desk drawer, or even, dare one say it, a module box. It involves countless exchanges with journalists and/or others, and it hopefully exploits (or suffers from) changing circumstances in the media and elsewhere as it unfolds over time. Nothing is certain: the media (and others) may be indifferent, or hostile. The fruits of PR are usually indirect and hard to discern, located as they are in the output of others. Its real achievement may be that nothing appears in the media, or that hostile coverage is minimised. Hence the exact achievements of PR work are the subject of endless claims and counterclaims.

The best university exercise can only very loosely simulate the media pond in which the PR practitioner swims (let alone the broader social swamps through which they wade) – far more loosely than a journalism course can simulate the editor's spike. Certainly students can practise writing press releases, but these are only a humble building block in the construction of PR, not the be-all and end-all that the printed word is in print journalism.

All of these obstacles have major implications for the teaching of ethics. So much of PR involves private interaction – unrecorded meetings and conversations, phone calls, emails (which have admittedly proved leaky). It is here that the critical judgment calls and many of the commonly criticised aspects of PR lurk, and it is precisely these elements of the work that cannot truly be replicated in the classroom. It is all very well to assemble models of ethical perfection at one's leisure, as part of one's teaching, but such models are seldom robust enough to survive the bombardment of reality – the time pressures and the demands of bosses, clients and journalists and others which afflict one at times when one's very career seems to be upon the line. Lest anyone think that work experience for students – however valuable – is an easy way round this problem, let them reflect again on the difficulty of judging PR's effectiveness, and the near-impossibility of an outsider knowing the full inside story of a PR campaign, not least its ethical dimensions. Were Alastair Campbell a student, how would we assess his performance, ethical and otherwise?

DOES AN INFINITY OF CODES MAKE PR PROFOUNDLY ETHICAL?

PR's own propagandists duck and dive around these issues. What practices, precisely, are unethical? Well, PR has certainly generated numerous codes of conduct – a suspiciously large number, one might conclude, if one is of a cynical disposition. A PR practitioner in the UK might well be subject to codes devised by the Chartered Institute of Public Relations (www.ipr.org.uk), the Public Relations Consultants Association (www.prca.org.uk), the International Communications Consultancies Organisation (www.iccopr.com), the International Public Relations Association (with two main codes – www.ipra.org) and the European Public Relations Confederation (www.cerp.org), and others as well. Enforcement of these codes is in inverse proportion to the number of them. It is rare for PR practitioners to be investigated, and rarer still for them to be disciplined – which might mean that PR is, indeed, profoundly ethical.

The real problem is, of course, more complex. For the reasons described above much of the most sensitive PR work takes place in private and involves deniable conversations. As we all know, private conversations can be recalled in many ways and are capable of an infinite number of interpretations. It is no accident that several notorious recent scandals have been the result of controversial practices being inadvertently placed on the record. Sophie Wessex's business partner surely did not know he was being recorded when he offered to procure gay partners for the *News of the World*'s fake sheikh in 2001. One might argue that it was the tape-recording rather than the offer to procure men which led to his expulsion from the IPR. Similarly, that distinguished alumna of the University of Westminster's media studies programme, Jo Moore, may not have started on the downward path which led to her losing her job as one of New Labour's political advisors had she popped her head round an office door and simply said what she wanted to suggest about burying bad news about local government amid the events of 9/11 in 2001, rather than documenting it in her fateful email.

So misdemeanours are difficult to detect and prove. But one might also question the will of PR organisations seriously to enforce their codes. Although their titles are designed to suggest otherwise, PR organisations are in reality trade associations rather than professional bodies. They have no right to control entry to the practice of public relations – and no ability to exclude anybody from practising it – and it is difficult to see how this could ever change. Of course even established professional bodies – the Law Society, for example – are suspected of favouring the interests of their members over those of their clients. For PR organisations this is even more the case. They are powerless, and are entirely dependent on seeking recruits and retaining their membership (and their subscriptions). Not surprisingly, this has hardly been a recipe for stern discipline.

In this atmosphere PR codes could be likened to a series of Potemkin villages: although their injunctions do no harm and may even have some positive effects (I'm not going altogether to gainsay the advantages of urging people to be well-behaved), their real purpose is display. They seek to show that public relations is − or is on the brink of becoming − the profession it will never be. PR organisations, of course, protest the contrary: it was, I understand, a past President of the Institute of Public Relations who prompted the presenter of Radio 4's World at One to conclude that "Nelson Mandela and Mother Theresa would have struggled to qualify for admittance to the Institute for Public Relations".[7]

The preamble to the code of ethics of the world's biggest PR organisation, the Public Relations Society of America, illustrates this polarisation between high principle and impotence when it says: "Ethical practice is the most important obligation of a PRSA member." But it goes on to explain:

> Emphasis on enforcement of the Code has been eliminated. But, the PRSA Board of Directors retains the right to bar from membership or expel from the Society any individual who has been or is sanctioned by a government agency or convicted in a court of law of an action that is in violation of this Code.[8]

WE ALL TELL LIES

Precisely what activities are frowned upon by the PR industry's own organisations? Well, some are quite narrow and technical and I don't intend to go into them all here, but PR's attitude to the truth is perhaps worth focusing on. Telling lies is outlawed by most of the codes. This might seem unexceptional − until one starts to think about it. As Pontius Pilate pointed out: "What is truth?".[9] Rather more recently one well-known PR practitioner thought it was time to answer the question with the establishment of a Truth Institute[10], although nothing seems to have come of it so far. On the other hand, as one of the best-known − and most controversial − PR people in contemporary Britain, Max Clifford, famously said:

> I stand up and say that an important part of public relations is lies and deceit. We all know that but they won't ever admit it (Moloney 2000: 23).

Fortunately it was a well-known journalist, not a PR person, who wrote the following:

> Try, for just a day, a policy of absolute honesty. You think the
> neighbours are dreary or obese? For God's sake, don't hide it. You find
> your daughter wittering? Tell her – never mind the tears. Your boss
> has a bad body odour problem? Tell the brute, as frankly as you inhale
> it. A day of honesty would be enough to finish most of us (Marr op
> cit: 164).

So we all lie. Even those who invoke the thinking of Immanuel Kant on this issue
are, I'm told, and perhaps without knowing it, guilty of dishonesty, simply by
choosing to pronounce his name politely but inaccurately. Some lies are clearly
more acceptable than others, and some are expected, enabling us to discount the
information we receive. Lying about specific facts – and especially figures – may
be inadvisable and sometimes even illegal, but no competent PR person would
advise his or her employer or client to offer full details on every problem or
internal disagreement.

For example, and as a rule of thumb, when someone expresses full
confidence in a subordinate a lie is involved: they have only been asked the
question because that confidence has been undermined. One could say that the
notion of the Cabinet's collective responsibility institutionalises such lies, and all
organisations have cultivated similar ways of coping with the dilemmas Andrew
Marr describes. Normally, when difficulties are acknowledged it is because they
can no longer be hidden, and we are usually told that the problem has been – or
shortly will be – resolved. Often this involves a lie, but it's lie that can be
anticipated and is therefore deemed socially acceptable, even by journalists.

THE WHIG INTERPRETATION OF PR HISTORY

It's not just PR codes of ethics, with their abstract and unthought-through
approach, that sometimes seem unreal. Far too much purportedly academic
writing about public relations stops little short of drivel as it seeks – cackhandedly
– to propagandise for the industry, promoting a Whig interpretation of PR history,
where PR has risen from the slough of propaganda towards the sunny uplands of
something called "two-way symmetric communication" (Grunig and Hunt 1984).
In this Shangri-la of public relations mutual understanding between organisations
and their publics is achieved and peace and happiness will reign for ever more.
(Although, interestingly, even proponents of this view argue that PR is always just
about to arrive at this destination but has never quite got there.) For such people:

> Public relations…should be ethical in that helps build caring – even
> loving – relationships with other individuals and groups they affect in
> a society or the world…(quoted in L'Etang and Pieczka op cit: 31).

Others have claimed that PR should have nothing to do with persuasion (for example Harrison 1995: 3, 7[11]). These efforts seem to me self-defeating as well as unreal. People quickly see through them and, far from improving PR's standing, they further undermine the discipline's credibility. Better to try to be honest even if it seems hard than to make spurious claims to saintliness: I don't think many people expect PR practitioners to behave like Nelson Mandela or Mother Theresa (see above), so why pretend? Sadly, those PR people who espouse such views and who, as mentioned, seem to see their occupation as akin to a new religion, have become believers and are no longer sceptical and duly critical seekers after the truth (even if just occasionally one suspects one or two of them of being like revivalist preachers who rage against sin while casting a lascivious eye over members of the choir). As has been said:

> The theologian may indulge the pleasing task of describing Religion as she descended from Heaven, arrayed in her native purity. A more melancholy duty is imposed on the historian. He must discover the inevitable mixture of error and corruption which she contracted in a long residence upon earth, among a weak and degenerate race of beings (Gibbon 1993: 488).

Indeed, a little more serious history and a little less pontification might help the cause of PR. The attempts of PR's own trade associations to control the way in which PR is studied also do the discipline a disservice. The aim of the main PR organisation accrediting UK university courses is to "improve the standing of public relations as a strategic and rigorous management discipline".[12] Industry capture of an academic subject area is hardly a recipe for free intellectual enquiry.

THE INSECURITIES OF A FLEDGLING ACADEMIC DISCIPLINE

There are other dangers. In this chapter I have sought to ground my observations upon real dilemmas, drawn from the myriad of problems a PR practitioner might face. Too often "academic" PR shuns or dodges these brutal realities. With all the insecurity of a fledgling academic discipline which lacks a secure research base and is uncertain of its place within contemporary academia it seeks to make up for its lack of critically tested knowledge by laboriously erecting edifices of theory.[13] These are frequently founded upon dreary and second-rate logic chopping, with inflated language to match (as Orwell put it, "A mass of Latin words falls upon the facts like soft snow, blurring the outline and covering up all the details" (Orwell 1946)), and adorned with plenty of half-digested name-droppings. An excessive readiness to hide behind famous names rather than tackling difficult issues for oneself is not unique to PR academics, and may be an understandable way of preening oneself, but I'm not sure obscuring the debate in this way helps the discipline of public relations – nor does it do much for those facing, or preparing to face, the practical problems of working life. In the end, too much Kant can truly sound like cant.

Lest some of the above sounds cynical, negative or nihilistic I want to conclude by suggesting the – limited – role that PR educators can play in inculcating ethical practice. I tend to think that a country gets the PR practitioners it deserves. Students come to us as young adults, products of the society which we and they inhabit, having already absorbed most of the ideas of right and wrong which are going to guide them through life. They will of course have to apply this moral framework to their chosen occupations. I'm not a great fan of preaching to them or imposing some kind of generational imperialism, but certainly studying and discussing some of the moral mazes in which PR practitioners lose themselves is perfectly proper.

Jettisoning as much as possible of the lush and unreal moralistic vegetation described above would serve to clear the air. More thoughtful, critical PR case studies would be helpful, but for reasons alluded to elsewhere in this paper that will always be a problem. In particular, self-serving accounts of practitioners' own work should be treated with extreme caution: self-congratulation certainly presents ethical problems. So my credo is to give students the chance to explore ethical issues and to hear and read a range of different views. The aim should be to produce thoughtful, questioning graduates, not happy hypocrites. If we adopt this approach at least we can say that students are aware of the issues and have reflected upon them. But from then on, it's up to them.

NOTES

1. For the purposes of this paper I see little point in getting bogged down in competing definitions of ethics. The important point here is the commonly understood meaning of ethics among people who are not obsessed with definitional issues. I am happy to go along with the definitions provided by the *Shorter Oxford English Dictionary*. Of those offered, the notions that ethics comprises "the science of morals"; "the moral principles by which any particular person is guided"; and "the rules of conduct recognised in a particular profession or area of human life" seem particularly relevant.

2. My scenario is not entirely fanciful. In 2003 the Director General of the Institute of Public Relations pointed to the increased opportunities for PR in sectors such as tobacco and alcohol, as regulation increasingly excludes the use of advertising (http://www.ipr.org.uk/news/index.htm, accessed 26 March 2005).

3 . I recall an external examiner deploring the unethical practices of some journalism students. In the view of their tutor it was precisely those students who had the best career prospects.

4. http://www.prweek.com/news/news_story.cfm?ID=221739&site=1, accessed 30 March 2005
5. For more on this topic see the present writer's "PR: an infant learning to walk in the groves of academe?" (*Media Education Journal*, Issue 34, Autumn 2003 pp 12-13)
6. Although the notion of journalism finding its social meaning can be exaggerated: as one long-serving foreign correspondent put it, his work was like peeing off the Grand Canyon – he assumed something had reached the bottom but could not be sure. (*Guardian*, 21 May 2005, p.13)
7. http://www.guardian.co.uk/tv_and_radio/story/0,3604,1088095,00.html, published 19 November 2003, accessed 10 April 2004
8. http://www.prsa.org/_About/ethics/preamble.asp?ident=eth3 , accessed 25 March 2005.
9. The Gospel according to John, Ch. 18 v. 38
10. http://www.anti-spin.com/index.cfm?SECONDARY_ID=0&PRIMARY_ID=19, accessed 25 March 2005
11. Interestingly Harrison watered down this repudiation of persuasion in the second edition of her book published in 2000
12 . Criteria and Procedures for IPR Recognition of Diploma and Degree Programmes in Public Relations, June 2000 p.3
13. A short chapter on ethics in *The Public Relations Handbook* invokes Kant at least 21 times. The same chapter offers a single two paragraph case study. (Ian Somerville in Theaker, Alison, ed, 2002 pp 107-118)

REFERENCES

Bernays, Edward L (1928) *Propaganda,* New York, Horace Liveright

Buckley, Christopher (2003) *Thank You for Smoking,* London, Allison and Busby

Gibbon, Edward (1993) *The Decline and Fall of the Roman Empire,* London, David Campbell (Everyman's Library Edition)

Grunig, James E, and Hunt, Todd (1984) *Managing Public Relations,* New York, Holt, Rinehart and Winston

Harrison, Shirley (1995) *Public Relations: An Introduction,* London and New York, Routledge (second edition published by Thomson Learning in 2000)

L'Etang, Jacquie and Pieczka, Magda (eds) (1996) *Critical Perspectives in Public Relations,* London and Boston MA, International Thomson Business Press

Marr, Andrew (2004) *My Trade: A Short History of British Journalism,* London, Macmillan

Moloney, Kevin (2000) *Rethinking Public Relations: The Spin and the Substance,* London and New York, Routledge

Orwell, George (1946) *Politics and the English Language.* Available online at http://orwell.ru/library/essays/politics/english/e_polit, accessed on14 May 2005

Theaker, Alison (ed.) (2002) *The Public Relations Handbook,* London and New York, Routledge

NOTE ON AUTHOR

Simon Goldsworthy is Senior Lecturer in Public Communication at the University of Westminster, where he established the MA in Public Communication and Public Relations in 2000 and the PR pathway on the University's BA Media Studies programme. He also lectures regularly on political communication at the Sorbonne. He was a member of the Government Information Service between 1990 and 1997 and has also worked in PR in the private sector. His publications include: "PR: an infant learning to walk in the groves of academe?" (*Media Education Journal*, Issue 34, Autumn 2003 pp. 12-13); "Advertising as the fall guy for consumerism: the real and perceived roles of public relations and advertising in contemporary 'propaganda' " (*La Revue LISA*, Volume IV – No. 3, 2006); and, with Trevor Morris, *Public Relations for Asia*, Palgrave Macmillan, 2007. Contact details: Department of Journalism and Mass Communication, University of Westminster, Harrow Campus, Watford Road, Harrow HA1 3TP. Email: simongoldsworthy@aol.com.

19

Involving vulnerable communities in organisational decisions: Communication ethics in action

Anne Gregory

Public relations is a developing field of study and there is still debate about its role in organisations and society. Part of this debate is whether and how it can assist organisations to engage with stakeholders in an ethical manner. This chapter explores some of these issues, using a teaching case study to describe how one large Mental Health NHS Trust has implemented its public relations-led involvement policy. It illustrates how involving stakeholders at a deep level places ethical obligations on organisations that must then be honoured, both in terms of the process of engagement and its outcome.

INTRODUCTION

There can be little doubt that public relations has an image problem. Books such as *Sultans of Sleaze: Public Relations and the Media* (Nelson 1989), *PR A Social History of Spin* (Ewen 1996), *Trust Us, We're the Experts* (Rampton and Stauber 2002) and *Tailspin* (McClusker 2005) chronicle the problems and issues in detail. Indeed, as Parsons (2004) puts it, public relations ethics is regarded by many as an oxymoron.

Against this background, the UK Chartered Institute of Public Relations, in a major report co-produced by the government's Department of Trade and Industry stated that "more urgency and effort is required by individual practitioners, organisations and public relations industry bodies to communicate a modern and ethical profession" (DTI/IPR 2003:6). The Institute made a commitment, in the same report, to introduce an ethics module in its Continuing Professional Development programme.

Recognising the genuine ethical issues that surround the practice of public relations, the teaching of ethics has been an essential part of many of the public relations courses in the UK and around the world. For example, the undergraduate course at Leeds Metropolitan University has a Politics, Philosophy and Public Relations module that specifically addresses ethics, and ethical perspectives are embedded in the course as a core element of teaching professional practice. Professional codes of conduct, relations with the media, corporate social responsibility, the role of the public relations practitioner as ethical guardian (L'Etang 2003) for the organisation, are just some of the themes that are explored.

PUBLIC RELATIONS AS A FIELD OF STUDY

Public relations is an emerging discipline and there is still much discussion about its role in organisations and society (Moloney 2000, Cornelissen 2004). This is exemplified in the on-going debates about definitions. In 1976 Harlow (1976) had identified 472 definitions of public relations and there have been many more since. At the heart of the discussion is a conceptual debate about the nature and purpose of public relations. Cornelissen (2004) articulates it well. There are two dominant theoretical strands in the public relations field of study. One strand, which can be identified as the rhetorical and critical perspective, emanates from communication theory and focuses on "the phenomenon, process and effects of communications" (ibid: 17). Rhetoricians ascribe to the view that the symbolism contained within behaviour and communication is the crux of how relationships between organisations and stakeholders are initiated, maintained and changed.

The other main strand originates in management theory and focuses "on the analysis, planning and programming, tactical and evaluative activities engaged in for communications campaigns" (ibid). For those in the management tradition, the symbolic act of communication is seen only as part of the *process*, not the end point, which is the building and maintaining of beneficial relationships with stakeholders.

The rhetorical and critical school of public relations came to prominence in the 1990s. Scholars such as Pearson (2000), Heath (2001) and Toth (1992) argue that public relations involves people making sense of the symbols produced by organisations – whether they be verbal, written, visual or behavioural. To this school of thought, the *process* of communication constitutes the ethical core of public relations. Drawing on the work of Habermas (1984), rhetorical scholars place great emphasis on the rules of engagement for ethical dialogue, stressing that participants should be able to test and probe ideas, have equal freedom to initiate and continue dialogue, to set the discussion agenda and to challenge and/or explain.

To do this they must have freedom from manipulation and equality of power. They also have a responsibility for comprehensibility (ensuring they are understood), truth (factual accuracy), rightness (appropriate to those receiving the communication) and truthfulness (sincerity). To arrive at a position of agreed meaning, or truth, it is important that all parties to the dialogue advocate their position with as much vigour and persuasion as possible. Thus, arguments can then be tested and countered by other participants so that at the end of the process the best argument emerges.

The practical application of this position has difficulties as Somerville (2004) points out. In reality power is not equal, some organisations are extremely powerful and indeed act to close down opposing voices. While dialogue might be seen as a "good thing"; often there isn't time to have protracted debates, decisions have to be made. Sometimes these will be made in the interests of the majority or the most powerful because it is not possible to reconcile and agree a way forward that satisfies the interests of everyone.

Management theory is much more interested in the *ends* than the process *per se*. Ultimately an organisation has to survive and prosper if it is to continue in existence. In recent years the stakeholding view of the firm articulated by Freeman (1984) has become a prevailing management theory and it has particular relevance to public relations because of the conflation of the concept of stakeholders with publics. In simple terms, stakeholders are "any individual or group who can affect or is affected by the actions, decisions, policies, practices or goals of the organisation" (Freeman 1984: 25).

Central to the notion in stakeholding is that the organisation is part of an interdependent web of relationships with a range of individuals and groups who see benefits in those relationships and who, ultimately, decide whether or not the organisation is legitimate. If they decide it is not, they will withdraw the organisation's "licence to operate" and it will cease to exist. Stakeholding theory itself is not without controversy. Although as conceptualised originally and still proposed by Freeman (Phillips, Freeman and Wicks 2003) as a theory of organisational management and ethics, he accepts that in its "instrumental" variation (i.e. that managers should attend stakeholders as a means to achieving other organisational goals such as profit or shareholder wealth maximisation) stakeholder theory stands virtually unopposed (ibid: 479).

However, accusations of instrumentalism can be levelled at other management theories, for example those that conceptualise organisations through the marketing lens. The fact that stakeholding has at its core an ethical element is in itself pertinent to communication ethics. Stakeholding theory sees a role for public relations in maintaining and enhancing relationships in order to protect the legitimacy of the organisation. Communication is a key *means* by which this is achieved.

Of course the rhetorical and management perspectives, while different, are not mutually exclusive. In reality unless the *process* of dialogue is undertaken ethically, ethical *ends* are less likely to be achieved. To achieve mutually beneficial relationships, communication based on trust and integrity is essential.

SOME ISSUES OF PRACTICE

This theoretical debate is played out in public relations practice. The realm of politics is not an area for consideration in this paper, but in the organisational arena the main debate is around the nature and extent of advocacy. Some (for example, Gregory 2002) would argue that the first ethical choice is for whom the practitioner works. The fact that an organisation is legal, does not necessarily mean they should be represented. Typically tobacco companies, arms manufacturers and alcoholic drinks distillers and distributors are cited as obvious examples where moral choices are to be made. There are however, more difficult choices. For example, what enquiries should be made (if any) about where an organisation sources its raw materials, or what its employment practices are?

Having made the choice about client/employer, the question about whether loyalties should be to employer or society can be addressed. The DTI/IPR report referred to earlier gives its definition of public relations as "influencing behaviour to achieve objectives through the effective management of relationships and communication" (p.10). The implied orientation here is organisational. Furthermore, the CIPR's current Code of Conduct [1] does not refer to a duty to society. However, most of the standard and ethics text books on public relations, for example (Grunig and Hunt 1984; Seib and Fitzpatrick 1995; Cutlip, Center and Broom 2000; McElreath 2000; Parsons 2004) state that the practitioner's highest duty is to society. This ambiguity is itself is worthy of exploration.

Within this context the main practice issue about advocacy is confronted. Clearly public relations professionals are hired to represent organisations. They are not neutral bystanders, they are there to explain, defend and promote their organisations. This opens up a major debate on issues such as parallels with the law, defining and telling the truth, the extent to which all the facts are revealed, the timing of information release and who the information is released to. Alongside, there are issues about the use of front organisations, lobbying activities and third party advocacy. Academics such as Martinson (1999), Edgett (2002), Gregory (2003) and Parsons (2004) have sought to bring some practice principles to this debate.

By definition practitioners operate where there are tensions. They are classic boundary spanners with one foot in the organisation and one foot outside. They balance the interests of multiple stakeholders, making subtle judgements about their relative importance in any situation. They also balance the interests of organisation, stakeholders and society. They deal with issues and people, they manage crises. Their remit, along with others in the organisation, covers managing an organisation's relationships and legitimacy. The Canadian academic Ron Pearson summarised it well when he said:

Public relations practice is situated at precisely that point where competing issues collide. Indeed, public relations problems can be defined in terms of the collision, or potential collision of these interests (Pearson 2000: 67).

Teaching ethics in public relations

It is against this contextual, theoretical and practice background that teaching public relations ethics takes place and, indeed, is part of the content of that teaching. There isn't space in this chapter to examine all the various areas that lend themselves to ethical input. However, in broad terms they can be summarised as falling into three main areas:

Technical competence – being up-to-date with the latest practice techniques and being competent in their use. In practice this means refusing work for which the practitioner is not competent. This is an ethical issue because it is about providing the best possible professional service to clients and society.

Practice (or process) integrity – ensuring that the way that practice is conducted is ethical. This includes truth-telling, promise keeping, respect for others, arriving at sound judgements (rhetorical and critical theory perspectives).

Outcome legitimacy – ensuring that the outcome builds organisational legitimacy, that relationships are maintained or enhanced and that the "licence to operate" is supported (management theory perspective). This includes building a relationship of trust and integrity, not purely instrumental ones. In addition an open, democratic and participative society is to be aimed for, based upon the free flow of a multiplicity of ideas and views.

A powerful way to ground these concepts in reality is to use cases, an accepted and practical pedagogical device. The following case is used by the author to draw out some of the issues outlined earlier, but also as a vehicle for identifying principles of best practice in public relations. It is used in undergraduate, postgraduate and professional courses. It focuses on work led by the public relations department of South West Yorkshire Mental Health NHS Trust (SWYMHT), who were responsible for the stakeholder involvement activities surrounding the establishment of the trust's founding Vision, Values and Goals and their subsequent embedding within the organisation.

The public relations department is led by a board level director who has worked in the NHS for many years and is familiar with the ethical issues involved in working with vulnerable service users. The public relations department in the trust covers all stakeholder communication including press, internal communication, advertising and design. There is no separate marketing department.

SOUTH WEST YORKSHIRE MENTAL HEALTH NHS TRUST

SWYMHT was formed on 1 April 2002. It was an amalgam of the mental health services of four Health Trusts in South and West Yorkshire and when formed had no formal organisational infrastructure and only a chairman and CEO in post at director level. A priority task set by the chair and CEO was to agree the Vision, Values and Goals of the organisation, which would provide direction and cultural coherence whilst at the same time serving as a yardstick for performance management and accountability. The Vision, Values and Goals would have practical ramifications in that they would determine the organisational structure and the nature of the services provided within a framework laid down by government. It was felt that involving stakeholders in framing the Vision, Values and Goals was essential, not only because they were knowledgeable and passionate about the nature of the services that should be provided (and therefore their input would help better decision-making), but in order to obtain their support for the organisation's direction and structure (organisational legitimacy).

Before the Trust was launched, there had been a formal and legally required consultation process conducted by the National Health Service. Numerous stakeholder groups in the area had been asked about the structure and nature of the mental health and learning disability services they would prefer. Based on this information and discussions with staff and stakeholder groups, the CEO and new senior management team constructed initial Vision, Values and Goals statements, which were agreed by the board as a basis for wider discussion.

In July 2002 a large-scale multi-stakeholder event was held. Its purpose was to discuss the Vision, Values and Goals and how best to communicate with stakeholders. Those involved included: service users, their carers, voluntary organisations, advocacy organisations, self-help groups, staff and their representatives, community health councils, primary care trusts, local authorities and executive and non-executive directors.

At the event, the CEO presented the Vision, Values and Goals, then various stakeholder groupings discussed the statements in workshops and detailed feedback was provided. Vision, Values and Goals are not easy concepts to describe, but a minimum of jargon was used and clarification and explanations were given by the CEO as required. The Vision was described as "where we are heading", the Values as "how we will behave along the way" and the Goals as "what we will do which moves us to where we want to be". It was thought vitally important that the CEO led the event.

The event itself could have been daunting to those service users and carers involved, many of whom live with profound and longstanding illnesses and whose contact with the service is not always enjoyable. People who use the service are often vulnerable and dependent. However, carers and service users able to articulate their views are usually passionate about the service they receive, highly vocal and keen to be involved in shaping provision. Feedback from the event was broadly supportive of the proposed Vision, Values and Goals, but a number of changes in priorities and wording were recommended. A feedback document capturing comments and issues was sent to event attendees and all those invited, along with a revised set of statements and a communication plan.

In addition to this event, the CEO also led five internal events for staff. The Vision, Values, and Goals were placed on the website with comments being invited from all stakeholders. Staff also elicited feedback during their routine work and visits. Informal soundings from the various stakeholding groups were also taken by senior managers throughout the consultation period. All the feedback was then reviewed and a final version was produced and approved by the trust board in September 2002. To close the loop a further multi-stakeholder event was held in November 2002 to feed back results, and to ask for involvement in the work of the trust.

Since the Vision, Values and Goals were agreed, the trust has been developing a programme of stakeholder engagement and involvement. In particular, in early 2005 a major re-shaping of the service has been under discussion, which involves moving from an institution-based service to a community-based one. In the meantime, the results of the Vision, Values and Goals engagement are being embedded in the trust. Key elements of the statements were around partnership working, championing equality, encouraging involvement, supporting and valuing diverse lives (the trust operates in a mixed ethnic community) and increasing choice. The practical outworking of this has included:

- a devolved service structure which is organisationally more resource demanding than a centralised one;
- structuring the corporate plan and responses to government performance measures around the agreed Vision, Values and Goals;
- having service user representatives on trust committees, appointment panels and local partnership arrangements;
- trust-wide training in diversity, starting at board level;
- involvement of service users in the life of the trust, for example, the new visual identity was designed by a service user and service users are given employment opportunities with the trust as appropriate;
- challenging behaviour and language in the trust that does not uphold the Vision, Values and Goals agreed by stakeholders.

ETHICAL ISSUES DRAWN FROM THE CASE

The case is used to prompt discussion on a number of ethical issues. There are a large number of facets to this case, therefore, just an indicative selection of the issues raised is explored here.

Communication in society

The European articulation of public relations coming from a communication theory perspective is quite different from the Anglo-American view. In Europe, (see van Ruler and Vercic 2004) public relations is interpreted as working in the public sphere for the public good. The German word for public relations is *Oftenlichkeitsarbeit*, literally "public work" and is explained as "working in public, with the public and for the public" (Nessman 2004). This case opens up the discussion of the role of public relations in society and the way that it can contribute to or hinder public debate and understanding. Mental health is the subject of much media coverage and debate – usually negative. The trust sees part of its role as informing a debate that is often based on fear and prejudice. Getting the facts about mental health into the public area is regarded as one of its key responsibilities. Specifically in this case, there is good practice that can be explored.

While government has a policy that public organisations should consult on significant matters, the trust has gone beyond its legal obligations. It has embraced a culture of engagement based on a sense of duty and obligation (duty ethics) and is attempting to build a broad-based stakeholding community founded on mutual trust and responsibility. This fulfils the ambition of public relations ethicists Kruckeburg and Starck (1988) who said:

> A community is achieved when people are aware of and interested in common ends, and regulate their activity in view of those ends. Communication plays a vital role as people try to regulate their own activity and to participate in efforts to reach common ends (ibid: 53).

Communication with the vulnerable and disenfranchised

One of the standard tools that management theorists use to prioritise stakeholders is the power/interest matrix. Those with most power and most interest demand more of the organisation's attention. Those with least power and least interest require least attention. While many of the trust's service users are voluntary patients, some are compulsorily detained under the Mental Health Act. They have no power, and because of their condition, sometimes have little interest in their treatment or the service. Giving those (or those who represent them), who have ostensively little power a voice in deciding the nature of the organisation and its services is a moral act.

Not only does it follow the Golden Rule (do unto others as you would have them do unto you), it ascribes to the position taken by the BBC's Reith lecturer, moral philosopher Onora O'Neill (2002), who states that rights can only exist where people regard it as their duty to secure those rights on behalf of all.

The rights of those vulnerable and disenfranchised stakeholders are secured by the trust who regard it as their obligation to provide a forum where users, carers and those who support them can voice their views and then uses management machinery to ensure those views are taken forward.

This point introduces a discussion about the relative power and rights of stakeholding groups and what obligation (or not) public relations practitioners have to ensure the voice of minorities is heard. It also raises the issue of the extent of advocacy. Powerful and resource rich organisations can drown out or seek to emasculate opposition groups who have legitimate points to raise.

Technical competence

The technical ability to organise the trust's communication activities and implement them appropriately is discussed. For example, this case describes the organisation of large scale events management for people who have special needs. The nature of the stakeholding group means that special attention has to be given to the technical skills required. For example, the writing has to be accessible but not patronising, websites are user-friendly and designed for diverse audiences. This demonstrates a commitment to professional standards, underlines the ethical responsibility for the practitioner to be competent in their particular sphere of work and the fact that the competency list will be different depending on the nature of the organisation being worked for. The requirement for professional training is emphasised with the CIPR's training framework referred to, along with an encouragement for students to maintain Continuing Professional Development (CPD) activities.

Practice integrity

The case allows the principles of ethical dialogue to be drawn out. Not only are there clear pointers in the case to the relationship-building model of public relations (Dozier, Grunig and Grunig 1995, Ledingham and Bruning 2000), but it provides the opportunity to discuss Habermas's (1984) notion of the ethical and ideal communication situation. In addition, the practical realities of government regulation and the pressures of timescales can also be explored with their ethical implications.

Outcome legitimacy

The real test of whether communication is being used instrumentally by an organisation, is the extent to which communication can be seen to build trust and commitment and re-enforce organisational legitimacy. There are two clear indicators of this;

- the organisation changes as a result of stakeholder input, and changes of its own volition, not because it has to;

- stakeholders remain engaged and become advocates of the organisation.

By examining the actions of the trust, by reviewing its literature which shows exemplars of the extent of stakeholder involvement and by analysing third party reports from, for example, the media, government regulators and collaborating organisations, the delivery of the moral contract can be tested.

STUDENT REACTION TO THE CASE

Student reaction to this case is interesting. It provokes intense discussion about the nature of the profession and the ethical issues that are raised by its critics. Specifically it encourages them to consider the different modes of practice (i.e. advocacy or relationship-building). It challenges them to consider their professional and moral obligation to less powerful stakeholders and embraces a wider discussion of the "rights" of different stakeholders. It highlights the difference between communication as a "good thing" in its own right and the instrumental way that it is used by many organisations. It illustrates how the *methods* used in communication have ethical implications. The case also raises interesting issues about the differences of working in the private and public sectors. From a teaching perspective, it is a rich case providing opportunities to discuss different theoretical and practice perspectives whilst being able to provide pointers to good practice.

CONCLUSION

The field of public relations is an emerging study area. Theoretical underpinnings are being developed as the practice moves on. The DTI/IPR Study (2003) states public relations is the third most popular career choice for graduates and the industry itself continues to grow despite the image problems that dog its progress. Ethics has become a key area for discussion and consideration, increasingly so since public instances of misconduct are often attributed rightly or wrongly at least in substantial part, to public relations or communication professionals, especially in the political and business arenas. The teaching of ethics is a core part of the public relations curriculum both as a subject in its own right, but also as an integral part of theory and practice. Cases such as the one outlined here attempt both to indicate the complexity of the issues involved and to provide an exemplar of ethical public relations in practice.

The aim of public relations educators is that those students who progress through public relations courses understand and can articulate the ethical issues in the profession, are equipped with an intellectual toolkit that can help them make sound judgements in difficult situations and can refer to examples of good practice that will provide solid blueprints for how they might conduct their own professional lives.

NOTES

To view the Code of Conduct see www.cipr.co.uk

To see the training framework see www.Martex.co.uk/prcareerdevelopment/index.htm

REFERENCES

Cornelissen, J. (2004) *Corporate Communication*, London, Sage.

Cutlip, S.M, Center, A.H. and Broom G.M. (2000) *Effective Public Relations*, 8th edition, Englewood Cliffs, NJ, Prentice Hall

Dozier, D.M., Grunig, L.A. and Grunig, J.E. (1995) *Manager's Guide to Excellence in Public Relations and Communication Management*, Mahwah, NJ., Lawrence Erlbaum Associates

DTI/ IPR (2003) *Unlocking the Potential of PR*, London, IPR

Edgett, R. (2002) "Towards an Ethical Framework for Advocacy in Public Relations", *Journal of Public Relations Research*, Vol. 14 pp 1-26

Ewen, S. (1996) *PR! A Social History of Spin*, New York, Baric Books

Freeman, R.E. (1984) *Strategic Management: A Stakeholder Approach*, Boston, Pitman

Gregory, A. (2002) "To spin or not to spin: The ethics of public relations", inaugural AGM lecture of the Institute of Public relations, London, UK, May

Gregory, A. (2003) "Public Relations and the Age of Spin", inaugural lecture, Leeds Metropolitan University, Leeds, UK, March

Grunig, J.E. and Hunt, T. (1984) *Managing Public Relations*, Fort Worth, Holt, Rinehart and Winston

Habermas, J. (1984) *The Theory of Communicative Action I: Reason and the Rationalisation of Society*, Boston, MA, Beacon Press

Harlow, R.F. (1976) "Building a public relations definition", *Public Relations Review*, No. 2 pp 34-42

Heath, R.L. (2001) "Shifting Foundations", *Handbook of Public Relations*, Heath, R.L. (ed.), Thousand Oaks, Sage

Kruckeberg, D. and Starck, K. (1988) *Public Relations and Community: A Reconstructed Theory*, New York, Praeger

Ledingham, J.A. and Bruning, S.D. (2000) *Relationship building: a relational approach to public relations*, Mahwah, NJ., Lawrence Erlbaum Associates

L'Etang, J. (2003) "The myth of the 'ethical guardian': An examination of its origins, potency and illusions", *Journal of Communication Management*, Vol. 8 pp 53-67

Martinson, D.C. (1999) "Is it ethical for practitioners to represent 'bad' clients?" *Public*

Relations Quarterly, Vol. 44, No.4 pp 22-25

McClusker, G. (2005) *PR in a Tailspin*, London, Kogan Page

McElreath, M. P. (1997) *Managing Systematic and Ethical Public Relations Campaigns*, 2nd edition, Dublique, IA, Brown and Benchmark

Moloney, K. (2000) *Rethinking Public Relations*, London, Routledge

Nelson, J. (1989) *Sultans of Sleaze: Public Relations and the Media*, Toronto, Between the Lines Press

Nessman, K. (2000) "The origins and development of public relations in Germany and Austria", *Perspectives on PublicRelations Research*, Moss, D., Vercic, D. and Warnaby, G. (eds), London, Routledge

O'Neil, O. (2002), "A Question of Trust", Lecture 2: Trust and Terror, Reith Lectures. Available online at www.bbc.co.uk/radio 4/reith2002/2.shtml, accessed on 15 May 2005

Parsons, P.J. (2004) *Ethics in Public Relations*, London, Kogan Page

Pearson, R. (2000) "Beyond Ethical Relativism in Public Relations", *Public Relations Research Annual*, Grunig, J.E. and Grunig, L. (eds), Vol. 1 pp 67-86

Phillips, R., Freeman, R.E. and Wicks, A.C. (2003) "What Stakeholder theory is not", *Business Ethics Quarterly*, Vol. 13 pp 479-502

Rampton, S. and Stauber, R. (2002) *Trust Us, We're Experts*, WI, Tarcher

Seib, P. and Fitzpatrick, K. (1995) *Public Relation Ethics*, Fort Worth, Harcourt Brace

Somerville, I. (2004) "Business Ethics, Public Relations and Corporate Social Responsibility", *The Public Relations Handbook*, Theaker, A. (ed.), London, Routledge

Toth, E. and Heath R. (1992) *Rhetorical and Critical Approaches to Public Relations*, Hillsdale, NJ, Lawrence Erlbaum Associates

van Ruler, B. and Vercic, D. (2004) *Public Relations and Communication Management in Europe*, The Hague, Mouton de Gruyter

NOTE ON AUTHOR

Anne Gregory is the UK's only full-time Professor of Public Relations and Director of the Centre for Public Relations Studies at Leeds Metropolitan University, which has the largest department of public relations in the UK. Before moving into academic life, she spent 12 years as a full-time public relations practitioner, holding senior appointments both in-house and in consultancy. She is still involved in practice on a consultancy basis. She is Vice-President of the UK Institute of Public Relations, editor of the Institute's Public Relations in Practice series of books and editor of the *Journal of Communication Management*. She has published two books: *Planning and Managing Public Relations Campaigns*, (Kogan Page, 2000) and *Public Relations Practice*, (Kogan Page 2004) Her numerous articles include "The Scope and Structure of Public Relations: a technology driven view" (2004), *Public Relations Review*, Vol. 30, pp 245-254 and "Communication and the

Machine of Government", *Ethical Space*, No. 1, pp 20-25. She has also written 10 chapters in books. Contact details: Centre for Public Relations Studies, Leeds Business School, Leeds Metropolitan University, Bronte Hall, Headingley Campus, Leeds LS6 3QS. Tel: 0113-283 7520. Fax: 0113 283 1751; e-mail: a.gregory@lmu.ac.uk.

PART 4

COMMUNICATION ETHICS:
PHILOSOPHICAL EXPLORATIONS

20

Ethics in journalism: False dichotomies, uncertain goals

Karen Saunders

Discussion of ethics in journalism often turns around a series of dichotomies which can seem to undermine the very possibility of a conversation. The individual responsibility and autonomy of the journalist is set against the collective responsibility of companies or audiences; the merits of the "freedom paradigm" of the Enlightenment contrasted to the authoritarian paradigm of communitarian thought; the possibility of objective, "good" journalism contrasted to that of subjective, "bad" journalism. This chapter argues that unless we agree what journalism is for we will find it difficult to develop a framework for evaluating the practice of ethical journalism.

INTRODUCTION

The examination of ethics in journalism is a relatively new area of study in the UK, reflecting the fact that the study of journalism as such only recently moved into the academy.[1] In the US, on the other hand, journalism ethics has long been an area of scholarly interest (see Christians 1995). However, notwithstanding the considerable work achieved by theorists, there is a still remoteness between their work and that of the practitioners. In his valuable review of scholarship in the field of journalism ethics research, Kenneth Starck, concluded, among other things, that "a disquieting aspect of journalism ethics – in practice or research – is the disconnection between application and theory" (2001: 144).

One strategy for ensuring that theory is practical for journalism is the promotion of an ongoing dialogue between journalism educators, researchers and practitioners which also could also contribute to two key tasks: first, a clarification of concepts to ensure we are talking about similar issues; second, an exploration of some of the apparent dichotomies found in thinking about journalism ethics to examine whether the contradictions sometimes posed in debate are, in fact, false. These two steps will contribute to the clarity of the conversation between all of those concerned with ethics and journalism.

Clarifying the terms of the debate leads to what I consider to be a third, related issue namely, the discussion of what journalism is for. It seems to be difficult to make ethical assessments where there is no clear view of the purpose of a practice.

CLARIFYING CONCEPTS

What do we mean when we refer to ethics in journalism? If we discount the "Mackenzie" response,[2] in Britain – depending on whether those asked were journalists or members of the public – the answers would probably variously refer to the PCC's code of practice,[3] good, or usually bad, instances of journalistic practice (whatever this might mean), tabloid sensationalism, the Producers' Guidelines and so on. Little research has been carried out into what people consider to be ethical practice in journalism; even less has been done to examine what is the underlying conceptual backdrop and coherence to that thinking. If we start to do this, we can begin to find examples which show a less than certain sense of why or what is considered ethically in or out.

Take one example: in the entire editors' PCC code of practice there is only one clause which is considered to be a "moral obligation". This is clause 14 which states that journalists have a "moral obligation to protect confidential sources of information". What is meant by the use of the word "moral" here? Do the rest of the code's clauses not enjoin "moral" duties? If not, what kind of injunctions are they? When we claim something to be a "moral" duty, we say that a given action is obligatory. This, in turn, implies that some rule, law or principle requires that it be done. What is the source of authority for this rule, law or principle that confidential sources should be protected?

Does the notion of "moral" obligation, in fact, make any sense? Many moral philosophers would suggest that it does not since it derives ultimately from a theological view of the world. Thus, as Statman puts it: "People still regard moral obligation as universally valid and as overriding, although they deny the very frame of thought that gives sense to this view. Hence the emptiness of the concept" (2003: 4). On what, then, do we base what is considered to be the fundamental ethical principle in journalism to protect confidential sources? There may be several answers to this but it will be helpful to begin by establishing what it is we are talking about.

We can begin to do this by tackling some of the fundamental questions posed by discussion of ethics in journalism. Here I briefly tackle just three: first, we can ask about the epistemological status of ethics. Second, we can examine what is the scope and focus of ethics in journalism. And the third, related question is to understand what is the unit of study for ethics in journalism. Each of these questions would merit a book-length study. My excuse for introducing them in such desultory fashion is to begin a conversation about them which will allow us to speak sensibly about journalism ethics.

ETHICS AS KNOWLEDGE

The first question we can ask is whether ethics is a domain where we can obtain knowledge, where what can be called truth and error exists (see Lovibond 2002: 16). Is it, on the other hand, an area where the most we can hope to do is to compare notes? This fundamental question will have a decisive impact on whether it is possible to have a conversation about ethics at all. Ethical relativists[4] and nihilists would reply that it is not (see Sanders 2003: chapter 2). In their view, appeals to principles and establishment of common standards all founder on the idea that all moral assumptions are equally valid, meaningless or concerned with upholding vested interests.

There are, however, good reasons to suggest that there is more to ethics than these views would allow. When, for example we examine ethical language and discussion we find they have a curious feature: they appear to be about certain kinds of facts which have a singular force in our lives. The motivational aspect of ethical thought has been interpreted from various perspectives but one of particular interest to us here is the view that a certain act was performed because of the value the agent saw in it (see Lovibond op cit: 5-7). It appears to be the case that if we consider something valuable, we are ready to consider that it is of constant and permanent value. In the ethical outlook, there is a commitment to the notion that it is possible to identify shared and permanent values which arise out of our humanity (see Warnock 1998:163). For these kinds of explanations to have purchase at all, the reasons put forward for the value of an act must be in some way accessible. What count as reasons for being compassionate, not using torture, keeping a promise are recognisable to others.

Of course, it is also true that different people have different sensitivities and that values emerge through our involvement in specific communities. In this sense, then, we can say with Lovibond that: "The ethical...pertains to what people learn to value through immersion in a community acquainted with ideas of right, duty, justice, solidarity, and common social or cultural interests extending beyond the lifetime of the present generation" (2001: 33).

Thus, if we think of knowledge as being about how things are in the world, then we can say that ethics is about a certain kind of knowledge and therefore has an identifiable rational structure. We will sometimes disagree because, as thinkers like Raz have pointed out, the question of the universality of value is a complex one to which one can answer both yes and no (2001: 2): values change over time, our ethical notions may be rationalisations of culturally inculcated views. This is all true. Yet it is possible to construct a space where reflective scrutiny of prevailing ethical values takes place and where revision can occur even from within one's own ethical outlook. If we accept, then, that ethics provides us with knowledge about certain aspects of the world, we can begin to explore with confidence what it might tell us about the world of journalism.

ETHICS AS CONDUCT

The second area I will examine is that of the scope and focus of ethics in journalism. It seems to me that the primary, albeit by no means exclusive, focus of ethics is human conduct. The very notion of moral life refers to that area of conduct to which there is an alternative and in which behaviour is directed not by nature but by art. The notion of human conduct refers not only to the individual level but also to that of the corporative and social levels. A corporation's conduct has as much an ethical dimension as does a person's. This was interestingly illustrated by the *Sun* newspaper's coverage of the Hillsborough tragedy and the subsequent controversy. Its notorious headline about the Hillsborough football stadium tragedy, "THE TRUTH" (19 April 1989) and its one-sided attack on the behaviour of Liverpool fans – 96 of whom died in Sheffield – provoked disbelief and anger on Merseyside and the paper's sales dropped accordingly (Chippindale and Horrie 1999: 371).

In 2004 the paper signed up the serialisation rights to Wayne Rooney's autobiography, again provoking indignation in Liverpool for whom Rooney was a home-grown football hero who had been bought out by the enemy. The paper's subsequent apology for its original coverage of Hillsborough made a distinction between the conduct of the paper and the people employed by it: it began by making an apology for the actions of the *Sun* newspaper:

> IT is 15 years since the *Sun* committed the most terrible mistake in its history. By making grave and untrue allegations about the behaviour of Liverpool fans during the Hillsborough disaster, we enraged the city. We long ago apologised publicly to the victims' families, friends and to the city of Liverpool for our awful error. We gladly say sorry again today: fully, openly, honestly and without reservation (7 July 2004).

The apology is for the conduct of a company but not, as the *Sun*'s editorial later goes on to make clear, for the conduct of the journalists now working there:

The *Sun* of 2004 no more deserves to be hated on Merseyside than Wayne Rooney does. For a start, most of today's staff weren't on the *Sun* in 1989 and today's Editor was a 20-year-old student (7 July 2004).

Institutions, corporations and individuals are judged on their conduct for at the heart of ethical thinking is the view that alternatives exist; danger lies along that path which would lead us to the idea that ethical alternatives do not exist in our lives. This holds true for institutions, corporations and human beings.

Understanding conduct to be the focus of ethics highlights the role of education. Here we can understand education in a larger sense than simply the kind of education directed toward knowledge about ethics. Indeed, as Oakeshott states: "It is impossible to engage in any activity whatsoever without contributing to this kind of moral education" (1991: 63). In other words, if we take the case of journalism, all learning about journalism in whatever forum or by whatever means (the class-room, the media, peers and the workplace), works toward habits of emotion and conduct which come to configure our ethical space. This moral education could be said to be most perfectly acquired when to act wrongly is seen as a diminution of self rather than a failure to obey a rule.

Regarding conduct as the chief focus of ethics does not imply an atomised, individualistic vision. Nor does it suggest that questions about principles, codes, rights, evaluative terms and regulations are not part of the subject matter of ethics. All these areas are, of course, open to and have been subject to ethical inquiry. Indeed, ethics itself implies judgement and reasoning and hence is a theoretical but also a practical enterprise.

ETHICS AS THE PERSONAL AND THE POLITICAL

A second and related point to the preceding discussion is to emphasise that the focus and scope of ethics and journalism is not limited to either personal or social ethics. Other areas of professional ethics' scholarship – particularly business and medical ethics – are already leading the way in showing that concerns with ethics should encompass both the "personal" and "political". Solomon, a business ethicist, has argued that: "the concepts and values that define individual responsibilities and role behaviour as opposed to the already well-developed theories of macro-business ethics" (2003: 207) have been neglected. In journalism we must make sure that we explore ethics in both the realm of the personal and, what I call, the "political", that larger corporate, institutional and political sphere which we all inhabit. Thus, the study of ethics recognises in part the truth of the Greeks' view that "to live the good life one must live in a great city" (cited by Solomon 2003: 215), while understanding that it is human beings who must live this good life. Taken together, these characterisations of the nature and subject matter of ethics may allow us to clarify certain areas of debate which can at times become rather muddled.

FALSE DICHOTOMIES

As we know, dichotomies bifurcate reality and offer us two usually contradictory parts or opinions. All too frequently, however, *false* dichotomies are established offering phoney alternatives on any given issue: "You're either with us, or with the terrorists." False dichotomies simplify and polarise. They force opponents into extreme positions. They disguise the possibility that there may be more than two parts to a question or that each of the two parts offered may overlap. I will examine now three false dichotomies which bedevil discussion of ethics in journalism.

PERSONALLY POLITICAL

It is not uncommon for discussions of ethics in journalism to pose the questions in terms either of collective endeavour or individual struggle, the latter often considered futile in the face of super-charged turbo-capitalism. The individual responsibility and autonomy of the journalist is set against the collective responsibility of companies or audiences, with the former in an almost hopeless situation. It is, of course, true that journalists are in many ways far less powerful than we would sometimes imagine. Except for the privileged few, most journalists have precarious working conditions (Glover 1999: 295). In his research on the role of the British National Union of Journalists (NUJ) in raising ethical concerns, Harcup rightly states that "journalistic ethics cannot be divorced from everyday economic realities such as understaffing, job insecurity, casualised labour, bullying and unconstrained management prerogative" (2002: 112).

Questions of macro-ethics – the workings of the market economy, the institutional setting, the regulatory environment – are also the province of ethical inquiry. However, the fact that we need to consider the "macro-ethics" of political economy does not rule out the accompanying need to examine "micro-ethics", focusing on the concepts, values and dilemmas which define personal roles and responsibilities. The latter has long been the domain of moral philosophy and it would seem curious indeed not to wish to explore its insights and possible elucidation of ethical issues in journalism.

One example of an area of ethical discussion in moral philosophy which might shed light on our tendency to dichotomise the personal from the political is the paradox of moral luck (see Williams 1972/1993). The paradox of "moral luck" centres on the incompatibility of two assumptions: first, talk of ethical behaviour only makes sense with reference to conduct for which we can be held responsible; second, in fact, we are not in control of our lives because luck governs so much of what might happen to us.

This conundrum is of the kind which could lead us to cease to talk of ethics at all. Certainly, it can make us feel less than comfortable when speaking of ethics in relation to individual human actions. What, in an example explored by Hursthouse (1999), if I have been unlucky enough to be educated as a racist? My whole stock of emotions has been corrupted and with them "my reasons" too. How do I overcome this and indeed can I? Perhaps we need to accept, as Hursthouse does, that "those of us who have had racism inculcated in us early are unlucky; through no fault of own, and despite our greatest efforts, we may remain morally inferior (thought not thereby necessarily blameworthy) to those who, in virtue of good training in childhood and rational principle, achieve complete harmony between their emotions and reason and thereby full virtue" (1999: 116). *Mutatis mutandi* we can apply this argument in discussing ethical issues in journalism. We can debate the extent to which ethical lapses are partly due to moral luck – inadequate training, fierce competition, faulty management procedures, overweening government pressure – while at the same time recognising that, however finely balanced, discernment and analysis of the ethical features of human conduct are possible. If this is so, ethical journalism implies both an individual burden and collective responsibility.

SUBJECTIVE OBJECTIVITY

One common theme of debate of ethics in journalism is the contraposition of the notions of subjectivity and objectivity. The lack of objectivity in newspaper reporting is sometimes used as a stick with which to beat newspaper journalists. The BBC is berated when it fails to be objective. Subjectivity is considered to be bad and objectivity good. Another possibility, and one which I argue in favour of, is that both may be good or bad depending on how the terms are understood and how and by whom they are employed.

In one view of things, all journalism is necessarily subjective. All story-telling, including journalism, implies a story teller and every story teller has an implicit or explicit intentionality when telling the story. For this reason, all story tellers also act as moral observers: in telling a story, whether it be historical, journalistic or literary, the teller takes a position, has an intention in which a view of human conduct is inevitably expressed. The story teller's intentionality can be more or less explicit – the story can be written or presented in a "neutral" style or in a way which allocates praise or blame – but it is inescapable. For this reason, truly neutral stories do not exist and journalism is subjective.

However, to accept that all narrations have a narrator does not entail that practices aimed at truthfulness should be thrown overboard. Subjectivity is not antithetical to truthfulness but where it is not counteracted by conventions such as objectivity and accuracy, it may become so. Objectivity is an unattainable yet useful lode-stone for truthful reporting. It is particularly valuable for media enterprises in which a specific public trust has been placed. It is not, however, an unequivocal good set against the unequivocal badness of subjectivity. Where matters are open to interpretation – as so many are – setting "good" objectivity against "bad" subjectivity makes no sense.

TRUTHFUL INTERPRETATION

Linked to the issue just discussed, are the debates which surround the relationship in journalism between interpretation and truthfulness. As we have seen, subjectivity is part and parcel of story-telling in journalism and news stories have an intrinsic narrative structure. Of course, the difference between journalists and other story-tellers is that the former tell stories which have some (however spurious) connection to things which have happened. In doing this journalists act as interpreters and interpretation is itself an activity to which we bring premises, prejudices in the sense of pre-judgements. Some are personal, others are a kind of implicit background knowledge. Writing in an "objective" way, for example, is a cultural practice which is learnt. In this sense, as we have seen, we are all, and journalists are no exception, subjective and all of us necessarily interpret.

The question is, then, not whether interpretation is ranged against truthfulness. It cannot be so, otherwise none of us would be able to know the truth about anything. The question is more likely to centre on how our limitations as subjective interpreters can be offset by practices that ensure some connection of what is reported to what is truthful and real. Of course, some postmodern thought would argue that all "facts" are simply another kind of fiction. From this perspective, journalists are not only literally story-tellers, in the sense that their stories are narratives, but also in the sense that their stories are fiction.

There is some truth in this. Many stories can be woven from the same material and they disclose reality to a lesser or greater degree. But to admit subjectivity, recognise journalists' role as interpreters, acknowledge that they can never be complete masters of meaning, does not entail that we should abandon a commitment to understanding journalism as a cultural practice aimed at providing us with information about things that have in fact happened. Indeed, to argue this is to ask one of the central questions of this article namely, whether it is the case that it is necessary to understand journalism's goals in order for us to be able to formulate ethical arguments with which to judge it.

However, returning to the discussion about the distinction between fact and fiction in journalism, the question appears to be, as asked by a judge to a journalist: "So a novelist is the same as a journalist, then. Is that what you're saying?" If our answer is affirmative, it appears that we subscribe to a view of journalism as pure entertainment. If our answer is negative, it will indicate a view of journalism in which invented material has no place. This view of journalism understands that reporting has an exterior reference, a reference to the world of events about which it provides information to others. Fictional literature, on the other hand, refers to creations of the imagination.

Using invented material, as the *Mirror* did when it published the posed Iraq torture photographs (1 May 2004), however true the story it told might have been, represents a step beyond reporting into the world of fiction.

ACCOUNTABLE FREEDOM

A constant theme of discussion of ethics in journalism is the tension between the requirement for press freedom as against the call for the media to be responsible and somehow accountable for their actions. Here, it can be fairly claimed, there is a dichotomy. On the one hand, the media seek to maximise their freedom, largely understood as freedom of expression. On the other, the public and their representatives may try to set limits to this freedom. However, there are examples in which this dichotomy has been expressed in what I believe to be a misleading way.

The distinguished American scholar, John Merrill, contrasts the merits of the "freedom paradigm" of the Enlightenment to the authoritarian paradigm of communitarian thought, regarding the latter as inimical to the existence of a free press (2002). In broad terms, his argument is that the world is moving away from the libertarian press model favoured by the West in which maximum freedom, individualism, autonomy and competition are favoured. In its place, many parts of the world are adopting what he describes as an "Order" paradigm in which restrained freedom, cooperation and discipline are the norms. He identifies the "public journalism" movement of the 1990s as part of the shift away from the libertarian press model to a "more responsive and therefore a more responsible press" (2002:28).

I will not attempt to assess the correctness of his analysis but rather question the stark contrast he draws between the presence of freedom in each model. According to Merrill, the more responsible and responsive the press is, the more its freedom of expression is circumscribed and the opposite also holds true. The more freedom of expression you have, the less responsible you are. This, however, suggests a curious reification of freedom which disconnects it from what freedom means in a phenomonological sense. When we are free, we experience dominion, choice and consequences. Freedom as experienced by human beings is not to be free of consequences. Every action we take as free beings implies a choice and therefore a selection or exclusion of other acts. In other words, freedom is not opposed to responsibility or accountability. The latter are the other side of the coin of freedom, in tension with it but called into existence (however we then respond) by the very existence of freedom.

UNCERTAIN GOALS

Running through the discussion is a suggestion that one of the sources of our disagreements about ethics in journalism is an uncertainty about what journalism is for. If there is no consensus about journalism's goals, it is not clear to me how we can be clear in our ethical assessments. Are newspapers entertainment, news or money-making enterprises or, most probably, all three? Each of these areas enjoins a certain set of practices, distinct, oriented to achieve specific goals. Understanding what these are places us in a stronger position to understand why, or not, such and such a practice is ethical.

CONCLUSIONS: OCCUPATIONAL GOALS AND GOOD JOURNALISM

Holding up a notion of occupational excellence linked to occupational goals – knowing what journalism is for – may be one way of promoting ethical practice in journalism. We can think of the notion of professional or occupational goals as a regulative ideal: an occupational role, if it is to count as a good occupation, is one which contributes to a key human good and acting well in an occupational role will be judged by how it contributes to achieving the goals of the occupation. So, for doctors it has been suggested that the substantive human good aimed at is health, for lawyers justice (Oakley and Cocking 2001).

The content of the regulative ideals of a good journalist will be determined by a model of what reporting or journalism is. There are limits to what a doctor can do and still be said to be a doctor. If making money or making people laugh becomes a journalist's governing regulative ideal we say they are a good something else - a good "buisnalist" or "infotainer", for example (see Oakley and Cocking 2001: 89) – but we would not say the person was a journalist.

Can we agree that there are universal standards regarding what is good and bad journalism? We cannot ignore that journalism is a culturally established practice which has developed in the particular historical circumstances of each country (see Conboy 2004): Chinese journalism *is* very different to American journalism; British broadsheets are very different to their scholarly German counterparts. Do any of these traditions represent good or better journalism; bad or worse journalism? Of course, we might want to argue that this is indeed the case. And this returns us to the issue of agreeing what journalism is for. However, even if we can't all agree in every respect on this, I think we are still able to find values that all good journalism should share, the chief of which is the commitment to truthfulness. Simply put, novelists invent, journalists shouldn't.

NOTES

1. There is a great deal of American work in the area of media ethics. British pioneers are Belsey and Chadwick (1992), Kieran (1997, 1998), Frost (2000) and Keeble (2001). To these can now be added Sanders (2003), Conboy and Alia (2004). The big expansion of journalism studies in British universities began in the 1990s.
2. "Ethics? As far as I'm concerned that's that place to the east of London where people wear white socks." Kelvin MacKenzie, former editor of the *Sun*.
3. It is, of course, the editors' code of practice which is upheld by the Press Complaints Commission. For ease of reference, however, it will be referred to here as the PCC's code of practice.
4. We must be careful not to confuse relativism with a commitment to an ethic of toleration. Toleration involves a specific moral commitment, not relativist at all, to tolerate other ethical viewpoints without necessarily endorsing them.
5. A question asked by Judge William J. Rea during the MacDonald-McGinniss trial 7 July 1987 cited in Janet Malcolm's *The Journalist and the Murderer* (1990).

REFERENCES

Chippindale, Peter and Horrie, Chris (1999) *Stick It Up Your Punter! The uncut story of the Sun newspaper*, London, Pocket Books

Christians, Clifford G. (1995) "Review Essay: current trends in media ethics", *European Journal of Communication*, Vol. 10, No. 4 pp 545-558

Conboy, Martin (2004) *Journalism:. A Critical History*, London, Sage

Glover, Stephen (ed.) (1999) *Secrets of the Press: Journalists on Journalism*, London, Allen Lane

Harcup, Tony (2002) "Journalists and Ethics: the quest for a collective voice", *Journalism Studies*, Vol. 3, No. 1 pp 101-114

Hursthouse, Rosalind (1999) *On Virtue Ethics*, Oxford, Oxford University Press

Lovibond, Sabina (2002) *Ethical Formation*, Cambridge, MA, Harvard University Press

Merrill, John C. (2002) "Chaos and Order: Sacrificing the Individual for the Sake of Social Harmony", *The Mission. Journalism, Ethics and the World*, Atkins, Joseph B. (ed.) Iowa, Iowa State Press pp 17-35

Oakley, Justin and Cocking, Dean (2001) *Virtue Ethics and Professional Roles*, Cambridge, Cambridge University Press

Oakeshott, Michael (1991) *Rationalism in politics and other essays*, Indianapolis, Liberty Press

Raz, Joseph (2001) *Value, Respect and Attachment*, Cambridge, Cambridge University Press

Sanders, Karen (2003) *Ethics and Journalism*, London, Sage

Solomon, Robert C. (2003) "Corporate Roles, Personal Virtues: An Aristotelian Approach to Business Ethics", *Virtue Ethics. A Critical Reader*. Statman, Daniel (ed.), Edinburgh, Edinburgh University Press pp 205-226

Starck, Kenneth (2001) "What's Right/Wrong with Journalism Ethics Research", *Journalism Studies*, Vol. 2. No. 1 pp 133-152

Statman, Daniel (2003) "Introduction to Virtue Ethics", *Virtue Ethics. A Critical Reader*, Statman, Daniel (ed.), Edinburgh, Edinburgh University Press pp 1-41

Warnock, Mary (1998) *An Intelligent Person's Guide to Ethics*, London, Duckworth

Williams, Bernard (1972/1993) *Morality. An Introduction to Ethics*, Cambridge, Cambridge University Press

NOTE ON AUTHOR

Professor Karen Sanders is dean of the Faulty of Humanities and Communication, San Pablo University, Madrid. Her books include *Ethics & Journalism* (Sage). Contact details: kbfsanders@googlemail.com.

21

How linking happiness and ethics can help communication practitioners today

Dr. Hallvard Johnnes Fossheim (in conversation with Kristine Lowe)

The Oslo Happiness Project, based at the University of Oslo, aims to investigate ancient conceptions of the good life and to create greater awareness of ancient insights into ethics. The project was started in 2003 by a group of scholars in philosophy and antique languages. One of them, Dr Hallvard Johannes Fossheim, is a lecturer in philosophy at the University of Oslo having completed his PhD thesis on Nature and Habituation in Aristotle's Theory of Human Development. He talks here to Kristine Lowe.

The Oslo Happiness Project looks at ancient conceptions of happiness, ethics, moral education and the links between these areas. How are these ideas relevant to us today and, more specifically, relevant to us as communication practitioners?

The issue of how to lead a good life is as relevant today as it was in antiquity, although opinions differ as to what constitutes a good life. The role virtues play in antique thinking about ethics indicates that it is your character traits that determine whether or not you are going to be happy. A key idea in antiquity, not least in Plato and Aristotle, is that you become what you do. How you act and live will influence who you are. Virtue is not linked to money and fame: the idea is that being a good person is a precondition for leading a good life, for being happy.

When we eulogise someone, we don't talk about what rules he or she abided by, but what kind of person he or she was: what kind of virtues the person possessed. One of the easiest ways to see the relevance of such thinking in a specific practice, like journalism, is to look at virtues you need to do a good job: virtues like truthfulness, integrity, justice and the courage not to reveal your confidential sources. In any kind of profession there are certain virtues or characteristics that are valued more than others.

The word "paradigm" is certainly much used and abused in contemporary discourse. It is most commonly associated with Thomas Kuhn's seminal work *The Structure of Scientific Revolutions*, where Kuhn uses the word to describe the model that scientists hold about a particular area of knowledge. Is there a connection here?

The concept of paradigms is, indeed, central to understanding the way ethics was taught and discussed in antiquity. The term literally means examples, primarily examples to be followed. It is customary in contemporary moral philosophy to think primarily in terms of rules of conduct, whereas in antiquity it was customary to start with examples meant to inspire or deter. This was the starting point for ethical reflection.

Some of the contemporary critique of Kuhn is that he, in the book you mention, used the concept "paradigm" in something like 20 different ways. At least one of the ways in which he used the concept was as a kind of example and in that respect there is a resemblance, or continuity, with antiquity's concept of paradigm, which it is most appropriate to translate as "example". I think such paradigms reveal a central way in which social reality is shaped – the way in which we ourselves are shaped and shape our concepts of right and wrong.

In antiquity poetry was considered a main source of human beings' conditioning by paradigms. Especially Homer was an important figure in this respect. If you try to draw parallels to today, media and popular culture do a lot of the same job as Homer did in his time. The media contribute mental pictures that become the platform for discussion – often very simple images, but still examples through which we condition reality and are ourselves conditioned.

The media are often accused of providing a very simplified representation of reality. A friend of mine once said: "In the media we like black and white stories with obvious heroes and villains, a cartoon-script-like treatment of the issues." Could this not become very problematic if the media provide the starting point, and most of the raw material, for all public discourse?

True, but the media also provide a very important, positive, platform. They provide a shared basis for interpretations, discussion and dialogue. The very fact that we are having a discussion about the media's representation of reality only illustrates my point about the media providing a shared platform for discussion. Anything can be abused and exploited. But one of the good things about the culture of paradigms is that the example is meant as a platform for further reflection and discussion. If you are looking for a way to understand our culture, there's nothing wrong, I think, in starting with what is popular – just as Homer and Shakespeare were scions of popular culture in their times.

Could this view of the media and popular culture as today's main social conditioners not be taken as a very elitist perspective on what drives public discourse?

If we today think back to earlier historical periods, it is easy to take for granted that Homer and Shakespeare were part of the elite culture in their time, but it is not that simple: both of these were also conveyors of what we might call popular culture. I think it is valid to say that a lot of the representations we find in the media are the representations of the elite, but I do not think that this is the whole story:

If you look at an expression of popular culture, such as movies, you get another example of how cultural expressions do not have to be seen simply as a one-sided process, something we get top-down. Movies can both influence and change us, but are also an expression of trends and interests which are already there. This way of thinking about cultural expressions prevents you from ending up with the fallacy of seeing them as either cause or effect. Movies can be both at the same time: an often very well articulated expression of change, something which is happening here and now, but simultaneously something that will cause, and further shape, continued change.

Going back to the media as a platform for public discourse: what if the media are biased or only cover a small slice of reality?

That only goes to show the importance of the media's role, and their immense responsibilities. In such cases, all of the premises have already been laid down, as in a political debate where the participants are more interested in hitting each other over the head with repetitive slogans than in having a genuine dialogue. This brings us to the importance of practical reason. In Plato and Aristotle, practical reason is thought of not least as receptiveness to good arguments. When you have receptiveness you do not get this sort of static situation.

One can speculate that this is one of the main reasons why Plato chooses dialogue as the form in which to present his philosophy: perhaps he did not want it to appear as a closed argument. It is a form of inclusive reason: you make the best out of what you have and retain a certain openness. It is possible that Socrates in these dialogues is supposed to be a kind of ideal character in terms of critical openness: he is the one who enters into real dialogue, who sacrifices everything, even his life in the end, to remain in search of truth, without purporting to own the truth himself. In this way Plato is using Socrates as a paradigm in his works, indicating a way to proceed, without purporting to have found all the right answers once and for all. The dialogue accepts arguments from several different places and treats them seriously.

What about the Greek concept of *paideia*: what can we learn from the antique philosophers about teaching ethics? From our discussion so far I gather that providing examples of good practice might play a key role.

Paideia translates as upbringing, education, conditioning, shaping of the individual. It is not an education you can take in a certain amount of time, or could divide over a number of hours a week. It happens from earliest childhood on, through practice and examples provided by the culture, whether by examples of everyday manners or by narratives of heroic actions and defeat.

We might tentatively say that ethical forming by paradigms comes from at least three main sources: 1) Concrete people you know/things you can identify with. 2) People you read about or hear about. 3) Fictitious persons from literature or movies. Often, if you are faced with difficult situations – such as being asked to write about something you do not believe in, or represent a client you think is a crook - you think of concrete ideals you have encountered through your ethical forming, your *paideia*, as examples of how to act.

It has been argued that within large media corporations, like the BBC, the fact that many journalists arrive there straight from universities make them easy to imprint with the organisation's strong corporate values, and you end up with a news coverage that might be slanted, but not consciously so from the point of the journalist.

Again, if we try to consider situations like the one you describe in light of the notion of paradigms, such conditioning is neither subjective nor objective, but a common understanding which is upheld exactly because it is shared.

Allowing for this, how can you reach objective ethics? Many people see tolerance for different cultures as a logical corollary of relativism?

Ethics is often determined as dealing in universal principles of precepts. I think it is a constructive thing in the antique way of thinking that practical reason is thought of as discursive receptiveness. Tolerance and relativism are often seen as two sides of the same coin. However, being tolerant is not the same as being a relativist. Correspondingly, it is certainly possible to combine an objective platform for good and bad with tolerance. Here again, we have a constructive source in the ancients' presentation of practical reason as reaching for a solution through dialogue, even though the participants might have different starting points. Relativism is a form of defeatism. It is a way to give up on the effort of trying to reach a common platform and thereby to cut off dialogue. Ultimately, there is much to be said for the idea that it is objectivism, not relativism, which goes most naturally with tolerance.

For more details on the Oslo Happiness Project see http://www.hf.uio.no/ forskningsprosjekter/happiness/

22

Communication ethics and the dialectic

Robert Beckett

After two and a half millennia, the dialectic remains a controversial subject. Today, what is different is the changed information environment which, this chapter suggests, requires a reconsideration of dialectics. Noting the transition in the social and natural sciences from a physical to an informational universe, dialethic logic offers a methodological perspective to identify ongoing tensions in both knowledge and language formation. The techniques employed in this chapter aim to confront the ambiguity, paradox and uncertainty at the heart of post-structuralist critique and thereby locate new approaches for interdisciplinary analyses, even while remaining wary of universalist claims to hidden resources of certainty. A renewed study of dialectics may offer teacher and student of communication ethics a practical method for the evaluation and dissemination of the rich sources that inform the discipline, thereby aiding examination of a discipline that is itself, arguably, full of dialectical tension.

INTRODUCTION

Blackburn's dictionary (1994) describes dialethic logic as the formal study of opposites, with "de dicto" (logical distinctions) reflecting "de re" (natural dualisms). For a long line of theorists, C. S. Peirce (1878), De Saussure (1916), Shannon and Weaver (1946), Jakobson (1956), Sartre (1960), Greimas (1977), Laclau (1983) and Luhmann (1987), binary thought, or dialectical reason − founded in dialethic logic − forms a distinct platform for analyses. Dialectical conception is a methodological enquiry dating back to the Ancient Greeks, with Aristotle originally dividing propositions "held by all men" (Book 1, Topics I 0, L. 3) in a "...subject of inquiry that contributes either to choice and avoidance, or to truth and knowledge" (Book 1, Topics I I, L.1). Following from Aristotle, the

natural sciences have adopted dialectical distinctions as an essential methodological programme, while use of the dialectic generates a greater dispute in the discussion of social reality.

Dialectical distinctions described by Engels (1883) in his famous treatise on dialectics as "...the science of interconnections", are embedded in a variety of discourses, for instance, Gadamer (1975) has called the continuous process of knowledge formation, "the dialectic of question and answer" (1975: 472), while Buber (1966), recognising the Platonic relation between dialogue and dialectic, called us to a communicative life founded in twin dialogue that works to find the "unity of contraries" (Buber 1966: 111). The dialectic has also been appropriated by communication studies, for example in the study of semiotics and hermeneutics. In the simplified presentation below, dialectical reason (the study of difference) is differentiated from hermeneutics (the study of interpretation) and semiotics (the study of significance), displaying how each communicative analyses are situated alongside each other and are used together.

Examination of complex interactions between these three theory/methods remains beyond the scope of this chapter, although broadly, if hermeneutics concerns the examination of texts, and semiotics the examination of signs, then dialectics is the examination of discourse/knowledge; the underlying language formations and balance of concepts in creating theory and describing practice. The three, however, appear to work in a complex inter-relationship, linked to other theoretical domains – linguistics and pragmatics in the model below – each in turn revealing underlying meaning in discourse/knowledge through the employment of conceptual/material distinctions.

From an understanding of how dialectics define conceptual categories, "field dialectics" can be mapped for each subject area and each unique field study compared for utility. Individual authors might even be described, in summary, by the key dialectics of their various theoretical proposals. For Descartes (self/reason), Kant (self/other), Hegel (subject/intersubjective), Nietzsche (subjectivity/objectivity), Marx and Engels (use value/exchange value, capital/labour), Freud (unconscious/conscious), thinking may even be explored, stripped of the often disguised problematic of mistranslation through exegesis; the historicist dilemma reduced, if not completely avoided.

DIALECTICAL DISPUTE

Yet the dialectic causes as much dispute as agreement. Dispute arises in the search for epistemological distinctions that often fail to describe movement in interpretative reality – what Adorno calls negative dialectics, the "unstable relationship of contradictions between concepts and objects" (quoted in Denzin and Lincoln 1994: 140) and Derrida calls "unities of iterability" (1982: 318), the continuous underlying movement of signals and signs. Zima (2002) denies the Hegelian dialectical synthesis (thesis/antithesis), citing the influence of Nietzsche, who he says "…develops an open dialectics starting from a radical ambivalence, an irreconcilable unity of opposites which functions destructively rather than in a system-generating fashion" (Zima 2002: 17).

Nietzsche's "irreconcilable ambivalence" embodied in later post-structuralism, appears to contradict a "dialectical positivist" rule, thereby curtailing essentialist foundations for knowledge acquisition using dialectics. Echoing the Nietzschean critique, Popper has commented forcefully on the dialectic of knowledge formation:

> The whole development of dialectic should be a warning against the dangers inherent in philosophical system building.…philosophers should be much more modest in their claims. One task which they can fulfil quite usefully is the study of the critical methods of science (1962: 335).

In a proposal for a disciplinary application of dialectics for communication ethics, Popper's comment is thought provoking. In seeking to build not a philosophical system, but a methodology for examining dynamic socio-linguistic reality, Popper's comments might serve as a warning, and a signpost, towards a dialectical method that embodies the modus operandi of critical thinking, freed, as far as possible, from humanist universalisations. In fact, dialectical reason can be connected with the emergence of postmodern critique – according to Engels (1883) the dialectic acts as "transformation of quantity into quality", "the interpenetration of opposites" and "the negation of the negation" – by this move avoiding claims to complete or unitary knowledge, positioning dialectics as a technique for revealing knowledge by:

- bringing to light critical language concepts;
- making distinctions between terms;
- identifying tensions in knowledge/language formation;
- offering heuristics for comparative evaluation;
- reducing exegetic confusion and historicism.

This thesis regards concept formation embedded in "binary opposition" as critical in predominantly ideational/nomothetic domains, such as the social sciences, and particularly for discourse evaluation across new informational scapes (Appadurai 1996). For instance, in the Platonic dialogue, Phaedrus, Socrates comments that less dispute occurs about the concept of silver, while disagreement is more common in subtle distinctions, for instance to identify notions of the good (Cooper 1997: 540). For Sartre, whose *Dialectics of Reason*, is an exacting attempt to address the nature of dialectics, value derives from its deep connection between knowledge creation and these essential critical tensions:

> ...the dialectic is both a method and a movement in the object. For the dialectician, it is grounded in a fundamental claim both about the structure of the real and about that of our praxis. We assert simultaneously that the process of knowledge is dialectical, that the movement of the object (whatever it may be) is itself dialectical, and that these two dialetics are one and the same. Taken together these propositions have a material content; they themselves are a form of organised knowledge, or, to put it differently, they define a rationality of the world. (2004: 20 [1960])

THE DESTABILISATION OF MEANING

Three controversial themes are apparent in dialectical knowledge formation:

a. the dangers of a universal humanism reduced to technique;
b. the destabilisation associated with revolutionary Marxist ideologies and
c. the fear of a futuristic, machine-like techniques designed to capture all human thought.

Meanwhile, Foucault (1972) suggests that much knowledge has already been captured in "power-knowledge" regimes where it offers expedient access and historical advantage to particular social elites. Opposing the tendency of ideological structures to capture existing, or reject new knowledge, the recently dynamic information environment, the "space of flows" according to Castells (1996), generates a dynamic in which information is released from traditional structures and historic agreements. In the infoverse, or what Norbert Weiner called "the economy of the signal" (Durham Peters 1999: 94), Zima describes how the "temporal-spatial variability of signs" destabilises the formation of meaning (2002: 35). By employing the full semiotic encoding/decoding (Hall 1980) possibilities of technology, revised principles of knowledge formation such as digital replication, dematerialisation and dis-aggregation appear to upend former certainties and call into question powerful scientific, environmental and socio-economic orthodoxies (Ormorod 1996; Kelley 1996). Such diagnosis fits with the breakdown of certainty prescribed in postmodern critique and reflects a deeper commitment to the uncertainty and ambivalence that protects against authoritarian control and appropriation that positivist knowledge regimes imply.

Dialectical reason avoids the embedding of knowledge in permanent structures of certainty, by assessing the tensions in knowledge/language, rather than proclaiming their permanence, offering in the process the means to make detailed evaluations of continuous movement in meaning formation. For people living in a newly dynamic relationship between self and information communication technology (ICT), such a powerful method uncovers the existing sedimentations of knowledge through the simple technique of concentrating on dialectical formations, resulting in profound implications for human/technology centred knowledge re-evaluation.

THE RECREATION OF DIALOGUE

A break-down in the conditions and rules of knowledge formation combines with a break-up of human experience, where a chaotic information space puts in doubt socially constructed agreement and even human identity itself (Baudrillard 1986; de Zengotita 2005). For dialectics, like communication ethics, the question is can a new real-time onto/epistemological analysis give the "self-constructing identity" (formally the individual) a controllable dialethic logic by which to ethically/logically examine, devise and revise the individual/social contract, without reducing all knowledge to instrumentality? Implied in any such renegotiation is the need for a new social space where individuals are not the subject of the system, but its co-creators. Dialectical thinking of the sort proposed here, may challenge ideologies and structures of modernism that remain dominant in today's socio-political landscape, through a radical openness.

This movement suggests that individuals supported by technical information systems are able to process information and make decisions applying

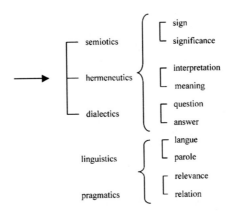

Figure 1 Implications for communication

the type of tests/ethical stipulations proposed by Habermas (1990) in the discourse ethics and Benhabib (1992) in the principle of enlarged thought. A clear result of post-structuralist critique is one of gaining critical high ground in the discourse of modernism, of diminution of statutory and authoritative knowledge formation and by inserting the interests of otherness e.g. feminism, ethnicity, class, ethics and ambivalence, into historic ideologies. Jacque Derrida's concept of *la différance* (1967: 227) implies a new reality where, binary opposites (signifier/signified) in dynamic semiotic associations (linguistic/symbolic) establish a continuous information/communication spectrum, where in Foucault's words, "everything is dangerous" (1984: 343). Orthodox interpretation (dogma/doctrine) in this way can be transformed into openness (communication) with uncertainty re-established as the prevailing condition for all knowledge.

In *Simulacra and Simulation*, Jean Baudrillard describes Marshall McLuhan's famous dialectic, "the medium, is the message", as "the key formula of the era of simulation" (1994: 82). The era of information is also the era of diversity, where the system is composed of digital dialectics (0-1) that spawn spatiotemporal discontinuities, and in turn define a new socio-dialectical reality. For individual conscious/unconscious responsiveness to a new continuous mediated/unmediated reality, a new critique is required, that will identify fundamental complexity in human information/communication resources. Bernstein's voice/message dialect (1990: 35), Austin's (1961) dialectic of speech acts and Wittgenstein's (1953) language games describe the syntax for a new language of informationalism and even a new methodological science founded in human discourse (Kroger and Wood 2000; Fairclough 1995). Underpinning the dialectical nature of language formation,

symbolic- *linguistic*	*mediated* *unmediated*
information *misinformation*	*communication* *miscommunication*

Figure 2 Dialectics for communication (example only)

McCarthy (1996) describes a double-structure of communicative interaction:

> If speaker and hearer are to reach an understanding they must communicate simultaneously at two levels: a) the level of intersubjectivity on which speaker and hearer, through illocutionary acts, establish the relations that permit them to come to an understanding with one another; and b) the level of experiences and state of affairs about which they want to reach an understanding in the communicative function determined by a) (1996: 282).

Describing a widespread dialectical reality captured in communicative analyses, a brief overview of some of the many models available can be conducted. For instance, Cronkite's model of human communication balances responsiveness/intention in communicative interaction:

A dialectical method exists in the theory of critical discourse analysis (CDA) proposed by Fairclough (1995).

In an informational world, simple binary distinctions (analytical logic) are found wanting, because distinctions that aim to reduce/control knowledge rather than expose and re-create it, are susceptible to reductionist argument. For instance, a typical distinction might be made in dialogue between two choices, an either/or decision may be called for? A reframing of the distinction using dialectical reason might encourage another distinction to be drawn, that between both/and, i.e. the reconstitution of the choice from one of mutual exclusivity, to one of mutual interdependence, the dialectical tension being moved from analytical certainty to dialectical ambivalence . This is an insight many communication scholars have shared. For instance, Wilden explains: "Such oscillations [between yes–no choices]

Cronkite's 1976 Human communication model

intentional	*unintentional*
active *response*	*passive* *response*

Figure 3 Dialectical representation of communication model (cited in Burgoon 1994: 19)

do not present a problem for dialectical logic, which is of a higher logical type than analytical logic and (paradoxically) subsumes it" (Wilden 1972: 123).

For information society reassessment, such an insight is essential, to demonstrate how science, technology, government and social organisation are often devised using traditional forms of analytical reason; one that seeks completion/control, rather than openness/uncertainty. Powerfully, the dialectical-relational realm enables an informationalism able to balance the expedience of logic with the "natural turn" of ethics, where as Christians proposes an *altheia* (Gk. def: truth) "…more relational than propositional" (Christians 2005). The relational realm, between things rather than in them, overcomes the propositional in a new dialectical formation that promotes association over authority, values over certainties and people over possessions. Drawing from an older tradition of communication while embodying a revelation that is fundamental to communication ethics analysis, Wilden makes a similar point: "In spite of Aristotle, Hegel and Marx, the truth that entities do not create relationships as much as relationships create entities was (and still remains) generally obscured" (1972: 215). The reframing of knowledge claims is emphasised by researchers critical of a traditional-reductionist dialectic which shapes all human thought. Pasquali (1997) for instance emphasises the power of a new dialectically informed consciousness for communication ethics where:

> We must rethink the world, no longer in the traditional way as "the whole of all phenomena" but as "the whole of all human beings"…retrieving the post war concept of the "human family" which was soon substituted by

New distinctions, new dialogue

text *production*	*text* *consumption*
discourse *practice*	*sociocultural* *practice*

Figure 4 Dialectical formation of communication theory discourse analysis (Fairclough 1995:59)

"globalisation" a mercantile term. This commitment, in fact, implies that we remake the entire theme of intersubjective relationships from subject to subject and not from subject to object, or to reason, to law, to mediation, to being, and so forth (1997: 36).

THE HERMENEUTIC CIRCLE AND THE DIALECTIC

In response to the issue of a controlling logic that threatens any potential gain from dialectical analyses, a number of researchers have promulgated the essentially creative experience of communication freed from analytic/dialectical limitation. For instance, Baudrillard (1983) calls this pataphysics, "…a science of imaginary solutions, a science of the simulation or hypersimulation of an exact, true, objective world, with its universal laws" (1983b: 33-4). While Lyotard (1979) describes a "parology" where, "Science is a model of an 'open system', in which a statement becomes relevant if it generates ideas, that is if it generates other statements and other game rules" (1979: 64).

Likewise, Ricoeur (1989) avoids the double-bind of language by calling for "super abundant thinking". According to these researchers, assessment of knowledge and/or dialogue should account for a level of creative/heuristic openness, aiming to bring the participants to a position where they can appreciate the issues themselves. Reading between our lines, interpretive critique, requires a freeing from the potential limitations imposed by all forms of logic including the dialectic. One of the foundational dilemmas for dialectical reasoning has been how to move from the powerful, but limiting, oscillations of binary thought, to a more complex reasoning that explains how knowledge moves in emergent reality (hermeneutics); in Fibonacci terms from − 1,1, 2, 5, 8, etc.

Dewey (1896) attempted an early move from analytical/dialectical logic in the famous "reflex arc" concept in which he replaced the stimulus/response oppositions of binary thought with a "self-adjusting circle', in a move that reminds of the hermeneutic circle, Dilthey, Scheliermacher's and even earlier, Spinoza's, identification of circularity in interpretation. Following Dilthey, this essay argues that the use of the hermeneutic circle is quite compatible with dialectical reasoning, explaining dialectics in terms of the tension between terms that creative experience and communicative interaction encourage. This relation reduces the opportunity for dialectical closure and opens the dialectic to creative expression/ revision.

This crucial balance in hermeneutic/dialectical reality is identified in Simon Rogerson's DICKJ model, which uses the 5circle (see below) to present dimensions of dialectical concept formation; in the process bringing to light not only tension between terms, but also tension in language and concept formation (Rogerson 2004). Reading around the circle, transitions of thought are emphasised; e.g. between data and information, or information/communication −

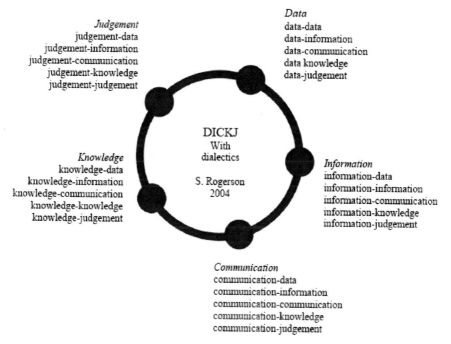

Figure 5   A cycle of data knowledge formation (S. Rogerson. 2004).

creating questions about the nature of each and the transitions between states; when does one become the other for instance? Under each heading in the model, is a set of dialectics that describe how terms exist in tension within themselves; ergo, defining data requires to define its prior conceptual relations.

The argument is not between simple binary oppositions (e.g. right and wrong), the argument is about a more complex association of ideas that ground conceptual development. The hermeneutic circle acknowledges ongoing complexity in language and knowledge formation and replaces a method of certainty acquisition with that of critical heuristic analysis. Formally put, in the light of ontological/epistemological reflexivity, it is essential to privilege the mediating-relational world over the material/objectifying world and in so doing, to balance hermeneutic closure with dialectical ambivalence.

In keeping with the aims of communication ethics analyses, emphasising communication as a creative-hermeneutic task where *différance* is examined and protected, the dialectic even encourages the re-introduction of ethical reason. Ethics are re-transposed from the instrumental/legal realm to the decisional/relational realm and become part of a dialectics that embodies social thinking (ethico/logical) rather than reduces it. Equally, communication dialectics are held – temporarily – in hermeneutic creations and instead of certainty, what emerges is critical openness, the ability to display concept development outside subject/object narrative obligations, and thus to open thought to both critique and to reintroduce the human/creative principle. In such a powerful move, ethical evaluation finds a reemphasised role equally in the provision of new possibilities and for the assessment of methodological justifications.

ETHICAL AND COMMUNICATIVE DIALECTICS

In the informational world ethical language is revived through reorientation towards inter-subjective/intra-subjective claims, those specifying the knowable/unknowable contingencies of "I/we" relations. The dialectical position is central to conceptions of the other in ethics (Socrates, 470-399BCE; Buber 1966; Levinas 1969) and equally to feminist concepts of a new subject/subject orientation in fundamental human ontology (Benhabib 1992; Gilligan 1980; Kristeva 1968). In an age of information "human relation" is one of the few certainties we all possess, an insight sponsored by Heidegger's early formulation "man is language" (Ricoeur 1989: x). Or, in other words, wo/man is not substance, she is energy understood as relation. This revises the epistemological value of ethics in an energetic dialectical movement. Ethics "examined values" (ICE 2001) find expression in an information age where clear distinctions between means/ends, right/wrong, good/bad, fact/values etc. continuously adjust knowledge across fluid boundaries and in dynamic relations.

　　While logical process is employed in ethical reasoning (e.g. the utilitarian judgement), counter intuitive, social knowledge is equally valued, in part, as a force against the burden of analytical logic and the appropriation of all human significance by powerful authorities using closed tools of reason. Unfortunately, traditions of reason that prize exact alternatives have reduced much thought to a pathological degree of rationality, despite Foucault's (1973) admonition, "the diacritical principle of medical observation...the only pathological fact is a comparative fact" (1973: 134). The hermeneutic judgement is thereby essential to deny closure in analyses and to lend colour/detail to comparative and to interdisciplinary knowledge formation.

　　For historic interest, the study of dialectics is traced to before Plato and Aristotle. The Pre-Socratics, particularly Heraclites and Pythagoras, are credited with arithmetical philosophy that exerted contemporary influence, in a moral impulse that spanned the ancient world; interestingly in a single "long" century, in which at least three of the world's great religions emerged.

COMMUNICATION ETHICS AND THE DIALECTIC

THE DIALECT

Aristotle quotes the Pythagoreans as possessing a dialectical knowledge that combined material/spiritual foundations; "…the Pythagoreans have said in the same way that there are two principles, but added this much, which is peculiar to them, that they thought finitude and infinity were not attributes of certain other things, e.g. of earth or fire… but the infinity itself and unity itself were the substance of the things which they are predicated. This is why the number was the substance of all things" (Barnes 1997: 1561).

Communication ethics dialectics ethics/communication communication/ethics	*dialogic ethics* *K.O. Apel* *1972*	*communicative* *action* *Habermas* *1984/7* *discourse ethics* *1979*	*communicative* *ethics* *Banhabib 1992*	*communicative* *ethics* *Christians 1997*
Standpoint theory *Wood 1997*	*contingency of* *language* *Rorty 1989*	*strategic* *communicative* *action* *Habermas* *1984/87*	*original* *position* *Rawls 1972*	*community of* *communication* *K.O. Apel 1972*
medium message *McLuhan 1964*	*speech act* *Austin 1962*	*self-other* *Buber 1961*	*language* *games* *Wittgenstein* *1953*	*community of* *interpretation* *C.S. Peirce* *1898*

Figure 6 Communication ethics dialectics (e.g. only, no priority)

According to Aristotle the pre-eminent concern of the Pythagoreans was duality, embodied in the Tectractys (fourness) even while, "...other members of this same school [Pythagoreans] say there are ten principles, which they arrange in two columns of cognates, limited and unlimited, odd and even, one and plurality..." (Barnes 1997: 1560). Despite earlier thinkers, the precise identification of dialectical reasoning is peculiar to Plato, according to Aristotle because, "earlier thinkers had no tincture of dialectic'"(ibid: 1562). Both Plato and Aristotle employ dialectical reasoning in establishing the very foundation for Western rationality.

While Plato remained committed to a philosophical practice of dialectics, for instance, in the Socratic "elenchus", apparently the dialectic remained submerged, perhaps conforming to the Pythagorean principle of remaining silent about technique? (see introduction, in Barnes 1997). Aristotle's contribution to science and logic can arguably be traced to a mathematical understanding underpinned with dialectical principles. An insight of this type, accords with post-structuralist understanding of dialectics that generate dynamic and continuous knowledge formation and which remain resilient to closure. Despite this, the tendency of dominant discourses and institutions to enclose all knowledge in regimes that limit both use and change – institutions/professions – has subverted and even damaged the creative potential of dialectical knowledge freed from disciplinary interests.

While this essay has not the means to cover either the use of ancient dialetics or to introduce a discussion of dialectics in modern or postmodern ethical theory, the technique of visualising dialectics and hermeneutic reasoning can be extrapolated to these subjects within the discipline of communication ethics.

COMMUNICATION ETHICS AND DIALECTICS

In communication ethics, a critical distinction is held that false dichotomies inhere in much "instrumental reasoning" and that strategic action denies the possibility of communicative action (Habermas 1984/7, 1990). In the new global-technological space where new informational logics apply and where in the words of Seyla Benhabib (1992) we move "from legislative to interactive rationalism" (1992: 2) dialectical reason moves beyond duality, in doing so identifying it and remarking on its passing. Change of the fundamental order found in postmodern information societies requires new responses that address the ambiguity, paradox and ambivalence now recognised as the basis of the postmodern condition.

Citizens, as legally constituted actors rather than socialised individuals, act across an information realm without a ruler, requiring onto-ethical explanations for contemporary life. In an overwhelming information environment, identity, trust, certainty and agreement are human ethical needs that demand to be addressed, while equally being freed from distortion, privilege, control and arbitration by powerful authorities, including the media itself (Habermas 1968 [62]). Within a lifeworld where "argumentation is designed to make possible not impartiality of judgement, but freedom from influence or autonomy in will formation" (Habermas 1990: 71), the concept of freedom from distorting authority is critical. In fact, Habermas's discourse ethics play a key role in the epistemological foundation for the new discipline of communication ethics, offering insight into the objectivist/subjectivist, universal/relative dialectics that have plagued the social sciences throughout a disputed history.

For Habermas, critique "has taken hold of and demolished the sorts of concepts by which those aspects could be distinguished from one another, so that their paradoxical entanglement became visible" (1987: 338). It may be that a central purpose for communication ethics is to identify the critical distinctions inherent in knowledge and to expose the fractures of knowledge sterilised of moral action, thereby to re-establish/re-balance human being/knowing, in renewed ethics/communicative resources. By proposing dialectics as a practical resource for communication ethics, the notion of convivial tools might be called on. Christians (2004) quotes Ivan Illich as promoting "…convivial tools – those responsibly limited and thereby empowering. Convivial technology respects the dignity of human work, needs little specialized training to operate, and is generally accessible" (2004: 8-9). If it is possible to discern knowledge using convivial "dialectical tools",

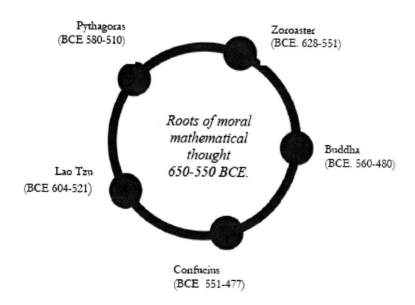

Figure 7 Roots of moral mathematical thought. Actual dates disputed.

without submitting to finality, communication ethics may propose/protect, heuristic knowledge that reflects the dynamics of an information age, where human mind and knowledge are otherwise displaced. For Ricoeur the problems of double meaning in knowledge persist in a continuous equivocal relationship:

> …for the theoretical distinction between two kinds of equivocalness – equivocalness through a surplus of meaning, founding in the exegetic sciences, and equivocalness through the confusion of meaning, which logic chases away – cannot be justified at the level of semantics alone. Two logics cannot exist at the same level. Only a problematic of reflection justifies the semantics of double meaning (Ricoeur 2004 [1981]:18).

We cannot escape from the dialectic, in Ricoeur's words, the semantics of double meaning. The only opportunity is to employ it legitimately, transparently and creatively, to unpick knowledge interests and to design new temporal knowledge structures, providing for a human reality where global knowledge resources, like economic resources, are shared and equitably distributed. For instance, imagine a government institution publishing its dialetics in the same way it publishes its financial accounts; or a corporation communicating its foundational research design using dialectical structures; or a group dialogue using dialectics to assess the alternative courses of action open to participants. Uses for the dialectic are endless, the question remains, does such methodological openness reveal meaning and enable further interpretative potential?

Aristotle's dialectical reason		
	demonstrative	dialectical (dialectic-rhetoric)
	contentions	mis-reasoning

Figure 8 Four means of reasoning, Aristotle. Topics

CONCLUSION

Emerging from the womb, every human begins a struggle to identify the dynamic/complex world we each inhabit. On one hand a critical faculty that examines/explains a physical universe; what the senses register; and on the other a bio-creative faculty that supports consciousness founded in abundance and complexity; communication as "the study of mutual imaginations" (Durham Peters 1999: 186). From a child's first experience, natural duality is a primary means of language formation and of experiential learning. Our perceptual universe appears founded in essential differences that reveal as well as obscure what passes for human knowledge. To appropriate Marcuse's (1964) critical insight, in order to move from individual perception to shared agreement, we might usefully move from "one dimensional man'" to five-dimensional human beings through multiple, open, methodological techniques that privilege the lifeworld.

Today, the information universe is different from the material universe in ways that are only now becoming clear and, as Lyotard has claimed, demand a different type of knowledge formation/control. As the informational and immaterial grows in value in simple mercantilist terms, so does the social–ethical world of values, Popper's (1972) second world, where new knowledge, relations and services actually evolve. The bringing together of two foundational disciplines, communication and ethics, at a time of massive information availability gives the background for a new navigational practice (dialectics/hermeneutics) for those looking to make sense of an informational world, where complexity/certainty are balanced and where individual knowledge, group judgement and systematic knowledge resources are integrated into a process of continuous co-creating. Overcoming the dialectical nature of many assumptions in communication gives a more refined purpose for communication itself; a notion endorsed by Bokeno and Gannt (2000):

Dialogic relationships understand simply that that there are better things to do with contradictions than resolve them; that there is much more to explore in the confrontation of contradictory views than in the collapse of one or compromise of both (2000: 253).

This move also avoids the great humanist dilemma of knowledge formation, that of certainty and offers a role for a dialectics combined with interpretative hermeneutics which encourage, not closure but openness, not certainty but creativity, not concrete rules but active heuristics. Such a position is compatible with Denzin and Lincoln (1994), who are sceptical about simple 'binary opposition' and yet who themselves identify the tendency to "…frame up the debate in strictly (and naively) modernist terminology which employs exhaustive binary oppositions privileging one set of terms against the other" (1994: 143). The point being that if the dialectics exist, they should be admitted into the house of analyses, while readily admitting that such analyses will never be a faithful reproduction of all human reality.

In summary, dialectics exist across human thought, language, systems and social organisation. They can be discerned and isolated as can the elements on the periodic table, and to mix a metaphor, can be used like the points in a map to distinguish the underlying structures and assumptions of knowledge. Unlike the purely philosophical task of' "interpretation of interpretation", communication ethics is grounded in practical concerns which alter the task from one of system building to one of creative/critical revelation, showing the roots of knowledge for what they are, unstable energetic agreements about the nature of life. In this case, the dialectic/hermeneutic may perform a valuable task within a new discipline of communication ethics, to encourage the shared examination of communicative reality founded in an open balance between the ethical/logical domains of human communication.

REFERENCES

Appadurai, A. (1996) *Modernity at Large: Cultural Dimensions of Globalization*. Minneapolis, University of Minnesota Press

Aristotle, (circa 350 BCE) *Topics* (trans.) W.A. Pickard-Cambridge. Available online at www.libertyonline.hypermail.com/Aristotle/Logic/Topics.html, accessed 6 February 2006

Austin, J. L. (1962) *How to do things with words,* London, Oxford University Press

Barnes, J. (ed.) (1984) *The Complete Works of Aristotle.* (Vol. 2), The revised Oxford Translation, Princeton, Princeton University Press

Baudrillard, J. (1981 [1972]) *For a Critique of the Political Economy of the Sign.* (trans. Levin, C.) St. Louis, Telos Press

Baudrillard, J. (1983) *Simulations.* (trans. Foss, P. and Beitchman, P.), New York, Semiotext. pp 33-34

Baudrillard, J. (1994) *Simulacra and Simulation.* (trans. Glaser, S. F. and Arbor, A.), Michigan, University of Michigan Press

Benhabib, S. (1992) *Situating the Self. Gender, Community and Postmodernism in Contemporary Ethics,* New York, Routledge

Bernstein, B. B. (1990) The *structuring of pedagogic discourse,* London, New York, Routledge

Blackburn, S. (1994) *The Oxford Dictionary of Philosophy.* Oxford, Oxford University Press

Bokeno, M. and Gantt, V. (2000) "Dialogic Mentoring: Core relationships for organizational learning", *Management Communication Quarterly*, Vol. 14, No. 2, November 2000 pp 237-270

Buber, M. (1973 [1966]) *Between Man And Man.* (trans. Smith, R. G.), London, Collins

Buck-Morss, S. (1977) *The Origin of Negative Dialectics. Theodore W. Adorno, Walter Benjamin, and the Frankfurt Institute.* London, the Free Press, Collier MacMillan

Burgoon, M., Hunsaker, F. G. and Dawson, E. J. (1994) *Human Communication.*, Thousand Oaks, Sage Publications

Castells, M. (1996) *The Information Age: economy society and culture*, Malden Massachusetts, Blackwell

Christians, C. G. (2004) *Social Justice and Internet Technology.* Available online at www.wmich.edu/comm/ethics/christians, accessed on 6 February 2006

Christians, C. G. (2005) "Social Dialogue and Media Ethics", *Ethical Perspectives*, Vol. 7, Nos 2-3, June-September pp.182-193

Cooper, J. M. (ed.) (1997) *Plato Complete Works.* Indianapolis, Indiana, Hackett Publishing Company

Denzin, N. K. and Lincoln, Y. S. (1994) *Handbook of Qualitative Research*, Thousand Oaks, Sage Publishing

Derrida, J. (1976 [1967]) *Of Grammatology* (trans. Spivak, G. C.), Baltimore, John Hopkins University Press

Derrida, J. (1982) *Margins of Philosophy.* (trans. Bass, A), Chicago, University of Chicago Press

Dewey, J. (1896) "The Reflex Arc Concept in Psychology", *Psychological Review*, Vol. 3 pp 357-370

de Zengotita, T. (2005) *Mediated: how the Media shapes your world and the way you live in it,* London, Bloomsbury

Dilthey, W. (1996) *Selections. Essays.* Princeton, N.J., Princeton University Press

Durham Peters, J. (1999) *Speaking Into The Air: A History of The Idea Of Communication.* London, University of Chicago Press

Du Saussure, F. (1966 [1916]) *Course in General Linguistics* (ed.) Charles Ballt and Albert Sechehaye and Albert Riedlinger (trans. Baskin, W.), New York, McGraw-Hill

Engels, F. (1883) *Dialectics of Nature.* Available online at www.marxists.org/archive/marx/works/1883/don/, accessed on 6 February 2006

Fairclough N.(1995) *Analysing Discourse: Textual Analysis For Social Research,* New York. Routledge

Foucault, M. (1970 [1966]) *The Order Of Things: an archaeology of the human sciences,* London, Tavistock Publications

Foucault, M.(1973) *The Birth Of The Clinic: An Archaeology Of Medical Perception.* (trans. Sheridan Smith, A. M.), New York, Vintage Books

Foucault, M. (1984) *The Foucault Reader.* Rabinow, P., (ed.) New York, Pantheon Books

Gadamer, H-G. (1993 [1975]) *Truth and Method.* 2nd revised edition. (trans. Weinsheimer, J. and Marshall, D.G.), London, Sheed and Ward

Gilligan, C. (1982) *In a Different Voice: Psychological theory and women's development,* Cambridge, MA, Harvard University Press

Greimas, A. J. and Coutés, J. (1982 [1977]) *Semitics and Language: An Analytical dictionary.* (trans. Crist, L. et al.) Bloomington, Indiana University Press

Habermas, J. (1968 [62]) *The Structural Transformation of the Public Sphere: A Inquiry Into A Category Of Bourgeois Society* (trans. Burger, J. and Lawrence, F.), Polity Press Cambridge

Habermas, J. (1990) *Moral Consciousness and Communicative Action,* (trans. Nicholsen, S, W), Polity Press, Cambridge

Habermas, J. (1984) *The theory of communicative action. Reason and the rationalization of society.* Vol. 1. (trans. McCarthy, T.), Cambridge, Polity

Habermas, J. (1987) *The theory of communicative action. Lifeworld and system a critique of functionalist reason.* Vol 2. (trans. McCarthy, T.), Cambridge, Polity

Hall, S. (1980) "Encoding and Decoding in the Television Discourse", *Culture, Media, Language,* Hall, S., Hobson, D., Lowe, A. and Willis, P. (eds), London, Hutchinson pp 128-38

Heidegger, M. (1971) *What are Poets for? Poetry Language and Thought,* New York: Harper and Row

Institute of Communication Ethics (2001) *Establishment Papers,* 16 November, 2001. London, UK

Jakobson, R. (1973) *Main trends in the science of language,* London, Allen and Unwin

Kelley, K. (1994) *Out of Control: The Rise of Neo-Biological Civilization,* Wokingham, Addison Wesley

Kristeva, J. (1977) *About Chinese Women.* New York, Urizen Books

Kroger, R., Wood, L. (2000) *Discourse Analysis.* London, Sage Publications

Levinas, E. (1969) *Totality and Infinity.* (trans. Lingis, A.), Pittsburgh, Duquesne University Press

Lacan, J. (1987[1979]) *The four fundamental concepts of psycho-analysis.* Miller, J.-A. (ed.) (trans. Sheridan, A.), London, Penguin

Laclau, E. (1977) *Politics and ideology in Marxist theory: capitalism, fascism, populism,* London, NLB

Luhmann, N. (1995) *Social Systems* (trans. Bednarz Jr. J. and Baecker, D.), Stanford, California, Stanford University Press

Lyotard, F. (1982[1979]) *The Postmodern Condition: A Report on Knowledge.* (trans. Bennington, G. and Massumi, B.), Minneapolis, University of Minnesota Press

McCarthy, T. (1996[1978]) *The Critical Theory of Jurgen Habermas.* Cambridge MA, MIT Press

Marcuse, H. (1964) *One-Dimensional Man.* London, Sphere

Ormorod, P. (1994*) The Death of Economics,* London, Faber and Faber

Pasquali, A. (1997) "The Moral Dimension of Communicating", Christians, C. and Traber, M. (eds) *Communication Ethics and Universal Values,* Thousand Oaks, CA., Sage pp 46-67

Peirce, C. S. (1982 [1878]) *Writings of Charles S. Peirce: a chronological edition.,* edited by Fisch, M., Bloomington, Indiana University Press

Popper, K. (1968 [1935]) *The Logic of Scientific Discovery,* London, Hutchinson

Popper, K. (1962) *Conjectures and refutations: the growth of scientific knowledge.* London,

Routledge and Kegan and Paul

Popper, K. (1972) *Objective Knowledge*. Oxford, Oxford University Press.

Rogerson, S. (2004). Unpublished seminar material, held at the Centre for Computing and Social Responsibility, at De Montfort University, Leicester, UK. June 2004

Riceour, P. (2004 [1989]) *The Conflict of Interpretations: essays in hermeneutics*. London, Continuum

Sartre, J.-P. (1960) *Critique of Dialectical Reason*. London, Verso

Schleiermacher, F.D.E (1986) *Hermeneutics: The Handwritten Manuscripts*, (edited by Duke, J. and Forstman, J.), Atlanta, Atlanta Press

Shannon, C. E. and Weaver, W. (1964 [1946]) *The mathematical theory of communication*, Urbana, University of Illinois Press

Wilden, A. (1972) *System and Structure: Essays in Communication And Exchange*. London, Tavistock

Zima, P.V. (2002) *Deconstruction and Critical Theory*. London, Continuum

Wittgenstein, L. (1968) *Philosophical Investigations*. Oxford, Basil Blackwell

NOTE ON AUTHOR

Robert Beckett is a member of the Institute of Communication Ethics. He is an associate of the Centre of Computing Social Responsibility at De Montfort University, UK, and is undertaking postgraduate research through Rambaud University at Nijmegen, Netherlands. His research interests include diagnosis, dialectics, dialogue and discourse in communication ethics and in the relations between political, media, organisation, group and interpersonal communicative standpoints. His work aims to develop these techniques into an integrated graphic language and database, 5systems, which may be viewed at www.5systems.net. Contact details: One Station Road, Lewes, East Sussex, UK BN7 2YY. Email robertbeckett55@yahoo.co.uk.

23

Cyberspace as an excuse from responsibilty

Moira Carroll-Mayer and Bernd Carsten Stahl

This chapter discusses the question of whether involvement in cyberspace or virtual environments can be seen as an excuse from responsibility. It will start by discussing the concept of responsibility and concentrate on the question of when and why subjects may be excused from being responsible. Against this background, the chapter will examine the cases of Rusnak and Leeson, two online traders successfully prosecuted in the criminal courts for having lost huge sums of money. It will be argued that the effects of being online can in large part explain their actions and that these effects are such that they could constitute an excuse from responsibility. Nevertheless, the legal system does not recognise cyberspace as an excuse. The chapter will conclude that it may be worthwhile reflecting upon our concept of responsibility ascription and asking whether this should be developed in light of the effects of extreme immersion in cyberspace.

INTRODUCTION

The concept of responsibility facilitates the ascription of moral, legal and other norms. Within the information society it provides a medium for the discussion of factual and normative problems. The concept has an impact on the way we deal with media and communication; for example in content selection and questions of access. Thereby technology become simultaneously a means of responsibility ascription and reason for ascription.

We will focus on whether the use of ICT can count as an excuse against responsibility. More specifically whether an agent immersed in cyberspace should be less eligible for responsibility ascription by the courts than one from a non-virtual environment. The chapter argues there are stimuli unique to cyberspace that induce psychological disturbance and moral ambiguity synonymous with postmodern ennui. It posits these should be taken account of by courts in the apportionment of responsibility.

The chapter provides a description of the theory of responsibility. It then adduces information from the case studies of defendants. These cases exemplify the effects of cyberspace and societies assessment of the evidential value of these effects. Information from research in the postmodern trading environment will be analysed and adduced. We conclude by asking whether the legal formulae for responsibility ascription should assimilate stimuli unique to cyberspace.

METHODOLOGY

This chapter is interdisciplinary; it applies critical methodology to research of the law, an area traditionally immune to the penetrative gaze of sociological methods. The results are more informative than they would otherwise have been, revealing a rich vein for research. It is concerned with the conflict that arises when the motives, morality and values of the real world and cyber world clash. The presence of structural conflict provides the ideal milieu for the conduct of critical research (Fay 1987: 27). The chapter considers how inhabitants of the cyber world are held hostage by "real world" norms and suggests solutions that are inclusive of the inhabitants of both societies. It was, therefore, necessary to employ a methodology that permits identification and investigation of ills and prescription, (ibid: 36). Critical research methodology is the only mainstream methodology that admits all these initiatives (ibid: 34).

The paper analyses the understanding of the "real" and cyber societies, in particular subjective statements of members of the cyber society. Critical methodology admits subjective understandings. The consequences of legal policy for cyber society are evaluated from case studies. Critical research enables judgments of effects *outside* the boundaries of origin. The research draws upon a range of material, biography, law reports and academic journals. Critical research admits a range of source materials. It refuses to take for granted what is said in hegemonic material (Van Dijk 2004: 7). Critical research considers the contribution of ideology to societal crisis (Fay op cit: 30). This paper considers the inadequacy in cyberspace of laws informed by Cartesian ideology. Ideological information elucidates understanding of how far dominant ideologies go in satisfying the norms of society (Potter 1996: 18).

RESPONSIBILITY

Responsibility can be defined as the social construct of ascription that links an object to a subject. The subject is the entity (usually a person) said to be responsible for the object (usually an inanimate or insentient thing). Ascription of responsibility by society will involve normative aspects such as law, morality or custom. Responsibility is usually ascribed after behaviour has been scrutinised by an authority endowed by society with the power to decide an outcome. The ascription of legal responsibility requires the scrutiny of judge or jury. Responsibility can be ascribed retrospectively or prospectively. Moral or legal responsibility may coincide or be contradictory.

There are aspects that most ascriptions share. Responsibility ascription is open; it reflects different values in different cultures and epochs (Holland and Webb 2003: 3). It is, therefore, impossible to predict ascription or the outcomes of ascription. Secondly, ascription unlike other moral frameworks seeks outcomes. Thirdly, ascription of responsibility is a teleological concept meant to further the good life shared by the participants. A thorough review of the concept requires detailed discussion (cf. Stahl 2004). Since we are only interested in excuse from responsibility within the context of the law we will restrict our discussion to that context.

EXCUSES FROM RESPONSIBILITY

We understand as excuses from responsibility facts or circumstances that render ascription unhelpful from society's perspective. The existence of such prevents ascription or ameliorates its consequences. Such facts or circumstances typically arise in the subject or affect his relationship with the object. An example is mental imbalance. The rationale of the criminal courts' refusal to ascribe responsibility here can be understood by looking at the aims of the criminal law, deterrence and retribution (Townsend 2005: 1). A disturbed person who does not understand the relationship between ascription and his action cannot be deterred; therefore ascription is otiose. This illustrates the relationship between the aim of ascription, the subject and the object. Actions for which the law might hold the mentally disturbed responsible are those attracting strict liability, where a societal vested interest outweighs societal interest in protecting the mentally disturbed. Offences of strict liability include unauthorised possession of drugs or possessing a firearm without a certificate (Card Cross and Jones 2001: 144).

Excuses from responsibility can be understood by looking at conditions the guilty subject is usually deemed to fulfil and the relationship between subject and the object. Among these we typically find causality, freedom, power and knowledge. Causality implies the subject has influence on the object and the freedom to have avoided the action/event complained of (Goldman 1999; Moore 1999). The guilty subject is normally taken to have freedom of will and the ability to act according to his preferences (Staddon 1999; Neuberg 1997; Bayertz 1993), without external constraints (Fischer 1999; Wunenburger 1993). It is often argued the more power over an object the subject has, the more responsible he should be for it (Ricoeur 1995). Another element is knowledge. The extent of the knowledge that the subject has regarding the object's proclivity for power, freedom, and causality should be accounted for (Hubig 1995; Held 1991).

In the courts an excuse is usually accepted or consequences of responsibility ascription ameliorated when emotion, motive, intention, self-control or physical capacity are modified without the complicity of an accused. The digital trader is the consummate "normative post-modern social subject. He [the postmodern social subject] is peculiarly vulnerable to the new forms of chronic ennui that are part and parcel of...Information/Computer Age technological developments" (Irvine 1999: 4). Postmodern ennui modifying emotion, motive, intention, self-control and physical capacity are disregarded however by the courts.

This chapter echoes the post-structuralist claims of Derrida (1974), Baudrillard (1983; 1993), Heidegger (1977), Lacan (1993) and Virilio (1989; 2002) arguing that postmodern ennui is more virulent than that of earlier societal phases. It represents "a specific disintegrative response to the particular social formations characteristic of advanced capitalism" (Irvine op cit: 11). The sufferer posses a fragmented self that is a law unto itself. It does not see the big picture; it does not seek to understand wholes or even to find its own true self; it is unwilling to believe in any certainty other than uncertainty. Postmodern ennui breeds in postmodern trading houses, it resonates in online traders Leeson and Rusnak. The response of the legal system is manifest in the guilty verdicts delivered after their trials.

THE POSTMODERN BROKERAGE HOUSE

Psychologists (Orzack 1998, Wilson 2005) and philosophers (Virilio 1989; 2002; Heidegger 1977) attest to the erosion of free will concomitant with high levels of involvement with technology. In the age of expert witnesses the courts consistently fail to relate the implications of this evidence to guilt assessment. This represents the value judgement of a society where 85 per cent by value of all money transfers are handled electronically and entire foreign reserves are transferable abroad within fifteen minutes.

The judgement is reinforced by protocol that makes electronic transfers irrevocable (Lloyd 2000). But by tilting with the law at the technological reality we are at the losing end of a war with technology (Lenk 1997: 126). Our laws are not tailored to assimilate the reality of technology; we use them in blind self-defence, failing to understand the complexities, fearing to confront it, our capitulation veiled by modernist law in a postmodern battle. Strait-jacketed by outmoded Cartesian theories of human supremacy and separation of mind, body and environment, the law evolves ever further from reality in cyberspace (Clayton 2002).

In 2003 the US General Accounting Office released estimates of losses in accounting scandals. At about $100 billion, almost twice the value of the Irish stock market, losses are unlikely to lead societies away from zero tolerance. There arises a duty to look at the affects of relentless exposure to IT and how these effect responsibility. This is urgent: cases are conducted within a no tolerance climate, normal evidential standards are abandoned and sentences extended, in the US, beyond those for first-degree murder and other homicides (Channel Four News, 8 August 2005). The UK Financial Services and Markets Act 2000 replaces *mens rea* with the 'regular market user test' and the normal standard of proof "beyond reasonable doubt" with the civil standard "on the balance of probability".

STICKY EFFECTS OF HIGH TECHNOLOGY

The effects of high technology are uniquely "sticky", with one in sleep and while awake, while the narrow bandwidths of electronic trading reduce signalling channels and block normalising activities usually available to the brain (Stone 1996:17). Of all the professions time is of most relevance to traders (Knorr-Cetina and Bruegger 2000). From the markets' inception they have looked to the past and to the future simultaneously, moulding the future in biased directions through record and anticipation. In the temporal immediacy of real time decisions are taken upon information received from second to second, without history and models previously available to traders. Accounts and values, the knowledge bases of the markets are, for the first time in history, truly indecipherable to traders. Demski sums up the position (Demski et al 2002: 11):

> My fear is that we are in the information business, intellectually and professionally, but have become addicted to thinking, regulating and communicating as if we were in the valuation business.

Yudkowsky (2006:1) also chastises the mismatch of high technology to critical risk response. "Artificial Intelligence is not *settled* science; it belongs to the frontier, not to the textbook...We cannot discuss actuarial statistics to assign small annual probabilities of catastrophe, as with asteroid strikes. We cannot use calculations from a precise, precisely confirmed model to rule out events or place infinitesimal upper bounds on their probability, as with proposed physics disasters. But this makes AI catastrophes more worrisome not less. The effect of many cognitive biases has been found to increase with time pressure, cognitive busyness, or sparse information. Which is to say that the more difficult the analytic challenge, the more important it is to avoid or reduce bias".

Traders as a group are involved in what Schutz (1964: 54) calls the "we relation". Contemporaneously they experience the market as it assembles in replicate action, focused in collective anticipation and preparation for the next event. For cyber traders the intensity is extreme. Leeson and Rusnak had been supplied with the Travel Bloomberg system in contravention of global banking regulations. Travel Bloomberg provides insight and means to manipulate markets so pervasively that its use is restricted to the heads of stock exchanges and central banks (Creaton and O'Leary 2002: 91). This system allowed them to penetrate more intensively and for longer periods than ordinary traders, thereby increasing the already intense effects of online trading.

The type of traders upon whom no tolerance ascription impacts most set the trends and make the markets. Technology connects them to the World Bank; it provides them with specialist information and brokerage services through Reuters, Bloomberg and Telerate. They are always in the process of defining the market, reading it, trying to understand, articulating it, testing it, moving and manipulating it. In turn the market displays itself, altering what is seen, raising question after question. Incapable of being understood it calls for understanding from moment to moment as new properties are acquired, situations change and events unfold around the globe. In a nightmarish dance of the seven veils it reveals everything yet nothing. A notion of lack and wanting informs the relationship between trader and technology binding them together physically and mentally (Knorr-Knorr-Cetina and Bruegger op cit). Traders are in a post modern nightmare rivalling that in Lacan's Seminars *Sur Psychoses* (1993), the narcissistic human ego, dependent on other human beings as significant others and achievable goals (Lacan 1993) is constantly suppressed. The market is everything yet it is nothing. Knorr-Cetina (2000: 154) asked a Zurich trader what the digital market meant to him:

KC: What is the market to you?
Z: Everything, everything.

Knorr–Cetina persisted:

KC: It has a form and meaning which is independent of you? You
           can't control it is that the point?
Z: Right. Exactly right! It has a life in and of itself you know.
           Sometimes it all comes together and sometimes it's all sort of
           dispersed, arbitrary and random, directionless and lacking
           cohesion.
KC: But you see it as a third thing? Or do you mean the being as
           a whole?
Z: I mean the being as a whole.

Like the disembodied satellite man of Baudrillard's *Transparency of Evil*, Leeson and Rusnak dealt within a cybernetic value system where morality, law, human relationships, reason itself are redundant (Baudrillard 1993). Baudrillard speaks of technology reducing individuals to self-referential operatives, in communication not in touch, terminal subjects, flat and blank as the screen, transfixed by a monitor that supplants experience. When Leeson created Error Account 88888 to contain and conceal his losses he did so without reference to another human being. He was self referential to a terminal self, engaged in an automated battle with the real numbers of the true digital accounts. He reflects that his actions will variously protect colleagues' reputations or incur wrath in far off London. Yet the depth of these references to these people and place, that by now had become "the other" are flimsy, betraying an inability to see the other as real. Neither Leeson nor Rusnak appear to have been motivated by personal gain neither had hoarded money in anticipation of a "get away".

Significantly it is when Leeson enters a limbo, neither affiliated with the cyber world of Simex nor yet with the real human world, at the moment he must leave the Simex building forever that he is able to confront the notion of criminality. It is as though his divorce from the temple of technology allowed a re-emergence of understanding of human mores and sanctions. That Leeson was undergoing "divorce" is arguably true. Computers are the ultimate post − social objects, they replace other human beings as the most fascinating part of technologically orientated lives. Nowhere is this greater than postmodern trading houses where interaction, time, space and communication are altered by technology. Traders relate to their technology not as an instrument but experience it as a feeling, reflexive being. They can spend 18 hours a day in the presence of a "voice-broker" that continuously shouts prices and demands deals, all the while confronted with five or more screens each containing sub-screens. These display rapidly changing market prices and myriad of randomly fluctuating information with which he must keep pace. Knorr-Cetina's and Bruegger's portrait (op cit: 149) brings home the intensity of the relationship that the researchers believe is unparalleled anywhere in either the real or virtual world,

When traders arrive in the morning they strap themselves to their seats figuratively speaking, they bring up their screens and from then on their eyes will be glued to those screens, their visual regard captured by them even when they talk or shout to each other, their body and the screen world melting together in what appears to be a total immersion in the actions in which they are taking part...

DEFINING MOOD OF POSTMODERNISM

Leeson's words exude the defining mood of postmodernism, fear, brought about by uncertainty between the boundaries of self and technology, affected not by modernist biomedical illness but a postmodern syndrome aroused by the invisible latent threat of loss of self, mind and even body to technology (Clayton 2002).

> I'd lost millions of pounds … the figures scared me to death…I turned off my Reuters screen and the green flickering figures died an instant, quiet death. They were just numbers on a screen, nothing to do with real cash … I was living in a hermetically sealed world where I breathed no fresh air and handled no real money…Rationally I knew I should sell…Hold up my hands and be escorted off the trading floor into a police van or into a padded cell... (Leeson 1996: 3).

THE RAFTS OF JUSTICE

Having argued that the effects of immersion in cyberspace be taken into account in the assessment of guilt, the paper will now focus upon the jurisdictions within which the prosecution of online traders is most likely, namely those in the UK and the US. Within their criminal processes two aspects of cyberspace are pertinent: when the defence of automatism is raised in a UK court and the cultural defence in a US court.

AUTOMATISM

Under the Attorney General's Reference of 1992 the defence of automatism was limited to complete loss of voluntary control. Before that deprivation of *effective control* sufficed. The Reference was sought following a case where automatism was successfully argued to defeat the charge of causing death by dangerous driving. The defence presented psychiatric evidence that the driver was reduced to a trance by the repetitive stimuli of a straight, flat, featureless motorway. The focal point of vision had gradually become closer until just ahead of the windscreen. Peripheral vision had continued to send signals to the brain with which it dealt subconsciously, enabling him to drive the vehicle while largely unaware of what was happening. On the basis of this evidence the driver was acquitted. Net artists Cosic and Lialina demonstrate the hypnotic, disassociative forces of computer images in Deep ASCII and Agatha Appears (Berry 2001).

　　The unresolved struggle to make sense of what is shown induces an autonomist state (Knorr-Cetina and Bruegger op cit). The random, rapid appearance and disappearance of numbers on a traders screen as they flash and change value induce mental struggle familiar to fans of Cosic and Lialina. The repetitive, mechanistic effort of the brain to reconcile the irreconcilable brings it to virtual unconsciousness. Consider the trader, more adrift than the driver for whom stimuli, lines, tarmac and cats eyes, flow like a river, none the less transferring him from one location to the other, closer to destination. Not for the trader a journey inherent with meaning of destination, the flickering, random, ultimately meaningless digits consume his being, offering neither destination nor closure.

Policy makers are considering a return to the pre-Reference standard, loss of effective control (Card et al 2001). The defence of automatism based upon the effects of immersion in cyberspace may one day be presented. Objections to raising automatism in defence of cyber traders are anticipated. An obstacle is adherence to the theories of Descartes (1644). His theory that a place exists if it is reducible to coordinates remains entrenched in legal thought. Shields (1996: 9) looks at Derrida's work (1974) describing hypertext carried out in a different organisation of space, capable of being read in chaos and with infinite variety. This implies Cartesian space is not a universal truth, there is a new, equally valid perception undelineated by co-ordinates. The movements of the trader occur outside Cartesian space, carried out in chaos, in a place that exists nonetheless.

If the effects of exposure to IT are to form a defence Cartesian assumptions that humans are privileged, the nature/culture, mind/body dichotomies must be abandoned. In R v Quick Bridge. J (*ratio decidendi*) held:

> A malfunctioning of the mind…caused by the application to the body of some *external factor* such as violence, drugs, alcohol or hypnotic influences cannot fairly be said to be due to disease.

Bridge's assessment precludes the effects of surroundings. But illness and environment are conjoined in human beings, their intertextuality unaffected by theory. Traders' bodies are sites of metamorphosis, boundaries of self and other melded into new existence. There is a liquidation of referentials from an oversupply of images replacing previous notions of truth with shallow simulation. Traders' fear, depression, panic, obsessiveness and claustrophobia, rooted in technology, are articulated through the text of the body as madness (Clayton op cit: 840) that courts will not recognise.

In 1993 Paul Bedworth was acquitted by a jury of hacking after argument that he was addicted to computers at the time of the alleged crime (Bainbridge 2004: 384). Bedworth, unique, unsupported by precedent, labelled perverse, is the fleck of sand at the heart of a pearl. Herman (1995: 22) warns: "If the criminal law does not provide…legal solutions to cultural changes and conflicts then it will become irrelevant."

Bedworth indicates society does not have faith in current legal theory to deal with the complexities of cyber life. There must be reformulation of "disease of the mind" that recognises the intertextuality of man and technology. The symptoms emergent in traders have no relation to illness that comes from within while no persuasive evidence linking psychiatric illness to any single locus has emerged (Clayton op cit: 851). It is less than certain psychological illness obtains to a biomedical explanation. Trauma in the postmodern sense is not the disruption of a stable psyche, but unbounded experience of constant disaffection, unrecognised by judicial thought. The disturbances associated with Baudrillarian disaffection have no known location or exactly identifiable source. Clayton suspects disease recognition reflects societies obsession with a belief or a way of life. If he is right this explains the paucity of research into the negative affects of technology. Globally there is tremendous investment in technological systems; concomitantly there is a desire not to undermine that investment, now in the time of its devastatingly triumphant infancy.

THE CULTURAL DEFENCE

Phillips and Eisenberg (1993) assert email lacks the paralingualism of letters and phone calls; it enables concealment of emotional information, uncertainty and lack of conviction. It allows traditional and functional lines to be crossed with ease; it increases opportunities for abuse of those down the chain of command (Barron and Yechiam 2002: 507). The US House Financial Services Committee refused to press the prosecution of Brabbs World Com's manager of European and Asian accounts for obeying emails ordering illegal concealment. House spokesperson Peterson referred to Brabbs's subjection "to serious opposition and intimidation via email". The opposition and intimidation spoken of may constitute backdoor recognition that Brabbs was not part of mainstream American culture, but a vulnerable member of a separate cyborg culture.

The concept of a separate culture may open the door for cyborgs that fall foul of regulations and societies vested interests. Reddy (2002) describes how cultural difference moved centre stage in the American courts so that it constitutes a defence. In the People v Chen (1989) the jury found the accused did not possess the *mens rea* for murder. They found the motive was desire to conform to a culture. In the People v. Hamoukai (1986) culture progressed to being the problem itself. The US Model Penal Code adopted, by 13 states, has prepared for the inclusion of the cultural defence. These developments have implications for the defence of online traders in the US. Research indicates a separate culture. Knorr-Cetina and Bruegger (2002) found traders' existence satisfied the three criteria of Schutz's formula for a separate culture:

1. A tension of consciousness i.e. wide-awakeness; traders give the screen full attention and are aroused and awakened by it more than during everyday wide-awakeness. Traders remain transfixed by the screens, immersed by the action on them.

2. Intentionality geared to the outer world; traders continually keep pace with markets and develop empathy with them. Analysis renders them permanence for a second or two, it passes and they again move forward.

3. A time frame in which the inhabitants act. A specific time frame in which the inhabitants act in unison. Schutz refers to normal time, Knorr-Cetina and Bruegger (op cit: 158) transpose real-time. They conclude that the compression of action there intensifies the sense of a culture separate from the "real" world.

In theory there appears no reason why the cultural defence cannot embrace the effects of cyberspace. The practice may require much more.

THE WAY FORWARD

The post-structuralist critique provides a theoretical foundation from which it is possible to understand life in cyberspace. From the post-structuralist perspective the case studies of Leeson, Rusnak and Bedworth are prisms through which it is possible to examine the postmodern condition and the inability of the legal system to reconcile that reality. The challenge is to rescue (without compromising others) the sufferer of postmodernist ennui who is eschewed by Cartesian justice and trapped in the, so far, fatalistic spiral of post-structuralism. The defences in the end rest upon the acceptance of difference. The understanding made possible by post-structuralist critique can be built on. Benko (2005), while discarding Cartesian humanism, does not accept that post humanism (derived from post-structuralism) will address the needs of a society where we are to *varying degrees* cyborgs, where there may be some who are not cyborgs. "Posthumanists rush to embrace technology as that which saves us from humanism… a future where the human body has been left behind…In doing so posthumanism has not articulated a comprehensive ethics for how individuals should respond to technology…" (Benko 2005: 3). The challenge to ensure justice must be informed by an equitable critique.

Best and Kellner (2001: 265) posit a reconsideration that does not squander the understanding of the post-structuralist critique: "Traditionally the riddle of human identity has been resolved through religion and philosophy, today technology challenges us and forces us to reconsider how the human body, the human community and what it means to be human is understood." This implies a reconstitution of what it means to be ethical. According to Benko (op cit: 19): "The ethical community is a community of people that adopts and amends laws that ensure the voices of the marginalised others will be heard, not to protect an exclusionary vision of human nature." The law should not be designed for those whose morality arises from the human or cyborg world. For Benko this requires an ethical critical theory of technology that maps the increasingly technological/human hybrid society, that resolves neither in Cartesian stagnation nor capitulation to technology.

CONCLUSION

This chapter looks at the concept of responsibility, the effects of immersion in cyberspace and the implications of these for the ascription of responsibility in the courts, concluding that in cyberspace some conditions of responsibility no longer pertain. These refer to knowledge and causality, more importantly to how individuals perceive and deal with reality. Most theories of responsibility argue absence of the conditions of responsibility count against ascription. *Prima facie* the effects of extreme involvement in cyberspace should count against ascription.

     Prompted by post-structuralist claims, the critical analysis of the Leeson, Rusnak and Bedworth cases has enabled a microscopic examination of the macroscopic concerns of post-structuralism. The implications stretch beyond the defendants. They highlight deficiencies in legal policy that render it inadequate for the postmodern world. The chapter proffers solutions based on existing law, their implementation requires acceptance of difference. There is a maxim at the root of defence, *audi alterum partem* (let the other side be heard). Perhaps that is all we seek: a hybrid solution for a hybrid world.

REFERENCES

Bainbridge, David (2004) *Computers and Law, London and New York*, Pearson Longman

Barron, Greg and Yechiam, Eldad (2002) "Private Email Requests and the Diffusion of Responsibility", *Computers and Human Behaviour*, September pp 507-520

Baudrillard, Jean (1983a) *The Procession of Simulacra*, Paris, Galilee

Baudrillard, Jean (1993b) *The Transparency of Evil*, London, Verso

Bayertz, Kurt (1993) "Evolution und Ethik. Größe und Grenzen eines philosophischen Forschungsprogramms". Bayertz, Kurt (ed) *Evolution und Ethik*, Stuttgart, Reclam Stuttgart pp 7-37

Benko, Steven (2005) "Ethics Technology and Posthuman Communities", *Essays in Philosophy, A Biannual Journal, Humboldt State University*, Vol. 6, No. 1 pp 1-27. Available online at 2005@http://www.stevequayle.com/News.alert/05, accessed 22 September 2005

Berry, Josephine (2001) Automatism, Autonomy and Virtual Unconsciousness. Available online at www.nettime.org/Lists/Archives/nettime-0108msg00093.html, accessed April 2005

Best, Steven and Kellner, Douglas (2001) *The Postmodern Adventure: Science Technology and Cultural Studies at the Third Millenium*, New York, Guildford Press

Card, Richard, Cross, Rupert and Jones, Philip Asterley (2001) *Criminal Law*, London, Butterworths

Clayton, Belinda (2002) "Rethinking Postmodern Maladies", *Current Sociology*, Vol. 50, No. 6 pp 820-839

Creaton, Siobham and O'Clery, Conor (2002) *Panic at the Bank*, Dublin, Gill and MacMillan

Demski, Joel, Fellingham, John, Yuji, Tjuri and Sunder, Shyam (2002) "Some Thoughts on the Intellectual Foundations of Accounting", *Accounting Horizons*, Vol. 16, No. 2 pp 157-168

Descartes, Renee (1644/1983) *Principia Philosphiae, The Philosophical Writings of Descartes*, Vol 3 (trans by Cottingham, John, Stoothoff, Robert and Murdoch, Dugald), Cambridge, Cambridge University Press

Derrida Jean (1974) *Of Grammatology*, Maryland, John Hopkins University Press

Fay, Brian (1987) *Critical Social Science: Liberation and Its Limits, Cambridge*, Polity Press

Fischer, John Martin. (1999) "Recent Work on Moral Responsibility", *Ethics*, Vol. 110, No. 1 pp 93-139

Goldman, Alvin (1999) "Why Citizens Should Vote: A Causal Responsibility Approach", Paul, Ellen Frankel, Miller, Fred D. and Paul, Jeffrey (eds) *Responsibility*, Cambridge, Cambridge University Press pp 201-217

Heidegger, Martin (1977) *The Question Concerning Technology*, (trans by Lovitt, W.), New York and London, Harper and Rowe

Held, Virginia (1991) "Can a Random Collection of Individuals be Morally Responsible?", May, Larry and Hoffman, Stacey (eds), *Collective Responsibility: Five Decades of Debate in Theoretical and Applied Ethics*, Savage, Maryland, Rowman and Littlefield Publishers Inc pp 89-100

Herman, Ellen (1995) *The Romance of American Psychology: Political Culture in the Age of Experts*, Berkeley, University of California Press

Hubig, Christoph (1995) *Technik und Wissenschaftsethik*, Berlin, Heidelberg, New York, Springer Verlag, second edition

Holland, James and Webb, Julian (2003) *Learning Legal Rules*, Oxford, Oxford University Press

Irvine Ian (1999) "Towards an Outline of Postmodern Ennui", *The Antigonish Review*, Issue 116 pp 1-18. Available online at www.antigonishreview.com/bi-116/116-irvine.html, accessed August 2005

Knorr-Cetina, Karin and Bruegger, Urs (2002) "Inhabiting Technology: The Global Lifeform of the Financial Market", *Current Sociology*, Vol. 50, No. 3 pp 389-405. Available online at www.ucm.es/BUC/compludoc/W/10207/00113921_3.htm, accessed February 2005

Knorr-Cetina, Karin and Bruegger, Urs (2000) "The Market as an Object of Attachment", *Canadian Journal of Sociology*, Vol. 25, No. 2 pp 141-168. Available online at www.arts.ualberta.ca/cjscopy/articles/Knorr.html, accessed January 2005

Lacan, Jean (1993) *Seminar III Psychoses*, New York, Norton

Leeson, Nick (1996) *Rogue Trader*, London, Warner Books

Lenk, Klaus (1997) "The Challenge of Cyberspatial Forms of Human Interaction to Territorial Governance and Policing", Loader, Brian (ed.), *The Governance of Cyberspace*, New York, Routledge pp 126-135

Moore, Michael S. (1999) "Causation and Responsibility", Paul, Ellen Frankel; Miller, Fred D. and Paul, Jeffrey (eds) *Responsibility*, Cambridge, Cambridge University Press pp 1-51

Neuberg, Marc (1997) Introduction, *La responsabilité – questions philosophiques*, Paris, Presses Universitaires de France pp 1-24

Orzack, Maressa Hecht (1998) "Computer Addiction: What Is It?", *Psychiatric Times*, August 1998, Vol XV No 8. Available online at @http://www.psychiatrictimes.com/p980852.html, accessed 5 December 2004

Phillips, Steven R and Eisenberg, Eric M (1993) "Strategic Uses of Electronic Mail in Organisations", *Electronic Journal of Commerce*, Vol. 3, No 2 pp 1-3. Available online at @www.cios.org, accessed 6 August 2005

Potter, Jonathon (1996) Discourse Analysis and Constructionist Approaches, John Richardson (ed.) *Handbook of Qualitative Research*, Leicester pp 12-22

Reddy, Sitta (2002) Pathologising Cultural Differences in American Criminal Courts, *Journal of Health and Illness*, Vol. 24, No 5 pp 667-686

Ricoeur, Paul (1995) "Le concept de responsabilité – Essai d'analyse sémantique", *Le Juste*, Paris, Editions Esprit pp 41-70

Schutz, Alfred (1964) "Concept and Theory Formation in the Social Sciences", Natanson, Maurice (ed.), *The Problems of Social Reality: Collected Papers 1*, The Hague, Nihoff pp 50-56

Shields, Richard (1996) *Cultures of the Internet*, London, Sage

Staddon, John (1999) "On Responsibility in Science and Law", Paul, Ellen Frankel, Miller, Fred D. and Paul, Jeffrey (eds) (1999) *Responsibility*, Cambridge, Cambridge University Press pp 146-174

Stahl, Bernd Carsten. (2004) *Responsible Management of Information Systems*, Hershey, Idea Group

Stone. Allucquere Rose (1996) *The War of Desire and Technology at the Close of the Mechanical Age*, Cambridge MA, MIT

Townsend Christopher (2005) *The Morality of Punishment*. Available online at www.leaderu.com/humanities/moralityofpunishment.html, accessed 7 August 2005

Van Djik, Teu (2004) From Text Grammar to Learning Discourse Analysis. Available online at www.discourse-insociety.org/beliar-ctm.htm, accessed 12 August 2005

Virilio, Paul (1989) *War and Cinema* (trans. by Camiller, P.) London and New York, Verso

Virilio, Paul (2002) *Ground Zero*, translated by C. Turner, London and New York, Verso

Wilson, Glen. (2005) *Report commissioned by TNS Research for Hewlett Packard into the effects of technology*, Kings College, London. Available online at www.timesonline.co.uk, accessed 18 August 2005

Wunenburger, Jean Jacques (1993) *Questions d'éthique*, Paris, Presses Universitaires de France, PUF

Yudkowsky Eliezer (2006) *Artificial Intelligence as a Positive and Negative Factor in Global*

Risk, forthcoming in Global Catastrophic Risks, eds. Nick Bostrom and Milan Cirkovic (draft as of 31 August, 2006. Available online at http://www.singist.org/upload/artificial-intelligence-r..., accessed 2 October 2007

CASES

Attorney General's Reference No 2 of 1992
People v Apayath (1986)
People v Leeson (1996) Singapore
People v Rusnak (2003) Maryland
R v Quick (1973) QB 910

LEGISLATION

The Financial Services and Markets Act (UK) 2002

NOTES ON AUTHORS

Moira Carroll-Mayer BA, MA, LLB, LLM is a lecturer in the Substantive and Procedural Law of Forensic Computing at De Montfort University in Leicester. She is the content designer of the Procedural and Substantive Law module. Moira is completing Doctoral research into the Legal and Ethical Implications of Autonomous Weaponry at the Centre for Computing and Social Responsibility at the Faculty of Computer Sciences and Engineering, De Montfort University. She took degrees in Literature, Politics and Law at the University of Ulster, London Guildhall University, the University of Westminster and the Queen's University of Belfast respectively. Her main areas of interest are the legal and ethical implications of autonomous weaponry and the effects of technology upon human behaviour and institutions. Before commencing doctoral research in 2003 Moira was a commercial lawyer. Contact details: Centre for Computing and Social Responsibility, Faculty of Computer Science, The Gateway Building, De Montfort University, Leicester LE1 9BH. Telephone: 00353861695672 or 01162556143. Email: moiracaroll2000@yahoo.co.uk.

Bernd Carsten Stahl is a Reader in Critical Research in Technology in the Centre for Computing and Social Responsibility at De Montfort University, Leicester, UK. His interests cover philosophical issues arising from the intersections of business, technology, and information. This includes the ethics of computing and critical approaches to information systems. He is the Editor-in-Chief of the

International Journal of Technology and Human Interaction. Contact details: Centre for Computing and Social Responsibility, Faculty of Computer Science, Gateway Building, De Montfort University, Leicester LE1 9BH. Telephone: 01162556143 or 01162551551. Email: bstahl@dmu.ac.uk. URL http://www.cse.dmu.ac.uk/~bstahl/,

PART 5

BUSINESS AND COMMUNICATION ETHICS

24

Making a firm commitment to trust

Kristine Lowe interviews Paul Jackson

Corporate Social Responsibility (CSR), ethical codes, ethics officers — these days all companies have to have them, and business ethics is a fast growing industry. But has the corporate landscape really changed, or is it only skin deep? Can you legislate for companies to behave well, and how do these new ethical codes fare when western companies meet cultures with widely different value systems? Kristine Lowe raises these issues (and many more) with Professor Paul Jackson, of the Manchester Business School (formerly School of Management, UMIST) at the University of Manchester

Why do we need business ethics?
Ethics for me is part of business practices, it is how you do business: you do not wake up one day and suddenly think "I am going to do ethics". Ethics is just a slant, a way of thinking about what business does.

In what way have you come to work with business ethics?
My speciality is internal communications. I am interested in relationships, trust relationships within companies and lately I have become more interested in mergers and joint ventures, so trust between companies. I mainly have students from East-Asia who look at doing business across different cultures. And that is very much about trust. If you look at relationships, lasting relationships such as marriage, they are all based on trust and the commitment that people make to each other.

Why do Western companies get into difficulties when trying to capitalise on the huge potential in the Chinese market?
I think the big reason, the biggest one, is that Western companies do not understand the Chinese, which is hardly surprising. Secondly, they do not spend

the time and effort to build a trusting relationship with their Chinese stakeholders, to build what they call *guan xi*. You cannot buy your way into China: you cannot buy *guan xi*. Even if you are rich, famous, or both, it does not mean that anyone will trust you.

What you will see if two Western companies are bidding for business is that the one that has been there, on the ground, visible, present, for a length of time – that's the company that will get the business. When IKEA went to Russia, which I think has many similarities to China, there were lots of problems with the transition from communism. But once they were there they refused to leave. Other Western companies did leave. Then, when things became better and it was a question of whom to give business to, well IKEA got the business and was allowed to set up on a larger scale because they had persevered. I do not know what they call it in Russia, it's not *guan xi*, but it is a term with a similar sort of meaning.

When I interviewed a top British businessman, whom everyone thought a bit of a nutter when he set up business in Russia in 1994, he said that with the Russians you have to meet the family and share a drink of vodka – then the business deal would be cast in iron...
There is a saying that an Englishman's word is his bond, so if he shakes hands on something then that is it: there is agreement. You still get all the paperwork and all of that, but still, I think in this way Russia, China and England are the same. You cannot just walk in off the street and expect to get new business because of the money behind you, or expect people will give you respect.

The problem with China is that the legal system, banking, insurance, intellectual property and all the rest are almost non-existent. There is very little respect for them, and that is why *guan xi* is so important. When you cannot trust the banks, the legal system, or anybody else, then you have to be very careful about whom you do trust. In economics they talk about transaction costs: *guan xi* lowers the transactions costs – you shake hands or drink some vodka; it is much cheaper than paying a lawyer who charges I do not know how much to draw up the contracts. If you then hold to it because you shook hands then it lowers the cost of transactions. It makes sense economically. In China, if you shake hands then you have this special relationship with people. It is not always just positive, there are lots of negative aspects to it as well: it makes for lack of transparency and it makes for what we call bribery and corruption.

So back to the issue of business ethics, do we need a genre or discipline called business ethics, or is that superfluous on the basis of what you just said?
I do not know if it is a discipline. I think the answer is almost certainly yes, because ethics is so important. However, it is not separate from business. You cannot say: "Well these things are ethics and these are not" but you do need people who think

through what the ethical implications of business decisions are. I think we do need specialists, for instance, to think through different ethical codes within different countries. How do we understand ethics?

Particularly when we have globalisation you get a situation aptly described by the term "glocal" which is a made-up word for global and local. Companies want to be global but recognise they cannot do it like McDonald's and be the same everywhere – so you get commercials like those of HSBC, "the local bank" on a global scale. They have to be grounded in the society they are in, to respect the local history and the traditions. That immediately brings dilemmas and you get, for instance, a discussion of how Nike manages their factories in East Asia and elsewhere.

It is easy for us to be imperialistic and apply our value sets globally: just because it does not feel right to us we assume it must be wrong in Thailand or Pakistan or anywhere else. The concept of global and local means that you need to respect the ethical, philosophical and cultural traditions of the society you are in or work with. That immediately creates conflicts we have not had before.

Given what you've just said, do you think it possible to create a universal ethical code in a world where so many different cultures meet so much more dramatically, or come closer to each other than they have ever done before?

I think the answer is that, yes, you can have ethics that are universal but they are going to be on such a level of generality that they do not actually coerce anybody: they do not actually define what you should do. There are not many absolutes that people would agree on, and if there are they tend to boil down to treating people the way you would like to be treated or the equivalent of that.

In the wake of recent high profile business scandals, highlighting malpractice by the likes of Enron, Worldcom and Citigroup, there has been a flurry of new legislation. But can you legislate companies to behave well? John Plender and Avinash Persaud argue in a forthcoming book, *The Missing Moral Compass: A Reality Check On Business and Finance Ethics*, that "the Sarbanes-Oxley Act in the US assumes that you can legislate companies into good behaviour, but the extraordinary expansion of legislation and governance codes since Enron has only exacerbated the problem by encouraging a compliance culture". Would you agree?

I think you have to have legislation to define that something is illegal and something is wrong, but at the same time you obviously cannot legislate people into morality. What we often seek to do, either through laws or other means, is look to mould people into doing what we would like them to do. You make it so that it is easier for them to do what you want them to do. If legislation can create systems and procedures so that it is easier, cheaper and in your best interest for you to do what is right, I think that is preferable to a system where behaving unethically is the easiest.

A lot of companies now have their own ethical officers and there are lots of companies that specialise in business ethics and hire out their services, in addition to all the new legislation. When it all comes down to it, though, has it really improved ethical behaviour in the marketplace?
Yes, but obviously not everywhere and not universally. Having an ethics officer could well mean that people think: "Oh well, we just carry on doing what we are doing, ethics is his job, so we do not have to care." If that is the effect it will be like a million other initiatives like environmental standards, accounting standards – you get a tick-box mentality. Then it will be absolutely and definitely harmful because it will give the impression that you do not have to think about ethics because that is a different category over there, handled by the person down the end of the corridor or the by consultant in another company.

It has indeed been argued that many ethical codes are nothing more than cynical public relations exercises, and that they do not to amount to any difference in a company's day-to-day practice. Do you think this can sometimes be the case?
Oh yes, absolutely. Enron had a beautiful ethics code yet some people were actively undermining it for their own benefit. Ethics codes can be immensely damaging, a bit like papering over the cracks at the Titanic. You have lots of examples of that: for instance, with Citigroup: people acting on their own, not necessarily fraudulent, but acting autonomously when they should not have been, and nobody noticing.

Now that we have the internet and blogosphere, consumer awareness is certainly more readily available, and only increasing. Will it not eventually become impossible to operate on a collision course with what is accepted as normal ethical guidelines?
Society is much more transparent which means biases are more transparent as well, but there is a lot on the internet you cannot trust. It is almost entirely a good thing because it means that companies cannot assume they can behave however they like without anyone finding out. The Internet must have changed everyone's life in the West, even those who do not use it, because people behave in a different way. There is much more discussion and transparency and readily available information. It gives a voice to people who previously did not have one. It does not equalise the playing field, but it does make it easier to make your voice heard. I think the consequences are very healthy.

Lightning Source UK Ltd.
Milton Keynes UK
25 August 2009

143069UK00001B/75/P